DI807652

Dear Alice,

Thank you very much for your trust, it is a great honour for me to be a Chair at the School of Education, University of Leeds & I look very much forward to working with you for the many years to come ✠

Michaela R.

Children, Development and Education

International Perspectives on Early Childhood Education and Development

Volume 3

Series Editors

Professor Marilyn Fleer, *Monash University, Australia*
Professor Ingrid Pramling-Samuelsson, *Gothenburg University, Sweden*

Editorial Board

Professor Joy Cullen, *Massey University, New Zealand*
Professor Yukiko Mastsukawa, *Rak-Rak University, Japan*
Professor Rebeca Mejía Arauz, *ITESO, Mexico*
Professor Nirmala Rao, *University of Hong Kong, China*
Professor Anne B. Smith, *Formally from the Children's Issues Centre, University of Otago, New Zealand*
Professor Collette Tayler, *Queensland University of Technology, Australia*
Associate Professor Eva Johansson, *Gothenburg University, Sweden*
Professor Lilian G. Katz, *Ph.D. Professor Emerita of Early Childhood Education, University of Illinois, USA*

Early childhood education in many countries has been built upon a strong tradition of a materially rich and active play-based pedagogy and environment. Yet what has become visible within the profession, is essentially a Western view of childhood preschool education and school education.

It is timely that a series of books be published which present a broader view of early childhood education. This series, seeks to provide an international perspective on early childhood education. In particular, the books published in this series will:

- Examine how learning is organized across a range of cultures, particularly Indigenous communities
- Make visible a range of ways in which early childhood pedagogy is framed and enacted across countries, including the majority poor countries
- Critique how particular forms of knowledge are constructed in curriculum within and across countries
- Explore policy imperatives which shape and have shaped how early childhood education is enacted across countries
- Examine how early childhood education is researched locally and globally
- Examine the theoretical informants driving pedagogy and practice, and seek to find alternative perspectives from those that dominate many Western heritage countries
- Critique assessment practices and consider a broader set of ways of measuring children's learning
- Examine concept formation from within the context of country-specific pedagogy and learning outcomes

The series will cover theoretical works, evidence-based pedagogical research, and international research studies. The series will also cover a broad range of countries, including poor majority countries. Classical areas of interest, such as play, the images of childhood, and family studies will also be examined. However the focus will be critical and international (not Western-centric).

Michalis Kontopodis · Christoph Wulf ·
Bernd Fichtner

Editors

Children, Development and Education

Cultural, Historical, Anthropological Perspectives

 Springer

Editors
Dr. Michalis Kontopodis
Department of European Ethnology
Humboldt University
Mohrenstrasse 40/41
10117 Berlin
Germany
michaliskonto@googlemail.com

Prof. Christoph Wulf
Department of Educational Science and Ps
Free University
Arnimallee 11
14195 Berlin
Germany
chrwulf@zedat.fu-berlin.de

Prof. Bernd Fichtner
Department of Education
University of Siegen
Adolf-Reichwein-strasse 2
57076 Siegen
Germany
fichtner@paedagogik.uni-siegen.de

ISBN 978-94-007-0242-4   e-ISBN 978-94-007-0243-1
DOI 10.1007/978-94-007-0243-1
Springer Dordrecht Heidelberg London New York

Library of Congress Control Number: 2011925155

© Springer Science+Business Media B.V. 2011
No part of this work may be reproduced, stored in a retrieval system, or transmitted in any form or by any means, electronic, mechanical, photocopying, microfilming, recording or otherwise, without written permission from the Publisher, with the exception of any material supplied specifically for the purpose of being entered and executed on a computer system, for exclusive use by the purchaser of the work.

Printed on acid-free paper

Springer is part of Springer Science+Business Media (www.springer.com)

Contents

Contributors

Birgit Althans Universität Trier, Trier, Germany, althans@uni-trier.de

Katrin Audehm Free University Berlin, Berlin, Germany, kathrin_audehm@web.de

Seth Chaiklin University of Bath, Bath, UK, s.chaiklin@bath.ac.uk

Anna Chronaki University of Thessaly, Volos, Greece, chronaki@uth.gc

Bernd Fichtner University of Siegen, Siegen, Germany, fichtner@paedagogik.uni-siegen.de

Gabrielle Ivinson Cardiff School of Social Sciences, Wales, UK, ivinsong@Cardiff.ac.uk

Mariane Hedegaard University of Copenhagen, Copenhagen, Denmark, Mariane.Hedegaard@psy.ku.dk

Martin Hildebrand-Nilshon Free University Berlin, Berlin, Germany, hildenil@zedat.fu-berlin.de

Sigrid Klasen Free University Berlin, Berlin, Germany, sigiclasen@yahoo.de

Michalis Kontopodis Humboldt University Berlin, Berlin, Germany, michaliskonto@googlemail.com

Christiane Moro Université de Lausanne, Lausanne, Switzerland, Christiane.Moro@unil.ch

Falk Seeger University of Bielefeld, Bielefeld, Germany, falk.seeger@uni-bielefeld.de

Estrid Sørensen Ruhr-Universtiät Bochum, Bochum, Germany, estrid.sorensen@rub.de

Anna Stetsenko The Graduate Center, The City University of New York, New York, NY, USA, astetsenko@gc.cuny.edu

Christoph Wulf Free University Berlin, Berlin, Germany, chrwulf@zedat.fu-berlin.de

Chapter 1
Introduction: Children, Development and Education – A Dialogue Between Cultural Psychology and Historical Anthropology

Michalis Kontopodis, Christoph Wulf, and Bernd Fichtner

Introduction

> Children are particularly literary, for they say what they feel and not what someone has taught them to feel. Once I heard a child, who wished to say that he was on the verge of tears, say not "I feel like crying", which is what an adult, i.e. an idiot, would say, but rather "I feel like tears." And this phrase – so literary it would seem affected in a well-known poet, if he could ever invent it – decisively refers to the warm presence of tears about to burst from eyelids that feel the liquid bitterness. (Pessoa, 2001, p. 108)

Reading this passage by Fernando Pessoa, a passage from *The Book of Disquiet by Bernardo Soares, Assistant Bookkeeper in the City of Lisbon*, we are surprised by the way Pessoa (or Soares) manages in a few lines to manifest everything our book is about. Pessoa refers in a poetic way to children and adults as speaking subjects, to the differences in the way they use language and to the importance of the senses in child experience. This quote is situated in the context of a longer work that reflects on power relations and implies an understanding of human history as not yet ended – which, as we will see, are also important arguments presented in our edited volume.

In the above-presented quote, Pessoa refers to the fact that children and adults are speaking subjects. An important argument presented in this book is that children and adults become subjects and experience the world through speaking. Speaking involves mimetic and metaphoric processes as well as the creative appropriation of utterances already used by others (cf. Bakhtin, 1973). As Gebauer and Wulf write:

> Only in interaction with the outer world does the individual come to acquire his or her subjectivity (. . .). The development of the human individual's complex of impulses takes place in language, which is also responsible for conducting interaction with the world. Thus does there arise within a single system both the formation of the self and discrepancies between the self and the outer world. (Gebauer & Wulf, 1995, p. 275)

Gebauer and Wulf outline here an important thesis of the school of "historical anthropology," a school of thought developed at the Free University Berlin in

M. Kontopodis (✉)
Humboldt University Berlin, Berlin, Germany
e-mail: michaliskonto@googlemail.com

M. Kontopodis et al. (eds.), *Children, Development and Education*, International Perspectives on Early Childhood Education and Development 3, DOI 10.1007/978-94-007-0243-1_1, © Springer Science+Business Media B.V. 2011

Germany over the course of the last 30 years. This school of thought can be seen as a revision of the German philosophical anthropology under the influences of the French historical school of Annales and the Anglo-Saxon cultural anthropology. Historical anthropology examines the historical and cultural situation of humankind today as connected with the significance of signs (gestures, oral and written language and pictures) in social evolution, especially in western civilizations (Dux, 2000; Gebauer & Kamper, 1989; Gebauer & Wulf, 1995; Wulf, 1997, 2009; Wulf & Kamper, 2002). In this context, the relations between child development and culture have become a particular focus for a great deal of historical anthropological theory and research (Wulf, 2004, 2007, 2010; Wulf, Göhlich, & Zirfas, 2001).

The primacy of language and signs for the constitution of human subjectivity was also the main research subject of another school of thought that emerged in the context of the Soviet revolution and deeply affected the discipline of psychology in the twentieth century. The experienced reader will understand that we refer here to the approach of Vygotsky and his colleagues and students, as well as to what has later been called the "cultural-historical school," "cultural-historical activity theory," "post-Vygotskian research," or simply "non-classical psychology" (Chaiklin, 2001; Daniels, 2008; Daniels, Cole, & Wertsch, 2007; Fichtner, 1996; Fleer, Hedegaard, & Tudge, 2009; Lompscher, 1989; Robbins & Stetsenko, 2002; Stetsenko & Arievitch, in press; van Oers, Elbers, Wardekker, & van der Veer, 2008).

According to Vygotsky, development occurs *in* the relationship between the child and its environment (Vygotsky, 1931/1997, 1934/1987). Post-Vygotskian approaches to teaching, learning, and development have thoroughly studied how signs and tools mediate the communication between teachers and students, adults and children, as well as between one's 'inner speech' and oneself, shaping one's thinking and imagination. According to this approach, the very 'nature' of subjectivity, i.e. psychological processes such as thinking, imagination, or motivation, is constituted through the use of the signs and tools available in a civilization at a particular historical moment (Hildebrand-Nilshon, 1980; Hildebrand-Nilshon, Kim, & Papadopoulos, 2002; Seeger, Voigt, & Waschescio, 1998; van Oers et al., 2008; see also Chapter 4, this book). Concepts such as appropriation, agency, activity, and semiotic mediation have been central to this kind of theory and research.

The edited volume *Children, Development and Education: Cultural, Historical, Anthropological Perspectives* brings together these two approaches to children and child development so similar to each other: historical anthropology and cultural-historical psychology. The history of the ideas of both approaches can be traced back to the German classical philosophy of the late eighteenth and nineteenth centuries. W. Benjamin's works are of particular importance for historical anthropology, while the works of L.S. Vygotsky and activity theory are central for the cultural-historical approaches to child development. At the same time each approach has specific strengths – theoretical, methodological or empirical – that, when combined, can prove of particular importance for the further development of childhood research and educational practice.

Cultural-historical psychology has developed theoretical tools with which to study subjective phenomena such as the development of abstract thinking or of imagination. It has also studied collective subjectivity (or subjectivities) and its (i.e. their) active contribution to societal change and the making of history. These theoretical and methodological accomplishments advance the understanding of current society and minimize the "great divide" between theory and practice, thus suggesting novel forms of social organization.

Anthropology, on the other hand, has developed a theoretical and methodological sensitivity to children's alterity. It has also developed a great sensitivity towards alterity in general, which depending on the particular context of investigation can be alterity of gender, class, (sub-)culture, race, color, or age. It is obvious, even in an era of globalization deeply marked in its content and form by Western culture, that different forms of human life exist today, influenced by various local, regional, and national cultures. Within this framework, the focus of anthropological research lies on the social and cultural diversity of human life. Quite apart from creating sensitivity for the strange and foreign character of other cultures, anthropological work also creates sensitivity for that which is strange and foreign in one's own culture. The (self-)reflexive point of view adopted by cultural and historical anthropology towards European cultures has contributed to the considerable evolution and advancement of anthropological knowledge (cf. Evans-Pritchard, 1965; Harris, 2001; Lévi-Strauss, 1992; Malinowski, 1922; Mead, 1950; Sahlins, 1976).

This sensitivity has not been adequately elaborated in cultural-historical psychology. Cultural-historical psychology "grew up" in a "modern" context, never questioning objectivity in general and the scientific representation of childhood, gender, race, or class in the radical way anthropology has (Marcus, 1986; Wulf, 2002; Wulf et al., 2001). Furthermore, cultural-historical psychology has not widely studied the senses and embodiment to which Pessoa so poetically refers in the introductory quote and which play an important role in everyday rituals and ritualizations and have thus always been a major object of study for anthropology (Wulf, 1997, 2001; Wulf & Kamper, 2002).

Despite the aforementioned minor differences or specific strengths of these approaches, it is quite obvious that cultural-historical psychology and historical anthropology are grounded on similar theoretical prerequisites, share a similar interest for children and education, and, as we will see, involve similar methodologies. However, until now they have never been in dialogue. While literally working next to each other at the Free University of Berlin, the editors and authors of this volume soon realized that cultural-historical psychology and historical anthropology could be complementary to each other. This edited book is the result of this local interdisciplinary research cooperation between German anthropologists, educational scientists, and cultural psychologists. This research cooperation has slowly grown into an international endeavor and dealt with theoretical and empirical issues related to early child development, the history of childhood, everyday child-related practices, and emerging educational challenges (2004 until today)[1]. In the following we will refer more analytically to the main ideas of this interdisciplinary work: subjectivity, performativity, infans absconditus, and historicity.

---

[1] See acknowledgements for details.

First Motion: Subjectivity

In the above-presented quote, Pessoa echoes Walter Benjamin in his *Berlin Childhood around 1900* (Benjamin, 2006). Benjamin shows in this autobiography how children appropriate the world mimetically: like a poet they establish similarities between themselves and the outer world; mimetically they discover streets, squares, and the various rooms of their home. Children's poetic and metaphoric interpretation of the world, which views the world of objects as something that is animated and responsive to themselves, is established by making themselves similar to the objects. In this process, children extend themselves into the world, accord it a place in their own internal imaginary worlds, and educate themselves. As this world is always historically and culturally determined and its objects endowed with meaning therefore symbolically encoded, these mimetic processes also lead to the *enculturation* of children. With the help of their mimetic abilities, children acquire the meaning of objects and forms of representation and action. A mimetic movement thus serves as a bridge between a child and the outer world (see also Chapter 5 by Wulf, this book).

For Vygotsky, theoretically grasping a particular developmental level involves discovering the transformations in a child's *entire personality*. It means understanding a special kind of *drama* with its major and minor roles, central and peripheral lines of development, evolutionary and involutionary elements. The specific *social situation of development* is to be understood as a dynamic system, as a context in which a child effects his or her own development by engaging in a dialogue with his or her environment (van Oers, 1998; Vygotsky, 1934/1987; Wygotski, 1987a). Placed in the broader context of spinozic monism (Spinoza & Curley, 1994), development for Vygotsky is not about the development of cognitive or professional skills, but about the development of a child or an adolescent as a whole person *in relation to* other persons and to the society as a whole (Kotik-Friedgut & Friedgut, 2008; Robbins, 2001, 2003; Vygotsky, 1933/2002). Vygotsky is especially interested in "critical age levels" in which the "dialectical laws of development" are manifest (Wygotski, 1987b).

A much-disputed concept that belongs in this framework and carries revolutionary implications for developmental theory and educational practice (cf. Newman & Holzman, 1993) is the Vygotskian notion of the "zone of proximal development" (Vygotsky, 1929/2005, 1930–1934/1998, 1934/1987, 1934/1999). Chaiklin has reviewed all of Vygotsky's texts in which this term appears and questions the definition of the term, since Vygotsky himself does not provide it and there is no outline of the theory of the "zone of proximal development" (Chaiklin, 2003). Chaiklin argues against the various "common sense" interpretations of the "zone of proximal development" and their implications for educational practice. The main features of the "zone of proximal development" as summarized by Chaiklin are the following: (a) it involves the whole child, (b) development is concerned with the relations between psychological functions and not the psychological functions as such, (c) development takes place as a qualitative change in these relationships, (d) change is brought about by the child's actions in the social situation of development, and (e) each age period is characterized by a leading activity/contradiction that organizes the child's actions through which new functions develop (Chaiklin, 2003, p. 50).

In the psychology of Vygotsky, development is not considered to be an inner progression of states that follow one another; Vygotsky's psychology is processual and relational. We would like to emphasize here that seen from our perspective, the notion of proximity in development indicates not a following *temporal* phase but the *space* of social relations that can be further developed. Proximity understood in this sense is *proximity to the unknown* – and not to the known. The "zone of proximal development" is thus defined as the distance between the known and the unknown. The dialogue and tension between the given and the forthcoming, the past and the future fascinates Benjamin in the analysis of his own childhood under the threat of fascism (Adorno & Benjamin, 2005; Benjamin, 2006). It also fascinates Vygotsky in his analysis of the tragedy of Hamlet (Vygotsky, 1925/1971) and of the crises of development (Vygotsky, 1932–1934/1998). These dynamic and conflicting aspects of child development and everyday action in educational institutions are given particular emphasis in the second part of this book.

An important idea implied in concepts such as "mimesis," "zone of proximal development" (see above), "appropriation" (Stetsenko & Arievitch, 2010), or "motive" (Hedegaard, 2001; Leont'ev, 1978), is *active subjectivity*, i.e. the idea that children and youngsters as well as scientists or teachers act according to their own intentions and motivations, actively participating in defining how signs and tools are used (Stetsenko, 2005). Active subjectivity can thus transform a given social situation so that new practices emerge. Being in the world is transforming the world, not adapting to it (Freire, 1973, 1986; Kontopodis, 2009a). Human development is the process of the purposeful transformation of the world, a process which is collaborative per definitionem (Liberali & Rahmilevitz, 2007; Stetsenko, 2008; Vianna & Stetsenko, 2006). Desires, affects, and emotions play here a very important role[2]. In this regard, one could argue that Vygotsky's approach shares a great proximity with Benjamin's approach, whose work is one of the cornerstones of historical anthropology, as we mentioned above. Emotions and affects are what bring different people to act together, thus transforming themselves as well as social and societal relations (cf. Chapter 12 by Kontopodis, this book).

It is quite well known that Vygotsky tries to conceptualize child development in terms of *drama* – a drama in terms of theatre and performativity during which different tensions collide and novelty is generated. Very recently Veresov (2004) has pointed out an aspect of the "zone of proximal development" which has hitherto been overlooked: emphasizing the influence of art on Vygotsky, Veresov interprets

---

[2]Vygotsky studied intensively Spinoza and Nietzsche and was affiliated with Trotsky. This last influence is made explicit in his texts about emotions and art, which were censored by th ideological machine of the Soviet Union (for details see: Dafermos, 2002, p. 81, Keiler, 2002).

Vygotsky's work as a psychology in terms of "drama." He uses the term "emotionally colored experience" (perezhevanie) to refer to development according to Vygotsky as a process that is dynamic and lived-through. In the zone of proximal development, as Veresov argues, *"dramatic events"* occur and contradictory aspects collide – crisis and conflict arise and thus development emerges. There is no way of predicting or foreseeing the outcome of these dramatic events. After a dramatic event, nothing is as it was. In this context, Vygotsky attributes particular attention in his developmental theory to emotions, intensity, and desire (Delari, 2009; Puzyrei, 2007; Veresov, 2004; Vygotsky, 1929/2005). He considers play the cornerstone of development:

> "An idea that has become an affect, a concept that has turned into a passion" – this ideal of Spinoza's finds its prototype in play, which is the realm of spontaneity and freedom. (...)
> In short, play gives the child a new form of desires, i.e., teaches him to desire by relating his desires to a fictitious "I" – to his role in the game and its rules. Therefore, a child's greatest achievements are possible in play – achievements that tomorrow will become his average level of real action and his morality (Vygotsky, 1933/2002, online).

Seen from this perspective, child development is studied and conceptualized not only in terms of plurality but also in terms of intensity, conflict, and controversy between different value positions, the outcome of which nobody can predict (Dafermos, 2002; Gebauer & Wulf, 1995; Vygotsky, 1929/2005). As becomes evident in most chapters of this book, the process of merging the subjective and the cultural-historical includes biographical ruptures; it embodies social controversies and reflects power relations.

Second Motion: Performativity

However important signs, metaphors and language might be, the senses and the body – in the quote by Pessoa the tears and their liquid bitterness – are central to mimetic processes and to ritualized situations that involve particular emotions and feelings. Historical anthropology does not employ the notion of *drama* – however, it has developed a methodology for the study of everyday *rituals,* which are hardly different from dramas. Rituals and ritualizations have a beginning and an end. They are characterized by their dynamics, which cause adaptations and changes in child behavior. Their corporeal practices create forms of action, images, and schemata, which children identify with, which they remember, and the performance and enactment of which bring forth new forms of actions. During the performance of rituals and ritual practices, the participants relate immediately and directly to the actions of other participants. This takes place in a largely mimetic manner, using the senses, the movements of the body and the common understanding of words, sounds, tastes, smells, language, and music. Rituals can be conceived as small, everyday performances that include conflict potential, express power relations and at the same time accept and question a given social order (Wulf, 2004, 2010; Wulf & Zirfas, 2004; Wulf et al., 2001).

Geertz regarded culture as an "assembly of texts" and saw a necessity for a "thick description" (Geertz, 1975, 1995). On the basis of a similar background, classic hermeneutics assumed the existence of a deeper structure of meaning that was contained in (educational) reality and has to be brought to light by the researcher. However, extensive discussions about the "crisis of representation" (Berg & Fuchs, 1993) and the so-called "performative turn" moved the focus of attention from meanings and representations themselves to the ways in which they are performed, employed, and enacted to constitute realities. In this context, historical anthropology shifted its attention from the *hermeneutics* of pedagogic and educational reality to the *performativity* of pedagogic and educational practice (Wulf, 2003; Wulf & Zirfas, 2007).

Departing from a performative understanding of culture historical anthropological research has recently looked into *how* children learn, *how* they perform their learning, and *how* this manifests itself in their interactions with other children. It is only in interaction with other children that children pursue their own learning program. Historical anthropological research here begins to resemble Vygotskyan and post-Vygotskian research. However, it sheds another light on development by focusing on the performativity of *difference* in everyday interactions. For example, the question of *how* boys distance themselves from girls and *how* girls distance themselves from boys during class activities has been crucial in a series of recent studies (Tervooren, 2006; Wagner-Willi, 2005; Wulf, 2010).

Rituals in education always relate to other rituals that have already taken place – either rituals in which one has participated or rituals of which one has heard an account. This makes the historical dimension a basic condition of rituals. Ritual actions involve mimetic references to earlier rituals. As these references are made mimetically, they create an "impression" of earlier performances of the ritual that is then adapted to suit the current context. Creating a mimetic link between the current and previous world ensures historical continuity in education thus legitimizing the current ritual activity, even if it differs from its predecessor. Mimetic referencing is "taking on similarities," i.e. the repetition of a similar action that would not be possible if the previous ritual activity had not taken place. Mimetic reference does not mean that the ritual is recreated in exactly the same way every time.

In some cases the result of this mimetic referencing also leads to critical distancing from the reference point of the ritual, without this point of reference becoming superfluous. Mimetic referencing enables the current figurations and arrangements of ritual practices in education to be updated and modified to suit the context of the current instance. Mimetic constellations, staging styles and types of movement are adapted and changed according to necessity or taste. The "repetition" of earlier rituals does not result in a copy of this ritual in the sense of a copy as made by a photocopier. Rather, this repetition, which makes use of mimetically transferred and assimilated elements, creates something new for all participants although the predecessor is dialectically upheld. The ritual that has been updated by this mimetic process integrates the old ritual with a new purpose and a new appearance (Wulf, 2005; Wulf et al., 2001). The staging of rituals in education is always conducted in the context of previous ritual performances. However, these can differ enormously.

In some cases the relationship between old and new ritual performances is very close, and in other cases very loose.

Rituals do not only guard societal and cultural continuity, they also cause change. The practical knowledge required for their performance, which is acquired in mimetic processes, means that they are social dramas, and the performative character of these dramas changes social orders. Without rituals, social relations and communities would be unthinkable. Educational and social communities are formed in ritualized practices. Communities are the cause, the action, and the effect of rituals. These practices are creating an order, for the emergence of which power relations play an important role. Through regularity and repetition, the relationships between children and between children and adults are confirmed as well as modified.

Power issues between the genders and generations are also dealt with in everyday rituals such as at the family breakfast table (see Chapter 9 by Audehm, this book); this occurs in a seemingly casual manner that is all the more effective for its relaxed appearance. Ritual staging and performance allow several matters to be handled simultaneously in education. For example, children may demonstrate that they are no longer children and are on their way to the next stage of psychological development. They enact this passage through rituals, playfully making it public for their relatives and for their school community (Wulf, 2001).

To sum up, during the performative arrangement of rituals, a new social and educational reality is created. This reality is not completely new – previous models of it have existed before. However, it has not been present in this particular form at this particular location before this particular time. Taking earlier rituals as a basis, every performative arrangement in education creates a new ritual reality and a new ritual community. This ritual community can develop for the first time among the children or people who carry out the ritual practices, but it can also be a repetition of itself, whereby the community confirms its status as such.

The performative turn does not only draw our attention to rituals but in general to the question how semiotic, material and corporeal relations are performed in the classroom, at school or in other educational settings as well as to the question how can qualitatively new relations emerge. This has recently also been the focus of science and technology studies (Bowker & Star, 1999; Kontopodis & Niewöhner, 2011; Latour, 1994; Law, 2004), of post-feminist theory (Haraway, 1997; Wolfe, 2010), of performativity theory (Barad, 2003; Butler, 1997; Conquergood, 2002) and can be seen as a research direction that can prove very fruitful and significant in educational and psychological research (cf. Chapter 13 by Chronaki, this book; Chapter 8 by Ivinson, this book; Chapter 12 by Kontopodis, this book).

Third Motion: Infans Absconditus

Pessoa's quote at the very beginning of this introduction brings our attention to a further aspect of childhood: *infans absconditus*. Since children and adults live in modern societies and use language in different ways, children and adults have become radically different from each other. To adults, children and childhood display a confusing strangeness and heterogeneity, an absolute difference in relationship to them and their world. The mysterious presence of childhood and children is the presence of something that is *radically and irreducibly Other*. In communities, however, that have been less affected by European modernity, we do not encounter this radical strangeness and otherness of children in comparison to adults.

Researchers and educational practitioners participate in defining, generating or limiting otherness by means of scientific knowledge, methodology, and educational approach. Modern science, as a *form of knowledge* and a *process,* attempts to arrive at ever more precise approximations of reality. In doing so, it must presume that the essence of reality has already been determined, thus separating reality from its intrinsic becoming different-to-itself. This means that developmental psychology must already know what a "child" or "adolescent" is. Pedagogy assumes that it is known what kind of institution and organization a "school" is. The emergence of educational science and developmental psychology has long been associated with the establishment of public education in the eighteenth century as well as with European modernity in general. In this context, mainstream childhood research has thus been based on the western idea of the "general child" that finds itself in the process of developing into an adult. Educational and psychological research has thus often been criticized for relying on the normative conception of a universal, a-historical, rational human being, thereby reproducing power relations, defining and at the same time excluding otherness (Morss, 1990; Walkerdine, 1993; Wulf, 2002).

Neither the concept of mimesis, so crucial in Benjamin's work and further developed by Christoph Wulf and his colleagues (Gebauer & Wulf, 1995; Wulf, 2005), nor the concept of the "zone of proximal development" of Vygotsky (cf. Chaiklin, 2003) reduce children to predictable objects of knowledge or offer a way to exactly predict how a child is going to appropriate a given sign. Not only is childhood and child development a cultural-historical phenomenon (as claimed by post-Vygotskian and historical anthropological research); the methodologies and models employed for the study of children and childhood have also been *cultural-historically developed* and are also *cultural-historically situated*. There is thus a dialectical relation between the cultural-historical aspects of the phenomena studied and the cultural-historical specificity of the knowledge produced about it. We define this relation as "double culturality and historicity" (Wulf, 2009, p. 129). The epistemological position of double culturality and historicity enables cultural-historical scholars to reflect on both the cultural-historical character of childhood, education, and child development, *and* the cultural-historical specificity of their own discourses and methodologies.

This modest and reflective approach is very different from dominant modern childhood research; it cannot avoid making its own values explicit and becoming political. An emphasis is thus given to qualitative and interpretative methodologies that examine the different value positions of research subjectivities with sensitivity and reflectivity, such as qualitative or quasi-experiment, case-study analysis, ethnographic fieldwork, interpretative video-supported observation, and the analysis of photographs, interviews and group discussions. These methods should be combined wherever possible and are indispensable for obtaining complex and methodologically transparent research results. The methodologies followed by the authors in this volume provide an overview of the different methodological possibilities provided in cultural-historical and historical-anthropological research and reveal different aspects of the ways in which culture affects children's and young people's everyday lives and development.

Fourth Motion: Historicity

In his psychology, Vygotsky employs a concept of history stemming from Hegelian philosophy that Dafermos has examined in great detail (Dafermos, 2002, pp. 35–38). Also influenced by Marx's political economy as well as by the theory of evolution, Vygotsky introduced the "genetic historical approach" to developmental psychology. In Vygotsky's words:

> To study something historically means to study it in the process of change; that is the dialectical method's basic demand. To encompass in research the process of a given thing's development in all its phases and changes – from birth to death – fundamentally means to discover its nature, its essence, for it is only in movement that a body shows what it is. Thus, the historical study of behaviour is not an auxiliary aspect of theoretical study, but rather forms its very base (Vygotsky, 1930/1978, pp. 64–65).

Not only does Vygotsky conceive child development and schooling as cultural-historical phenomena, he also poses the question as to how human history can lead to a new type of society and a new type of human being (Vygotsky, 1934/1994). Critical educational (Davydov, 2008; Fichtner, 1996) and critical psychological research (Holzkamp, 1993) have been much inspired by Vygotsky as well as by the entire Soviet school of psychology (Davydov, 2008; Leont'ev, 1978; Lompscher & Galperin, 1972).

A quick review of cultural-historical psychological literature reveals, however, that the understanding of history of most cultural-historically oriented studies is very abstract and is not translated into a concrete methodology for the analysis of historical data[3]. Such an approach would investigate the history of childhood, disability, schooling and other related phenomena in combination with the history of the discipline *and* the history of local practices and traditions. It would have to be able to face the challenges and dilemmas such an investigation would pose.

Anthropology quite recently underwent a significant *historical turn*, as is apparent in the historical treatments of anthropological topics by the *Annales School* and the history of mentalities that flowed from it (Ariès & Duby, 1985; Burke, 1991). Fernand Braudel's study of the Mediterranean (Braudel, 1949), Emmanuel Le Roy Ladurie's of the village of Montaillou (Ladurie, 1979), Carlo Ginzburg's of the world of millers around 1600 (Ginzburg, 1980) may be cited as successful examples of this kind of approach. Under this influence, historical anthropology nowadays

---

[3]As an exception to this one might regard the work of Valsiner (1998) which offers a general methodological frame for the study of historical processes as well as enters into dialogue with anthropological approaches.

attempts, to bring into accord the historical and cultural determination of its perspectives and methods with the historical and cultural determination of its object of study. As a consequence, historical anthropology can harness insights gleaned in the humanities with those yielded by a critique of anthropology based on the history of philosophy. It can combine them to create new perspectives and lines of inquiry out of a new consciousness for methodological problems [4]. Historical anthropology is limited neither to certain spatial frames nor to particular epochs. Reflecting on its own historicity and its own cultural condition, it succeeds both in leaving behind the eurocentrism of the humanities and an antiquated view of history, and focuses on examining and discussing current and future problems (Wulf, 1997, 2009; Wulf & Kamper, 2002).

The critique of anthropology is itself a constituent part of historical anthropology, which leads to an epistemological uncertainty. At the same time, it is important – especially in the context of the present economic crisis – to emphasize, as Vygotsky did, that history has not yet come to an end, that human development is a process of purposeful collaborative transformation (Stetsenko, 2008) and we (can) actively contribute to the making of history and human development (see also: Kontopodis, 2009b).

Such an understanding of historicity goes together with the notions of "active subjectivity" and "drama" briefly introduced above. Furthermore, the notion of *practice*, not as opposed to *theory* but as dialectically related to it (Chaiklin & Lave, 1993), is very important here. From a Marxian/Hegelian point of view, theory is only meaningful to the extent in which it advances practice in the creation of a more equal society (Chapter 14 by Chaiklin, this book). Theoretical concepts such as those of situated cognition, of peripheral participation, or of communities of practice have long been employed in psychology as well as in anthropology in order to develop an understanding as to how people participate in practices that are cultural-historically rooted and at the same time transform these practices in emancipatory ways (Dreier, 2008; Hedegaard & Chaiklin, 2005; Lave & Wenger, 1991; van Oers, 2009).

Taking these terms seriously one could speak of a "cultural-historical science" as Seth Chaiklin does in the "instead of an epilogue" part of this book. On the basis of the ideas presented so far a cultural-historical science would try not only to analyze human practices but also to develop them thus participating in satisfying societally meaningful needs. In this regard, the book *Children, Development and Education: Cultural, Historical, Anthropological Perspectives* advances current scholarship and criticizes mainstream western developmental theories and educational practices by bringing into dialogue cultural-historical psychology and historical anthropology. By emphasizing communication, semiotic processes, and the use of artifacts, pictures, and technologies the edited volume places special focus on performativity, everyday action, school, family and community practices, and changing educational institutions. Divided into two main parts, "Culture, History and Child

---

[4]The study of Althans presented in Chapter 7 (this book) provides an example of this approach by exploring the double historicity and culturality of western childhood.

Development," "Gender, Performativity and Educational Practice" the book may be seen as an important contribution to the fields of cultural-historical research, educational science, developmental psychology, and childhood studies.

The Contents of This Volume

Part I: Culture, History and Child Development

The first part "Culture, History and Child Development" presents a compination of theoretical and empirical theoretical works that examine childhood and child development as products of the transformative powers of history, culture and society over nature. It enacts a dialogue between classical texts of Vygotsky and/or Benjamin and current research from disciplines as diverse as developmental psychology, the anthropology of childhood, and evolutionary anthropology. Human development is thus explored and conceptualized in regard to its interrelated semiotic, material/embodied, mimetic and performative aspects.

In her opening paper "Darwin and Vygotsky on Development: An Exegesis on Human Nature" *Anna Stetsenko* suggests an alternative to the evolutionary and neurological reductionisms that are currently becoming dominant in psychology. She charts an approach to the human mind and to development in which people are revealed as being shaped by history, culture, and society at the same time as they themselves create and continue these processes in the ever-expanding fabric of their communal life.

In the framework provided by Stetsenko, *Falk Seeger & Martin Hildebrand-Nilshon* examine in their paper "Two Lines of Development: Reconsidering and Updating Vygotsky's Argument" how Vygotsky's example of the development of the pointing gesture is situated within more recent developments in developmental psychology, comparative psychology, and the analytical philosophy of language. Drawing on these approaches and findings, Seeger and Hildebrand-Nilshon develop the Vygotskian argument of two lines of development (natural and social/cultural) and claim that from the moment of birth – and possibly even before – human infants turn out to be super-social attractors. Being born into an environment so deeply saturated with signs and meaning requires intentional understanding as basic to all other human activity.

Seeger & Martin Hildebrand-Nilshon's analysis is continued in the chapter **Material Culture, Semiotics and Early Childhood Development** by *Christiane Moro*. Moro focuses on the materiality, variety, and complexity of semiotic systems and their interactions as source and resource for psychological development in early infancy. She explores human thoughts and matter as mutually constitutive. She analyses a series of everyday observations of children dealing with material objects such as telephone devices under the guidance of adults in quasi-experimental settings and contributes to theory building about the material aspects of mediation thus criticizing speech-centric developmental psychological and educational approaches.

Within a similar perspective, the next chapter by *Sigrid Klasen* analyzes the early communication between mother and child while employing micro-sequential video analysis. In her study "Touching Each Other: Video analysis of Mother–Infant Interaction after the Birth," Klasen examines the mimetical, performative, and embodied aspects of early mother–child communication and how these contribute to the establishment of community relations between the mother and the newborn.

Concluding those critical to speech - centric approaches studies *Christoph Wulf* in his paper "Mimesis in Early Childhood: Enculturation, Practical Knowledge and Performativity" elaborates on the notion of "mimesis." On the basis of a historical analysis of the term in western philosophy (Aristotle, Plato, Benjamin) and by taking a critical look at recent findings of evolutionary anthropology, Wulf argues the importance of mimesis for human evolution and development. Wulf's analysis leads to similar conclusions as those of Stetsenko and Hildebrand and Seeger: it foregrounds the social character of developmental processes. At the same time, Wulf also examines the corporeal aspects and the creative potential of mimesis. The chapter by Wulf can thus be read as a "conclusion" or an "outlook" to the first part of this book.

Part II: Performativity and Educational Practice

As a transition from the first to the second part, the next paper "Speculative Imaginations: Infancy in Educational Discourse of Early Modern Germany," by *Birgit Althans* examines how scientific and pictorial representations simultaneously express and form understandings of childhood and shape associated cultural practices. Althans' study illuminates the interrelation between scientific and artistic *images* of childhood and scientific and artistic *imagination* and enables a critical analysis of current western childhood-related practices (medicalization, scientification, objectification).

The chapter by Althans adds a historical or – better say – genealogical dimension to the account developed in the first part of this book. It opens the second part "Gender, Performativity and Educational Practice" which reveals multiple aspects of the ways in which children's and young people's everyday lives and development are shaped in-between and through various institutional practices. While the first part of this volume focuses more on infancy and early childhood development (as also does the transitory chapter by Althans), the second part focuses more on qualitative studies of school-aged children and young people. While the possibilities to escape given power relations are investigated and/or discussed, a specific focus is given here on multiple identities, difference, materiality and performativity[5].

---

[5]Although many types or modes of "difference" are investigated, we decided to use the word "gender" in the title of this part in order to make clear the connection to feminist scholarship and especially the so-called "third wave" of feminism.

In her study "A Cultural-historical Approach to Children's Development of Multiple Cultural Identities," *Mariane Hedegaard* analyzes interviews with children from Turkish cultural minority families who have just completed 9 years in a Danish school. Hedegaard explores conflicting situations in which the institutional demands of a concrete school practice are in conflict with the student's own motives. Instead of defining this conflict as "cultural", she suggests a cultural-historical activity approach that moves beyond the given anthropological and psychological understandings of identity. In this frame, Hedegaard suggests that the conflict is about how participants in school practice (Danish teachers and students from immigrant families) should develop a shared practice.

The next chapter of the book moves from the study of cultural differences to the study of age-related differences, and focuses on family settings. Kathrin Audehm analyzes the ritualized performance of children and their parents during eating. In her paper "Under The Sign of the Coffee Pot: Mealtime Rituals as Performative Practices," Audehm interprets ethnographic material of a German middle-class family's breakfast. By making use of Bourdieu's concept of social magic, she analyzes the performative effects of rituals of the table and argues that what is going on during rituals of the table is education.

Maintaining the focus upon difference, the study by *Gabrielle Ivinson* brings together cultural-historical theory and feminist approaches in order to examine how gender emerges in classroom practices and how boys and girls recognize and access different kinds of semiotic assemblages during different curriculum activities. Under the title "School Curriculum as Developmental Resource: Gender and Knowledge," Ivinson draws on ethnographic work in year 8 (students aged 12/13) single-sex drama classes at a British comprehensive secondary school. She investigates the classrooms as semiotic fields with a range of linguistic and non-linguistic signifiers and demonstrates how historical legacies that intermesh gender with knowledge are embodied and performed in curricular subjects.

Both historical anthropology and cultural-historical psychology emphasize that neither subjectivities nor objectivities (signs, tools etc.) exist outside of practice (Chapter 14 by Chaiklin, this book, Papadopoulos, 1999; Wulf & Zirfas, 2004). Children and youngsters as well as scientists and teachers not only actively participate in defining how signs and tools are used in everyday practices, but are also shaped through these practices. This twofold character of practice, which includes uncertainty, has been thoroughly examined not only by cultural-historical approaches but also by Foucault, Martin, Gutman, and Hutton (1988) and Foucault, Gros, Ewald, and Fontana (2005) and by process philosophy (Badiou, 2005; Deleuze & Guattari, 1980/1987). It has recently been the focus of science and technology studies (Bowker & Star, 1999; Kontopodis & Niewöhner, 2011; Latour, 1999; Law & Mol, 2002; Mol, 2002), of feminist theory (Blackman & Walkerdine, 2001; Haraway, 1997; Walkerdine, 1998), of performativity theory (Barad, 2003; Butler, 1997; Conquergood, 2002), and of critical psychology (Dreier, 2008; Stephenson & Papadopoulos, 2006).

In this broader frame *Estrid Sørensen's* paper "Configuration of Ontologies: an Inquiry into Learning Designs," takes as its point of departure the well-known 5th

Dimension learning design (Cole, 1996), which is founded on cultural-historical activity theory but applies an actor-network theory approach in analyzing the ordering of the 5th Dimension game as well as another internet-based project, Femtedit, which shares a lot of 5th Dimension's features but provides a much more flexible virtual environment. Sørensen analyzes the ways in which the different environments lead to different kinds of activities, and suggests that children and materials, humans and artifacts are co-constituted so that different human–artifact configurations lead to different distributions of agency.

As a further contribution to the discussion about educational practice, *Michalis Kontopodis*, in his paper "Enacting Human Developments: from Representation to Virtuality," brings together materials from two different research projects: ethnographic research that took place at an experimental vocational school in Germany from 2004 till 2005, and a literature-based analysis of a similar school project that took place in the Woodrow Wilson School in Long Beach California, USA from 1994 till 1998. The analysis of the presented material points out that "development" is not something happening "out-there," in the school or in everyday life; nor is it just a discursive category specialists use "in-here" to describe what is happening "out-there." Development is instead the product, the enactment, or the relation between the "in-here" and the "out-there." This relation is mediated through documents, diaries, photos, CVs, and other tools.

The attempt to bring together cultural-historical thinking with actor-network theory and performativity theory continues in the next chapter of the book, "Troubling' Essentialist Identities: Performative Mathematics and the Politics of Possibility." *Anna Chronaki* analyzes three cases of Tsiggano children who deal with school mathematics in distinct ways. Chronaki examines how participating in school arithmetic rituals involves performing certain learning identities and in some situations disrupts norms, and "troubles" - in Butler's (1990) words - hegemonic discourses about who is able, and who is not, to do well in school mathematics.

Instead of an Epilogue

Our edited volume concludes with the chapter "The Role of 'Practice' in Cultural-historical Science," by *Seth Chaiklin*. This chapter can be read as an epilogue to the whole book and claims that it is possible to conceive of "cultural-historical science" as a science directed at the study of human practices. Chaiklin elaborates on the epistemological and methodological implications of this theoretical position, and formulates some general principles of investigation in cultural-historical science. He claims that research in cultural-historical science should not just lead to a better understanding of existing human practices, but also to the development of new ones.

One could thus say that with a special focus on late-modern European societies with their multiplicity of inner societal groups and communities, the book *Children, Development and Education: Cultural, Historical, Anthropological Perspectives* does not only present reports from the cutting edge of developmental and educational psychological and anthropological research but constitutes a whole that is more than its parts. The edited volume highlights differences in ethos that depend on where, how, and with whom someone lives. Such an approach sets cultural-historical practice at the center and employs it as an organizing principle for conducting research. It also makes clear that practice is always to be thought of in terms of diversity and heterogeneity. Distinguished contributors highlight the dynamic and creative aspects of everyday action and the dramatic aspects of child development and search for innovative ways to translate cultural-historical and historical anthropological theory and research findings into a thorough understanding of emerging phenomena in the fields of childhood and youth education and development.

Acknowledgements The work presented here is the result of long interdisciplinary research cooperation between anthropologists, educational scientists, and psychologists and has its origins at two international conferences funded by the German Research Foundation and co-organized by Michalis Kontopodis, Christoph Wulf, Bernd Fichtner, Martin Hildebrand-Nilshon, and Maria Benites at the Free University Berlin (2006) and at the University of Siegen (2007) as well as at further meetings held in the context of International Conferences in Toronto (ISTP, 2007) and San Diego (ISCAR, 2008). We would like to thank the German Research Foundation, the Faculty of Education and Psychology at the Free University Berlin, the Department of Educational Science at the University of Siegen and the Department of European Ethnology at the Humboldt University Berlin for making this long international scientific exchange possible, as well as for funding the translation and proof-reading of the chapters of this book. Special thanks are due to Kareth Schaffer, Diana Aurisch, and Thomas La Presti for their patience in dealing with all the challenges of translation and proof-reading, and for the excellence of their work. Last but not least we would like to thank the Springer Series' "International Perspectives on Early Childhood Education and Development" editors, Marilyn Fleer and Ingrid Pramling, for their kind cooperation in publishing this book.

References

Adorno, G., & Benjamin, W. (2005). *W. Benjamin: Briefwechsel 1930–1940*. Frankfurt am Main: Suhrkamp.

Ariès, P., & Duby, G. (1985). *Histoire de la vie privée*, vol. 1–5. Paris: Seuil.

Badiou, A. (2005). *Being and event*. London and New York: Continuum.

Bakhtin, M. (1973). *Problems of Dostoevsky's poetics*. Ann Arbor: Ardis.

Barad, K. (2003). Posthumanist performativity: Toward an understanding of how matter comes to matter. *Signs: Journal of Women in Culture and Society, 28*, 801–831.

Benjamin, W. (2006). *Berlin Childhood around 1900*. Cambridge, MA: Belknap Press of Harvard University Press.

Berg, E., & Fuchs, M. (Eds.). (1993). *Kultur, Soziale Praxis, Text: Die Krise der Ethnographischen Repräsentation*. Frankfurt am Main: Suhrkamp.

Blackman, L., & Walkerdine, V. (2001). *Mass Hysteria: Critical Psychology and Media Studies*. Houndmills and New York: Palgrave.

Bowker, G., & Star, S. L. (1999). *Sorting things out: Classification and its consequences*. Cambridge, MA: MIT Press.

Braudel, F. (1949). *La Méditerranée et le monde méditerranéen à l'époque de Philippe II*. Paris: A. Colin.

Burke, P. (1991). *The French historical revolution: The Annales school, 1929–89*. Stanford: Stanford University Press.

Butler, J. (1990). *Gender trouble: Feminism and the subversion of identity*. New York. Routledge.

Butler, J. (1997). *Excitable speech: A politics of the performative*. London and New York: Routledge.

Chaiklin, S. (2001). *The theory and practice of cultural-historical psychology*. Aarhus: Aarhus University Press.

Chaiklin, S. (2003). The Zone of Proximal Development in Vygotsky's analysis of learning and instruction. In A. Kozulin, B. Gindis, V. Ageyey, & S. Miller (Eds.), *Vygotsky's educational theory in cultural context* (pp. 39–64). Cambridge: Cambridge University Press.

Chaiklin, S., & Lave, J. (1993). *Understanding practice: Perspectives on activity and context*. Cambridge; New York: Cambridge University Press.

Cole, M. (1996). *Cultural psychology: A once and future discipline*. Cambridge, MA: Belknap Press of Harvard University Press.

Conquergood, D. (2002). Performance studies: Interventions and radical research. *The Drama Review, 46*(2), 145–156.

Dafermos, M. (2002). *The cultural-historical theory of Vytgotsky: Philosophical, psychological and pedagogical aspects*. Athens: Atrapos.

Daniels, H. (2008). *Vygotsky and research*. London: Routledge.

Daniels, H., Cole, M., & Wertsch, J. V. (Eds.). (2007). *The Cambridge companion to Vygotsky*. Cambridge and New York: Cambridge University Press.

Davydov, V. (2008). *Problems of developmental instruction: A theoretical and experimental psychological study*. Hauppauge, NY: Nova Science Publishers.

Delari, A. Jr., Passos, B., & Vladimirovna, I. (2009). *Alguns sentidos da palavra perejivanie em L. S. Vigotski: notas para estudo futuro junto á psicologia russa*. Accessed November 21, 2010, from http://www.vigotski.net/casa.htm

Deleuze, G., & Guattari, F. (1980/1987). *A thousand plateaus: Capitalism and Schizophrenia* (B. Massumi, Trans.). Minneapolis: University of Minnesota Press.

Dreier, O. (2008). *Psychotherapy in everyday life*. Cambridge and New York: Cambridge University Press.

Dux, G. (2000). *Historisch-Genetische Theorie Der Kultur*. Weilerwist: Velbrück.

Evans-Pritchard, E. E. (1965). *Theories of primitive religion*. Oxford: Oxford University Press.

Fichtner, B. (1996). *Lernen Und Lerntätigkeit. Phylogenetische, Ontogenetische Und Epistemologische Studien*. Magburg: BdWi-Verlag.

Fleer, M., Hedegaard, M., & Tudge, J. (2009). *World yearbook of education 2009: Childhood studies and the impact of globalization: Policies and practices at global and local levels*. New York: Routledge.

Foucault, M., Gros, F., Ewald, F., & Fontana, A. (2005). *The Hermeneutics of the subject: Lectures at the Collège De France, 1981–1982*. New York: Palgrave-Macmillan.

Foucault, M., Martin, L. H., Gutman, H., & Hutton, P. H. (1988). *Technologies of the self: A seminar with Michel Foucault*. Amherst: University of Massachusetts Press.

Freire, P. (1973). *Education for critical consciousness*. New York: Seabury Press.

Freire, P. (1986). *Pedagogy of the oppressed*. New York: Continuum.

Gebauer, G., & Kamper, D. (Eds.). (1989). *Historische Anthropologie. Zum Problem Der Humanwissenschaften Heute Oder Versuche Einer Neubegründung*. Reinbek: Rowohlt-Taschenbuch.

Gebauer, G., & Wulf, C. (1995). *Mimesis: Culture, art, society*. Berkeley: University of California Press.

Geertz, C. (1975). *The interpretation of cultures: Selected essays*. London: Hutchinson.

Geertz, C. (1995). *After the fact: Two countries, four decades, one anthropologist*. Cambridge, MA: Harvard University Press.

Ginzburg, C. (1980). *The cheese and the worms. The cosmos of a sixteenth-century Miller*. Baltimore: Johns Hopkins University Press.

Haraway, D. (1997). *Modest_Witness@Second_Millennium. Femaleman© Meets Oncomouse*™. New York: Routledge.

Harris, M. (2001). *The rise of anthropological theory. A history of theories of cultures.* Walnut Creek, CA: Altamira Press.

Hedegaard, M. (2001). *Learning in classrooms: A cultural-historical approach.* Aarhus: Aarhus University Press.

Hedegaard, M., & Chaiklin, S. (2005). *Radical-local teaching and learning: A cultural-historical approach.* Aarhus: Aarhus University Press.

Hildebrand-Nilshon, M. (1980). *Die Entwicklung der Sprache: Phylogenese und Ontogenese.* Frankfurt/Main: Campus.

Hildebrand-Nilshon, M., Kim, C.-W., & Papadopoulos, D. (2002). *Kultur (in) Der Psychologie: Über Das Abenteuer Des Kulturbegriffs in Der Psychologischen Theorienbildung.* Heidelberg: Asanger.

Holzkamp, K. (1993). *Lernen: Subjektwissenschaftliche Grundlegung.* Frankfurt am Main: Campus.

Holzman, L. (2009). *Vygotsky at work and play.* London and New York: Routledge.

Hüppauf, B., & Wulf, C. (Eds.). (2009). *Dynamics and performativity of imagination: The image between the visible and the invisible.* New York: Routledge.

Keiler, P. (2002). *Lev Vygotsky: Ein Leben Für Die Psychologie.* Weinheim: Beltz.

Kontopodis, M. (2009a). Culture, dialogue and emerging educational challenges: An introduction. In M. Kontopodis (Ed.), *Children, culture & emerging educational challenges: A dialogue with Brazil* (pp. 9–23). Berlin: Lehmanns Media.

Kontopodis, M. (Ed.). (2009b). *Children, culture and emerging educational challenges: A dialogue with Latin America.* Berlin: Lehmanns Media.

Kontopodis, M., & Newnham, D. S. (Guest Eds.). (2011). Expanding Cultural-historical and Critical Perspectives on Child and Youth Development/ Introduction to Ethos Dialogue 2011. *Ethos, 35*(3).

Kontopodis, M., & Niewöhner, J. (Eds.). (2011). *Das Selbst als Netzwerk: Zum Einsatz von Körpern und Dingen im Alltag.* Bielefeld: transcript.

Kotik-Friedgut, B., & Friedgut, T. H. (2008). A man of his country and his time: Jewish influences on Lev Semionovich Vygotsky's world view. *History of Psychology, 11*(1), 15–39.

Ladurie, Le Roy E. (1978). *Montaillou: Cathars and catholics in a French village, 1294–1324.* London: Scolar Press.

Latour, B. (1994). Les Objets Ont-Ils Une Histoire? Rencontre De Pasteur Et De Whitehead Dans Un Bain D' Acide Lactique. In I. Stengers (Ed.), *L'effet Whitehead* (pp. 197–217). Paris: Vrin.

Latour, B. (1999). *Pandora's hope: Essays on the reality of science studies.* Cambridge, MA: Harvard University Press.

Lave, J., & Wenger, E. (1991). *Situated learning: Legitimate peripheral participation.* Cambridge and New York: Cambridge University Press.

Law, J. (2004). *After method: Mess in social science research.* London: Routledge.

Law, J., & Mol, A. (2002). *Complexities: Social studies of knowledge practices.* Durham: Duke University Press.

Lévi-Strauss, C. (1992). *Tristes tropiques.* New York: Atheneum.

Leont'ev, A. (1978). *Activity, consciousness, and personality.* Englewood Cliffs, NJ: Prentice and Hall.

Liberali, F., & Rahmilevitz, E. (2007). Shared creativity in Brazilian schools: Different contexts, one pursuit. In V. Kalnberzina (Ed.), *Radosa Personiba (Creative Personality)* (pp. 261–266). Riga: SIA.

Lompscher, J. (1989). *Psychologische Analysen der Lerntätigkeit.* Berlin: Volk und Wissen.

Lompscher, J., & Galperin, P. J. (1972). *Probleme der Ausbildung Geistiger Handlungen: Neuere Untersuchungen zur Anwendung der Lerntheorie Galperins.* Berlin: Volk und Wissen.

Malinowski, B. (1922). *Argonauts of the Western Pacific.* London: Routledge.

Marcus, G. E. (1986). Contemporary problems of ethnography in the modern world system. In J. Clifford & G. E. Marcus (Eds.), *Writing culture: The poetics and politics of ethnography* (pp. 165–193). Berkeley, CA: University of California Press.

Mead, M. (1950). *Sex and temperament in three primitive societies*. New York: New American Library.

Mol, A. (2002). *The body multiple: Ontology in medical practice*. Durham: Duke University Press.

Morss, J. (1990). *The biologising of childhood: Developmental psychology and the Darwinian myth*. Hove and East Sussex: Erlbaum.

Newman, F., & Holzman, L. (1993). *Lev Vygotsky: Revolutionary scientist*. London: Routledge.

Papadopoulos, D. (1999). *Lew S. Wygotski: Werk Und Wirkung*. Frankfurt am Main: Campus.

Pessoa, F. (2001). *The book of disquiet by Bernardo Soares, assistant bookkeeper in the city of Lisbon* (R. Zenith, Trans.). London and New York: Penguin.

Puzyrei, A. A. (2007). Contemporary psychology and Vygotsky's cultural-historical theory. *Journal of Russian and East European Psychology, 45*(1), 8–93.

Robbins, D. (2001). *Vygotsky's psychology-philosophy: A metaphor for language theory and learning*. New York: Kluwer Academic/Plenum Publishers.

Robbins, D. (2003). *Vygotsky's and A.A. Leontiev's semiotics and psycholinguistics: Applications for education, second language acquisition, and theories of language*. Westport: Praeger Publishers.

Robbins, D., & Stetsenko, A. (Eds.). (2002). *Voices within Vygotsky's non-classical psychology: Past, present, future*. New York: Nova Science.

Sahlins, M. (1976). *Culture and practical reason*. Chicago: Chicago University Press.

Seeger, F., Voigt, J., & Waschescio, U. (1998). *The culture of the mathematics classroom*. Cambridge and New York: Cambridge University Press.

Spinoza, B. de, & Curley, E. M. (1994). *A Spinoza reader: The ethics and other works*. Princeton, NJ: Princeton University Press.

Stephenson, N., & Papadopoulos, D. (2006). *Analysing everyday experience: Social research and political change*. London: Palgrave Macmillan.

Stetsenko, A. (2005). Activity as object-related: Resolving the dichotomy of individual and collective planes of activity. *Mind, Culture and Activity, 12*(1), 70–88.

Stetsenko, A. (2008). From relational ontology to transformative activist stance on development and learning: Expanding Vygotsky's (CHAT) project. *Cultural Studies of Science Education, 3*, 471–491.

Stetsenko, A., & Arievitch, I. (2010). Cultural-historical activity theory: Foundational worldview and major principles. In J. Martin & S. Kirschner (Eds.), *Sociocultural Perspectives in Psychology* (pp. 231–253). New York, NY: Columbia University Press.

Tervooren, A. (2006). *Im Spielraum von Geschlecht und Begehren: Ethnographie Der Ausgehenden Kindheit*. Weinheim: Juventa.

Valsiner, J. (1998). *The guided mind: A sociogenetic approach to personality*. Cambridge, MA: Harvard University Press.

van Oers, B. (1998). From context to contextualizing. *Learning and Instruction, 8*(6), 473–488.

van Oers, B. (2009). Developmental education: Improving participation in cultural practices. In M. Fleer, M. Hedegaard, & J. Tudge (Eds.), *Childhood studies and the impact of globalization: Policies and practices at global and local levels (World yearbook of education 2009)* (pp. 293–317). New York: Routledge.

van Oers, B., Elbers, E., Wardekker, W., & van der Veer, R. (Eds.). (2008). *The transformation of learning: Advances in cultural-historical activity theory*. Cambridge and New York: Cambridge University Press.

Veresov, N. (2004). Zone of Proximal Development (ZPD): The Hidden Dimension? In A.-L. Ostern & R. Heila-Ylikalko (Eds.), *Sprak Som Kultur – Brytningar I Tid Och Rum (Language as Culture – Tensions in Time and Space)* (pp. 13–30). Vasa: ABO Akademi.

Vianna, E., & Stetsenko, A. (2006). Embracing history through transforming it: Contrasting Piagetian versus Vygotskian (activity) theories of learning and development to expand constructivism within a dialectical view of history. *Theory & Psychology, 16*(1), 81–108.

Vygotsky, L. (1978). Mind in society: the development of higher psychological processes. Collection and Trans. of Original Texts Ed. by M. Cole. Cambridge, MA: Harvard University Press.

Vygotsky, L. S. (1925/1971). *The psychology of art*. Cambridge, MA: MIT Press.

Vygotsky, L. S. (1929/2005). Concrete human psychology: An unpublished manuscript Publication. Retrieved May 25, 2009, from The Laboratory of Comparative Human Cognition: http://lchc.ucsd.edu/MCA/Paper/Vygotsky1986b.pdf

Vygotsky, L. S. (1930/1978). Tool and symbol in child development. In L. S. Vygotsky (Ed.), *Mind in society: The development of higher psychological processes* (pp. 19–30). Cambridge, MA: Harvard University Press.

Vygotsky, L. S. (1930–1934/1998). Child psychology (S. Sochinenij, Trans.). In L. S. Vygotsky (Ed.), *The collected works* (Vol. 5). New York and London: Plenum.

Vygotsky, L. S. (1931/1997). The history of development of higher mental functions (M. Hall, Trans.). In R. Rieber (Ed.), *The collected works* (Vol. 4, pp. 1–251). London and New York: Plenum.

Vygotsky, L. S. (1932–1934/1998). The problem of age (S. Sochinenij, Trans.). In L. S. Vygotsky (Ed.), *The collected works: Vol. 5. Child Psychology* (pp. 187–206). New York and London: Plenum.

Vygotsky, L. S. (1933/2002). Play and its role in the mental development of the child: Psychology and Marxism internet archive. Published online: http://www.marx.org/archive/vygotsky/works/1933/play.htm date of access: 2006-11-22

Vygotsky, L. S. (1934/1987). Thinking and speech (N. Minick, Trans.). In R. Rieber (Ed.), *The collected works of Vygotsky: Vol. 1. Problems of general psychology* (pp. 39–288). New York and London: Plenum.

Vygotsky, L. S. (1934/1994). The socialist alteration of man. In R. van der Veer & J. Valsiner (Eds.), *The Vygotsky reader* (pp. 338–354). Oxford and Cambridge: Blackwell.

Vygotsky, L. S. (1934/1999). The teaching about emotions: Historical-psychological studies (S. Sochinenij, Trans.). In R. Rieber & M. J. Hall (Eds.), *The collected works* (Vol. 6, pp. 69–235). New York and London: Plenum.

Wagner-Willi, M. (2005). *Kinder-Rituale Zwischen Vorder-Und Hinterbühne: Der Übergang von Der Pause Zum Unterricht*. Wiesbaden: Verlag für Sozialwissenschaften.

Walkerdine, V. (1993). Beyond developmentalism? *Theory & Psychology, 3*(4), 451–469.

Walkerdine, V. (1998). *Counting girls out: Girls and mathematics* (New ed.). London and Bristol, PA: Falmer Press.

Wittgenstein, L., & Anscombe, G. E. M. (2003). *Philosophical investigations: The German text, with a revised English translation* (3rd ed.). Malden, MA: Blackwell.

Wolfe, C. (2010). *What is posthumanism?* Minnesota: University of Minnesota Press.

Wulf, C. (2002). *Educational anthropology*. Münster and New York: Lit.

Wulf, C. (2003). *Educational science: Hermeneutics, empirical research, critical theory*. Münster and New York: Waxmann.

Wulf, C. (2005). *Zur Genese Des Sozialen: Mimesis, Performativität, Ritual*. Bielefeld: transcript.

Wulf, C. (2009). *Anthropologie: Geschichte, Kultur, Philosophie*. Köln: Anaconda.

Wulf, C. (Ed.). (1997). *Vom Menschen. Handbuch Historische Anthropologie*. Weinheim: Beltz.

Wulf, C. (Ed.). (2001). *Das Soziale als Ritual: Zur Performativen Bildung von Gemeinschaften*. Opladen: Leske + Budrich.

Wulf, C. (Ed.). (2004). *Bildung im Ritual: Schule, Familie, Jugend, Medien*. Wiesbaden: Verlag für Sozialwissenschaften.

Wulf, C. (Ed.). (2007). *Lernkulturen im Umbruch: Rituelle Praktiken in Schule, Medien, Familie Und Jugend*. Wiesbaden: Verlag für Sozialwissenschaften.

Wulf, C. (Ed.). (2010). *Gesten in Erziehung, Bildung, Sozialisation*. Wiesbaden: Verlag für Sozialwissenschaften.

Wulf, C., Göhlich, M., & Zirfas, J. (Eds.). (2001). *Grundlagen Des Performativen: Eine Einführung in die Zusammenhänge von Sprache, Macht Und Handeln*. Weinheim: Juventa.

Wulf, C., & Kamper, D. (Eds.). (2002). *Logik und Leidenschaft. Erträge Historischer Anthropologie*. Berlin: Reimer.

Wulf, C., & Zirfas, J. (Eds.). (2004). *Die Kultur des Rituals: Inszenierungen, Praktiken, Symbole*. München: Fink.

Wulf, C., & Zirfas, J. (Eds.). (2007). *Pädagogik des Performativen. Theorien, Methoden, Perspektiven*. Weinheim and Basel: Beltz.

Wygotski, L. (1987a). Das Problem der Alterstufen. In J. Lompscher (Ed.), *Lew Wygotski. Ausgewählte Schriften* (Vol. 2, pp. 53–90). Köln: Rugenstein.

Wygotski, L. (1987b). Die Krise des Einjährigen. In J. Lompscher (Ed.), *Lew Wygotski. Ausgewählte Schriften* (Vol. 2, pp. 163–199). Köln: Rugenstein.

Part I
Culture, History and Child Development

Chapter 2
Darwin and Vygotsky on Development: An Exegesis on Human Nature

Anna Stetsenko

Introduction

The role and place of evolution in human development and, concomitantly, the role and place of human beings in nature have been highly debated at least since the publication of Darwin's works culminating in controversies surrounding the notion of "human nature" – a truly contested terrain enmeshed with issues of morals, ethics, and politics. Recent debates on these topics are being channeled into vitriolic and bitter fights between the left and the right of the political spectrum about the origins of life, morality, consciousness, bioethics, and stem cell research spilling even into Supreme Court decisions and presidential elections. It is not unusual for both sides in the debate to draw on evolutionary theory to support diametrically opposed views. Whereas Darwinism traditionally has been associated with resistance to the narrowly understood religious dogmas about the divine nature of humans and associated with social and political innovations, more recently it has been recruited to support starkly conservative positions that declare unregulated market economy, private property, and traditional social and sex roles as the ultimate – and convenient for preserving the status quo – expressions of human nature.

The stakes in the debates are very high, proving ever again that broad theoretical ideas and principles are not merely abstract and inconsequential speculations. Instead, they are the real players in the worldly matters of politics, ideologies, and everyday life. This makes urgent the task of developing a progressive notion of human nature that could be employed in approaches underpinned by ideology of social justice and equality. The challenge is to develop the notion of human nature that reveals human beings as belonging to nature yet not fully determined by it – that is, as beings whose existence is *in* but not *of* nature. Such a notion should be able to account for human consciousness, self-determination, and freedom while positing these features of human existence as neither supra-natural nor merely

A. Stetsenko (✉)
The Graduate Center, The City University of New York, New York, NY, USA
e-mail: astetsenko@gc.cuny.edu

M. Kontopodis et al. (eds.), *Children, Development and Education*, International Perspectives on Early Childhood Education and Development 3, DOI 10.1007/978-94-007-0243-1_2, © Springer Science+Business Media B.V. 2011

mechanistic and rigidly determined. Above all, this notion of human nature should be able to counter the now popular trend that severs it from culture, history, ideology, and politics and uses it to justify existing social order, eviscerate politics, and preclude social innovation. The critical task today is to reject the idea that nature is an incontestable "given" existing apart and independently from politics and culture and instead, to offer an alternative notion of human nature while being aware of its grounding in and implications for both science and politics.

In this chapter, I re-visit Vygotsky's cultural-historical activity theory and expand its approach to human nature and development in which evolutionary origins of humanity in the animal world are acknowledged yet human nature is seen as superseding these origins and transcending any biological imperatives, allowing for a leap into the realm of freedom and self-determination. This unique ability to transcend biological constraints has to do with the advent of human beings' *new relationship to the world* and their *new mode of existence* – realized through collaborative labor mediated by collectively invented cultural tools. This new relationship represents a unified realm where forces of history, culture, and society reign and is, therefore, not rigidly predetermined by any initial conditions and endowments. It consists in an active transformation of environment – a process through which human beings create their world while at the same time creating themselves and essentially coming into Being as agents of their own development and history. This approach opens up ways to employ the notion of evolution in ways that are radically different from the ones dominating evolutionary psychology and much of the popular discourse today. In other words, the framework developed herein acknowledges the importance of adopting an evolutionary perspective in understanding human development, yet suggests the model that integrates human agency, self-determination, and freedom.

Along with other issues, I will consider how Darwinian ideas about nature as a historicized and relational process have been assimilated by Vygotsky (primarily through the works of Marx and Engels) and put to use in addressing the twofold dialectical idea highlighting (a) the continuity of human development with the preceding evolutionary history and (b) the qualitative leap in transition to humanity associated with the emergence of labor as a new mode of existence and the linchpin of human nature and development. While re-visiting Vygotsky's project and delineating its core foundation, I will expansively reconstruct the notion of human nature implied in this project including a number of implications that are still in need of articulation.

Darwinian Roots: The Historicity of Nature

One of the key features of Vygotsky's theory is that it firmly roots human development within the realm of continuously evolving through time, and therefore historicized and open-ended, natural processes taking place in the animate world, while at the same time, this theory assigns humans a number of unique features that reflect their historical Becoming and allow them to transcend natural constraints imposed by biology. In this respect, Vygotsky followed the new mode of thinking in the steps of the Darwinian revolution in natural sciences that took place in the mid-nineteenth century. Such a characterization does not mean that Vygotsky uncritically took Darwinian ideas and integrated them into his system of views without profoundly changing them. Rather, pointing to similarities at the worldview level between cultural-historical and evolutionary theory implies that there are several deep currents common to them, without making a presumption that the overall edifice of Vygotsky's works significantly overlaps with that of Darwin. In fact, they do not overlap and in a number of ways Vygotsky moves far beyond Darwinism, both absorbing and abolishing, preserving and transcending Darwinian thinking. However, it is precisely in light of their common foundation that the differences between Vygotsky and Darwin can be revealed and appreciated better than if this foundation were to be overlooked.

The links between Vygotskian and Darwinian thinking have not been sufficiently explored in the past, with many current expositions of Vygotsky's theory not mentioning Darwin at all (including the treatment in textbooks, see e.g., Dixon & Lerner, 1999). When comparisons have been drawn between the two theories (e.g., Cole, 1996; van der Veer & Valsiner, 1991), the analysis has focused on a limited range of issues. Namely, it predominantly focused on comparing human and animal behavior, for example, noting that Vygotsky accepted the Darwinian ideas of animal–man continuity and of random variation coupled with natural selection as the driving force in phylogeny. Such interpretations, their importance notwithstanding, do not do full justice to the profound influence that the Darwinian revolution had on Vygotsky's thinking and the worldview underpinning his works.

It is not difficult to underestimate the impact of Darwin's theory on Vygotsky at the worldview level because discerning this impact requires going beyond traditional compilations of what is taken to be the central principles developed by these two scholars: (a) variation, natural selection, and survival of the fittest in Darwin's theory and (b) mediation (or the role of context in development) in Vygotsky's theory. What I want to draw attention to instead, in a somewhat non-traditional interpretation of these two theories, is that both of them are grounded in a profoundly *historicized view of nature*, and thus, that both capitalize on nature being continuous, fluid, dynamic, and open-ended. In both theories, nature is taken to be neither immutable nor preordained; instead, nature is in a constant flux, subject to change, variation, and development which entails that it neither has predestined constraints nor follows preprogrammed paths, algorithms, and ordered stages. This is a point that often goes unnoticed in many accounts of Darwinism in biology and especially in the socio-biological incarnations of (pseudo)-Darwinism such as the recently popular brand of evolutionary psychology where the ideas of immutability and determinacy of nature are seen as central. This is also true of interpretations of Vygotsky's theory that draw attention to the historicized character of human development rather than of nature at large. In other words, what goes unnoticed in both cases is that these two scholars endorsed the dynamical and relational worldview in their accounts, opposing characterizations of human nature from the standpoint of the mechanistic worldview.

Vygotsky's worldview, however, is profoundly indebted to Darwin's ideas of evolution (and the same is true of James, Dewey, and Piaget). Namely, Vygotsky was able to appreciate the revolutionary breakthrough made by Darwin in terms of the very mode of thinking about nature that pertains to what makes evolution and ultimately human development itself possible. Before Darwin, the classical idea of species implied that they represent changeless, immutable forms – each with its own distinct and pre-established essence. The idea of humans as divine creatures separate from the rest of the animate world was perhaps the strongest rationale behind this view – consistent with teleological beliefs in the sense of both requiring and supporting these beliefs. Although certain developments in the forms of life were admitted (because the growth of separate organisms during their lifetime could not be ignored), these developments were seen as largely preprogrammed or arranged by some supreme force, and aimed at achieving a pre-given endpoint (telos) represented by mature forms existing in the present.

Darwin's theory posited – and essentially discovered – that organisms are not self-contained, preprogrammed and separate from the rest of life's "entities" with fixed essences. Instead, organisms are subject to change as *members of the species* who are immersed in historical development whereby they continuously evolve through time, with each successive generation taking over from the previous ones and setting the stage for developments within subsequent generations. A corollary of this view is that all species alive today are descendant from original forms of life and in this sense, are all interdependent and interrelated. Each given species and each particular organism within a given species represent a storehouse of previous interactions with and adaptations to the environment and thus embody histories of past developments while at the same time serving as springboards for further developments in subsequent generations. In this sense, species can be said to have *collective history* that unfolds through time. This collective history forms the context for understanding anything and everything in relation to organisms, species, and nature. It is in this sense that Darwin can be said to have historicized nature (cf. Costall, 1993, 2001; Lewontin, 2000).

Moreover, species evolve, according to Darwin but contrary to many common perceptions of his theory, due to events, processes, and developments essentially *outside of organisms*. That is, species originate, exist, develop, give rise to new species, and sometimes go extinct not because of anything inherent to themselves but instead, due to the processes that stretch beyond the confines of any particular species (let alone of single organisms) taken as a separate entity. The driving forces of evolution were sought by Darwin in events and developments – often dramatic and never pre-scripted – that take place at the *intersection*, or confluence, of contextual processes such as the geographical distribution of a given species on the one hand and the features of organisms such as their morphology, on the other. The key process at this intersection, according to Darwin, is adaptation – a process in which organisms face the demands of their environments and become selected based on the outcomes of them being more or less able to answer these demands. Note that both adaptation and selection are processes that depend neither solely on organisms nor solely on environments but precisely on the intermediary, that is, *relational realm* where the organisms and their environments *come together* in one unified system of "species-in-environment." That is, rather than focusing exclusively on external events (e.g., changing environments) or internal characteristics of organisms per se, the theory of evolution shifted the emphasis to processes in which organisms and their environments actively codetermine each other.

The idea about *collective history* (rather than inherent features of organisms or environments) being central to evolution was perhaps the key insight offered by Darwin. The relational and historical character of nature, interlinking all living forms through their history clearly comes through in that Darwin employs the notion of *co-adaptations* of organic beings to each other and to their physical conditions of life and laments "our ignorance of the *mutual relations* of all organic beings; a conviction as necessary, as it is difficult to acquire" – relations that are "of the highest importance, for they determine the present welfare and, as I believe, the future success and modification of every inhabitant of this world" (Darwin, 2009/1859, p. 12).

Darwin's idea about the collective, relational, and historicized dynamics of life was a decisive blow to the mechanistic worldview. Namely, this idea marked a dramatic departure away from the notions of nature as immutable and predetermined (intractable and fixed) and of organisms as simple mechanisms that exist separately from each other and independently from the world around them – these two pillars of the mechanistic worldview. All the related ideas of variation, adaptation, struggle for survival, and natural selection can be seen as being embedded in this overarching worldview.

Importantly, Darwin's views can be characterized as materialist yet not narrowly mechanical because it is in the *material order of history* that nature and evolution find their explanations according to his theory. That is, Darwin's nature is materialist yet neither mechanical nor inert; instead, nature is *animated* (or enchanted) with filaments, bonds, and meaning that accrue through *mutual relations* among all living forms – through togetherness, mutualism, and continuity in development. In this material order of history, all organisms and forms of life form one living compound – to which Darwin refers to as one tree "united by wonderful and mysterious manner" – where everything is animated through interconnections and interdependence.

As Jillian Beer (2000, p. 37), a literary scholar who studied Darwin in the context of his times, writes

> The evanishing of matter, even the most recalcitrantly enduring, gives a particular poignancy to Darwin's feeling for materiality. His materialism is a sensuously grounded response to the world of forms and life, not an excluding or purely subtracting force. . . .Darwin's romantic materialism. . .should be understood as part of a profound imaginative longing shared by a great number of his contemporaries. *Material was not simply an abstraction.* . . .The palpable, the particular, became not only evidence, but *ideal.* (emphasis added)

That is, although Darwin repudiates theological explanations, his account of evolution is not mechanically materialist, nor is it inert and devoid of meaning. On the contrary, his materialism resists attempts to eradicate meaning from matter. For Darwin, meaning inheres in interrelations and mutualism of processes and phenomena in nature. His zest for the observable world "lances him out not only into history but into the material of the present" and "warms the random, with its meagerness and insignificance, into profusion" (Beer, 2000, pp. 40–41).

This interpretation of Darwinism starkly differs from the traditional one according to which "Darwin's signal contribution to the concept of evolution was to mechanize it, to de-romanticize nature and capture evolution for the Newtonian world view" (Leahy, quoted in Costall, 1993, p. 113; cf. similar views in Dennett, 1996, among others). Even when Darwin's contribution is seen in a broader light, as one of the key precursors for developmental and historical thinking in psychology, the crux of Darwinism is limited to three ideas, namely, (a) the stress on the history of organisms (rather than the collective history of species), (b) the focus on the adaptive feature of behavioral and mental ontogeny, and (c) an interest in the study of the role of the environment or context in ontogeny (see Dixon & Lerner, 1999, p. 14). Missing is the idea of the relational character of evolution and nature at large, of the collective history of organisms and of the organism–environment nexus as the center stage (and often the battlefield) where the main drama of evolution unfolds.

Even more strikingly, Darwin's discovery that the general principles of how nature evolves reside in nature itself is taken by many today to mean that all developments in nature including in humans are based on a sober foundation of *mechanistic* materialism (Dennett, 1996). According to this view, these developments are algorithmic, trial-and-error processes of a robotic type not different from those involved in constructing a machine such as a clock. The implication of this view is that all the intricacies and vicissitudes of human development including the works of the human mind can be understood to be the mechanistically generated products of a cascade of generate-and-test algorithms.

This narrow, reductionist view pulls all nature "downwards" into the realm of mechanistic phenomena whereby all complex processes are taken to be akin to the ones that describe machines. Such an interpretation ignores that there can be a non-mechanistic materialism which, rather than pulling nature "downwards," raises it "upwards" into the mode of existence that is relational, historical, and dynamical. The narrow mechanistic view therefore ignores the very gist of Darwinism with its emphasis on dynamical, indeterminate, and open-ended processes at the core of evolution. Alexander Koyre's famous expression that the Newtonian synthesis "broke down the barriers that separated the heavens and the earth" could be fully applied to characterize Darwin's theory. However, it remained and still often remains unnoticed that there are two alternative ways to conceptualize nature *after* the breaking down of these barriers is achieved. One way is to harden nature into mechanistic imagery with its linear, static, deterministic, and immutable laws that govern machine-like fixed entities in a preprogrammed and preordained manner. The alternative way is to elevate nature within a new worldview that is nonmechanistic, dynamical, open-ended, indeterministic, and ever-evolving. The neo-Darwinists such as Dennett appear to follow the former path, portraying nature in the image of a machine, thus achieving the same result as the one Alexander Koyre ascribed to Newton – a synthesis which substitutes for our world "...in which we live and love and die, another world – the world of quantity, of reified geometry, a world in which, though there is a place for everything, there is no place for man" (quoted in Costall, 2001, p. 474).

At the end of his magnum opus, Darwin solemnly stated that "[t]here is grandeur in this view of life..." (Darwin, 2009/1859, p. 649). Indeed, there is. However, it is not an easy task to grasp this view because doing so entails going beyond the habitual dichotomous thinking in terms of two rigidly opposed and irreconcilable core metaphors – that of nature as a machine versus that of nature as a divine creation. The grandeur of evolutionary thinking suggests giving up both of these metaphors to instead view nature as a continuous and limitless process that stretches from the past into the future without breaks, thus uniting all living forms into one interrelated process, one web of connections without constrains imposed from outside by any rigid commands or predetermined design specifications. There is no mechanical analogy to this process because no machine is intimately related to all other machines that are and ever were in existence, and that co-depend on each other while co-adapting, together with others, to the world. It is precisely that there is no algorithm according to which life unfolds – instead, its course is anchored in a confluence of a de facto infinite number of forces of such different order and of such dynamism and constant change that it is impossible to apply any algorithm to describe, model, or predict this process.

In other worlds, the grandeur that Darwin's approach implies has to do with an intimate interconnectedness of each and every form of life with all of life; the interconnectedness of all that is alive with all that ever was, is, or ever will be alive. This is the grandeur of a *mutual interdependence* of all forms of life with all other forms, where the world itself is entangled with the unfolding life and co-implicated in its dynamics and its history. This is the grandeur of life and nature that are seen as being, at one and the same time, contingent and unpredictable, ever-changing and continuous, open-ended and ordered – with all of these polarities ceasing to be irreconcilable dimensions that exclude each other. It can be said that there is a place for humans within this view of nature because nature, thus understood, entails a human (ideal) dimension – the world in which "we live and love and die."

Vygotsky's Views on Human Nature Expanded

Vygotsky's theory, at its most fundamental level, endorsed the worldview permeated by the Darwinian type of thinking about nature as a constantly changing and fluid web of interconnections infused with dynamism and mutualism. In particular, Vygotsky relinquished the mechanistic worldview in one of its core components – the methodology of elementarism according to which the universe is composed of separate entities that exist and can be studied in isolation from each other, just as a clock or any other machine can be studied by looking at its parts. Vygotsky substituted for this the worldview of nature as a process in flux and constant change, with fluid and ever-changing, open-ended and nonlinear, indeterminate (i.e., neither preordained nor fixed) dynamical processes linking organisms and their environments at the center. For example, Vygotsky (1997, p. 100) challenged the view that development could be understood as a set of static, predetermined steps:

> Least of all does child development resemble a stereotypic process shielded from external influences; here [in child development], *in a living adaptation to the outside milieu* is the development and change of the child accomplished. In this process, ever newer forms arise, rather than the elements in the already preordained chain being simply stereotypically reproduced (emphasis added).

In this and similar instances, Vygotsky insisted that development cannot be seen as a preordained unfolding of pre-specified internal potentials enclosed in some "primordial essence" that putatively exists at preceding stages of development (let alone at birth); neither can it be seen as a natural and universal course toward maturity that proceeds progressively along a particular path toward the end goal. Such an understanding, according to Vygotsky, describes not so much a process of development as a process of growth and maturation. In the alternative account which Vygotsky began to chart, development is characterized as a process in which new stages arise not out of pre-specified potentials, but out of *an actual confrontation between the organism and the environment – an alive adaptation to the environment*. This is perhaps the reason why Vygotsky favored the notion of development as *drama* – not in the sense of plotted spectacle but as living performance and an ongoing affair in which events unfold on the moment-to-moment basis, where competing forces come into play and often collide, where everything emerges out of live relations among players participating within an ensemble, in an intricate balance of oppositions and reconciliations. In this rendition, the concept of relations and mutualism (even in the form of contradictions and struggles) takes the center stage conveying the sense that development is a constant process of transformation in which fixed entities, preordained stages, and teleological order are relinquished.

Moreover, whereas most relational and dynamic systems theories that are being developed today (including those following Dewey and Piaget and the Dynamic Systems Theory) treat human beings as not different from other biological organisms – thus maintaining the notion that "nature makes no drastic leaps" – Vygotsky and his followers postulated precisely such a leap and turned to exploring its implications. In doing so, these scholars followed the Marxist dialectical materialist view according to which "...[the] base for human thinking is precisely man changing nature and not nature alone as such, and the mind developed according to how human beings learned to change nature"(Engels quoted in Vygotsky, 1997, p. 56; italics in the original).

Vygotsky was strongly influenced by the Marxist account of human development and of the role of labor in it according to which the evolutionary origins of humans have to do with an emergence of *a unique relation to the world* realized not through adaptation but through the social practice of *human labor* – the collaborative (and therefore socio-cultural), transformative practice unfolding and expanding in history. Through this collaborative process – involving creation, expansive development and passing on, from generation to generation, of the collective experiences reified in cultural tools, including language – people not only constantly transform and create their environment; they also create and constantly transform their very life, consequently changing themselves in fundamental ways while, in and through this process, becoming human and gaining self-knowledge and knowledge about the world. Therefore, human activity – material, practical, and always by necessity social, collaborative process aimed at transforming the world – is taken to be the basic form of human relation to the world, that is, of human life itself.

Importantly, it is not just the mediation by cultural tools and artifacts that played a role in the advent of human species in evolution. An exclusive emphasis on artifacts of culture, all their significance notwithstanding, downplays the more general claim by Vygotsky that bears profound implications for interpreting human development. This claim has to do with the Darwinian-type view that the key to understanding human development lies in the processes that characterize *the very type of relationship between humans and their world* that goes beyond mere employment of artifacts while making their use both needed and possible.

It is the new transformative relation of human beings to their world, in which people change the world and reciprocally change themselves and thereby come into being, precisely as a *new form of life* that brings about the emergence of people as the new species. This form of life supersedes adaptation and natural selection, as well as the distinction between nature and culture, and establishes the centrality of human practice in its unity of history, society, and culture as a supreme ontological realm for development. The shift from adaptation to transformation can be understood to signify the end of biological evolution and a transition to processes now taking place in the realm where forces of history, culture, and society reign.

This turn by Vygotsky is of a truly dialectical sort because it posits that human development is both continuous with *and* radically different from the processes in the rest of the animate world. Human history and life entail a radical break with nature, while at the same time coming out of it and, in this sense, continuing it. Thus, with the transition to humans there is a drastic leap away from biological laws and regularities that govern in the animal world. In this leap, nature negates itself, turning into a radically new reality – the reality of cultural history of human civilization that proceeds in the form of a continuous flow of collaborative practices of people aimed at transforming their world. Human development, from this perspective, can be conceptualized as *a socio-historical project and a collaborative accomplishment* – that is, a continuously evolving process representing "a work-in-progress," a *historical Becoming* by people as agents who together change their world and, in and through this process, come to know themselves and their world, while ultimately becoming human.

It is the simultaneity, or in even stronger terms, the *unity* of human collaborative transformative practice on the one hand, and the process of Becoming (and being) human and of knowing oneself and the world on the other that is conveyed in this conception. Human beings come to be themselves and come to know their world and themselves *in the process and as the process* of collaboratively changing their world (while changing together with it) – in the midst of this process and as one of its facets – rather than outside of or merely in conjunction with it. This conceptualization of human development moves beyond the dualistic designation of nature and culture and does so not by simply stating their bi-directional interaction that produces a hybrid process. Instead, the collaborative human practice is posited as the *unified* (rather than bifurcated) and unique *ontological realm* that takes over and dialectically supersedes and transcends the very distinction between nature and culture, through absorbing and negating (though not eliminating) them within its own, radically new *transformative ontology of historical Becoming* represented by human collaborative practice aimed at transforming the world. This notion resolutely breaks with the double vision in which "an incontestable, raw nature" of a purely biological and mechanical order is pitted against the separate world of subjective phenomena such as mind, value, and reason.

Importantly, the social collaborative practice as a mode of human existence (*Lebensweise*) does not negate or eliminate natural phenomena but instead, incorporates and co-opts them *as its own constituents*, takes them into its orbit and transforms them on its own grounds in mutual alignment. In this process, "the natural" becomes infused with human relevance and significance, for example as instruments of achieving human goals and as social affordances, whereby things and phenomena in the outside world are endowed with meaning and value, parlayed into a realm where everything is colored by inclusion in and relevance to collaborative practices. In this realm, things are what they are in light of whether and how they matter to people by virtue of being included into human activity of transforming and ultimately creating the world. Human productive activity, their collectively produced life, represents an *amalgamation of natural and social dimensions of life*, of the biological and the cultural-social where these dimensions are united through and within historical practice. The world is thus enchanted and humanized in the sense that the natural is blended with the world of cultural practices on the basis of its relevance to these practices, especially vis-à-vis their goals and purposes.

Human nature, in this perspective, is not an immutable, pre-given evolutionary residue that rigidly defines development within the constraints of a biological endowment and functioning (even if aided by cultural mediation). Neither is it a product of various factors and influences acting on human beings from outside of and in abstraction from their own activity and relations to the world. Instead, human nature is a process of *overcoming and transcending its own limitations* through collaborative, continuous, and transformative practices mediated by cultural tools. In other words, it is a process of a historical Becoming of people not as creatures of nature but as agents of their own lives and development, that is, as *agents whose nature IS to purposefully transform their world and to thus come into Being and Becoming.*

That human development is grounded in the socio-historical project of people liberating themselves from the dictate of the brute forces of nature should not be equated with the idea that people struggle with nature itself or that they somehow break up with nature. The key process is that of engaging in the project of overcoming *the constraints* of nature and *the dictate* of its brute forces rather than nature itself. This process entails understanding the natural forces and learning how to control rather than eliminate them. This is a continuous and limitless process that can never be achieved in full, where each partial success is always accompanied by emerging new challenges. Thus, the notion of human nature as a process of overcoming its own limitations should not be interpreted as some sort of "utopian vision" in which human beings are thought to be completely liberated from the constraints of biology as would be the case if people achieved or aimed to achieve some "absolute conquest" over nature, taking a position over and above nature.

In fact, while withstanding the brute forces of nature and learning to understand and control them, people actually come ever closer to *a unity with nature*, transforming nature into an important *ally of humanity*, thus striving for an ever growing communion with it. The socio-historical practices are not separate from nature and instead, represent the continuation of nature by other means – they represent a "naturally" evolved way of humans' interrelating with their world which, however, is of a qualitatively new type in that it provides humans with the tools of acting in goal-directed and purposive ways. This view posits the inherent unity of humanity and nature where the two are blended in mutual interconnectedness yet allows for humans' ability to understand and mold nature according with their goals. It is in this sense that Engels (1939, pp. 125–126) spoke of "oneness with nature," envisioning a "real human freedom" based on "an existence in harmony with the established laws of nature."

This transformative ontology of human historical Becoming is deeply and profoundly cultural (as well as ineluctably social) but not for the simple reason that culture exerts influences on this process from outside, nor because these cultural influences are somehow more important than the biological ones. Nature (biology) too is inherent to collaborative transformative practices in the sense that humans develop as fully embodied, biological organisms and in the sense that their Becoming has to do with *relating to nature* while engaging in the project of overcoming its constraints. However, both cultural and natural factors per se, taken in abstraction from human activities and practices (as some abstract, de-humanized "givens") neither possess human relevance nor act to produce meaningful effects in human development. Instead, biology and culture coalesce within human Becoming and are co-opted into one unified epigenetic developmental system represented by dynamically emerging processes through which human beings engage with the world and come to actively transform it. In the ontology where collaborative transformation of the world is taken to constitute the primary and foundational realm of human Becoming, the very distinction (bifurcation) between nature and culture is eliminated. Instead, within this worldview, both culture and nature are understood as an *inherent dimension* of human collaborative practices rather than as outside sources of influence.

Culture in this sense is neither inside nor outside human beings; moreover, culture is neither something that people have nor just a milieu that people exist in or relate to – an extraneous world out there, such as a pool of artifacts, to be discovered and appropriated through some special processes or procedures. Instead, *culture is a quality of human life* and of their relationship with the world, something that people constantly and continuously *do and enact* (always together with others) – a unique quality of how people always *collaboratively* engage with their world through *collective* efforts to change it.

Yet human development is rightfully termed socio-cultural or cultural-historical in Vygotsky's project, rather than bio-cultural or bio-social. The reason for this, again, is not that some abstract "cultural influences" are more potent than the abstract biological ones. Instead, the key reason has to do with the ineluctable collectivity, or communality, of human beings in the sense of their fundamental dependence and reliance on each other (including reliance on cultural artifacts that embody experiences of others including from past generations) in transforming the world and achieving their humanness. It is because of the profound *"togetherness"* of human goals and means of Becoming – where everything happens together with, because of, and for the sake of others (including conflicts and struggles which are also deeply relational) – that human development is, at its core, socio-cultural or cultural-historical, rather than socio-biological or cultural-biological. Culture, understood as a quality of human relationships, bonds, and engagements constituted by collaborative practices of changing the world, is not an add-on layer to nature and evolution but is the inherent dimension of how human beings relate to their world, and therefore, *how they are in the world*.

This perspective is compatible with the recently evolved approach in biology that constitutes nothing less than a conceptual revolution in understanding developmental processes (Gottlieb, 2002; Lewontin, 2000; Lickliter & Berry, 1990; Lickliter & Honeycott, 2003a, 2003b; Oyama, 1985, 2000). While unfortunately overlooked by many psychologists who are still often unaware of the sweeping changes in neighboring disciplines, this approach provides an integrated account of human development and is associated with the ascendancy of relational and developmental systems approaches that move away from the assumptions typical of the mechanistic worldview that reifies and essentializes human nature.

According to this revolutionary approach, all and any organisms as well as physiological, behavioral, and cognitive processes never are, and in principle cannot be, pre-specified *in advance of individual development*. The hallmark of this approach is the "constructive interactionism" that argues against any pre-specification of traits, characteristics, or behaviors including psychological processes in even their "skeletal forms." Instead, development is posited to be a self-organizing, probabilistic process in which pattern and order emerge and undergo changes in the course of development as a result of complex interactions and relations with the world unique to each organism.

Importantly, these new advances in biology imply that development is not the result of the summation of genetic and environmental factors, because neither operates independently and cannot be seen as an alternative cause for the expression of traits, characteristics, or behavior. The importance of this position is not that genetic and environmental factors (nature and nurture) are claimed to interact or mesh with each other in individual development. Instead, the key message is much more radical, namely that the organism itself, together with all of its traits and characters, *must be constructed* – rather than expressed or brought to realization – *in individual ontogeny*. A focus on the organism coactively constructing itself in the course of its life undermines any claims that cognitive modules (or any other structures) preexist individual development and lie dormant awaiting mere activation or realization under certain conditions and extraneous influences. As Lickliter and Honeycutt (2003c, p. 869) state:

> [P]henotypic traits are *generated,* not expressed, in development. In the language of developmental dynamics, *form is an emergent property of the entire field of relationships within which the organism comes into being* ... This dynamic and contingent account of trait generation underscores the key insight that understanding the mechanisms of development and evolution requires *a relational concept* of causality ... The influence of genes, neuronal architecture, the physical surround, or any other factor in development can be understood only in relation to the developmental system of which they are part (emphasis added).

The stance of collaborative transformation of the world as the core grounding of "human nature" builds on this dynamic view of development while also delineating, within the same logic of constructive interactionism and relational causality, the specifics of human development. Importantly, within this stance, the notions of nature and culture are employed in a way that deconstructs their opposition and, moreover, problematizes the very idea that there is a "human nature" that is independent from collaborative practices of social transformation. This proposal overlaps with recent works that also problematize the received notions about nature and culture and emphasize creative and agentive qualities of human development, for example, in the notions of culture as cultivation (Eagleton, 2000), as mediation (Latour, 1994), and as a synthesis of these two notions in Derksen's (2007) idea of self-cultivation. All three notions draw attention to the central, mediating role of the human agent in determining human nature and relating it to culture (rather than to the mediating role of culture as in some post-Vygotskian works). All three also underscore that it is important to move away from putting too much store in the putative limitations of human nature posited by traditional approaches as is especially prominent in today's pseudo-evolutionary, reductivist frameworks described in the first section of this chapter.

However, the proposal offered herein is more radical than even these progressive notions of cultivation, mediation, and self-cultivation. If culture is taken to mean the active tending of *natural growth* (Eagleton, 2000), or if human beings are understood as mediators of mediators who create hybrid collectives of humans and nonhumans (Latour, 1994), or if the individual is understood as a mediator between nature and culture and therefore as a bio-cultural hybrid (Derksen, 2007), then there is still room to think of human nature as somehow existing apart from human practices (i.e., as a "*raw material*"). That is, human nature in these perspectives is conceptualized as malleable, not totally constrained by initial "givens," and in need of being cultivated and mediated by humans who can be effective actors in the play of biological and cultural processes. Yet culture and nature are still viewed as two distinct though highly interrelated realms of existence and types of phenomena.

The conceptualization suggested herein does more than establish a bi-directional (dialectical) relation between nature and culture; and it assigns to humans a role in their own Becoming that is more radical than that of mediating between nature and culture. The key point, again, is that the collaborative transformative practice constitutes a unique ontological realm that is not bifurcated because it represents the core human relation to the world – *the only process* of human Becoming. In other words, this practice supersedes the very distinction between nature and culture, fully encompassing while also transforming them, thus eschewing their bifurcation. This practice is therefore profoundly natural and humanist/cultural at the same time – as a unified and unique process through which people come into Being and that represents their ultimate mode of existence where distinctions between the biological and the cultural dissipate. The role of human beings is then unequivocal – they are creators of their own "nature" who come into Being precisely through (not in addition to) this creation which, importantly, is always a collaborative project carried out through individual contributions to it.

Conclusions

Positing a continuous flow of collaborative transformative practices as the foundation of human life and the substrate (or *fabric*) of their development entails a number of implications, for example, regarding the social and individual planes of activity (for details, see Stetsenko, 2005, 2007, 2008). Central to this chapter is the implication that human nature can be conceptualized without reducing it to either strictly mechanistic, inert materiality or to some mysterious supra-natural realm alien to other forms of life. This position assigns primary significance to human practice – with labor representing its generic form – that, having emerged in the course of natural evolution, gave rise to human consciousness that therefore does not constitute some supra-natural realm of unknown and mysterious origins, regularities, and laws. Instead, the human mind is understood to be fully a product of biological evolution and is therefore not posited outside of nature. Yet at the same time, labor represents a radically new form of relationships between humans and their world – namely, a collaborative process bound by, building on, and benefiting from experiences and efforts of other people extended in history and stretching from generation to generation through shared activities mediated by cultural tools including language. As such, labor is capable of superseding and transcending adaptation – its counterpart in the animal world where relationships of organisms to the world are realized through immediate processes of fitting in with the environment. Therefore, human consciousness too, having emerged in association with and out of relations of labor, transcends strictly deterministic forces of biological nature and allows for a leap into the realm of freedom and self-determination. In this sense, humanity can be said to have evolved naturally as the historically and culturally evolving species that is uniquely capable of transcending its own limitations and, moreover, that comes into Being precisely *through* such transcendence.

   This notion of human nature has its roots in Darwin's notion of nature as a relational, self-organizing, and dynamical process where relationships among organisms and between organisms and their environments drive evolution and development. At the same time, in the rendition suggested herein, human nature cannot be explained by the centrality of relations per se and instead is grounded in collaborative meaningful practices of humanity that necessarily entail purposes, directionality, and goals. As such, this account navigates the discourses of science, politics, and ethics and bridges the gap among them in an approach that simultaneously relies on the theory of evolution and the humanist view that posits human beings as agents of their own development and Becoming and in which the responsibility and accountability for human actions are not relinquished. What is relinquished instead is the idea about human nature as incontestable and inert – that is, as existing apart, prior to, and independent from social practices, politics, and culture.

This notion of human nature can be used, above all, to refute the now habitual ways of thinking about social inequality and injustice as representing inevitable outcomes of some blind forces of evolution and natural selection. For example, to explain unequal distribution of recourses or achievement gaps in disadvantaged populations by forces of nature (e.g., see Charlesworth, 1992) is to grossly mischaracterize what in reality are the workings of particular social and political institutions that create colossally increasing wealth surrounded by disastrously increasing poverty. The excuses for irresponsive policies based on claims about putatively incontestable human nature and forces of evolution that are beyond human control have to be abandoned in favor of developing strategies to combat inequalities and social injustice – exactly in the spirit of understanding human nature as a collaborative project of social transformation.

References

Beer, J. (2000). *Darwin's plots: Evolutionary narrative in Darwin, George Eliot and nineteenth century fiction*. New York: Cambridge University Press.

Charlesworth, W. R. (1992). Darwin and developmental psychology: Past and present. *Developmental Psychology, 28*, 5–16.

Cole, M. (1996). *Cultural psychology: A once and future discipline*. Cambridge, MA: Harvard University Press.

Costall, A. (1993). How Lloyd Morgan's canon backfired. *Journal of the History of the Behavioral Sciences, 29*, 113–122.

Costall, A. (2001). Darwin, ecological psychology, and the principle of animal-environment mutuality. *Psyke & Logos, 22*, 473–484.

Darwin, C. (2009/1859). *On the origin of species*. New York: Cambridge University Press.

Dennett, D. (1996). *Darwin's dangerous idea: Evolution and the meanings of life*. New York: Simon & Schuster.

Derksen, M. (2007). Cultivating human nature. *New Ideas in Psychology, 25*, 189–206.

Dixon, R. A., & Lerner, R. M. (1999). History and systems in developmental psychology. In M. H. Bornstein and M. E. Lamb (Eds.), *Developmental psychology: An advanced textbook* (4th ed.) pp. 3–45. Mahwah, NJ: Lawrence Erlbaum.

Eagleton, T. (2000). *The idea of culture*. Oxford: Blackwell.

Engels, F. (1939). Engels, *Anti-Dühring*. New York: International Publishers.

Gottlieb, G. (2002). Developmental–behavioral initiation of evolutionary change. *Psychological Review, 109*, 211–218.

Latour, B. (1994). Pragmatogonies—A mythical account of how humans and nonhumans swap properties. *American Behavioral Scientist, 37*, 791–808.

Lewontin, R. C. (2000). *The triple helix: Gene, organism, and environment*. Cambridge, MA: Harvard University Press.

Lickliter, R., & Berry, T. D. (1990). The phylogeny fallacy: Developmental psychology's misapplication of evolutionary theory. *Developmental Review, 10*, 348–364.

Lickliter, R., & Honeycutt, H. (2003a). Developmental dynamics: Towards a biologically plausible evolutionary psychology. *Psychological Bulletin, 129*, 819–838.

Lickliter, R., & Honeycutt, H. (2003b). Evolutionary approaches to cognitive development: Status and strategy. *Journal of Cognition and Development, 4*, 459–473.

Lickliter, R., & Honeycutt, H. (2003c). Developmental dynamics and contemporary evolutionary psychology: Status quo or irreconcilable views? *Psychological Bulletin, 129*, 866–872.

Oyama, S. (1985). *The ontogeny of information*. Cambridge: Cambridge University Press.

Oyama, S. (2000). *Evolution's eye*. Durham, NC: Duke University Press.

Stetsenko, A. (2005). Activity as object-related: Resolving the dichotomy of individual and collective types of activity. *Mind, Culture, and Activity, 12*, 70–88.

Stetsenko, A. (2007). Being-through-doing: Bakhtin and Vygotsky in dialogue. *Cultural Studies of Science Education, 2*, 25–37.

Stetsenko, A. (2008). From relational ontology to transformative activist stance: Expanding Vygotsky's (CHAT) project. *Cultural Studies of Science Education, 3*, 465–485.

van der Veer R., & Valsiner, J. (1991). *Understanding Vygotsky: A quest for synthesis*. Malden, MA: Blackwell Publishing, 1991.

Vygotsky, L. S. (1997). The problem of the development of higher mental functions. In R. W. Rieber (Ed.), *The collected works of L.S. Vygotsky: Vol. 4. The history of the development of higher mental functions: Cognition and language* (pp. 1–26). New York: Plenum.

Chapter 3
Two Lines of Development: Reconsidering and Updating Vygotsky's Argument

Falk Seeger and Martin Hildebrand-Nilshon

Introduction

In this paper we will pick up some lines of discussion started in our paper from 2006 (see Hildebrand-Nilshon & Seeger, 2006). In particular, we will have a closer look at how our critique and elaboration of Vygotsky's famous example of the development of the pointing gesture is situated within more recent developments in child developmental psychology, comparative psychology, and analytical philosophy of language.

In our paper from 2006, we began elaborating the difference between four types of triangulation: (1) attentional triangulation, (2) semiotic triangulation, (3) referential triangulation, and (4) dramatic triangulation. Realizing that we were trying to take a step forward without considering the wealth of possible contributions from others disciplines, today we would like to return to the original Vygotskyian idea of two lines of development, a natural line and a social line, so to speak – a line where the achievements of our animal ancestors are taken up and continued, and a line where we as humans break with the heritage of the great apes.

In a first attempt to come to grips with the problem of meaning we considered a comparison of Vygotsky and Leontiev. This seemed an obvious route to take because they both developed different ideas on how to deal with the problem of how meaning develops. We thought that it might be informative to put the question of how meaning that had existed between people can turn into meaning within one person and still continue to be as general as social meaning to both, Vygotsky and Leontiev. If social meaning creates individual meaning, how is it that individual meaning is still shared and not some mechanical taking over of prefabricated social meaning. We thought it might be instructive to compare Leontiev's idea of some form of prior existence of meaning in the form of the societal division of labor – that roughly corresponded to some form of top-down development, and Vygotsky's idea

F. Seeger (✉)
University of Bielefeld, Bielefeld, Germany
e-mail: falk.seeger@uni-bielefeld.de

M. Kontopodis et al. (eds.), *Children, Development and Education*, International
Perspectives on Early Childhood Education and Development 3,
DOI 10.1007/978-94-007-0243-1_3, © Springer Science+Business Media B.V. 2011

of a gradual formation of higher psychological functions starting from the example of the development of the pointing gesture – roughly corresponding to some sort of bottom-up development. At a closer reading, however, it turned out that along these lines of thinking it might be very difficult to integrate new research and new views on the nature of shared intentionality into this grid of top-down and bottom-up processes. It looks much more promising indeed to use Vygotsky's idea of the two lines of development as a background for the discussion.

We have at least two sources that demand and might feed an update or an elaboration of the discussion of the development of semiosis and language in cultural-historical psychology and developmental psychology. The challenge comes on the one hand from research in comparative psychology, developmental psychology, und the psychology of language development where the abilities of human children and great apes to grasp the intentions of others and to cooperate are studied. The research done by Michael Tomasello and his co-workers in the last 10 years or so is representative of this source of knowledge. Here one could separate the comparative research tradition from the developmental language-related strand of research. But as the work of Tomasello and his recent volume on language development (Tomasello, 2005) shows, no clear boundaries between the disciplines are apparent here. This is also true for the research of Tomasello and his colleagues on the development of children that clearly can be located within developmental psychology – even though it is done within a comparative context of research.

On the other hand, work done in the tradition of analytical philosophy and Wittgenstein is highly relevant for the issues discussed here. Here, the problem of meaning is tackled from an angle that might be highly informative for psychology, even though authors like Davidson, Brandom, or Wellmer did not have this issue on their agenda, but looked at the problem from the direction of the philosophy of language.

Shared Intentionality and the Two Lines of Development

One of the unique features of Vygotsky's approach to development is the "development of higher psychological functions." Higher psychological functions are, in his view, specifically human types of psychological functions compared (1) to the psychological functions of our animal forebears in phylogenesis, and (2) to the psychological functions of the youngest children in ontogenesis.

At the beginning of *The History of the Development of Higher Psychological (i.e. Mental) Functions*, published in 1960 as part of the first six-volume edition of his works, Vygotsky makes it clear that there is another dimension, in juxtaposition, so to speak:

> The concept "development of higher mental functions" and the subject of our research encompass two groups of phenomena that seem, at first glance, to be completely unrelated, but in fact represent two basic branches, two streams of the development of higher forms of behavior inseparably connected, but never merging into one. There are, first, the processes of mastering external materials of cultural development and thinking: language,

writing, arithmetic, drawing; second, the processes of development of special higher mental functions not delimited and not determined with any degree of precision and in traditional psychology termed voluntary attention, logical memory, formation of concepts, etc. Both of these taken together also form that which we conditionally call the process of development of higher forms of the child's behavior (Vygotsky, 1997, p. 14).

In the following quote Vygotsky painstakingly explains that he sees a significant difference between a biogenetic version[1] of human development, viewing ontogeny as a repetition of phylogeny, and his idea of an *analogy* between ontogenesis and phylogenesis:

> In the development of the child, two types of mental development are represented (not repeated) which we find in an isolated form in phylogenesis: biological and historical, or natural and cultural development of behavior. In ontogenesis both processes have their analogs (not parallels). This is a basic and central fact, a point of departure for our research: differentiating two lines of mental development of the child corresponding to the two lines of phylogenetic development of behavior. This idea, as far as we know, has never been expressed; nevertheless it seems to us to be completely obvious in the light of contemporary data from genetic psychology, and the circumstance that it has this far stubbornly escaped the attention of the researchers seems completely incomprehensible. By this, we do not mean to say that ontogenesis in any form or any degree repeats or produces phylogenesis or is its parallel. We have in mind something completely different which only by lazy thinking could be taken to be a return to the reasoning of biogenetic law. . . . Now it is enough to say that speaking of the analogous nature of the two lines of child development through two lines of phylogenesis, we do not in any way include in our analogy the structure and content of either process. We limit it exclusively to one point: the presence of two lines in phylo- and ontogenesis (Vygotsky, 1997, p. 19).

After reading Vygotsky's careful presentation of the concepts, we still need to know more about how exactly the second line of development, the cultural and historical line, evolves. We know that the two lines continue to coexist – or that they merge into one single line, depending on what part of Vygotsky's work we refer to. In a first attempt, one could say that the first line of development is the typical development of the biological basic equipment of humans, while the second line is development through and into culture. The demarcation criterion between these two developmental lines is not exactly the point when the human is given birth to – at least as far as learning is concerned. If a feature of biologically grounded functions is that they

---

[1] The biogenetic approach claimed that each successive stage in the development of an individual represents one of the adult forms that appeared in its evolutionary history. Haeckel formulated the slogan: "Ontogeny recapitulates phylogeny." The recapitulation theory has also been used as a model for arranging curricula in teaching and learning according to development. Correspondingly, lower grades had to be preoccupied with earlier stages of cultural development, while higher grades had to deal with more recent accomplishments. In the words of Herbert Spencer (1866): ". . . it follows that if there be an order in which the human race has mastered its various kinds of knowledge, there will arise in every child an aptitude to acquire these kinds of knowledge in the same order. So that even were the order intrinsically indifferent, it would facilitate education to lead the individual mind through the steps traversed by the general mind. But the order is not intrinsically indifferent; and hence the fundamental reason why education should be a repetition of civilization in little." (Spencer, 1866, p. 123).

do not have to rely on learning, learning does not begin with the child leaving the mother's womb. Learning is a typical feature of culture.

Intentionality and Shared Intentionality: Towards a Definition

Intentionality has recently become a research topic of considerable interest. The problems and ideas around the development of intentionality promise to give fuel to attempts to formulate Vygotsky's idea of the two lines of development in greater detail – at least as far as the "higher" psychological functions are concerned. It has been the decisive feature of a higher psychological function in Vygotsky's sense in that it separates humans and nonhumans. In the light of a cultural-historical perspective on "intentionality" (Tomasello, 1999) and "shared intentionality (Tomasello & Carpenter, 2007), it becomes evident that even though the great apes share many of the features of human intentional understanding, they fail to incorporate reflexive shared intentionality into their practical life. A couple of highlights may illustrate what we ware talking about here:

- chimpanzees can fully understand what another chimpanzee can see,[2] for example when food is presented in a place right in between the two animals, it is always the one with the higher rank that takes the food. The lower ranked chimpanzee would never take the food in the presence of a higher ranked chimpanzee. When a blind is used in such a way that the animal with the lower rank can see the food and the higher ranking chimpanzee cannot see it, the lower ranking chimpanzee takes the food – knowing that the other chimpanzee cannot see it (see Hare, Call, & Tomasello, 2001). This provides evidence for the extent to which chimpanzees are consciously acting;
- in contrast, chimpanzees cannot perform a relatively trivial gesture like pointing at a certain object. Referential pointing (we will come back to that later) is not an option for the great apes and Tomasello provides an answer to the question: "Why apes don't point" (Tomasello, 2006);
- chimpanzees have tremendous problems with working cooperatively if the social ranking does not fit. Melis, Hare, and Tomasello (2006) have demonstrated that chimpanzees are quite successful as pairs in a task requiring cooperation and coordination if they are tolerant and have no problems with the social rank of the cooperating partner. If they do have problems, cooperation is practically impossible.

Intentionality can be regarded as an individual or as a social construct depending on whether the context of activity is a more solitary one or a group situation. The type

---

[2] As it were, chimpanzees would do well in the three-mountain task which Piaget presented to children in order to determine whether they are still in an egocentric phase or whether they could de-center and put themselves in the position of an observer.

of *shared intentionality* we are dealing with here goes, however, beyond the mere sharing of goals in a social or a group situation. Shared intentionality as we discuss it here is defined by Tomasello as "two people experiencing the same thing at the same time *and knowing together that they are doing this*" (Tomasello & Carpenter, 2007, p. 121). In a new article, Tomasello, Carpenter, and Liszkowski (2007) return to our point of departure: infant pointing. Here they distinguish between a lean and rich interpretation of protoverbal forms of communication (like pointing). The lean position sees the relation of child and adult as merely instrumental: the child wants the adult to do something. The rich interpretation, however, sees that the child is acting on the basis of understanding the adult as a social being trying to influence her intentional/mental state. The rich interpretation requires that we take into account the shared context and its power to define relevance: a *common ground* is absolutely necessary for that. It is equally necessary for an account of what it means to "know something together."

Shared intentionality emerges on the basis of the belief that the other human being is "like me" (Meltzoff, 2002, 2007), that the other human being is a conspecific sharer in what I have in common with others. There is also a relation to the distinction between I-mode and We-mode shared intentionality introduced by Tuomela (2007). Obviously, one is not born with fully fledged shared intentionality. Shared intentionality has to develop in the early years – and it is a surprise how early certain functions are at the child's disposal – functions like empathy or helping being basic elements in the development of shared intentionality.

What we are going to do now is rephrase the problem of the two lines of development in two different parts: one part on cognitive core functions and their relation to shared intentionality, and one part on language and the two lines of development.

Core Functions and the Relation to Shared Intentionality

In this section, we would like to present some ideas about how one could imagine a relevant biological line of development. With "relevant" we mean that we are not talking about the necessity to eat and have water to drink and oxygen to breathe. We mean core psychological functions which we share with our animal forebears. We think that this is exactly the kind of "lower" psychological functions that Vygotsky discussed. A recent example of an attempt to synthesize research on these basic psychological functions is presented by Spelke and Kinzler (2007). While Spelke's first publications (see Spelke, 2000) focused on one single system, for example the number system, Spelke and Kinzler have identified four core knowledge systems: object representation, representation of agents and their actions, a core number system, and a system of representation of the geometry of the environment. We will briefly sketch the basic features of these four systems.

The core system which has received the widest attention is the system of *object representation*. In a sense, research on visual perception has spelled out most of the principles pertinent to this field. If one takes Gestalt psychology and Gibsonian psychology in relation to the cohesion of objects, the boundaries of objects, the constancy and illusion of object perception, the majority of what defines the field of object representation is covered. It is interesting to note that Spelke argues that the features of this system basically are the same whether one looks at a newborn infant or a newly hatched chick – and that they remain virtually unchanged during the life of the adult human being so that the core system of object representation remains constant over human development. This feature of object representation is in line with findings from very young children who seem to possess a rather vast amount of physical knowledge (like in the experiments of Wynn, 1992, 1995) without having had a chance to handle and manipulate objects – because their motor development has not enabled them to freely manipulate objects. This is in sharp contrast to a Piagetian view on the ontogenesis of physical knowledge which would presuppose extensive manipulation of objects.

The core system representing *agents and their actions* seems at first glance to overlap the system of object representation – if one thinks only of causation of movements and the like. Very young infants, however, interpret social and non-social actions, for example infants do not interpret the movement of an object as goal-directed and do not try to imitate those movements. All these representations of agents can also be found in newly hatched chicks, newborn monkeys, and so on. Mirroring behavior with a corresponding activity of mirror neurons seems to be an important and ancient part of adaptive behavior.[3]

The core *number system* is perhaps the most abstract of the core systems. We have to bear in mind, however, that we are talking here about numbers up to five, plus or minus two. For human infants, children, and adults and for adult non-human primates number representations have the same basic threefold property: First, number representations are imprecise and they become less precise the larger the cardinal value (scalar variability); second, number representations are abstract insofar as they apply to diverse entities, from stones, to apples, to cars and horses, to sequences of sound or sequences of light, and sequences of action: third, number systems can be compared and combined by operations of addition and subtraction. The above properties of number systems seem to prevail in all human cultures – whether they have number words for three plus or not.

The last core system has to do with orientation in the geometry of the environment. When infants, children, or adults lose orientation they start to reorient according to magnitudes of the geometry of the surface of the environment like distance, angle, and direction sensing. Landmarks play a much stronger role for adults in the case of disorientation.

If we add a fifth, tentative, element related to identifying and reasoning about potential social partners through *language*, we would get the following picture shown in Fig. 3.1:

---

[3] We cannot go into the interesting details and the role of research on mirror neurons here. For an interesting account see Rizzolatti, Fadiga, Fogassi, and Gallese (2002), Rizzolatti and Sinigaglia (2007), and Ramachandran (2000).

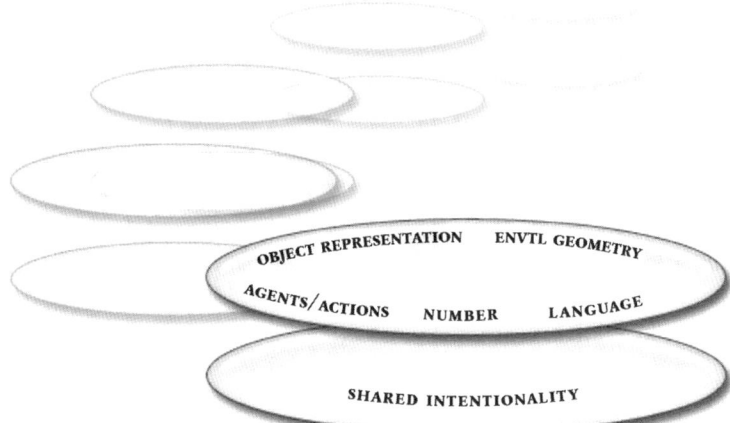

Fig. 3.1 Cognitive core systems and shared intentionality as two lines of development

Fig. 3.2 Cognitive core systems and shared intentionality as mediated by *Lebenspraxis* (life as praxis) and social semiosis

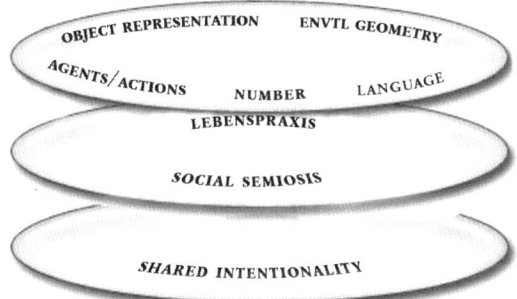

Figure 3.1 is an attempt to illustrate the fact that the further development of these core systems will not take place if it is not based on the common ground of shared intentionality.

The question now arises how shared intentionality succeeds in influencing the core functional systems. A tentative answer is given in Fig. 3.2: the social semiosis of the *Lebenspraxis* can be understood as mediating shared intentionality and the core functional system leading to a full development of those systems – turning it into the *cultural* line of development.

Cooperation, Language, and Development

Following the topics of shared intentionality and rich interpretation of communication through pointing we can show that the cooperation between child and caregiver forms the basis or the frame for further development. With both Vygotsky's cultural-historical psychology and Wittgenstein's Philosophy of Language in mind, we would like to interpret this cooperation in a specific way: The sharing of intentions takes place against the background of a linguistically structured life practice. Examining Fig. 3.2 showing intention sharing and the core knowledge systems as two intensely intertwined developmental levels, we added the linguistically structured life practice as an intermediate level. If we take the texts of Vygotsky and Wittgenstein seriously, we have to transform the figure: instead of using the level metaphor we see both basic levels embedded into an "envelope of consciousness" which surrounds the actors like the air they breathe. The cultural life practice of the child is constituted by the conscious acting of the adults, especially in their actions aimed at allowing the baby to thrive. What Wittgenstein calls "language-game" and Vygotsky the "higher psychological functions" (i.e. conscious attention, conscious memory, conscious emotion[4]) is in fact this embedding of the interactions between infant or child and adults in a conscious, language-permeated event – regardless of whether we call this a "philosophy of education" or "intuitive parenting." Besides the well-known mechanisms of automatically modulating the pitch of the parental voice or the distance to the child's face there must be a conscious, i.e. language-mediated, caregiving behavior – justified by religious, scientific, or other historically constituted attitudes.

Nobody would contradict this statement – so why will we now recourse to the Philosophy of Mind? In our opinion, it casts a positive light on the development of meaning in the first years of language development. We wish to explicate this in the following section because it could help to strengthen the persuasive power of Vygotsky's thesis of the development of the higher psychological functions in the child. The consequences for developmental psychology of a philosophy of language based on Wittgenstein and his successors (see the survey of Wellmer, 2006) are best demonstrated by examining some findings of current cognitive-psychological research. In so doing, we will revert to the already mentioned position of Elizabeth Spelke, i.e. her postulated five core knowledge systems representing objects, actions, number, space, and – last not least – social partners. We choose as an example the description of the system of object representation:

> It centers on the spatio-temporal principles of cohesion (objects move as connected and bounded wholes), continuity (objects move on connected, unobstructed paths), and contact (objects do not interact at a distance) (Spelke & Kinzler, 2007, p. 89).

These abilities are present in newly hatched chicks just as much as they are in human infants as they both can identify moving objects without previous experience. However, the post-natal incipient experience with objects does not immediately lead to a differentiated ability in object classification in human babies. Diverse studies concerning the development of object identity and object permanence, especially

---

[4]For reasons of space we have not focused on emotional development. The same principles apply here, beginning with the "precursor emotions" which then develop into complex culturally shaped emotions in social interaction (see Holodynski, 2006, pp. 81–168).

those of T.G.R. Bower and colleagues (cp. for example Wishardt & Bower, 1984, 1985) have shown early object-related behavior in babies – for Bower object identity follows object permanence, while for Piaget the former is a condition for the latter. In any case, objects can be differentiated on the basis of texture, form, and movement, partially hidden objects can be recovered, and children expect objects that have vanished to reappear. However, in spite of all those accomplishments, Piaget's famous A/not B error can be shown until the end of the first year: when the experimenter is hiding an object at place A, then visibly removes the object from place A and hides it visibly at place B, the children surprisingly look for the still hidden object at place A and not at place B.

What seems to be crucial here is the usage of the object concept. Reading the studies of Spelke, Bower, and colleagues you get the impression that babies can identify objects. In fact, babies can only recognize differences in the "object world" between different experimental arrangements, showing habituation or dishabituation or their preference of certain stimuli to others. Knowing that these differences are based on different objects or object features –mediated by our linguistically structured consciousness – we generalize our „objectified" adult worldview to the baby's worldview.

However, everybody knows that a child's perception is less differentiated than an adult's. But the difference is not seen as a qualitative one or caused by language. Rather, the child is provided with an already existing view on the three-dimensional object world which is stable in time and space and independent from one's self, which gradually develops into the adult form.

Could one say that these ideas correspond with the theories of Vygotsky? In this case, the natural developmental progression would equip the infant with object and person-related categories, accumulating and developing gradually through use until reaching an adult level. One would find an important explanation for the observable psychic development in these fundamental core knowledge systems of a modularly constructed neuronal system. Of course, this would not remove the role played by the physical and social environment for the success of this process. The structure of what developed would be found in these congenital cores, much as the structure of an apple tree lies in the core of an apple, although it still doesn't develop just anywhere and without the cooperation of the environment.

Social interaction and language learning would then work similarly. One would find the building blocks of development starting with early imitation processes and the preference for human faces and voices, as well as the recognition of human facial expression and the production of sounds at different levels of development and different adaptations to the proximate language (as well as Chomsky's language universals). Therefore, nature would effectively provide the material and building plan for development, while culture would produce the basic conditions and nutrients for the successful completion of it. Is this a model of Vygotsky's two lines of development? We doubt Vygotsky would find it to be so.

Before we return to Vygotsky, we would like to consider the terminological problems surrounding the object concept in current debates in the Philosophy of Mind. We will show that the presented model of a gradual concept formation process from simple perception to complex language mediation hasn't been thought through in cognitive developmental psychology. The core concept in these debates is the concept of meaning and the question of how meaning is linked to the problem of the object concept and the naming of objects. When are we allowed to characterize the perception of features in the object world as the perception of objects? When should we speak of knowledge systems, of object-related knowledge and of knowledge of objects? And what about Piaget's old category of the permanence of objects? Conceptual miniaturizations such as "proto-knowledge" or "precursor to the concept of object" miss the target because they give the impression that the essential components necessary for the development of the final product are present from the beginning. The Philosophy of Mind and the debate on the possibility or impossibility of private language shows that the object concept and the categorizing and naming of objects are inextricably intertwined (see Kripke, 1987).

One of the voices in the debate is Donald Davidson (2004). In the following citation he asks what it means to have a concept of something:

> To have a concept is to class things under it. This is not just a matter of being natively disposed, or having learned, to react in some specific way to items that fall under a concept; it is to *judge* or *believe* that certain items fall under the concept. If we do not make this a condition of having a concept, we will have to treat simple tendencies to eat berries, or to seek warmth and avoid cold, as having the concepts of a berry, or of warm, or of cold. I assume we don't want to view earthworms and sunflowers as having concepts. This would be a terminological mistake, for it would be to lose track of the fundamental distinction between a mindless disposition to respond differentially to the members of a class of stimuli, and a disposition to respond to those items *as* members of that class (137/38).

In our opinion, what Davidson formulates here for concepts could certainly be used for the word "object" in the perception of children. After all, the Spelke experiments testify to the fact that if the child can observe object X or Y, it must have a concept of the object that is the same as an adult's, albeit not so developed and complex. Cognitive developmental psychologists overlook the distinction made by Davidson between the ascertainment of an object and the ascertainment of an object *as an element of a category*. More precisely, the difference is between "recognizing an object" and "recognizing an object as an object."

This small but critical difference can be difficult to grasp. In the first instance, the child reacts to certain patterns or similarities in patterns and to certain object characteristics and their systematic appearance in the handling of the object, especially when these characteristics are isolated as such experimentally. The experimenters, effectively taking the position of objective observers, conclude from these reactions that the child is able to perceive an object because it reacts to certain characteristics of the object, for example the dynamics of its movements: "Object Elephant" disappears slowly behind a screen, reappearing, still at the same speed, as "Object Duck." The child recognizes this constantly moving stimulus as a pattern of movement and can anticipate its trajectory, even though it is ignoring form, color, and object category. In our opinion the children do not recognize objects, they recognize object-related features of a systematic experimental arrangement, which is reduced to that special feature.

Another example is demonstrated by habituation experiments. One can demonstrate that ten-month-old babies react to similarities in drawings of fantasy animals, which are grouped together according to similar legs, necks, tails, etc. Judged from differences in the length of fixation time, one can prove that the babies are able to systematically discern familiar and unfamiliar drawings, and can therefore recognize similarities and are able to accomplish certain visual feats of classification (Younger & Cohen, 1983). The authors speak here of correlative concept formation, others use the term "categorization" as one can see in the following quote from an actual textbook in developmental psychology:

> Findings reveal that 6- to 12-month-olds structure objects into an impressive array of meaningful categories – food items, furniture, birds, animals, vehicles, kitchen utensils, plants, spatial location („above", „below", „on", and „in"), and more (....). Besides organizing the physical world, infants of this age also categorize their emotional and social worlds. Their looking responses reveal that they sort people and their voices by gender and age (....), have begun to distinguish emotional expressions, and can separate people's natural movements from other motions (....). The baby's earliest categories are perceptual – based on similar overall appearance of prominent object part, such as legs for animals and wheels for vehicles. But by the second half of the first year, more categories are *conceptual* – based on common function and behavior. (Berk, 2006, 228/229; emphasis added)

Children older than 12 months are able to show active classification behavior (touching the classified objects), but only from 18 months onwards can they classify objects actively into two classes (putting the objects in two different baskets). Piaget would be satisfied because that corresponds with his theory of object permanence at 18 months, when mental processes are established on a representational basis – operating with mental imaginations. However Vygotsky considered *language* to be indispensable in this case, just like the Philosophy of Mind.

We are not of the opinion that children are unable to accomplish the cognitive feat known as non-verbal concept formation. We are, however, of the same opinion as Wittgenstein and Davidson in that what the children are demonstrating in these studies has nothing to do with concept formation and should not be designated as such. Separate criteria are applicable to concepts and to non-verbal classification processes with behavioral "answers" in the form of habituation or preference processes.

For Wittgenstein the ability to reconstruct objects as objects in space at the level of mental representations is unthinkable without linguistic representation. Only with the help of conscious processes can we imagine objects as objects, and for this language is the *conditio sine qua non*. Wittgenstein and his followers in Analytical Philosophy analyze this difference in great detail when they establish why a concept cannot originate by an associative linkage with a perceptual imagination. It is not true that a word–thing correlation, after it has been created, is then fed into a morphological rule system, for example designating that this particular word is to be used as a noun, adjective, or verb. The relationship between word and thing presupposes the linguistic permeation of the entire scene of action where the word is used. Without understanding the whole utterance within the communicative situation there will be no meaning of single words.

Wittgenstein expresses this in the following passage from the Blue Book (1984):

> The mistake we tend to make could be expressed as follows: we look for the use of a sign, but we look for it as if it were an object which coexists with the sign. (One of the reasons for this mistake is that we are looking for a "thing" that "corresponds with the noun"). The sign (the sentence) acquires its meaning from the system of signs, from the language it belongs to. In short: "to understand a sentence means to understand a language:" (The Blue Book, 1984, 19 ff, cited from Wellmer, 2006, p. 54); or if you take a quote from the Philosophical Investigations: "For a *large* class of cases – though not for all – in which we employ the word "meaning" it can be defined thus: the meaning of a word is its use in the language." (Wittgenstein, 1968, PI, § 43).

Concepts originate in social interaction as generalizations of experiences made in cooperation and communication. Concepts are defined through their relationships to other concepts. As it were, a concept does require a complex linguistic (language specific) fabric without which it cannot exist, even though it looks, at first glance, as if through pointing at an object and giving it a name, the origin of concepts could be understood and explained. However, the simple deictic sentence "This is a tree" will not be understood if the addressee does not know the function of pointing and does not know what "this" and "is" and "a" mean. In addition, most of the words in our language like, for example the ones just used, cannot be transmitted through gestures. Pointing at a tree in order to give it a name can only make sense if the addressee already knows how to use pointing as a gesture in communicative action. Even then, it is still relatively hard to decide whether the pointing person points at the tree, at the bark, at the treetop, at a bird, or at something hidden behind the tree.

Even if one imagines a cognitive process in which an infant first constitutes an non-verbal concept of an object or a living being, for example the mother, and only later links it to the auditory sequence, the infant must first have experienced a communicative situation applying this concept. The infant must have been part of a situation where the verbal structure "mama" – which is related to the averbal "object" or living being – receives a communicative function: calling mama, pointing at mama, talking about mama, and so on. Thus, understanding "mama" means to understand the entire communicative situation this word has been uttered in. Actively uttering "mama" also reflects the complex meaning of the entire communicative act: welcoming mama, pointing at mama, calling mama and so on. This means that those first "mama"-utterances cannot be understood as concepts of the "object mother" in the sense of referential acts, even though there are of course some referential elements in the utterance "mama."[5] Within the much more comprehensive final meaning of the utterance "mama," those referential elements form a kind of "guiding beam," directing the later development of the meaning of the single word "mama" out of the complex meaning of utterances situated within communication – opening up, at the same time, places for other differentiated word

---

[5]Evidence for the non-referential use of the word is the instance when infants call their fathers "mama" which can often be observed – assuming that the infant can discriminate both persons, which children of 12 months certainly can do.

meanings.[6] We could well replace the guiding beam metaphor with Vygotsky's "zone of proximal development," because it is the adults whose interpretations (in the sense of Bloom's "rich interpretation") externalize the meaning of the child's utterance presenting somehow to the child the „extended version" of what the utterance means – the „director's cut", so to speak.[7]

This is a decisive factor for the child about to learn the language, because the interpretation of the words she had uttered is actually enriching their meaning. On the one hand, the difference between the meanings of language in the child's utterances and the meaning of these or similar sounding utterances in the adult language result in the chance to identify linguistic elements with certain types of actions and features of the situation. On the other hand, the one-word sentence gives a clue to the adult about which shared actions the child wants to refer to. Because, in general, adults actually do interpret one-word sentences according to the intentions of the child: as sentences with complex meanings. The utterance "mama" in a certain situation will be understood as: „Look, Mama, what a big bird!" In this, the differences of meaning between the holophrase of the child and usage of the same word in the adult language constitute the dynamics of the language acquisition process. At the same time both processes are of critical relevance for its success:

- the active pars-pro-toto usage of a word with the meaning of a complex utterance, the interpretation of this utterance through the parents which leads to the success of the child's communicative intention, thus giving the child's utterance as it is used the meaning intended by the child, i.e., there is neither correction nor a lack of understanding of the child's construction.

In a sense, the same word ("mama") continues to exist in the communicative praxis for quite a while in two meanings:

- on the side of the child as a complex sentence with a variety of possible interpretations, because depending on the situation the meaning of "mama" may change,
- on the side of the parents as a single element of a complex utterance coupled through the experiences of shared cooperative actions with the communicational intentions of the child.

The common and successful life of those two meanings in societal praxis or, as Vygotsky would have it: in social intercourse between the individuals, is the basis for the constitution and development of meaning on the part of the child. The initial ambiguity of word meaning does not completely vanish but constitutes

---

[6]Tomasello (2005) has empirically demonstrated this phenomenon in the language acquisition process for the acquisition of verbs at the age of two and has given it the name "verb islands".

[7]See our critique of Vygotsky at the first Symposium 2006 in Berlin: we didn't criticize the role of the interpretation of the parents, but the non-communicative grasping movements of the child that it was related to.

what is special with language in its shared and non-shared meanings and reciprocal understanding – and proliferates a basis for metaphors and other creative applications.

We maintain that language and meaning, even just simple pointing, can only make sense psychologically in social use, in the communicative process. For the child, this sense does not exist in the relationship between an object or person-related bundle of characteristics and a sign. It lies in the long experience of interacting through joint action processes with competent speakers and actors. Here the child can achieve his goals by having something to show and something to say. The basis of this joint experience is the capacity of the infant for the "sharing of intentions, sharing of actions, sharing of emotions." Both the handling situation and communicative intention as a whole – including everything that belongs to the relevant context, place, time, partner, intent, prior experience and aim of the discourse – build upon this basis to create the meaning of an utterance. This is true even if only one single gesture or word is visible or audible. In this way, the production of a child's "one word sentence" follows the same principles as the daily discourse production of an adult or the new, metaphorical use of a concept in poetry or science.

Spelke and the above-mentioned perceptual abilities of the child shall not be falsified here. On the contrary, in the light of our two lines of development we are suggesting a conceptual differentiation, which purports that the human infant has a phylogenetic inheritance at its disposal that makes developmental processes possible in two areas of life:

- In relation to the object world he is able (contrary to one part of Piaget's findings) to look for things that have slipped out of his hand or otherwise disappeared because of crossmodal transfer. This transfer allows the infant to arrive at one modality by way of another and have them work together. The core knowledge systems postulated by Spelke and others also belong to this area, even though we would not call them knowledge systems. We would tend to reserve the concept of "knowledge" for explicit, conscious knowledge.
- In order to interact with his social environment, the infant has at his disposal a series of astounding abilities that allow him to appropriately react to social signals. In addition, he or she can also use behavioral systems to challenge his social environment into interacting with him or her when he/she smiles, makes sounds, establishes eye contact, imitates the expressions of adults, or heartrendingly cries and wails, allowing him- or herself to be calmed by a voice or a touch.

Even when one counts the sharing mechanisms as one of the biologically predisposed basic competencies, one should certainly keep in mind that the psychic development of these abilities into higher psychological functions through the embedding in a social or cultural environment does not happen automatically nor in linear fashion. This development needs the conscious "intervention" of the process in the form of linguistically structured communicative, cooperative, and evaluative acts. Two factors are decisive for this process. On the one hand there is the language and interaction community with its self-constituted social practice as the "cultural atmosphere," and on the other hand, the concrete person interacting with the child and this person's attitudes, values and experience affected by these actions. Language and the connected cultural life practice are therefore the medium, milieu and concrete equipment in which and by which the higher psychological functions can develop from the interindividual to the intraindividual.[8] To our understanding this is exactly how Vygotsky would also have sketched it. In other words: The speech for others which aims at the organization of social relations in the world acts back upon the speaking subject. This leads to a new means of organizing the sensorimotorically grounded experience of the speaking subject because he or she has sign sequences at his disposal which are able to reorganize episodic and procedural memory components with fitting symbolic means. In this the speaking subject acquires a new method and new means of actively expressing his experience for others and for himself – consciousness.

Concluding Remarks

Summarizing what we have done so far, we would express that shared intentionality is indeed at the center of those processes, which lead to the merging of the two lines of development. What is needed is more work on the role of imitation, on the definition of intentionality as active and passive, on the situatedness of intentionality, and the relation to other fields like autism or other emotional handicaps. We started with Vygotsky's phenomenal example of how sociality is becoming a fundamental feature of speaking and thinking and acting through the process of interiorization: what once was external, now is internal. Now, in the light of recent research, it seems that the social as "external" gives a slightly distorted picture. From the moment of birth – and possibly even before – human infants turn out to be supersocial attractors.

Being born into an environment so deeply saturated with signs and meaning, requires intentional understanding as basic to all other human activity. The psychology of perception and cognition have long treated inanimate objects and humans only as perceptual, they were alike in the sense that we can perceive them, think of them. But now, the difference between objects and humans seems to go deeper. One of the first major achievements of development of the infant after birth seems to be that they draw a line separating humans with intentions from objects without intentions, to separate objects from humans, from conspecifics.

---

[8]These terms should not be confused with interpsychological and intrapsychological (see other chapters). The authors try here to solve the problem how the interindividual/intraindividual becomes interpsychological/intrapsychological and believe that it is important to differentiate exactly between those terms.

References

Berk, L. E. (2006). *Child development* (7th ed.). Boston: Pearson.
Davidson, D. (2004). What thought requires. In D. Davidson (Ed.), *Problems of rationality* (pp. 135–149). Oxford: Clarendon Press.
Hare, B., Call, J., & Tomasello, M. (2001). Do chimpanzees know what conspecifics know? *Animal Behaviour, 61*, 139–151.
Hildebrand-Nilshon, M., & Seeger, F. (2006). *Sign and triangulation: From Vygotsky to Peirce and back.* Paper presented to the first international symposium of cultural-historical anthropology and cultural-historical psychology, December 1–2, Freie Universiät Berlin.
Holodynski, M. (2006). *Emotionen – Entwicklung und Regulation.* Berlin, New York: Springer.
Kripke, S. (1987). *Wittgenstein über Regeln und Privatsprache.* Frankfurt/Main: Suhrkamp.
Melis, A., Hare, B., & Tomasello, M. (2006). Engineering cooperation in chimpanzees: Tolerance constraints on cooperation. *Animal Behaviour, 72*(2), 275–286.
Meltzoff, A. N. (2002). Elements of a developmental theory of imitation. In: A. N. Meltzoff & W. Prinz (Eds.), *The imitative mind* (pp. 19–41). Cambridge: Cambridge University Press.
Meltzoff, A. N. (2007). 'Like me': A foundation for social cognition. *Developmental Science, 10*(1), 126–134.
Ramachandran, V. S. (2000). Mirror Neurons and imitation learning as the driving force behind the great leap forward in human evolution. Edge, No. 69, May 29.
Rizzolatti, G., Fadiga, L., Fogassi, L., & Gallese, V. (2002). From mirror neurons to imitation: Facts and speculations. In: A. N. Metzoff & W. Prinz (Eds.), *The imitative mind* (pp. 247–266). Cambridge: Cambridge University Press.
Rizzolatti, G., & Sinigaglia, C. (2007). *Mirrors in the brain: How our minds share actions, emotions, and experience.* Oxford: Oxford University Press.
Spelke, E. (2000). Core knowledge. *American Psychologist, 55*, 1233–1243.
Spelke, E. S., & Kinzler, K. D. (2007). Core knowledge. *Developmental Science, 10*(1), 89–96.
Spencer, H. (1866). *Education: Intellectual, moral, and physical.* New York: D. Appleton & Company.
Tomasello, M. (1999). *The cultural origins of human cognition.* Cambridge, MA: Harvard University Press.
Tomasello, M. (2005). *Constructing a language: A usage-based theory of language acquisition.* Cambridge, MA: Harvard University Press.
Tomasello, M. (2006). Why don't apes point? In: N. J. Enfield & S. C. Levinson (Eds.), *Roots of human sociality: Culture, congnition and interaction* (pp. 506–524). Oxford & New York: Berg.
Tomasello, M., & Carpenter, M. (2007). Shared intentionality. *Developmental Science, 10*(1), 121–125.
Tomasello, M., Carpenter, M., & Liszkowski, U. (2007). A new look at infant pointing. *Child Development, 78*(3), 705–722.
Tuomela, R. (2007). *The philosophy of sociality: The shared point of view.* New York: Oxford University Press.
Vygotsky, L. S. (1997). The history of the development of higher mental functions. In: R. W. Rieber (Ed.), *The collected works of L.S. Vygotsky* (Vol. 4). New York: Plenum Press.
Wellmer, A. (2006). *Sprachphilosophie. Eine Vorlesung.* Frankfurt: Suhrkamp TBW
Wishardt, J. G., & Bower, T. G. R. (1984). Spatial relations and the object concept: A normative study. In L. P. Lipsitt & C. Rovee-Collier (Eds.), *Advances in infancy research* (Vol. 3, pp. 57–123). Norwood, NJ: Ablex.
Wishardt, J. G., & Bower, T. G. R. (1985). Longitudinal study of the development of the object concept. *British Journal of Developmental Psychology, 3*, 243–258.
Wittgenstein, L. (1968). *Philosophical investigations.* New York: Macmillan.
Wittgenstein, L. (1984). Das *Blaue Buch.* Werkausgabe, Band 5, 15–116. Frankfurt: Suhrkamp.
Wynn, K. (1992). Addition and subtraction by human infants. *Nature, 358*, 749–750.
Wynn, K. (1995). Origins of numerical knowledge. *Mathematical Cognition, 1*, 35–603.
Younger, B. A., & Cohen, L. B. (1983). Infant perception of correlations among attributes. *Child Development, 54*, 858–867.

Chapter 4
Material Culture, Semiotics and Early Childhood Development

Christiane Moro

Vygotsky's major contribution to human development and consciousness is that it is socially and culturally mediated. Within the critical perspective that I am going to develop further on, it needs to be stated at the outset – in order to eliminate any misunderstanding – that I consider that the Vygotskian framework contains the very ingredients to overcoming the mainstream psychological focus on dualism that does not include an understanding of the psyche in what is essentially human, that is in its cultural-historical dimension.

Early in his career, Vygotsky (1925/1997c) posited an anti-dualistic conception of consciousness, notably influenced by Spinoza's and James' works. The characterization of consciousness as a function (James, 1912/1904) becomes of particular value to Vygotsky. With function, consciousness becomes methodologically accessible through practical human activity. Thus, for Vygotsky, a genuinely developmental approach relies less on the biological model or embryologic understanding of the potential deployment as contained in the germ (Vygotsky, 1934/1997a) and more on a definition of development in which culture structurally and functionally determines the human psyche, and thus consciousness.

Development related to culture, is closely linked to the mediation of psychological processes. Mediation is regarded by Vygotsky as the central fact of psychology. Two periods in Vygotsky's definition of cultural-historical development through mediation have been distinguished (Moro & Schneuwly, 1997; Moro & Rodríguez, 2004a). In a first period named 1st Vygotsky (Moro & Schneuwly, 1997), Vygotsky developed a tool-oriented concept of mediation of the psychological processes (Vygotsky, 1930); in a second period named 2nd Vygotsky (Moro & Schneuwly, 1997), Vygotsky focused on the content of the tool, that is, meaning (Vygotsky, 1934/1997a). The concept of mediation allowed Vygotsky (cf. the "base unit", Vygotsky, 1934/1997a) to include the cultural-historical dimension through the tool then through the sign (but centrally language-based) in his perspective of cultural-historical development. As such, semiotic mediation tends to be reduced

C. Moro (✉)
Université de Lausanne, Lausanne, Switzerland
e-mail: Christiane.Moro@unil.ch

M. Kontopodis et al. (eds.), *Children, Development and Education*, International
Perspectives on Early Childhood Education and Development 3,
DOI 10.1007/978-94-007-0243-1_4, © Springer Science+Business Media B.V. 2011

to the symbolic (conceived as linguistic) device while material artifacts are neither considered to involve public meaning nor to enhance cultural-historical development per se cf. Chapter 3, this book.

In this chapter, I focus on material objects as culturally oriented and as such as semiotic (Moro, 2000; see also Cole, 1996). In other words, I consider that objects and their uses cannot be reduced to simple instrumentality in a single physical-material sense (Moro, 2000) no more than to simple tools of communication or of social distinction (Barthes, 1985; Roche, 1997). It is through the prism of the construction of the objects through their uses, that I re-examine Vygotsky's conception of practical intelligence before language.

First, I refer to Vygotsky's design of ontogenetic psychological development of pre-verbal practical intelligence and discuss Vygotsky's conception of mediation of psychological processes entailed by his two successive theorizations of mediation through tools and through signs. Then, I develop the heuristic value of the semiotic mediation as developed in *Thought and Language* (1934/1997a) which can be considered as the heart of a new conceptual design of the psychological processes approach that Vygotsky was developing (Mecacci, 1983; Moro, 2000; Wertsch, 1979), in order to rethink culture in all its constitutive dimensions either identified as material or symbolic/ideational. I then point out what I consider to be the blind spot in Vygotsky's thesis, that is, the issue of the material object as culturally oriented and, as such, semiotic (and not merely instrumental), as the basis of psychological processes from early development. Object refers to culture in the sense that the material world involves shared meanings. Therefore, there is not an opposition between material culture and symbolic culture (Moro, 2000). Finally, I argue (based on the results of my research) for reconsidering cultural-historical development in relation to the diversity of semiotic systems available in culture. This proposal will engage a rethinking of the beginnings of psychological development and the concept of "practical intelligence" as well as the role of materiality in this development.

Practical Intelligence in Vygotsky's Framework at the Pre-Linguistic Level of Development

Vygotsky (1925/1997c, 1934/1997a) and Vygotsky and Luria (1930/1994) distinguished two types of development, *natural* – characterized by practical intelligence[1] based on the use of tools that are not yet conceived as the fruit of culture – and *linguistic* development dominated by the linguistic device with which maturation becomes cultural-historically oriented.

---

[1]Practical intelligence is one of two roots of development considered by Vygotsky as the source of language and verbal thinking. According to Vygotsky's developmental hypothesis, "non-verbal thought" develops in a phylogenetically different manner, distinct from the communication line, which is qualified by Vygotsky as "pre-intellectual language" (Vygotsky, 1934/1997a).

First, remember that Vygotsky established early on the uniqueness of human behavior, albeit still stated in primarily behavioral terms in 1925:

> [. . .] Finally, what is also essentially new for human behavior is that his adaptation and the behavior connected with it takes new forms in comparison to animals. In animals we have passive adaptation to the environment, in humans active adaptation of the environment to oneself. It is true that in animals as well we encounter rudimentary forms of active adaptation in instinctive behavior (nest building, the building of a dwelling, etc.), but in the animal kingdom these forms first are not of predominant, fundamental importance and, second, still remain passive in their essence and in the mechanism of their realization (Vygotsky, 1925/1997c, p. 68).

In this assertion, Vygotsky introduced a *rupture* between human and animal behavior from a psychological point of view. In 1930, Vygotsky and Luria (1930/1994) referring to Köhler's work with chimpanzees, later replicated with children and compared by Köhler himself, and by Bühler, infer the existence of thought implicated in the use of tools prior to language development. Also, research conducted in the field of phylogenetics, driven by ontogenetics demonstrated comparable results for both animals and humans during the pre-verbal period of development:

> "The child's use of tools is comparable to that of an ape's only *during the former's pre-speech period.*" (Vygotsky & Luria, 1930/1994, pp. 108–109, emphasis added)

For Vygotsky and Luria, practical intelligence at this stage of ontogenesis is not considered to enter the process of cultural-historical development. Experiments conducted were less concerned with tools as artifacts but more with "tools" as means of action and its goals:

> Some of the experiments may be regarded as directly transferred from Köhler's experiments (for instance, the experiment where a ring must be removed from a stick, or the series with the piece of toast attached to a string) (Vygotsky & Luria, 1930/1994, p. 111).
>
>   To understand the transformation of primary tool-oriented activity (i.e., preverbal) into tool activity that is cultural-historically oriented requires the introduction of external uniquely linguistic signs (Vygotsky & Luria, 1930/1994).
>
>   As soon as speech and the use of symbolic signs are included in this operation, it transforms itself along entirely new lines, overcoming the former natural laws and for the first time giving birth *to authentically human use of implements* [emphasis added]. From the moment the child *begins to master the situation with the help of speech, after mastering his own behavior* [in italics in the original text] a radically new organization of behavior appears, as well as new relations with the environment. We are witnessing the birth of those specifically human forms of behavior that, breaking away from animal forms of behavior, later create intellect and go on to become the base of labor: the specifically human forms of the use of tools (Vygotsky & Luria, 1930/1994, pp. 108–109).

Therefore, according to Vygotsky and Luria, the introduction of verbal elements in tool-oriented activity implicates a radical transformation of behavior, causing the child to enter into a process of cultural-historical development.

> Through the transformation of practical intelligence under the influence of language, it is the cultural mediation of the psychological process which defines a new, complex psychological unit "in which symbolic activity is directed toward organizing practical operations by means of the creation of secondary order stimuli and the planning of the subjects own behavior" (Vygotsky & Luria, 1930/1994).

> The child was thus given the possibility to solve practical problems of tool use outside
> its direct sensory field. The child mastered the external situation by first mastering itself and
> organizing its own behavior (Vygotsky & Luria, 1930/1994, p. 122).

From this point of view, it is less the tool as an artifact that is the object of
interest for Vygotsky than the psychological transformation implied by language
when integrated into tool-oriented behavior. I consider that this vision introduced a
developmental rupture in the evolutionary process during ontogenesis and poses a
theoretical problem with regard to the transformation of practical intelligence into
cultural-historically oriented intelligence. Moreover, this conception reduces the status of tools, which are not thought of as cultural products (the idea developed by
Vygotsky, in this sense is less aligned with Hegel and Marx and closer to Piaget's
stage V of sensory-motor ideas (1936/1977); see also Moro, 2000, 2002).

Beyond the Vygotskian conception and its paradoxes (Moro & Rodríguez, 2005),
is the problem of defining tools in terms of artifacts implicating public meanings
related to culture in its material dimension and consequently, the mediation of psychological processes (here, preverbal) by these artifacts in early development which
is questioned. I consider that in effect, culture has a tendency to be identified to a
particular class of artifacts, those that support the ideality or symbolism and do not
include that class of artifacts related to the material world.

Vygotsky's Semiotic Mediation of Psychological Functions and Its Heuristics for Studying the Psychological Processes Considered as a Whole

Vygotsky developed two conceptions of the mediation of psychological processes.
First a tool-oriented one (between 1927 and 1932) where Vygotsky introduced the
concept of psychological tools which he transposed, in the field of human psychological activity, from Hegel and Marx's conception of mediation concerning the role
played by work in the relation that man establishes with nature. Vygotsky insisted
on the analogy between the role of the tool in behavior and the role of the tool in
work. In tool-oriented action, tools, as artificial means elaborated through culture,
orient activity in an artificial direction. Therefore, Vygotsky identified the following
as psychological tools:

> The following may serve as examples of psychological tools and their complex systems:
> language, different forms of numeration and counting, mnemotechnic techniques, alge-
> braic symbolism, works of art, writing, schemes, diagrams, maps, blueprints, all sorts of
> conventional signs, etc. (Vygotsky online: 1930).

The class of artifacts related to materiality is not considered by Vygotsky in the
above tools. Furthermore, the sign is identified to the tool, and the meaning is not
implicated in this first definition of the mediation of the psychological processes
other than what Vygotsky mentioned finally himself:

> In our older work, we ignored that the sign has a meaning [...]. While our task was previously to demonstrate that which is common between the "knot of the tissue" and the logical memory, and now it is to demonstrate the differences that exist between them (Vygotsky, 1933/1968, p. 184).

At the end of the 1920s, Vygotsky (1931/1997b) attempts to clarify the differences between the tool and the sign. He argues on one hand, that the tool is externally oriented while on the other hand, the sign is internally oriented. This new theorization tends to reintroduce a kind of dualism in the conception of culture in the Vygotskian framework, and to counterpose material to symbolic culture.

A second conception of mediation – the semiotic mediation – is defined by Vygotsky where he reintroduced the meaning as the mean feature of the sign, considered as an instrument of communication and of thought. On the basis of the relationship between language and thought, Vygotsky (1934/1997a) defines "word meaning" which enters into the content of the tool and reconsiders the transformation of psychological functions. In the first theorization, psychological functions were taken in isolation: memory, attention, thought... as if they were autonomous systems independent from one another (Moro & Schneuwly, 1997). In his new (second) theorization, psychological functions are considered as intertwined (cf. studies on schizophrenia) (Moro & Schneuwly, 1997).

We can consider that through the notion of semiotic mediation – even oriented towards the analysis of the linguistic device in relation to the constitution of thought – Vygotsky sets the essential methodological foundations for a complete reconfiguration of the analysis of the pre-verbal instrumental period in which the material world, and more specifically objects with their uses considered as artifacts function as signifiers, and not just signifieds. For Vygotsky (1934/1997a), the development of the psychological functions is seen as the progressive appropriation of the culture though social interaction. In this respect, the conception of semiotic mediation becomes essential in the triptic composed by the child, the adult, and culture. The semiotic dimension is the core of the process of transmission–appropriation of the meaning of objects through their uses. As was noted by Lee (1985), Vygotsky sets the foundations for a functional semiotic psychology. Moreover, meaning is the right candidate to investigate the question of psychological functions as interfunctional systems. Psychological functioning is essentially considered as interfunctional and linked through meaning.

Material Culture as a Source of Development at Pre-Linguistic Stage: The Example of the Appropriation of the Use of Objects in Children Between 7 and 13 Months of Age in Triadic Interaction Child–Object–Adult

In this section, I will document with the support of research on the transmission–appropriation of the uses of an object by a child between 7 and 13 months old in the triadic interaction adult–object–child the role of material culture during the pre-verbal period, reconsidering the material object as a source for cultural-historical psychological development.

Presentation of the Research

In this investigation (Moro & Rodríguez, 1998, 2004a, 2004b, 2005), we show that pre-verbal psychological development is fundamentally oriented by culture through the appropriation of object use to which children are introduced by adults. In our conception, objects are social by virtue of their uses. Canonical and "symbolic" uses (redefined in a cultural sense) are generally shared by a community of subjects at a given time in collective history. Then, to be appropriated, use, or learning the rules for using the object, requires an educational intervention from people around a child.

The definition of the material object as an artifact moved us to methodologically distinguish the object from its use. Use is defined as a place of convention, communication, and public meaning which refers to the human community for its definition and transmission. The notion is inspired by Wittgenstein's (1961) where meaning is use. Early development is notably characterized by objects and their uses. Social uses (canonical and symbolic) concern the accomplishment of pure material functions of the object. Canonical uses are related to the construction of a primary state of things related to the immediate world in which the child is immersed. Symbolic uses (equally conceived as a cultural emanation) relate to the construction of alternative states of things which may refer to the generalization of canonical uses that exist in other objects (Rodríguez & Moro, 2002); or may also refer to the fact that the use is carried over to referential social practices that redefine the *hic et nunc* use of the object in a symbolic meaning (Moro, 2003; Moro & Rodríguez, 2004b). Symbolic uses may therefore include a semiotic stratification more or less complex, always implying a second meaning (Eco 2003). This complex (re)construction of the meanings of the material uses (canonical or symbolic) of objects by the child is considered to be established through the signs that the adults utilize in their educative mediations with the goal to intentionally transmit the uses of objects to the child.

In a general way, the questions that we formulate through this study are the following: How does a child construct the material world? How, during the period preceding language acquisition, do children learn about the objects surrounding them and their appropriate uses between 7 and 13 months old in the triadic interaction child–object–adult?

Data Collection

In order to master the uses of objects, the child must interact with adults. The resulting child–object–adult unit, called triadic interaction, constitutes the basic unit for the observation and analysis of children's behavior. Six dyads child–adult are longitudinally observed at 7, 10, and 13 months of age during the transmission – appropriation of social (canonical and symbolic) uses of objects. The data involve three female and three male Swiss children. The situations proposed involve the object as well as the mother (privileged adult partner). The adult is given the following instructions: "Play with your child as you usually do." To remain as close as possible to everyday life situations, the dyads are filmed within their home environment. Only one camera is used and the subjects are informed that the dyad will be filmed for 5 min and that if they wish (if they are tired) the session may be interrupted at any moment. The dyads are free to use objects as they wish. The recorded sessions are transcribed second-by-second using a timer and following a transcription method devised specifically for this purpose.

The object considered for this study is a Fisher Price telephone painted in vivid colors, with a red receiver. It has a traditional front that you have to turn to dial the number. It is set on four wheels and has a string inserted in the front so that it can be pulled and made to go like a car. It has a face painted on its front, with mobile eyes that animate when the phone is moved backwards and forwards. The string that goes to the receiver has been extended to make it easier to use by the dyad. The canonical use of the telephone consists in simulating *Saying hello*. This usage involves putting the receiver on the ear, using it alternatively with one's partner so that it creates something similar to a telephone conversation, with the related uses including *taking the receiver*; *dialing the number*; *talking on the phone*; *hanging up* (Fig. 4.1).

Semiotic Analysis Using Peirce's Conception of Sign

Unlike the conception of the sign seen as a resemblance or an identity (Kristeva, cited by Eco, 1998), Peirce's conception is essentially dynamic. It aims at describing

Fig. 4.1 The Telephone-toy used in our Experiments

"the semiosis, that is the process through which meaning occurs for an interpreter in a given context" (Everaert-Desmedt, 1990, p. 39). For Peirce, "a sign is something which once it is known allows to know something more" (Peirce, cited by Eco, 1998, p. 33).

The triadic conception of the sign according to the three terms of *representamen, object*, and *interpretant*, which constitute the foundations of Peircian semiotics, appears as essentially dynamic through the inferential process that subtends it. It appears to us quite adequate for the analysis of an online interaction process on a pre-linguistic level:

> A sign, or representamen, is something in some respect or capacity. It addresses somebody, that is, creates in the mind of that person an equivalent sign, or perhaps a more developed sign. That sign which it creates I call the interpretant of the first sign. The sign stands for something, its *object*. It stands for that object, not in all respects, but in reference to a sort of idea, which I have sometimes called the ground of the representamen (Peirce, 1931–1958, C.P. 2.228).

The Peircian sign conceived as inference is particularly useful for the description of development processes. In the examples proposed at the end of this chapter, we examine how the different inferences involved in semiotic processes at key points in development are elaborated. These inferences will allow the child to progressively acquire the meaning necessary for mastering the social (canonical and symbolic) uses of the objects. The Peircian semiotics allows one to follow nearly online the various inferential movements during play by the child in the course of construction of his or her cultural-historical knowledge relative to the material object during the appropriation of its uses.

The conception of the triadic sign issued from Peircian semiotics, adapted for communication and genesis, has been used to analyze the child's semiotic processes related to signs intentionally emitted by adults in order to transmit the use of the object to the child in the triadic child–object–adult interaction. In articulation with the three fundamental categories of phenomena advanced by Peirce (1931–1958), three types of relationships between the *representamen* (sign at the beginning of the process of interpretation) and the object of semiosis (i.e., what the sign represents) can be defined and further subdivided into three categories: *icon, index,* and *symbol*.[2] An *icon* refers to its object of semiosis by "resemblance" (for example, the smoking sign represents the smoking object); *an index* refers to an object of semiosis situated outside of itself under the pressure of its circumstances (the smoking sign represents the fire object in a purely circumstantial manner); a *symbol* refers to its object of semiosis by virtue of a law (the smoking sign represents the fire object independently of the circumstances). This trichotomy allows access to the

---

[2]The notion of symbol, in Peircian semiotics, is not identifiable as this (disputed elsewhere) used in psychology. Our concept of symbol is a cultural concept such that we have redefined it in the frame of this text. When Peirce speaks of symbol, he refers to the canonicity, as a rule to the Law. In our analysis, the two defined concepts are articulated.

reconstruction of public meaning in a child's interpretation of the adult's signs in the triadic interaction child–object–adult and, beyond that, to infer the type of semiotization of the material object (knowledge of the object through its use) by the child.

In concordance with Vygotsky's approach, different functions susceptible to intervene in the constitution of meaning are examined: attention, emotion, vocalizations – verbalizations; intentional signs from the adult related to the transmission of the use of the object to the child; and finally the status of the use of the object (noncanonical; precursors to canonical use; canonical use) effectuated by the child.

Presentation of the Examples

In what follows, I report several examples that illustrate this work on the transmission – appropriation of the use of the object in the triadic interaction child–object–adult in order to illustrate my proposal that material objects are the source of cultural-historical psychological development through semiosis during the pre-verbal period. On the contrary to Gibson's notion of affordance (1979), an object cannot tell the child how it should be used. In Gibson's theory, the meaning of objects is considered to be immediate and transparent to the child. For Gibson:

> Each thing says what it is... a fruit says "Eat me"; water says "Drink me"; thunder says "Fear me"; and a woman says "Love me" (Koffka cited by Gibson, 1979, p. 138).

The extracts presented here are parts of triadic interaction sessions that lasted 5 min that were videotaped as indicated supra. These examples demonstrate the child's progressive appropriation of canonical meanings till the uses of an object stabilizes. At 7 months of age, social uses (canonical and symbolic) of the object are not yet appropriated. We observe non-canonical uses, such as *rubbing, sucking, slapping, throwing*, which are applied to objects, no matter which objects are being used. The object considered in the examples is a Fisher Price toy telephone. The use concerned is "Saying hello" which, according to the circumstances, could be interpreted as canonical or symbolic. The first two examples illustrate that the use is not yet present on the intra-psychological plane (i.e. the object doesn't directly implicate its conventional uses) at 7 months of age whereas at 13 months the third example shows that the use (both in canonical and symbolical dimensions) is appropriated by the child and in consequence is present on the intra-psychological plane. The following examples illustrate the progress in the understanding of the conventional uses of the object through the interpretation of the signs intentionally emitted by the adult in the process of meaning-making by the child in relation to the transmission–appropriation of the uses of the object in the triadic interaction child–object–adult.

Elements of Analysis

Observation 1: Nelson, 7 months, Sequence 11, Duration: 33 s: Canonical use of combination under immediate demonstration of the use by the adult

> The adult turns the dial ("make the number"). Nelson puts his hand on the handset (mechanically displaying interest for the adult's action). The adult turns the dial a second time, seizing the handset, putting his ear to it while saying *allooo, allooo hello Nelson allo allo allooo hello Nelson* occasionally shaking the handset placed at his ear while the child sucks on the cord (on which the telephone base is fitted to the front to be rolled). Then the child moves his hand towards the adult's action, takes the cord (connecting the handset to the telephone), then the latch, then grabbing the cord again while continuing to look at the adult, who smiles. The adult, always with the receiver on the ear, says *aaaaah yes yes yes* while moving closer to the child. The adult lifts the receiver from his ear and says "you want to listen?" The child hangs up the phone then buries the cord in his mouth again. The adult places the receiver on the child's ear saying *allo alloo allooo allo alloo allooo who is it?* For four seconds, the child accepts this immediate demonstration of the use *saying hello*, effectuated by the adult. For the entire duration of the demonstration, except for a brief look at the adult's action of putting the receiver on his ear, the child looks straight at the adult in the posture of the person who telephones [. . .].

A first educative intervention (analyzed in terms of signs) is directly realized on the child's body by the adult when the canonical use of the object is made through a sign that we designate *immediate demonstration* which implicates the child's body. This immediate demonstration allows the child to enter into conventional meanings of the object under the whole control of the adult. During this immediate demonstration, after a brief look at the receiver, which is placed at his ear, the child enters into the use proposed by the adult *by accepting for 4 s* the receiver which was applied to his ear by the adult and by *looking straight at him* – that is, adopting the posture of the person who calls. The action of the adult (in *the hic et nunc*) becomes a sign of the conventional meanings of the object for the child, i.e. the immediate demonstration is interpreted by the child in relation to the canonical use of the object although he is not able to realize the canonical use of the object *on his own* at 7 months. The meaning at first iconic, (*the immediate demonstration* refers to itself), becomes indexical, the adult's sign being interpreted by the child as a reference to the use of the object (cf. *the child's acceptance* of the immediate demonstration produced by the adult and the child's adoption of the *looking straight ahead* of the person on the phone when the receiver is "put" on his ear). The child's interpretation of the immediate demonstration realized by the adult implicitly implies the inferential meaning *if it's a receiver, then put it on the ear*.

Observation 2: Nelson, 7 months, Sequence 9, Duration: 35 sec.: Approached "canonical" use of the receiver: initiation without specific intention

> The adult rolls the telephone base while making *rouuuuuu* [sounds], while also climbing it up one side of the child and down the other side, then climbing again while making *tourourourourourou ourourourou tourourourourou* [sounds]. The child looks at the adult's action then follows the adult's action with the help of [the adult's] hand. The child taps the dial with the receiver and while he taps, the receiver finds itself suddenly (and by chance)

positioned "upside-down" against the child's cheek, who says *euu*. The child looks for a brief moment straight ahead [in the posture of the person who telephones] all the while keeping the receiver on his cheek. Then, he looks again at the adult's action (who continues to roll the telephone) and puts down the receiver [. . .].

The use initiated by the child presents a dynamic that unfolds, at least from the beginning, almost despite him, that does not allow for him to be awarded the qualifier of intentionality at this stage. The consequence of the child's interest in the action of rolling the telephone, initiated by the adult, and the verbalizations that accompany it, leads the child serendipitously to effectuate *the action of putting the receiver on the ear* (in the approximate form). While the receiver is placed by the child himself against his cheek, the receiver solicited an interest, as evidenced by the child's reaction of surprise at his action (*euu*). This interest is linked to the feeling experienced with regard to his action, and refers to other feelings that the child could experience during previous *immediate demonstrations* (see Observation 1). This revival of sensations (of tactile and proprioceptive nature) that allows a type of past encroachment in the present constitutes one of the very first processes that allow the autonomy of meanings. Here, we can capture the first traces of an interpretation of the object in its conventional (canonical) meanings for the child *in an autonomous manner* at 7 months. The child's own action becomes a sign in a movement that goes from the *icon*, the *euu* relating to the action itself, to the *index*, as the posture of *looking straight ahead* relating to the canonical use of the object shows. This action is first made independently from any intention. It is the increasing complexity of the processes of interpretation that have been previously put into place by the child through the adult's signs (see Observation 1) that is at the origin of this production of meaning. The meaning *if receiver, then put it on the ear* appears and disappears in the course of action.

Observation 3: Justine, 13 months, Sequence 6, Duration: 7 sec.: Symbolic use of the telephone receiver by the child

> [The child, who rolls the telephone behind her while pulling the cord, moves again into view of the camera]. The child goes in front of the adult at full speed, making a detour to avoid being caught by the adult. The child says *daddy*. The adult says *well now then* while the child shakes the receiver in the air on the opposite side of where the adult is (all the while looking at the adult) while saying *a-te e-douu*. Then the child places the receiver on her shoulder. The adult [who tries to stop the child disappearing again] says *you could at least come and play with me, no, we're going to say hello* then he takes the child, who puts the receiver down [she keeps it 3 seconds on her shoulder].

In this observation, the child shows that she has constructed the public meaning of the object as it is implied in the semi-declarative gesture (e.g., the exhibition–ostension of the receiver made to the adult after the verbalization *daddy*) realized by the child before realizing the use. The canonical meaning *if it's a receiver, then put it on the ear* is appropriated to the conventional use of the object and enters here in the fictional play, which demonstrates that the child articulates (in action) two uses: one *hic et nunc* and the other not present, that is, the use implies the "telephone toy" and the "real telephone." The receiver takes on a double meaning, that of the toy object (with which one plays) and that of the real object (with which one telephones daddy). In that observation, the child utilizes the receiver as a substitute for the referent object "real receiver." The telephone-toy is essentially used by the child to *pretend* to call and the child *knows this*. Her verbalization *daddy* – the father is absent – intervenes beforehand into the receiver in the direction of the adult (in a type of exhibition of the object's meanings) – and signifies that with the receiver one can *pretend* to call daddy *who is not present*. In pursuing with canonical use, the child lets us believe that she understands *which game one plays with the receiver*. The child knows – which is confirmed by the analysis of other sequences – that the telephone toy is not the real object because one hears no one through the receiver and the child is otherwise engaged – in other sequences – in the alternating use of the receiver with the adult, characteristic of the fictional use of the object. The public meaning, now acquired, implicates that a rule is appropriated (symbol in a Peircian sense) and utilized here in a clearly symbolic way (in the psychological sense, classically understood).

Conclusion

In conclusion, this research on the transmission–appropriation of the use of the object demonstrates that the construction of public meaning (canonical and symbolic) of the object is achieved following a lengthy process involving the signs of other people. This construction is thus not immediate, to the contrary of the conception of Gibson's affordances (1979). This research shows that the construction of new manners of action relative to the object in a cultural-historical acceptance *proceeds to the meaning, that is, to the possibility to elaborate the shared meanings (implying complex sets of inference)*. The intention as it refers to a cultural-historical action is not a *primary process* but is always a *secondary process* (see the empirical study in Moro & Rodríguez, 2005 and critical theorizations in Moro, 2000). Thus, intention is a social construction resulting from the appropriation of socially shared meanings, that is, only public – we consider – the semiotic microgenetic analysis that brings it up to date. In addition, to respond to Vygotsky, we observe in the examples cited, that it is less the language which transforms the action into a cultural-historical one than the process of meaning-making related to non-verbal signs produced by other people in order to transmit the use of the objects to the child. The language presents a status more fundamentally iconic if not indexical "marrying" the meanings of the object – see the number of hyperboles used by the adult – shown or indicated through the non-verbal signs of the adult. The transformation of the child's action is then the consequence of the appropriation of the meanings related to the use of the objects transmitted by the adult specifically through non-verbal signs, allowing the child to enter material culture before language. These meanings which lead to new ways of acting with regard to the object in relation to culture are, therefore, at the origin of intentions in a cultural-historical way.

At this stage of development, we demonstrate that material culture has to be considered as semiotic through the objects and their uses in the process of the transmission–appropriation of their public meaning via non-verbal signs employed by other people surrounding the child. Meaning related to the use as an inferential construction through non-verbal signs (in line with Peircian semiotics) is fundamentally a source of cultural-historical development at pre-verbal age.

With the approach of the object conventional use, we show that pre-verbal intelligence as initially described by Vygotsky as merely instrumental needs to be reconsidered through the prism of semiotic mediation. During pre-verbal development, the mind is specifically mediated by material culture through artifacts and non-verbal signs other people use to transmit the use of the object in triadic interaction, allowing the construction of new inferences about the material world by the child. In this approach, evidence is provided that, at pre-verbal stage, the semiotic mediation of psychological functioning is not exclusively due to the advent of language but is based on a material object reinterpreted as an artifact. The material object is the source of cognitive development through signs and public meaning shapes the mind in the very early developing mind.

Acknowledgments   I am grateful to Michalis Kontopodis and Denise Shelley Newnham for their close reading of this text. I am indebted to Sarah Stauffer for her translation and Sophie Tapparel for her final reading and help in editing this paper.

References

Barthes, R. (1985). *L'aventure sémiologique*. Paris: Seuil.
Cole, M. (1996). *Cultural psychology: A once and future discipline*. Cambridge, MA; London: Belknap Press of Harvard University Press.
Eco, U. (1998). *Sémiotique et philosophie du langage*. Paris: Presses Universitaires de France.
Eco, U. (2003). *De la littérature*. Paris: Grasset.
Everaert-Desmedt, N. (1990). *Le processus interprétatif. Introduction à la sémiotique de Ch.S. Peirce*. Liège, Belgique: Mardaga.
Gibson, J. J. (1979). The theory of affordances. In R. Shaw & J. Bransford (Eds.). *An ecological approach to visual perception* (pp. 127–143). Boston: Houghton Mifflin.
James, W. (1912/1904). Does consciousness exist? Electronic document, Accessed July 20, http://psychclassics.yorku.ca/James/consciousness.htm
Lee, B. (1985). Intellectual origins of Vygotsky's semiotic analysis. In J. V. Wertsch (Ed.), *Culture, communication and cognition* (pp. 66–93). New York: Cambridge University Press.
Mecacci, L. (1983). *Vygotskij. Antologia di Scritti*. Bologne: Il Mulino.
Moro, C. (2000). *Vers une approche sémiotique intégrée du développement humain*. Habilitation à Diriger des Recherches en Psychologie. Université Bordeaux 2: UFR des sciences sociales et psychologiques Université Bordeaux 2.
Moro, C. (2002). Médiation et développement. Enjeux et perspectives de la théorie de L.S. Vygotski. In M. Wirthner & M. Zulauf (Ed.). *A la recherche du temps musical* (pp. 137–159). Paris: L'Harmattan.
Moro, C. (2003). L'action éducative et la médiation des significations des objets en crèche. In M. Saada-Robert et V. Solioz (Ed.), « L'intervention éducative en crèche et son rapport à l'observation. Confrontation de trois types d'analyse : sémiotique, didactique,

micro-génétique », *Actes du colloque du Service de la Recherche en Education (SRED): Constructivisme et Education. Scolariser la petite enfance, Genève, Septembre 2003*, 143–152.

Moro, C., & Rodríguez, C. (1998). Towards a pragmatical conception of the object: The construction of the uses of the objects by the baby in the pre-linguistic period. In M. C. D. P. Lyra & J. Valsiner (Eds.). *Child development within culturally structured environments. Construction of psychological processes in interpersonal communication* (Vol. 4, pp. 53–72). Stamford, Connecticut and London, England: Ablex Publishing Corporation.

Moro, C., & Rodríguez, C. (2004a). Formes sociales et (re)construction des significations dans la situation éducative. In C. Moro & R. Rickenmann (Ed.). *Situation éducative et significations* (pp. 221–245). Raisons Educatives No 8. Bruxelles: De Boeck.

Moro, C., & Rodríguez, C. (2004b). L'éducation et le signe comme conditions de possibilité du développement psychologique. Un questionnement qui transcende les frontières disciplinaires. In G. Chatelanat, C. Moro, & M. Saada-Robert (Ed.), *Unité et pluralité des sciences de l'éducation. Sondages au cœur de la recherche* (pp. 61–87). Berne: Peter Lang.

Moro, C., & Rodríguez, C. (2005). *L'objet et la construction de son usage chez le bébé. Une approche sémiotique du développement préverbal*. Berne: Peter Lang.

Moro, C., & Schneuwly, B. (1997). L'outil et le signe dans le développement psychologique. In C. Moro, B. Schneuwly, & M. Brossard (Ed.). *Outils et signes. Perspectives actuelles de la théorie de Vygotski* (pp. 1–17). Bern: Peter Lang.

Peirce, C. S. (1931-1958). *Collected papers*. Cambridge, MA: Harvard University Press.

Piaget, J. (1936/1977). *La naissance de l'intelligence chez l'enfant*. Neuchâtel-Paris: Delachaux & Niestlé.

Roche, D. (1997). *Histoire des choses banales. Naissance de la consommation XVIIème – XIXème siècle*. Paris: Fayard.

Rodríguez, C., & Moro, C. (2002). Objeto, communicación y símbolo.Una mirada a los primeros usos simbólicos de los objetos. *Estudios de psicología, 23/3*, 323–338.

Vygotsky, L. S. (1930). *The instrumental method in psychology*. Accessed July 24, 2009, Published online at: http://www.marxists.org/archive/vygotsky/works/1930/instrumental.htm

Vygotsky, L. S. (1933/1968). Problema soznanija [Le problème de la conscience]. In A. A. Léontiev et T. B. Riabovoï (Ed.), *Psychologija grammatiki* (pp. 182–196). Moscou: Isdatjelstvo Moskobskovo Universitjeta.

Vygotsky, L. S. (1934/1997a). *Pensée et langage*. Paris: La Dispute.

Vygotsky, L. S. (1931/1997b). *The history of the development of higher mental functions*. In R. W. Rieber (Ed.), *The collected works of L.S. Vygotsky* (Vol. 4). New York and London: Plenum Press.

Vygotsky, L. S. (1925/1997c). Mind, consciousness, the unconscious. In R. W. Rieber (Ed.), *Problems of the theory and history of psychology: Vol. 3. The collected works of L.S. Vygotsky* (pp. 62–90). New York and London: Plenum Press.

Vygotsky, L. S. (1930/1994). Tool and symbol in child development. In R. Van der Veer & J. Valsiner (Eds.), *The Vygosky reader* (pp. 99–174). Cambridge: Basil Blackwell.

Wertsch, J. V. (1979). The regulation of human action and the given new structure of private speech. In G. Zivin (Ed.) *The development of self-regulation through private speech* (pp. 79–98). New York: Wiley.

Wittgenstein, L. (1953/1961). *Investigations philosophiques*. Paris: Gallimard.

Chapter 5
Touching Each Other: Video Analysis of Mother–Infant Interaction After the Birth

Sigrid Klasen

Introduction

Research studies that deal with early child development can often be found to concentrate on gaze and voice, whereas bodily contact – the holding, stroking, embracing – as well as smelling and tasting as social phenomena are granted a rather marginal position; these are considered, if at all, as a framework in which the "actual" dialogical faculties are formed by seeing and hearing. This perspective does not seem surprising in a culture that is oriented to a great extent toward the visual while the spheres of touch, taste and smell are assigned to the lower senses and thus discriminated (Benthien, 1998; Diaconu, 2005; Kamper, 1984).

This study focuses on touch as an early means of communication used to establish a bond between the newborn and its caregivers.[1] In this respect, the first part of this chapter deals with theoretical assumptions that characterize in more detail the field of early communication where touching is taking place. The second part presents the microanalysis of a communicative situation between mother and daughter as an example in which the acts and activities described above play an essential role. The scene analyzed is part of a video recorded on the third day after the child's birth in a maternity unit of a large municipal hospital.

S. Klasen (✉)
Free University Berlin, Berlin, Germany
e-mail: sigiclasen@yahoo.de

[1]This study is a part of the DFG-project "Representations and practices of birth in families, obstetric institutions and media", lead by Christoph Wulf (see also my article in Wulf, 2008, pp. 85–125).

M. Kontopodis et al. (eds.), *Children, Development and Education*, International Perspectives on Early Childhood Education and Development 3, DOI 10.1007/978-94-007-0243-1_5, © Springer Science+Business Media B.V. 2011

Perceiving and Moving

In his representations of infants' early experiences, the psychoanalyst Daniel Stern has put the relationship at the centre of his theory (Stern, 1992).[2] Stern's theory states that cohabitation in the first months is affected by differentiated perceptions and interactions. Already in the first minutes after birth the infant is able to actively take part in forming the relationship by influencing the extent and the rhythms of the stimulation. She/he gives signals by turning her/his head towards and away from the caregivers, by tensing and relaxing her/his body, and by variations of vocalizations, screaming, etc. According to Tomasello, the meaning of this kind of communication for caregiver and infant essentially lies in sharing their behaviour and emotions (Tomasello, Carpenter, Call, Behne, & Moll, 2005). In doing so, the infant experiences the world in a form of microexchange that occurs continuously between her/him and her/his surroundings (Stern, 1979). Through this exchange, the infant receives a number of pieces of information, for example how the forms of thinking and feeling in her/his concrete familial community are dealt with or how the cultural surroundings treat social contacts.[3]

Stern has chosen the term "moving along" to designate the activities of relating and attuning in relationship situations, a concept that stresses their processual character (Stern, 2004). It refers to the flow of events and the way in which they follow or mesh with each other. The course of "moving along" is marked by fuzziness and nonlinearity because it takes its shape spontaneously and simultaneously with the events, so that the participants cannot clearly predict where this process will lead. Similarly, the ways in which participants relate to each other do not have any real beginning, since they always involve something that already exists. The manner in which they refer to each other is not in any causal relation, but follows the principle of contingence (Beebe & Lachmann, 2004). This is to say, the recognition of certain structures in the behaviour of the respective other enables both sides to predict the other participant's future behaviour with a certain probability. The ways in which they relate to each other allow coherences to occur through which the field of encounters between the adult and infant is gradually broadened. Within this field of communication, touches as tactile experiences have a special significance, especially pertaining to the establishment of a relationship to the newborn. But how can they be characterized in more detail?

To begin with, touches take place directly on the skin. They are based on the sense of touch, which develops in the womb after just two months as one of the first senses. After birth, too, tactile perception continues to play an essential role,

---

[2]Meanwhile, some recent studies on the development of emotions emphasize their relational aspect. They assume that emotions represent relationships that connect individuals with their surroundings. Thus, the emotions are developed by reciprocal formation processes with these surroundings, whereby cultural influences play a fundamental role (cf. Holodynski, 2006).

[3]This exchange of feelings can also be conceived as a base for the development of shared intentionality as it was discussed in the chapter by Seeger & Hildebrand-Nilshon (Chapter 3, this book).

as many experiments with newborn children have shown (Montagu, 1982; Oerter & Montada, 2002). What is special about the sense of touch is that it is characterized by a high structural complexity. Consequently, it represents a collective term for different sensory systems (Diaconu, 2005, p. 63 sqq.) such as the senses of temperature and pain, as well as the sensibility for depth (bathyaesthesia[4]). All of these sensory systems are placed in the skin as the most extended and perhaps the most important sense organ, enabling touches on the skin to be combined with the sensations of heat, coldness, pressure or pain. These, in turn, are furthermore connected to inner qualities of emotions.

Touches can essentially be characterized by two properties. On the one hand, they are always a matter of *movement*, which refers to their relation to gestures. On the other hand, they are intimately related to perception. In this respect they embody a relational act. They produce a dual perspective of *perception*, since someone who touches is at the same time someone who has a sensation of being touched. A clear division between an active and a passive role therefore appears to be impossible. Touches have their reflexive aspect, too, since one cannot sense something without sensing oneself. In this respect, touches establish a connection to the other's body and – by doing so – they also change the relationship to one's own body. From this point of view, the skin constitutes the first medium of social exchange: it separates one's own body with its sensations from the body of the other, but via the skin, there is also the potential to transcend the boundaries of one's own self.[5]

Synaesthetic Perception[6]

Senses are different modalities used to perceive the world. Through the intermodality of perception, the newborn already has the ability to coordinate different sense impressions of touching, tasting, smelling, hearing and seeing with each other and to combine them into perceptional entities (Stern, 1992). In the communication between caregiver and infant an intimate space is formed in which the bodies are at a short distance from each other. This allows the close senses to come forward more clearly; they unfold their power in the interaction with the distant senses of hearing and seeing. In this manner, the touches on the skin are mediated at the same time by voice and gaze.

---

[4]It concerns e.g. a sensation for the extension and spatial borders of one's own body.

[5]Cf. also Anzieu, who, from a psycho-analytic perspective, brought the skin together with the development of the self, whereby the borders between the physical and psychical appear indefinite (Anzieu, 1991).

[6]*Synaesthesia* is generally understood to be a conjunction of fields of perception deemed to be separate. Thus, for a synaesthetician e.g. certain noises can trigger colour perceptions. In this approach the synaesthesia is assigned to a specific realm of perception, a view not shared in this study.

In this context, it becomes obvious that in the perception of the other through touches, a sensuous dimension has been approached that cannot be reduced to individual elements. The sense data, such as tones, colours, odours or tactile qualities, are not simply synthesized to forms and shapes, but rather one should assume that the perception is able from the very beginning to "*sense*" situations in their actual arrangements. This happens in the process of coordinating the bodies with one another. From this a sphere of interrelation, a "temperedness of the space" or an *atmosphere* arises, whose meaning rests on the character of the "In-between" (Böhme, 1995, 2001). The space between caregiver and child as "tempered space" is thereby a constructed one; at the same time it appears against the background of a social world by which it is moulded.

In the manner described, atmospherically tempered spaces are also a part of staging practices and can be linked to mimetic and simulating acts, which will be discussed below in more detail. However, first attention will be called to a form of movement that can also be seen as an essential element in the formation of the space between caregiver and child: rhythmical movement.

Rhythms

Rhythms are based on temporal dynamic changes and make it possible to create order in the flow of events. Rhythm itself can even be considered a universal phenomenon of nature (Desain & Windsor, 2000).[7] Thus, a number of physiological processes in our bodies are organized rhythmically, like the heartbeat, breathing, the muscle contractions of the digestive tract, or the sleep–wake alternation. Intercellular processes or hormonal movements also belong to these processes.[8]

In the course of the communication between adult and child, rhythmic processes create accentuations in the sequences of movement by being related to a pulse, which expresses an alternation of closeness and distance, action and pause, or tension and relaxation. In exchange with other movements, social rhythms can emerge in this manner in terms of alternating movements that are synchronized with each other by the activity of reciprocal perception. On the other hand, these rhythms can be part of staging strategies as well and stimulate the other to bodily movements or challenge movements as reactions.

Rhythm itself does not necessarily consist of a regularity of exact repetitions but is rather characterized by a process-like nature and structural similarities (Brüstle, Ghattas, Risi, & Schouten, 2005). The single rhythmic movements do not regulate

---

[7] Dewey referred to this in his article "Art as Experience" from 1934 (Dewey, 1988).

[8] This has led the physiologist Baier to the view that the understanding of bodily processes requires sonoric forms of representation in addition to imaging procedures. According to him, the rhythmic organization of corporeal phenomena can be expressed more intensely aurally, since the ear can better perceive complex temporal structures than the eye (Baier, 2001).

themselves on the basis of achieving an aim, but are based on the *How* of the bodily movements and their temporal extensions. The rhythms are perceived by turning the attention to the course of temporal processes. What is essential here is that specific structures can be realized as similar in a sensuous manner. This comprises a creative internal activity, which establishes a connection with a past experience, the recollection of this experience, and an expectation directed to the future. The aspect of the similar appears here as an interplay, which alternates between expectation and surprise.

Mimesis and Simulation

Gestures as mimetic movements have a specific function in accessing the emotional world of the other.[9] This refers to an approach to the world of the other in the form of attuning, assimilation or correspondence. One relates to the other by adopting something of the latter's behaviour and by reshaping it into something new, which in turn can be "answered" by the other accordingly. In this manner reciprocity comes into being. According to Gebauer and Wulf, mimesis of the gesture is an act of the body through which the body accesses the world and in whose realization the body is accessed by the world (Gebauer & Wulf, 1998, p. 80 sqq.). In this sense, mimesis constitutes a mediating instance, whereby the emphasis of an act lies not in its outcome but in its process-like nature.

In the context of early communication, this applies above all to coordination in the form of temporal qualities, to which degrees of intensity in affects and rhythmic structures belong (Klasen, 2008a). Cultural patterns of order are imparted to the child through the manner in which gestures and parlances are expressed; at the same time, however, ad-hoc situations again and again amount to an exploration of leeways, and thus new forms of contact emerge.

Within the embodiment of communication, a further form of approach plays an essential role; this form, like the mimetic, is closely related to rhythmic processes and will here be called the simulation of a dialogue. This connotes a model that is introduced into the communication by the caregiver and refers to staging. Relevant in this context are the verbalizations, among which one can distinguish between the content of speech and the modality, meaning *how* this content is expressed, the verbal gesture. The latter refers to the melody and rhythm in the content of speech achieved by raising the pitch, by accentuating single words, accelerating and decelerating the rate of speech, varying the sound volume, or setting pauses in the flow of speech. Emotions can thus be transferred or intensified, especially when combined with immediate touches on the skin.[10] At the same time the speech represents, in

---

[9]See Chapter 6 by Wulf about mimetic learning as a practice of cultural learning, which encloses all the senses (in this book).

[10]Similarly, they play an important role in the acquisition of language and the learning of hearing (Horsch, 2004).

terms of content, a kind of performative excess that cannot be understood by the infant. For the caregiver, however, this excess is meaningful insofar as he or she tries to turn the infant into a "dialogue partner at the same eye level".[11]

Microanalysis of the Interaction Sequence

Methodical and Methodological Aspects

The video clip discussed below demonstrates the affective formation of a moment of encounter between mother and daughter (Ma and Li[12]), in which precisely those elements of communication described above, mediated through gestures of touching, become apparent.[13] Recording was carried out using a freely focusing camera direction. Besides Ma, Li and the observer, no other persons were present in the room. On the basis of this fact it can be assumed that in such an intimate situation, the presence of the observer was not forgotten, but, at the most, had taken a back seat. In the analysis this very fact has been taken into consideration, where it has gained relevance in the communication process itself.

The aim of the analysis was to clarify the performative character of the scene (Wulf, Göhlich, & Zirfas, 2001). In this context the body with its movements and performing actions constitutes the real medium of communication. On the basis of the way in which it is used, the body appears as an actor for establishing social processes (Hirschauer, 2004). Consequently the focus of the observation is directed to the "doing", and the question arises regarding *how* the participants form and maintain the process of communication. This refers to the fact that the meaning of the action lies within the dynamics of that action itself, within its development at the moment when it is performed. In this respect, communication takes place in a force field in which the body appears as a social factor that is already socialized and culturally formed from the very beginning. This applies not only to the adult body, but the body of the newborn child as well, in which the earliest experiences gained while inside the womb and during the birth have already been inscribed. The process of communication itself, however, is shaped by improvising action that again and again allows new leeways of behaviour to come into existence, which cause a change in pre-existing cultural and social orientations.

---

[11]In this context, a study of Keller, Demuth and Yovsi is interesting, in which the scientists analyzed mother–child interactions of the Nsos, a clan in Cameroon. There, kinesthetic stimulations play an important role in early communication to support the early motorical development of the children. During this the mother stimulates the baby by shaking it rhythmically on her lap. She accompanies this with similar rhythmic vocalizations. The mother does not comment on every expression of the child and makes no pauses in which the child can "reply", instead the rhythms initiate moments of unisono (Keller, Demuth, & Yovsi, 2008).

[12]In order to maintain the anonymity of the subjects, abbreviations have been used: Ma = mother and Li = daughter.

[13]Li is Ma's second child; Ma already has a nearly 2-year-old son (at the time of the video recording).

This interpretation of the scene between mother and daughter is a (re)construction of action based only on the context of the situation. It is assumed that the spatial arrangement of the bodies as well as the bodily and vocal relations of the actors create types of order whose meaning rests on the process-like course of the action itself (cf. Knoblauch, 2005). The transcription of the behavioural patterns was achieved by means of a software program.[14] In a tabular representation of the scene, mother and daughter are assigned to each other according to units of time. This makes the structure of the forms of expression visible in their sequential course. At the same time, capturing the temporal duration of the expressions will clearly show when they overlap.[15]

The description of the scene begins with a short overview of the content. The subsequent interpretation takes place at two levels. In the first step, the analysis is closely oriented to the course of the action and is documented here with photographic images. The second step represents an attempt to build a connection to the theoretical implications outlined in the first part. This kind of presentation and interpretation is meant to be comprehended as a work of translation, which tries to access the strangeness of the language of body. Translation as such is comprised of a reconstructive as well as a constructive element. At the same time, this highlights a situation within the research field in which an unbridgeable difference remains when approaching the body as a foreign entity. A reconstruction is thus always partly a construction, which makes one's self visible in the other.

The Play with the Grasp Reflex (Duration: 65.44 s)

Overview

The scene demonstrates in four variations (sequences A–D), how Ma initiates a playful action with the grasp reflex by means of touching. In the succession of the gestures, a development in regard to the intensity of the activity will appear. With Ma this manifests itself as an increase in her bodily and vocal gestures towards Li. With Li, a rising level of activity will become visible through her bodily movements and the opening of her eyes.

Sequence A

At the beginning of the scene Ma is sitting on the bed in an upright position and cradling her daughter in her arms. She keeps the baby at a short distance to her body and has turned her face towards Li. Li is lying in a straight position. She holds her

---

[14]INTERACT, Version 7.2 1991–2005, Mangold Software & Consulting GmbH. By decelerating the speed of the images, the temporal duration of Ma's and Li's activities was recorded and coded independently.

[15]On the preservation of interlacing in the sequentiality and simultaneity in the context of video interpretation, cf. Wagner-Willi (2004).

arms at a slight angle; her eyes are closed. She is awake, nevertheless, as can be seen by her slight facial movements.

As Li raises her arms, with eyes closed, Ma speaks to her in a very quiet voice. She asks: „*Guckst du denn?*" [*Are you looking then?*]. Each word is stressed in the same way and is spoken slowly. Then she touches Li's fingertips with her forefinger. Li's hand opens up and Li loosely encompasses Ma's forefinger, whereupon Ma strokes the palm of Li's hand. The impact of Ma's stroking activity can be seen in the relaxation of Li's posture: she drops the other arm, moves her head slightly to and fro and opens her mouth a little so that her tongue becomes visible. At the end of the sequence, both of them drop their hands with closed fingers. Ma's thumb is held flexed to the side, which announces the next sequence.

Fig. 5.1 04.88 s: Ma touches Li's hand with her forefinger (Sequence A)

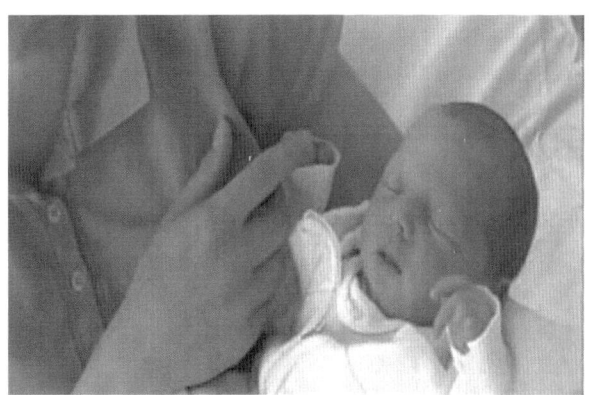

Fig. 5.2 06.24 s: Ma strokes the palm of Li's hand (Sequence A)

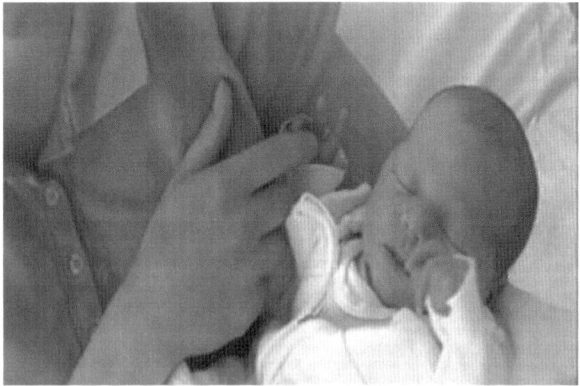

Fig. 5.3 07.40 s: Li encompasses Ma's forefinger. She drops the other arm (Sequence A)

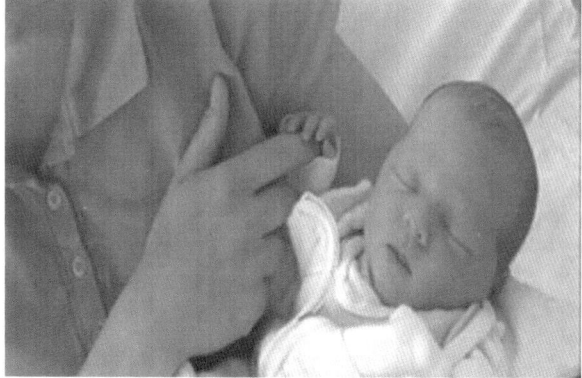

Fig. 5.4 09.80 s: End of gesture: expression of relaxation on Li's face (Sequence A)

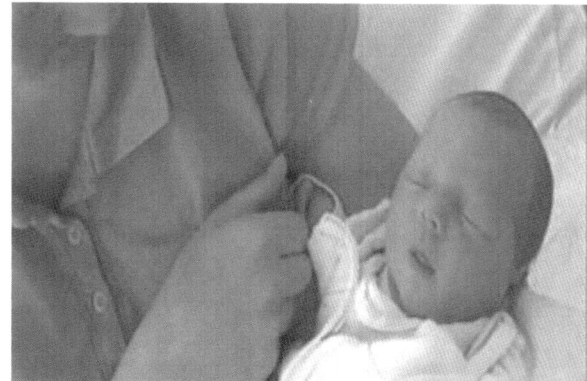

Sequence B

Ma now strokes Li's finger with her thumb. Li responds to this gesture by opening her hand wider than she had done during the preceding moment. At the moment when Li's hand has opened, Ma touches the palm of Li's hand, whereupon Li encompasses Ma's forefinger anew. This time, however, Li's gesture is slightly stronger, and emerges from the previous movement of the hand, which was opened wide before. During the gesture of grasping, Li slowly opens her eyes, though not entirely. She loosens her hand from Ma's contact and develops an activity on her own by opening her hand, clenching it to a fist, spreading her fingers, and turning the hand. At the same time her eyes open a little wider, still blinking at first. During this moment Ma leaves her hand in the same position as when Li had enclosed her finger in her hand.

After Li opens her eyes wider, Ma relates to this and asks with a very quiet voice: „*Doch ma' rausschielen?*" [*Are you peeking?*]. She holds her head at a slight angle and observes Li's gestures. Li simultaneously opens her eyes even more widely.

Fig. 5.5 11.52 s: Ma strokes Li's finger with her thumb (Sequence B)

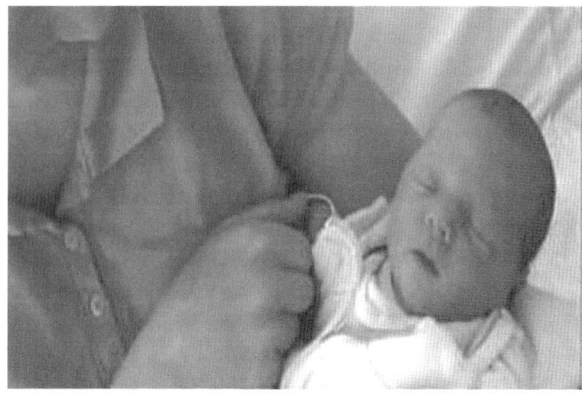

Fig. 5.6 14.36 s: Li opens her hand (Sequence B)

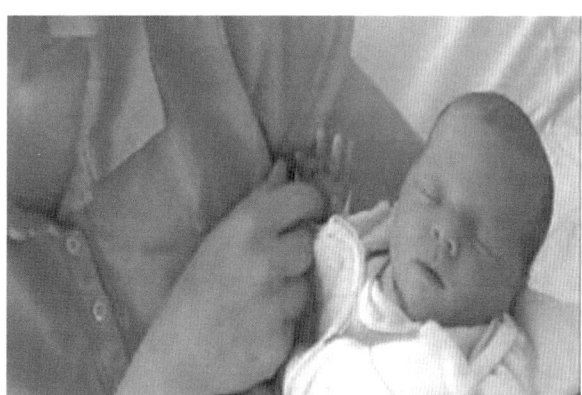

Fig. 5.7 17.12 s: Li encompasses Ma's forefinger and begins to open her eyes (Sequence B)

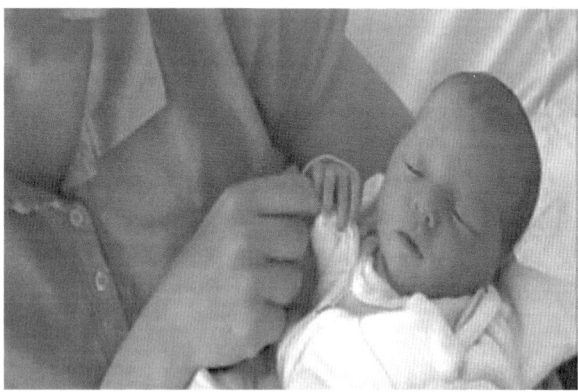

Fig. 5.8 18.96 s: Li loosens her hand from Ma's finger and develops her very own movements with it (Sequence B)

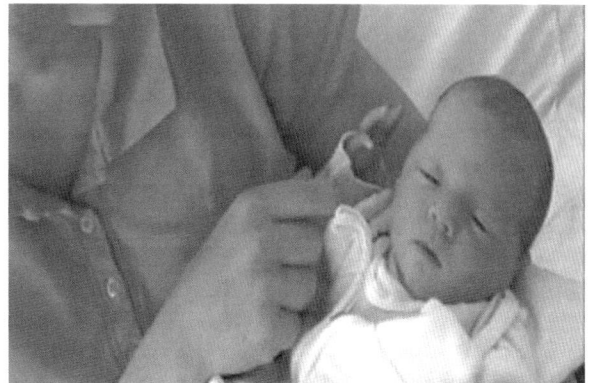

Sequence C

Ma now challenges Li a little more. She tilts her head in Li's direction and says invitingly and with an emphasized voice: „*Lächeln!*" [*Smile!*]. She smiles herself at the same time and shortly strokes the back of Li's hand once with her forefinger. Li responds by turning her head to the middle without establishing eye contact with the mother. At the end of her gesture, Ma slightly distances the upper part of her body from Li and observes Li. Li simultaneously turns her head again a little to the other direction and moves the finger of that hand which was touched by Ma. At this point the dialogue is interrupted by the observer, who states: „*Lächeln für den Fotografen!*" [*Smile for the photographer!*], upon which she and Ma laugh. Li thereby grasps at her head with both hands. Then she raises her arms once again and yawns. At the end of the yawn she looks in the direction of Ma's hand.

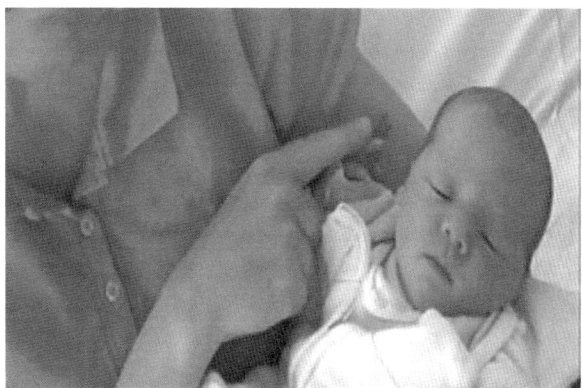

Fig. 5.9 31.80 s: Ma strokes the back of Li's hand with her forefinger (Sequence C)

Fig. 5.10 32.88 s: Li turns
her head in Ma's direction
(Sequence C)

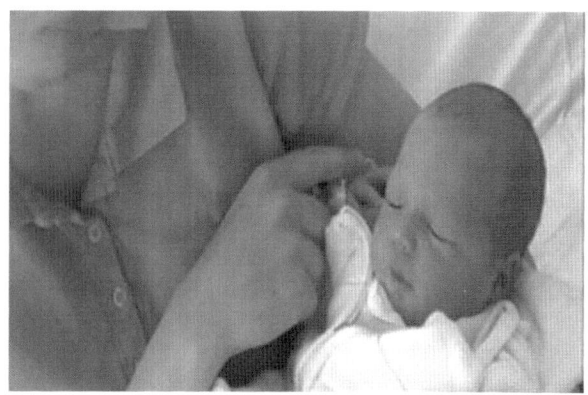

Fig. 5.11 45.60 s: Li
yawns... (Sequence C)

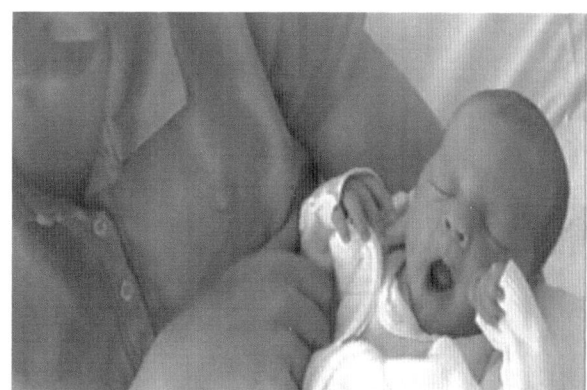

Fig. 5.12 48.68 s: ... and
then looks in the direction of
Ma's hand (Sequence C)

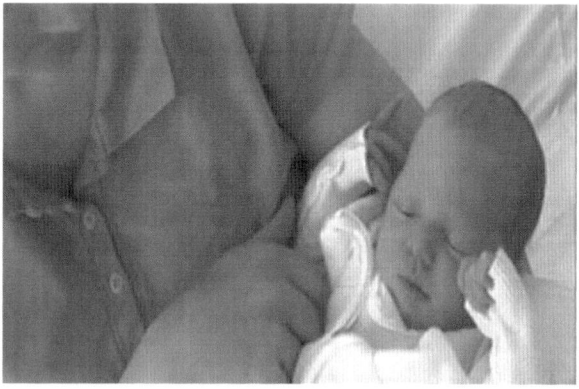

Sequence D

After Li has finished her yawning, Ma again begins to stroke Li's hand. She takes the hand between forefinger and middle finger. In response, Li encloses Ma's middle finger and turns her head away from Ma. Ma now gently strokes Li's finger with her forefinger. While doing so she holds Li's hand loosely between the two fingers. This creates a space for movement within which Li spreads her fingers in order to grasp at Ma's forefinger again. Simultaneously, Li guides her other hand to her mouth. Ma reacts to this by pausing with the stroking for a short while. As Li opens her hand again, she starts to suck loudly on the fingers of her other hand at the same time. In the end, Ma changes her gesture once again by pulling on Li's hand.

Fig. 5.13 52.88 s: Ma strokes the back of Li's hand (Sequence D)

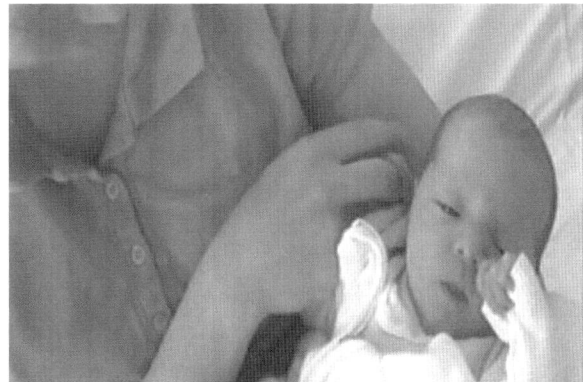

Fig. 5.14 64.04 s: Li sucks on the fingers of her left hand (Sequence D)

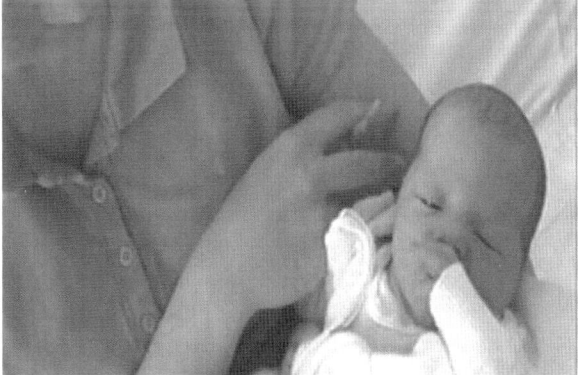

Tactile Contact as an Act of "World Disclosure"

When the four mini sequences A–D are considered in their succession, they reveal a development in the form of a slow crescendo. This development is essentially brought about by the variations in the miniature and defined-set tactile gestures of the mother, intensified by her voice and related pauses. This constitutes a space within which Li can create her own activities. Ma thereby takes up the gradual increase of Li's activity mimically, gesturally and vocally in her subsequent reactions. The action thus gains a structure that follows a dialogical pattern. This pattern is formed by Ma's interpretation of Li's expressions as "answers" to her "speech", which creates a kind of pseudo-dialogue between mother and daughter. From this point of view the scenic process turns out to be a highly detailed interplay of "speech and answer" between Ma and Li, whereby the degree of intensity in action continuously increases.

This play is begun in sequence A by Ma, who reduces her voice and gestures in order to adapt herself to the state of the infant, whose eyes are closed. In contrast to this state, the mother says: *„Guckst du denn!"* [*Are you looking then?*] and reveals in this way that her attention is focused on the gaze. Li "answers" by encompassing the forefinger loosely and taking up a relaxed bearing. They both drop their hands at the end of the dialogue.

Sequence B is once again initiated by Ma. Here a chain of "speech and answer" evolves from the immediate effect of tactile contact on the skin. At first Ma strokes Li's finger with her thumb. Li "answers" by opening her hand, to which Ma, in turn, "replies" by stroking the palm of Li's hand with her forefinger. After this, it is Li's turn again: she encompasses Ma's forefinger and narrowly opens her eyes. Finally, she loosens her hand from Ma's contact and makes rhythmical grasping movements in the air with it, which will last for a while. Simultaneously, she continues to open her eyes, still blinking at first. At this point Ma does not use stroking anymore, but makes a short pause and focuses once again on Li's gaze by asking her in a very quiet voice: *„Doch ma' rausschielen?"* [*Are you peeking?*] The steadily opening eyes of Li seem to be interpreted by Ma as an "answer", as she intensifies her communication in the next step by means of mimic, gesture and voice (Sequence C).

She smiles mischievously and strokes Li's hand once with her forefinger, the hand that Li is still moving. Ma demands in a drawl: *„Lächeln!"* [*„Smile!"*], whilst she tilts her head in Li's direction. Contrary to this stronger sign of attention, she subsequently slightly distances her body from Li and in this manner again emphasizes the very mode of "speech and answer". Li reacts to Ma's stroking hand with a different part of the body than the one she was touched on: she turns her head in Ma's direction and hereby expresses a growing activity of her body.

The request to smile that Ma expresses at this point is an indication of the fact that though she is situated in communication with Li, she is simultaneously acting in a "performance for a spectator", one for whom the mother is presenting and representing *her* form of relationship with Li. Her request is promptly completed by the spectator's comment: *"Lächeln für den Fotografen!"* [*Smile for the photographer*], at which Ma and B proceed to laugh. Li's grasping at her head and yawning, occurring shortly after that, may presumably be considered as an act of compensation due to the higher density of stimuli. This moment does not cause any interruption of the play, but only leads to a short delay before Ma again takes up the play with Li.

The play begins in Sequence D with Ma first starting a new action after Li has stopped yawning. Li's readiness for something new becomes obvious in the fact that she gazes into the direction of Ma's hand at the end of yawning. Ma now resumes the play with the grasp reflex through a further variant of her stroking gesture. As before, she leaves Li a space within which Li can develop her own form of movement: she holds Li's hand only loosely between her fingers and makes a pause with her stroking motion at the moment of child-like spreading and grasping movements, signalizing this time rather subtly, that "now it is your turn!"

It becomes obvious that Ma's dialogues as described above are generated by a rhythmic alternation of action–pause–action, etc. The tactile contacts of the mother, aided by the bodily and vocal gestures, are at first performed spontaneously. As these, however, achieve an (real or imagined) impact, they will animate to a repeated participation, which finally will bring about an instance of playing. These "repetitions", which can rather be characterized as variants of the previous actions, are formed by mimetic processes in that they will take up a part of the child's activity, and this activity will be integrated in the following action. In this manner the mother adjusts the way in which she relates to the intensities of Li's expressions, but still raises the intensities slightly in the very next moment. Mimetic activities can also be noticed on Li's part, since her behaviour co-performs the increasing activity in Ma's expressions. This is visible in her hand movements, gradually opening eyes, head movement, yawning, and finally in her gaze towards Ma's hand at the end of the yawning. In such a way a kind of joint play is generated, evoked by the immediate effect of touches. They are taken up and enhanced through dialogical and mimetic actions. The playing itself remains existent as long as the other participant reciprocates.

In the video sequence a further aspect is of interest: it concerns the grasping movements of Li. In order to discuss this it is necessary to regard the scene from another perspective. In Sequence A and at the beginning of Sequence B, the touches of Ma generate different forms of encompassing Ma's finger by Li, which differ from each other in their degree of intensity, whereby the form of encompassing in the latter sequence reveals a larger movement. This movement becomes the basis of the moment in which Li detaches her hand from Ma's hand and develops a movement on her own. At this moment something appears that can be understood as the dialectic of touch and resistance, as two forces opposite to each other and still linked together.[16] Li detaches her hand from the immediate impact of Ma's touch; at the same time, however, the touch is continued through the force mediated by it. This

---

[16]In an article on the sense of touch, Sennett points out the connection between touch and resistance in the context of sensual experience during the playing of a musical instrument (Sennett, 1998).

becomes visible in the expression of the child-like gesture, which varies grasping hand movements, and in the opening of the eyes. In a certain respect, this kind of moment can be understood, in an as of yet very rudimentary form, as an experience of difference emerging from intimacy. Specifically, the point is less the grasping movement in space as such, but the fact that this movement arises from a social situation and thereby partially loses its reflex-like structure.

Conclusion

The scene described above shows a play sequence between mother and daughter, which in several respects can be understood as a form through which to explore a relationship. The instances of playing are established by a communication between the bodies in interplay of facial expression, gesture, voice, speech and gaze, where touches, initially quite simply on the skin, are of great significance. The skin as a covering and as a surface provides, on the one hand, a protective border to the outside; on the other hand the skin, by means of its high sensitivity for touches, provides manifold possibilities of contact through which other modalities of perception – tasting, smelling, hearing and seeing – are incorporated (Anzieu, 1991). As the skin has the ability to combine different spheres of senses, it becomes the point of transfer for sensations and thereby, in addition, a place of transition between the familiar and the foreign.

Forms of approaching can be observed between mother and daughter, which, although arising from an improvised action and spontaneously built up on the foundation of the momentary situation, also reveal expressions of staging from the mother's side. The latter forms appear in the simulation of a dialogue, initiated by the mother, in which she interprets the expressions of the child as answers to her touches and playfully enhances them on that basis. By means of the dialogue, an existent reality is performed via simulation, and in this manner it becomes reality between mother and daughter. The simulation process as such makes clear that accessing the reality, in this case accessing the reality of the other, also always means producing the reality in certain respects.

Within the dialogue, mimetic forms of assimilation become apparent through which the communication is reciprocally formed. These mimetic acts are essentially determined by temporal dimensions and they are characterized by rhythmic and dynamic accentuations of the action. The rhythms, however, can also occur in a form of self-rhythmization, as the hand movements of the daughter show. These arise from the interrelation of touch and resistance that can be observed in many other scenes as well and that expresses both closeness and difference. Moreover, considering the dialogue itself, it is also based on a rhythmic structure.

By examining touches in early communication, an attempt has been undertaken to draw attention to the aesthetical aspects that constitute an experience of relationship. A certain concept of aesthetics serves as a starting point, one that cannot be limited to the arts and artistic experience, but encompasses the realm of the social as well. In this context, the term *atmosphere* in the sense used by Böhme becomes relevant. According to this point of view, the atmospheres are not something that exist independently of persons and objects in a space, but are created by and through these very persons and objects. Furthermore, of equal importance is the idea that perception itself is conceived as an active action, as an activity in process. Applied to the scene described above, the communicative interplay of facial expression, gesture, vocal timbre, movement of the body as well as the merging of different senses in the perception constitutes an atmosphere that is sensed by the participants and within which shared common experiences finally become possible.

When Merleau-Ponty in his philosophy of intercorporeality speaks about an "incorporation of the Seer to the Visible" in regard to the gaze "sampling" and "enclosing" things, he assumes that all cognitive processes are based on a tactile component (Merleau-Ponty, 1986).[17] Conversely, the analysis of this scene calls attention to the way in which the materiality of the body is pervaded by abstract processes. Hence the body itself should already be assigned a kind of reflexive quality.

References

Anzieu, D. (1991). *Das Haut-Ich*. Frankfurt am Main: Suhrkamp.
Baier, G. (2001). *Rhythmus. Tanz in Körper und Gehirn*. Hamburg: Reinbek.
Beebe, B., & Lachmann, F. M. (2004). *Säuglingsforschung und die Psychotherapie Erwachsener. Wie interaktive Prozesse entstehen und zu Veränderungen führen*. Stuttgart: Klett-Cotta.
Benthien, C. (1998). *Im Leibe wohnen. Literarische Imagologie und historische Anthropologie der Haut*. Körper, Zeichen, Kultur, Band 4. Berlin: Berlin Verlag.
Böhme, G. (1995). *Atmosphäre*. Frankfurt am Main: Suhrkamp.
Böhme, G. (2001). *Aisthetik. Vorlesungen über Ästhetik als allgemeine Wahrnehmungslehre*. München: Fink.
Brüstle, C., Ghattas, N., Risi, C., & Schouten, S. (Eds.). (2005). *Aus dem Takt. Rhythmus in Kunst, Kultur, Natur*. Bielefeld: transcript.
Desain, P. W. M., & Windsor W. L. (Eds.). (2000). *Rhythm perception and production. Studies on new music research, 3*. Lisse: Swets & Zeitlinger.
Dewey, J. (1988/1934). *Kunst als Erfahrung*. Frankfurt am Main: Suhrkamp.
Diaconu, M. (2005). *Tasten, Riechen, Schmecken. Eine Ästhetik der anästhesierten Sinne*. Würzburg: Königshausen & Neumann.
Gebauer, G., & Wulf, C. (1998). *Spiel, Ritual, Geste – Mimetisches Handeln in der sozialen Welt*. Hamburg: Rohwolt.
Hirschauer, S. (2004). Praktiken und ihre Körper. In K. Hörning, & J. Reuter (Eds.), *Doing culture. Neue Positionen zum Verhältnis von Kultur und sozialer Praxis* (pp. 73–91). Bielefeld: Transcript.
Holodynski, M. (2006). *Emotionen – Entwicklung und Regulation*. Heidelberg: Springer.
Horsch, U. (2004). Frühe Dialoge als Elemente der Hör- und Sprachentwicklung. In: U. Horsch (Ed.), *Frühe Dialoge. Früherziehung hörgeschädigter Säuglinge und Kleinkinder. Ein Handbuch* (pp. 121–137). Hamburg: Verlag Hörgeschädigte Kinder GmbH.

---

[17] According to Merleau-Ponty the relation between seeing and touching embodies a modality to recognize the world, which sublates a clear division between subject and object (Merleau-Ponty, 1986, pp. 172–203).

Kamper, D. (1984). *Das Schwinden der Sinne*. Frankfurt am Main: Suhrkamp.

Keller, H., Demuth, C., & Yovsi, R. D. (2008). The multi-voicedness of independence and interdependence – The case of Cameroonian Nso. *Culture & Psychology, 14*(1), 115–144.

Klasen, S. (2008a). *Mimesis in der frühen Kindheit. Mikroanalyse einer Spielsequenz zwischen Mutter und Kind*. Berlin: Logos.

Klasen, S. (2008b). Berührung als Kommunikation. In C. Wulf (Ed.), *Geburt in Familie, Klinik und Medien. Eine qualitative Untersuchung* (pp. 85–125). Opladen: Budrich.

Knoblauch, H. (2005). Video-Interaktions-Sequenzanalyse. In C. Wulf (Ed.), *Ikonologie des Performativen* (pp. 263–275). München: Fink.

Merleau-Ponty, M. (1986). Die Verflechtung – Der Chiasmus. In R. Grathoff & B. Waldenfels (Eds.), *Übergänge, Band 13: Das Sichtbare und das Unsichtbare* (pp. 172–203). München: Fink.

Montagu, A. (1982). *Körperkontakt. Die Bedeutung der Haut für die Entwicklung des Menschen*. Stuttgart: Klett-Cotta.

Oerter, R., & Montada, L. (2002). *Entwicklungspsychologie*. Weinheim, Basel and Berlin: Beltz.

Sennett, R. (1998). Der Tastsinn. In Kunst- und Ausstellungshalle der Bundesrepublik Deutschland GmbH (Ed.), *Der Sinn der Sinne* (pp. 479–495). Göttingen: Steidl.

Stern, D. N. (1979). *Mutter und Kind. Die erste Beziehung*. Stuttgart: Klett-Cotta.

Stern, D. N. (1992). *Die Lebenserfahrung des Säuglings*. Stuttgart: Klett-Cotta.

Stern, D. N. (2004). *The Present moment in psychotherapy and everyday life*. New York and London: Norton & Company.

Tomasello, M., Carpenter, M., Call, J., Behne, T., & Moll, H. (2005). Understanding and sharing intentions: The origins of cultural cognition. *Behavioral and Brain Sciences, 28*, 675–735.

Wagner-Willi, M. (2004). Videointerpretation als mehrdimensionale Mikroanalyse am Beispiel schulischer Alltagsszenen. *Zeitschrift für qualitative Bildungs-, Beratungs- und Sozialforschung, 5*, 49–66.

Wulf, C., Göhlich, M., & Zirfas, J. (Eds.). (2001). *Grundlagen des Performativen. Eine Einführung in die Zusammenhänge von Sprache, Macht und Handeln*. Weinheim, München: Juventa.

Other Media

INTERACT, Version 7.2 1991–2005, Mangold Software & Consulting GmbH.

Chapter 6
Mimesis in Early Childhood: Enculturation, Practical Knowledge and Performativity

Christoph Wulf

Mimesis and Education by Imitation in Antiquity

The frame outlined in the previous book chapters provides a fruitful ground for the development of more general conclusions about the various aspects of mimetic processes and their role in human development. As far as we know today, the idea of mimesis originated in Sicily. "Mimesis" there referred to the way the "mimos" staged a farce. It was derived from everyday popular culture, from scenes staged at the celebrations of the rich, and designed to entertain them. The stagings and performances developed in this context were frequently crude and disrespectful. Thus, the concept of mimesis originally refers to performative cultural practices and has connotations that are distinctively sensory and related to physical movements. During the fifth century BC, the term "mimesis" is used on a larger scale in Ionia and Attica. Even in pre-Platonic times, three nuances of its meaning can be distinguished, which even today still describe crucial aspects of mimesis. Mimetic behaviour here refers, first to, the direct imitation of animals and persons in speech, song and dancing, then, to the imitation of human actions, and finally, to the material recreation of images of persons or things (Else, 1958, p. 79). In Platonic times, the word is already commonly used to denote processes of imitation, emulation, representation and expression.

It is in the third book of Plato's *Republic* that the concept of mimesis is first extended to education. According to the views developed there, education principally works by mimesis. Mimetic processes are ascribed an extraordinary power. This view is based on the strong human disposition for mimesis, which, especially in early childhood, is what makes motor, sensual, linguistic, mental, social and personal development possible. In Plato's opinion, children and adolescents experience and acquire social behaviour in their contacts with other people and in the experience they gain of other people's behaviour. Plato therefore emphasises the importance music, and mimetically dealing with music, has for the development of

C. Wulf (✉)
Free University Berlin, Berlin, Germany
e-mail: chrwulf@zedat.fu-berlin.de

M. Kontopodis et al. (eds.), *Children, Development and Education*, International Perspectives on Early Childhood Education and Development 3, DOI 10.1007/978-94-007-0243-1_6, © Springer Science+Business Media B.V. 2011

the soul's ability to experience. He distinguishes different types of music, to which he ascribes diverse effects on young people's "souls".

According to the views developed in the *Republic*, young people's educational development and learning is made possible by their mimetic desire, which "forces" them to become similar to role models. By choosing the right role models, human shortcomings are to be overcome, and improvement is achieved. What is controversial about this view, though, is its radical nature, its way of determining young people's lives and experiences on the basis of a normative anthropology and a normative theory of education.

Aristotle contradicted this Platonic view. Although he was as convinced as Plato of the power of mimetic processes, he drew different conclusions from this: The inadequate and the incorrigible should not be excluded from the domain of experience; rather, they had to be confronted and dealt with, so that one could "immunise" oneself against their contagion. Not to avoid negative examples, but rather to confront them is an effective protection against their power. Otherwise, young persons remain susceptible to and defenceless against negative influences. It is only in dealing with negative role models that resistance to them and personal strength can develop. Today, similar considerations still play a role in political education. According to this view, steadfast political opinions do not develop by avoiding different opinions, but by critically dealing with them. The same is true of the opinions and values conveyed in other areas of education. Today, this position is supported by psychoanalytic knowledge, which has emphasised the negative consequences avoidance and rejection have in psychogenesis.

Because of the LASTING effects of processes of mimetic learning, Plato calls for strict control of the influence their objects and contents have on the imagination, and Aristotle demands that their effects must be dealt with intensively. Since Plato we have known that it is not just ideas, attitudes, and values, but also social forms of living and acting which are learned by way of mimetic processes. Because of the different preconditions young people start out with, however, what emerges is not simply a copy of a model; the mimetic process leads to a difference which ensures the autonomy and creativity of its results. The model appropriated in the mimetic act is, therefore, not simply a reproduction of external similarities; it is a construction on the part of the person who behaves mimetically – a construction which leaves room for difference, particularity and creativity.

Mimetic Processes in Early Childhood

Mimetic processes of learning, forming an integral part of one's corporeality, begin at a very early stage. They take place before the split into the Self and the Other and before the subject–object division, and they are an important factor in psycho-, socio-, and personal genesis. They extend into the preconscious. Being entwined with the earliest processes that constitute our bodily make up – birth, weaning and desire – they produce lasting effects. Even before the emergence of thought and language, we experience the world, ourselves and the Other mimetically. Mimetic processes are linked to the activity of the senses. It is especially in the learning of motor skills that mimetic abilities play an important role. However, language acquisition, too, would be impossible without them. In early childhood, children experience the world by way of mimetic forms of life.

Initially, mimetic processes are mainly directed towards other people. Through them babies and small children relate to the persons they live with: parents, older siblings, other relatives and acquaintances. The children attempt to make themselves similar to these persons, for example by answering a smile with a smile. However, by using their already acquired abilities, they also produce the corresponding reaction in adults. In these early processes of exchange, small children also learn emotions, among other things. They learn to create them in themselves in relation to others, and to evoke them in others. Their brain develops in this exchange with their environment, i.e. some of its possibilities are developed while others are neglected. The cultural conditions of this early life are inscribed in children's brains and bodies. If they haven't learned seeing, hearing, feeling or speaking at an early age, they will not be able to do so at a later point.

Recent research on primates has demonstrated that although elementary forms of mimesis can also be observed in other primates, human beings are particularly prone to learn mimetically. This insight comes as no surprise to scholars in cultural studies. During the last few years, developmental and cognitive psychologists, using insights into the social behaviour of primates and comparing it to human behaviour, have succeeded in discovering some characteristics of human learning at this early age, most specifically the distinctive character of mimesis in human infants and small children.

Michael Tomasello summarises these abilities in small children (cf. also Chapter 3, this book):

> they identify with other persons; perceive other persons as intentional agents like the self; engage with other persons in joint attentional activities; understand many of the causal relations that hold among physical objects and events in the world; understand the communicative intentions that other persons express in gestures, linguistic symbols, and constructions; and construct linguistically based object categories and event schemas. (Tomasello, 1999, p. 161)

These abilities enable small children to take part in cultural processes. They can participate in the performance of the practices and skills of the social group they live with, thereby appropriating its cultural knowledge. The abilities described here point to the crucial importance role models have for mimetic processes in small children. Their ability to identify with other persons, to perceive them as intentional agents, and to engage in joint attentional activities, is tied to their mimetic desire to emulate adults, and to make themselves similar to or become like them. This desire to become similar to their elders motivates children to comprehend causal relations between physical objects in the world, to understand the communicative intentions other persons express in gestures, symbols and constructions, and to establish object categories and event schemas like them. At the age of 9 months, infants have already achieved these abilities, which lie in the human potential for mimesis, and which primates have no command of at any stage of their lives.

In mimetic processes, children, adolescents, and adults learn the values, attitudes, and norms embodied in the institutions of the family, the school and the work-place. As the discussion about the "heimlichen Lehrplan" ("hidden curriculum"; Zinnecker, 1975) has demonstrated, the values actually at work in an institution may contradict the way it consciously sees itself. The analysis of institutions, critique of ideology, institutional consultation, and institutional change can raise awareness of these contradictions, and help to find a way of resolving them.

Analogous observations can be made about the educative and socialising effects individuals have. These work much more than it is commonly assumed by means of mimetic processes. Here, too, there is a discrepancy between the way teachers see themselves and the effects their actual behaviour has. Often, the unconscious and unwanted effects which may be imparted via the teachers' and parental figures' personalities have a lasting influence on children and adolescents. In particular the way individual teachers feel, think and judge is experienced and learned through mimetic processes. In these processes, adaptation and rejection will play a different role in each case, the consequences of which are therefore difficult to assess. Partly, this difficulty in judging the effects of teachers' behaviour results from the fact that the same behaviour in a teacher or parental figure will be assessed differently by persons in different phases of their lives.

Objects as well as institutions, imaginary characters and practical actions are embedded in the power relations at work in a given society, and these power relations are conveyed in the process of making oneself similar or alike to something. They are learned and experienced by means of mimetic processes, though normally without at first being understood. To comprehend what is experienced mimetically, analysis and reflection are necessary. In most cases things will only then be judged and evaluated appropriately. Mimetic processes represent an important condition for the emergence of vivid experience, but for it to develop, analysis and reflection are indispensable.

Mimetic Appropriation of the World and the Constitution of the Subject

The mimetic appropriation of places, rooms, and objects is of crucial importance for the development of the subject. From early childhood on, subjects relate mimetically to the surrounding world, which is experienced as "animated". In this process of making themselves similar or alike to this world, children extend themselves into it, accord it a place in their own internal imaginary worlds, and educate themselves in the process. As this world is always historically and culturally determined, its objects being endowed with meaning and therefore symbolically encoded, these mimetic processes also lead to children's and adolescents' enculturation.

Walter Benjamin's autobiography *Berlin Childhood around 1900* (Benjamin 2006) provides a good example of processes of mimetic learning which involve appropriation of the world. The author describes the ways in which he, in child-hood, related to places, rooms, streets, houses, objects and events, and how he made them part of his inner world of images, thereby individually "appropriating" them. Benjamin's memoirs show how the child experiences the world mimetically. Like a magician he establishes similarities between himself and the outside world; mimetically he discovers streets, squares and the various rooms of his home. His magic interpretation of the world, which views the world of things as something that is animated and responds to the child, is established in processes of making himself and the objects similar or alike: the child "reads" the world and "creates" correspondences in the process (cf. quotation by Pessoa, at the beginning of Chapter 1, this book).

For instance, he becomes a "windmill" by stretching out his arms and rotating them, while producing the necessary wind with his mouth. In this way, he broadens his experience: The child understands how the wind drives the mill; he learns something of the power of wind and of the power of human use of the forces of nature. In mimetically transforming himself into a "windmill", he experiences the possibility to exercise – at least in play – power over nature. In becoming a "windmill" with his body, the child begins to make himself familiar with machinery, and with the human body as a machine. At the same time he experiences his body as a means of representation and expression. Thus, he does not just gain concrete means of representation and expression – he also discovers he can make use of his body for a clearly defined purpose, and obtain social recognition by doing so. Such mimetic processes are accompanied by symbolic interpretations, so that thinking and speaking are also developed in them.

In this childhood world it is not just images but also sounds and noises as well as smells and the experience of touch, which play an important role. These non-visual impressions frequently make the images transcend into the unknown and the unconscious. Thus, the "intoxicating sound of the air" is referred to; the hum of the gas burner becomes the voice of the "little hunchback" whispering adjuratory words over the threshold of the century; and the world of visible and tangible things ends in the echo of the telephone, in its "nocturnal noises", in the invisible, the indiscernible, the anonymous.

By mimetic processes, some images and sounds of early childhood settle in the "deeper ego", from which they may be optically or acoustically recalled to consciousness. The act of remembering mimetically refers to the remembered material, which is thereby represented in a specific way, depending on the situation. Memories differ in the intensity and significance they acquire in the moment of remembering. The difference between various acts of remembering which refer to the same event can be seen as a difference in the way it is constructed by memory and represented mimetically.

According to Benjamin, children's mimetic ability to relate to the world, to make themselves similar to it, and to read it, is incorporated into language and writing. The "mimetic gift", once the "basis for clairvoyance", creates for itself in this process in language and writing the "most perfect archive of non-sensuous similarity". Thus, the language children learn is "the highest application of the mimetic faculty – a medium into which the earlier perceptual capacity for recognising the similar had, without residue, entered to such an extent that language now represents the medium in which objects encounter and come into relation with one another. No longer directly, as they once did in the mind of the augur or priest, but in their essences, in their most transient and delicate substances, even in their aromas." (Benjamin, 1999, p. 697) Being and becoming similar are factors which are essential for children's development, and gradually establish their relationship to the world, to themselves, and to language.

With the help of these processes, children place themselves inside the structural and power relations which are expressed in the symbolically encoded world, and which they are only able to distance themselves from, to criticise or to change at a later stage. With the help of their mimetic abilities, children acquire the meaning of objects and forms of representation and action. A mimetic movement serves as a bridge between children and the outside world. Their relationship to the Other – which is not to be incorporated but which they must make themselves similar to – is central to mimetic activity. This movement includes a pause in activity, a moment of passivity characteristic of the "mimetic impulse".

The use of the term "mimesis", differing in this from imitation and simulation, adheres to the idea of an "outside", to which one can come close and make oneself similar, but into which the subject cannot "dissolve". One's difference to it therefore necessarily remains. This "outside", to which subjects attempt to move closer, may be another person, some part of their environment, or an invented imaginary world. In each case, the subject is making an approach to an outside world. The senses and the imagination convert this outside into internal images, into the internal production of sounds, and internal worlds of touch, smell and taste, resulting in vivid experiences, which are tied to the ineluctable corporeality of the subject.

Having had the possibility to mimetically experience the world as a child constitutes a prerequisite for the quality of adults' later sensory and emotional sensitivity. This is especially true of the development of their aesthetic sensitivity and their ability to experience empathy, pity, affection, and love. Their mimetic abilities allow them to comprehend others' emotions without reifying them or hardening themselves against them.

Mimesis, Social Action and Practical Knowledge

The ability to act socially is acquired mimetically in cultural learning processes. This has been demonstrated in the large amount of research conducted during the last few years (see Wulf, 2009). The culturally variable human abilities of playing, of exchanging gifts, and of ritual action are developed by means of mimetic processes. To be able to act "correctly" under given circumstances, people need practical knowledge gained in the sensual and corporeal mimetic processes of learning that take place in the corresponding fields of action. The characteristics of social action in a given culture can also only be grasped by approaching them mimetically. Practical knowledge and social action are to a large extent the result of cultural and historical conditions (Bourdieu, 1977).

Social actions may provisionally be described as mimetic if, as gestures, they refer to other gestures; if they can be understood as a corporeal performance or staging; and if they are autonomous actions, comprehensible in their own right, and at the same time related to other actions or worlds. Wherever somebody's actions refer to a pre-existing social practice while at the same time creating a social practice in themselves, a mimetic relationship is established. This is the case when a social practice is performed, when one acts according to a social model, and when one expresses certain social conceptions with the help of the body. As we have already seen, these actions are not simply imitative. Mimetic actions are by no means only reproductions, faithfully copying a model. Rather, in social practices that are performed mimetically something entirely new is created.

In contrast to processes of mimicry, which involve a mere adaptation to pre-existing conditions, mimetic processes simultaneously create similarity to *and* difference from the situations or persons they refer to. By "making themselves similar" to previously experienced situations and culturally formed worlds, subjects acquire the ability to find their way around a certain social field. By taking part in the practices of other persons' lives, they expand their own world and create new possibilities of action and experience for themselves. Receptivity and activity thus coexist here; in this process, the pre-existing world and the individuality of those who mimetically relate to it are entwined with each other. People re-create previously experienced situations or the external world, and appropriate them in this process of redoubling. It is only in dealing with the earlier situation or the outside world that they develop their own individuality. Only in this process can a person's previously unrecognised energy take the form of individual desires and needs. Dealing with the outside world and forming the self are both part of the same system. The external and the internal world are constantly becoming similar to each other, and each can only be experienced in relation to the other. Similarities and correspondences between the external and the internal are developed. People make themselves similar to the external world and are changed in the process; this transformation alters their perception of the external world and of themselves.

In mimetic processes of learning, pre-existing social actions are repeated. In this case, reference is not established by theoretical thinking, but aesthetically, with the help of the senses. The second social action departs from the first in that it neither addresses it nor changes it, but simply repeats it; the mimetic action here is of an indicating and representing character and its performance produces its own aesthetic qualities. Mimetic processes refer to social worlds of human creation, which can be either factual or imaginary.

The following example illustrates the processes of mimetic learning: a group of eight to 12-year-old girls had rehearsed Lou Bega's "Mambo Nr. 5" by making references to the respective music video. This was realised in the context of a project week in preparation for a performance during the school's summer party. In the "song", the German-African singer is sweet-talked by several young women towards whom he displays varying attitudes of courtship and rejection. The music video shows the attractive young women charming the singer whilst moving to the rhythm of the mambo. During the school's summer party, the 12-year-old girls dance before the eyes of their fellow pupils, their teachers, and their parents on a stage built for occasions like this. In their dance they are mimicking the movements of the women in the video clip. They are showing to all that they are no longer children and that they are on their way to becoming young women. They enact this passage and playfully make it public for their relatives and for their school community (Wulf, Göhlich, & Zirfas, 2001).

The study, which this example is taken from, was realised at the Free University of Berlin in the context of the Collaborative Research Centre "Cultures of the Performative" in a study financed by the German Research Foundation. This research on an inner-city primary school has so far been evaluated four times and is projected to take 12 years. It investigates educational learning processes in the following four fields of socialisation: school, family, peer groups and the media. The three projected comprehensive studies (Wulf et al., 2001, 2004, 2007) and six individual research projects (Audehm, 2007; Bausch, 2006; Jörissen, 2007; Kellermann, 2008; Tervooren, 2006; Wagner-Willi, 2005) that have been realised to date display a complex emerging image of pedagogy, education, and learning by primary school children.

Central to these investigations has been an inner-city primary school of 340 children half of whom speak German as their mother tongue while the other half comes from about 20 different migrational backgrounds. The school is characterised by its tradition of reform pedagogy and by being a UNESCO model school. In some cases, youths from the wider context of the school were integrated into the investigation thereby broadening its case-study character (Diederich & Wulf, 1979; Kraimer, 2000). The results of this ethnographic project are of course extensive and cannot be covered in the framework of this chapter.

Coming back to the above-presented example, one could say that in mimetic processes, the children's desire is directed towards other people whom they want to resemble – a phenomenon which Vygotsky conceptualised so greatly with his notion of "Zone of Proximal Development" (Chaiklin, 2003; Vygotsky, 1934/1987, 1930/1997). In this way, children relate to parents, relatives, and other adults such as their teachers as well as to imaginative characters and media personages. They want to become like the people towards whom their desire is directed. As we were able to show in our study, mimetic processes do not only refer to other people in *face-to-face* situations, but also to places, spaces, things, imaginary actions, scenes, and themes. Institutions such as the family, the school, the role play that is implicit in the media, but also values, attitudes and norms, are learned and embodied by children through mimetic processes.

By way of such role-model-related mimetic processes children create themselves and develop their individuality and uniqueness. Without reference to other people children would not be able to develop, neither into individuals nor into social beings. The desire to become like others is often the point of departure for mimetic processes. What is decisive for the mimetic process, however, is not the wish to resemble but the relationship that mimetically behaving children build with other people; these may well contain elements of distance and demarcation (Wulf, 2005). Mimetic processes between pupils also take place in the core groups where younger children learn from the older ones and the older ones are confirmed in their development by the younger ones.

What is more: mimetic processes further the polycentricity of boys and girls. They reach levels of corporality, of sensuality, and desire where a different set of dynamics is at work, than those that dominate the realm of consciousness. Among them are aggression, violence, and destruction, which are also roused and learned by way of mimetic processes. In group situations, the individual's centre for steering and responsibility is replaced by a group instance. Destructive forces can thus come into effect particularly easily; by way of ecstatic contagion, actions become possible, which an individual would not have been able to commit. Functioning rituals and ritualisations can canalise these dynamics in such a way that their destructiveness is contained.

Practical knowledge that is so crucial for living together is to a great extent also acquired mimetically (Gebaur & Wulf, 1995, 2003; Wulf, 2006). It is only through participating in social practices that the competence to act autonomously can be attained. The same is true for the learning acquisition of poetic competences, that is, the ability to produce something (Suzuki & Wulf, 2007; Wulf, 2007). The dynamic nature of social actions results from the fact that the knowledge necessary for their staging is practical knowledge. As such, it is less subjected to rational control than analytical knowledge would be. This is also the case because practical ritual knowledge is not a reflective kind of knowledge, nor one which is aware of itself. It will only become so during conflicts and crises in which the actions resulting from this knowledge have to be justified. As long as the social practice is not questioned, however, the practical knowledge behind it remains, as it were, half-conscious. Like the knowledge which constitutes a habitus, it consists of images, concepts, and forms of action, which can be used in the scenic corporeal performance of social action without reflecting on their appropriateness. They simply are known and used for the staging of social practice (cf. Bourdieu, 1977).

Body movements, too, with the help of which scenes of social action are arranged, form part of practical knowledge. When movements of the body are subjected to discipline and control, a disciplined and controlled practical knowledge emerges, which – stored in the memory of the body – makes possible the staging of corresponding forms of symbolic scenic action. This practical knowledge refers to the forms of social action and representation belonging to a certain culture. Therefore, even though it is far-reaching, its possibilities are nonetheless limited by historical and social factors.

In mimetic processes, an imitative act of changing and organising pre-existing worlds takes place. This is where the innovative potential of mimetic acts lies. Social practices are mimetic if they refer to other actions and if they themselves can be understood as social arrangements which form social practices for themselves, in addition to referring to other actions. Social actions are only made possible by the emergence of practical knowledge taking place in the course of mimetic processes. The practical knowledge relevant to social actions is corporeal and ludic as well as historically and culturally determined; it emerges in *face-to-face* situations, and is semantically ambiguous; it has imaginary components, cannot be reduced to intentionality, contains a surplus of meaning, and can be observed in the social stagings and representations of religion, politics, and everyday life.

Outlook

Mimetic processes are ambivalent; an impulse of becoming similar is inherent in them, and this can also take place independently of the value of the world they refer to. Therefore, the subject can also make itself similar to something obsolete and lifeless, which can interrupt or misdirect its inner development. Mimesis can degenerate into simulation and mimicry. However, it can also lead to an extension of the subject into the surrounding world, and forge a link to the outside world and to new learning experiences. The mimetic approach to the outside world is characteristically nonviolent. The mimetic process is not about forming or changing the world. Rather, it is about development and education resulting from the encounter with the world.

Through mimetic processes, a non-instrumental approach to other people can be acquired. Mimetic action leaves the Other as he or she is, without trying to change them. It comprises an openness towards the unfamiliar, accepting its existence, approaching it, but not trying to resolve the difference. The mimetic impulse towards the Other accepts its nonidentity; it accepts ambiguity in favour of the Other's otherness, which could only be made unambiguous by reducing it to the same, to the known. The acceptance of ambiguity ensures the richness of experience and the otherness of the unfamiliar.

In the mimetic movement, learning takes place by interpreting, by means of a symbolically generated world, the prior world, which has itself already been interpreted. A world which has already been read is subjected to a re-reading. This is the case even with repetitions or simple reproductions. The repetition of a gesture creates meanings different from those of its first performance. It isolates an object or an event from its normal context, establishing a perspective of reception which differs from that in which the prior world is perceived. Both isolation and a change of perspective are characteristics of aesthetic processes which are derived from the close relationship existing between mimesis and aesthetics. Mimetic re-interpretation is a new kind of perception, a "seeing as" (Wittgenstein & Anscombe, 2003). Mimetic action involves the intention to show the symbolically generated world in such a way that it is regarded as a certain kind of world.

References

Audehm, K. (2007). *Erziehung Bei Tisch: Zur Sozialen Magie eines Familienrituals*. Bielefeld: Transcript.
Bausch, C. (2006). *Verkörperte Medien: Die Soziale Macht Televisueller Inszenierungen*. Bielefeld: Transcript.
Benjamin, W. (1999). Doctrine of the similar. In: M. W. Jennings, H. Eiland, & G. Smith. (Eds.). *Selected writings* (Vol. 2) (R. Livingstone, Trans.). Cambridge, MA and London: Harvard University Press.

Benjamin, W. (2006). *Berlin childhood around 1900* (H. Eiland, Trans.). Cambridge, MA and London: Harvard University Press.

Bourdieu, P. (1977). *Outline of a theory of practice*. Cambridge: Polity Press.

Chaiklin, S. (2003). The Zone of Proximal Development in Vytgotsky's analysis of learning and instruction. In A. Kozulin, B. Gindis, V. Ageyey, & S. Miller (Eds.), *Vygotsky's educational theory in cultural context* (pp. 39–64). Cambridge: Cambridge University Press.

Diederich, J., & Wulf, C. (1979). *Gesamtschulaltag. Die Fallstudie Kierspe. Lehr-Lern Und Sozialverhalten an Nordrhein-Westfälischen Gesamtschulen*. Paderborn, München, Wien and Zürich: Ferdinand Schöningh.

Else, G. F. (1958). Imitation in the 5th century. *Classical Philology, 53*, 73–90.

Gebauer, G., & Wulf, C. (1995). *Mimesis: Culture, art, society*. Berkeley, CA: University of California Press.

Gebauer, G., & Wulf, C. (2003). *Mimetische Weltzugänge*. Stuttgart: Kohlhammer.

Jörissen, B. (2007). *Beobachtungen der Realität: Die Frage nach der Wirklichkeit im Zeitalter Der Neuen Medien*. Bielefeld: Transcript.

Kellermann, I. (2008). *Vom Kind zum Schulkind. Die Rituelle Gestaltung des Schulanfangs in Einer Jahrgangsgemischten Lerngruppe. Eine Ethnographische Studie*. Opladen: Leske + Budrich.

Kraimer, K. (Ed.). (2000). *Die Fallrekonstruktion. Sinnverstehen in der Sozialwissenschaftlichen Forschung*. Frankfurt am Main: Suhrkamp.

Suzuki, S., & Wulf, C. (Eds.). (2007). *Mimesis, poiesis and performativity in education*. Münster and New York: Waxmann.

Tervooren, A. (2006). *Im Spielraum von Geschlecht und Begehren: Ethnographie Der Ausgehenden Kindheit*. Weinheim: Juventa.

Tomasello, M. (1999). *The cultural origins of human cognition*. Cambridge, MA and London: Harvard University Press.

Vygotsky, L. S. (1930/1997). On psychological systems (R. v. d. Veer, Trans.). In: *The collected works. Vol. 3: Problems of the theory and history of psychology* (pp. 91–107). London and New York: Plenum.

Vygotsky, L. S. (1934/1987). Thinking and speech (N. Minick, Trans.). In R. Rieber (Ed.), *The collected works of Vygotsky. Vol. 1 problems of general psychology* (pp. 39–288). New York and London: Plenum.

Wagner-Willi, M. (2005). *Kinder-Rituale Zwischen Vorder- Und Hinterbühne: Der Übergang von der Pause zum Unterricht*. Wiesbaden: Verlag für Sozialwissenschaften.

Wittgenstein, L., & Anscombe, G. E. M. (2003). *Philosophical investigations: The German text, with a Revised English Translation* (3rd ed.). Malden, MA: Blackwell.

Wulf, C. (2005). *Zur Genese des Sozialen. Mimesis, Performativität*. Ritual. Bielefeld: transcript.

Wulf, C. (2006). Praxis. In J. Kreinath, J. Snoek, & M. Strausberg (Eds.), *Theorizing rituals. Issues, topics, approaches, concepts* (pp. 395–411). Leiden and Boston: Brill.

Wulf, C. (2007). Une anthropologie historique et culturelle. Rituels, mimésis sociale et performativité. Paris: Téraédre.

Wulf, C. (2009). *Anthropologie. Geschichte, Kultur, Philosophie*. Köln: Anaconda.

Wulf, C., Althans, B., Audehm, K., Bausch, C., Göhlich, M., Jörissen, B., et al. (2004). *Bildung im Ritual. Schule, Familie, Jugend, Medien*. Wiesbaden: Verlag Sozialwissenschaften.

Wulf, C., Althans, B., Audehm, K., Bausch, C., Göhlich, M., Sting, St., et al. (2001). *Das Soziale als Ritual. Zur performativen Bildung von Gemeinschaften*. Opladen: Leske & Budrich.

Wulf, C., Althans, B., Blaschke, G., Ferrin, N., Göhlich, M., Jörissen, B., et al. (2007). *Lernkulturen Im Umbruch: Rituelle Praktiken in Schule, Medien, Familie Und Jugend*. Wiesbaden: Verlag für Sozialwissenschaften.

Wulf, C., Göhlich, M., & Zirfas, J. (Eds.). (2001). *Grundlagen des Performativen. Eine Einführung in die Zusammenhänge von Sprache, Macht und Handeln*. Weinheim and München: Juventa.

Zinnecker, J. (Ed.). (1975). *Der heimliche Lehrplan. Untersuchungen zum Schulunterricht*. Weinheim and Basel: Beltz.

Part II
Gender, Performativity and Educational Practice

Chapter 7
Speculative Fantasies: Infancy in the Educational Discourse of Early Modern Germany

Birgit Althans

If we look at current discourses related to the care of newborn infants we see the newborns firmly fixed in the hands of doctors, nurses and midwives. Medical experts can be seen as educators as well – for example they give advice to the mothers about the right way to handle their babies and show them how to hold, (breast-) feed or wash it. Later, during the prescribed checkups in the consulting rooms of the paediatricians one can also observe the pedagogical performance of doctoral consultants. The discourse of medicine seems thus to dominate the interaction between the mother and the child. Situated in this context and based on a twofold genealogy of philosophical and scientific texts and of artistic and scientific representations of children this chapter examines the works of Rousseau, Kant, and Hegel about the meaning of education in very early childhood in relation to the public imagination and pictorial representation of early childhood in that time. In a second step, the impact of these anthropological and pedagogical ideas on the women's liberation movement at the beginning of the twentieth century and on representative artistic pictorial representations is analysed. In the third and last step, current images of very early childhood, those of the ultrasound screen, and their influence on mothers and fathers-to-be are examined. Our study illuminates the interrelation between scientific and artistic images and scientific and artistic imagination and enables a critical analysis of current western childhood-related practices.

Introduction

The construction of infancy in the educational discourse of eighteenth and nineteenth century Germany was a battlefield of interweaving representational practices such as pictures, artefacts, languages and even academic discourse. The effects of these interrelations between discourse, objects and pictures still resound today in the popular collective imaginary of very early childhood. The main aim of this chapter

B. Althans (✉)
Universität Trier, Trier, Germany
e-mail: althans@uni-trier.de

M. Kontopodis et al. (eds.), *Children, Development and Education*, International
Perspectives on Early Childhood Education and Development 3,
DOI 10.1007/978-94-007-0243-1_7, © Springer Science+Business Media B.V. 2011

is to show "heterologies of representations" (de Certeau, 1986): in other words, to demonstrate how cultural practices and objects created for use in early childhood formed the beginnings of the discourse on modern pedagogy, how discursive practices produced by these collective mental images became reflected in paintings and how these paintings in turn had an impact on this discourse.

This chapter tries to combine Foucault's discourse analysis with W.J.T. Mitchell's approach to "*picture theory* as a practical activity in the formation of representations" (Mitchell, 1995, p. 6), which attempts to demonstrate how "the image confuses as much as it (re-)organises discursive boundaries" (Fluck, 2003, p. 8). This attempt is framed in the context of historical and pedagogical anthropology, which examine transformations of human body concepts in changing historical and cultural contexts. A central concept of pedagogical anthropology is the human faculty of imagination (Kant, 1800), which includes the potentials of the 'homo pictor' (Wulf, 2007). Even the German concept of "Bildung" (education) refers to a "Bild" (image) and underlines the impact of images of man (and woman) on educational processes.

The impact of interrelating pictures and discourses on an unnoticed sphere of educational practices, pregnancy and birth, will be examined from the perspective of pedagogical and historical anthropology. The main thesis of this paper is that giving birth has nowadays become *more* precarious for parents – despite optimised medical care and technology. This precariousness is attended by a popular discourse on the educational competences of parents. This discourse, based on knowledge generated by the neurosciences, emphasises the importance of development for the unborn and the very young child while questioning the educational abilities of parents to assist in its processes. Recent interviews[1] with parents-to-be unfold a strong need for educational advice that is currently completely controlled by the discourse of medicine (or developmental and cognition psychology see: Foltys, 2008; Foltys & Lamprecht, 2008a, 2008b; Lamprecht, 2008). The discourse of educational theory has no authority here – it is not expected to speak.

As a solution to this empirically ascertained need for educational support in situations around birth, in this paper I aim to resurrect a lost and forgotten tradition of educational theory – the meaning of education and development for very early childhood, the handling of the infant after birth and its impact on the relation between the child and its parents. This tradition waits to be rediscovered – excavated – from the classics of educational discourse. Its excavation might bring to light fascinating interrelations between materialisations of the collective imaginary (paintings and child-care tools) and educational philosophers, or a mutual influence between

---

[1]This paper refers to the results of a study financed by the German Research Foundation which analysed the "Representations of birth in families, institutions of midwifery and in the media". The research for this project was done in 2007 in Berlin as well as in some smaller cities of Germany. The data was interpreted from 2008 to 2009 at the Department of Education at the Free University Berlin. The methods included interviews (group discussions and narrative interviews in the tradition of the documentary method), video-ethnography of mother–child interactions and discourse analysis of media productions about practices and discourses surrounding birth.

recent images representing mothers and children and – corresponding ideas about education and development:

- I would like to reconstruct the "speculative ideas" discussing the meaning of education in very early childhood in the works of Rousseau, Kant and Hegel, viewing them as a response to the public imagination and representation of early childhood in the Age of Enlightenment, supplemented by examples of contemporary paintings and artefacts of child-care tools.
- In a second step I will demonstrate the impact of these anthropological and pedagogical ideas on the Women's Liberation movement at the beginning of the twentieth century and their corresponding ideas of "spiritual" and "organised motherhood" – complemented by some works from a contemporary German female artist. In these paintings, the rejection of the idealised frame of unity and view of the "holy" relation between mother and child is even more explicit and outspoken in its materialisation of collective imagination.
- In a third and last step, I will examine current images of very early childhood: ultrasound scans and their influence on expecting mothers and fathers and their impact on the development of the unborn child – with the ultrasound, I propose that we have returned to Hegel's ideas.

The Child as the Other: Collective Imagination, Artefacts and Pedagogical Discourse in the Age of Enlightenment

The Educational Ideas of J.-J. Rousseau

Jean-Jacques Rousseau's ideas on education are not only formulated as *Bildungsroman* (Althans, 2000, 2007), even his ideas about infancy are completely *fictitious*. William Boyd, the American translator and editor of Rousseau's *Emile,* found that the first drafts of *Emile* said nothing about the "nursling state". In his reconstruction of the writing of *Emile,* Boyd found one contemporary reader of the manuscript who suggested that Rousseau should tell something about the care of newborns. Rousseau answered that he knew nothing about the first stage of infant training. He started to read and to gather information from the mothers of his acquaintance, "and the outcome was an account of baby management which caught the imagination of his contemporaries and led many young mothers to reform their ways" (Rousseau & Boyd, 1962, p. 9).

Book one of Rousseau's *Emile* starts with an anthropological perspective on education:

> "Plants are fashioned by cultivation, men by education. We are born feeble and need strength – possessing nothing, we need assistance; beginning without intelligence, we need judgement. All that we lack at birth and need when grown up is given us by education. This education comes to us from nature, from men or from things. The internal development

of our faculties and organs is the education of nature. The use we learn to make from this
development is the education of men. What comes to us from our experience of the things
that affect us is the education of things." (Rousseau & Boyd, 1962, p. 11)

According to Rousseau, education can also mean subjection and alienation.
Rousseau uses the traditional child-care tool of the swaddling band as a metaphor
in his famous statement: "From the beginning to the end of life civilised man is a
slave. At birth he is sewn up in swaddling bands, and at death nailed down in a
coffin". (Rousseau & Boyd, 1962, p. 16). Rousseau states that this cultural practice
of sewing up children by means of swaddling bands is caused by "mothers scorn-
ing their first duty and not willing to suckle their own children", instead choosing
to give their children to hired nurses. Rousseau believes that a betterment of these
practices – and a revolution in society – can only become real with nursing mothers:

> Let mothers deign to nurse their babies and a general reform of morals will follow as a
> matter of course. The natural sentiments will re-awaken in all hearts and the population will
> increase. (Rousseau & Boyd, 1962, p. 16)

Rousseau leaves the job of freeing the child and its early movements, the very
early but fundamental steps of education by nature, to the mother. At the same
time he is quite sure that this can be a drudgery. Rousseau describes the interaction
between mother and child as a battle:

> The babe comes into the world with a cry and his first days are spent in tears. [. . .] He gives
> orders, or he gets them: there is no middle way for us. His first ideas are either of mastery
> or servitude. Before he can speak he commands, before he can act he obeys. (Rousseau &
> Boyd, 1962, p. 18)

But Rousseau makes it very clear at this point that he sees this early interaction
between mother and child as an important part of the education process:

> If you want the child to keep his original character watch over him from the moment he
> enters the world. Get hold of him as soon he is born and never leave him till he is a man,
> short of that you will not succeed. Just as the right nurse is the mother, the right teacher is
> the father (Rousseau & Boyd, 1962, 18).

This sentence from the very beginning of *Emile* is an early statement of his ideas
on negative education: leave the child to his own activities, but watch him carefully
in all his actions and reactions. This installation of the "pedagogical gaze" (Wulf,
2002) by Rousseau had a very deep influence on the idea of the "holy family", on the
ideal of motherhood and on the broader concept of education. The educator became
an "impartial spectator", (a figure which became famous later with Adam Smith's
(moral) economy) whose finest duty was to watch and to observe every action and
sentiment of the child. In his *Julie or the Nouvelle Heloise* (Rousseau's first and even
more popular Bildungsroman, that had a strong influence on the romantic movement
in Germany), Rousseau constructs the three states of the (pedagogical) gaze: seeing,
watching and observing (Rousseau, 1761/1988). Foucault later shows us how this
idea of pedagogy formed the panoptical architecture not only of jail-houses but of
boarding-school houses as well (Foucault, 1975).

The Educational Ideas of I. Kant

Immanuel Kant bases his pedagogy on Rousseau, following his anthropological perspective on education:

> "Man can become man only through education" that in fact "he is nothing else than what education makes him". "Whoever is not cultivated is crude (roh); whoever is not disciplined is lawless (wild)" (Kant, quoted in Bryant, 1896/1971, p. 82).

In his philosophy, Kant focuses on the phenomena of reason, the powers of judgement and human understanding; he implements Rousseau's ideas in his anthropology from a pragmatic point of view, systematising the different roles of the educator in the education process into:

- *caring* such as feeding, cleaning, entertaining (Wartung)
- *discipline* (Zucht)
- *instruction* (Unterweisung) and
- *education* (Bildung)

These steps include *physical* and *moral education*, which help the pupil pass through the four development stages that Kant states as the main parts of the education process: to be a member of society – a citizen – the human being must become *disciplined, cultivated, civilised* and *moralised*.

Wartung, the cultural practices of caring in early childhood, clearly belongs to physical education in Kant's system. Kant invests some pages in thinking about the meaning of these practices from the perspective of cultural anthropology. He compares German practices with those of other cultures, listing such "bad habits" as: keeping babies too warm, putting them in swaddling bands, putting children into earthen holes filled with leaves to keep them clean in native American communities, rocking them in cradles, tying them to apron strings or playing with, kissing or cuddling them too much. In all his anthropological reflections on these phenomena, Kant follows Rousseau's idea of negative education: "Do not disturb the provisions of nature; don't add anything new" (Kant, 1869, A 43–A 45).

The origins of the discourse of educational philosophy and pedagogical anthropology seem thus to rely very strongly on traditional artefacts and pictures of childcare – and in turn they became strong metaphors in the discourse of Infancy during the Age of Enlightenment.

The Educational Ideas of G. W. F. Hegel

For Hegel, moral education starts very early: in the mother's womb:

> On the one hand, there is the inner fundamental Type, the universal, all-comprehensive form or Ideal of Mind inherent in each individual mind as mind [...] On the other hand, so regarded, the individual mind is a "subject" – i.e. a self-conscious, self-active unit of energy – which finds itself in the midst of endlessly manifold "objects" with which it is

ceaselessly and vitally related by the very necessities of its own being. Mind, and above all, a merely rudimental mind, cannot exist in mere isolation. But neither can things utterly unlike be related. (Hegel, quoted in Bryant, 1896/1971, pp. 84–85).

In his anthropology,[2] Hegel (1930) starts with the development of the unborn's soul in his mother's womb. Hegel puts the development of "the feeling soul" (§ 403–405) into his conception of the "ages of man": the soul is set as an "agent" or a mediator between the "immediate sensation" and the "imaginary capacity of consciousness". The soul is an "embodied soul" and simultaneously an "organ of the developing mind". In the embryo state, the soul is in a passive position – embodied soul in another body. But from Hegel's point of view, the immediate relation between mother and unborn child is not to be seen as a mere bodily ("neither mere bodily nor merely mental but psychical", § 405) but as a "psychic relation", as an interaction between souls: "Here are two individuals, yet in a psychic unity where one is not 'self', not impenetrable but without resistance, the other is his subject, and the self of both of them" (Hegel, 1930, § 405, 125). Hegel describes the mother here as "genius" of the child, the subjective substance of the other, the totality of feeling and being, character, and abilities.

The relation between mother and unborn child is described as a "magical relation" (referring to magnetism) that has a strong influence on the later social and cognitive life of the child. Again we see a large amount of educational responsibility placed on the pregnant mother in the magical dependency of the child. In his overflowing amount of footnotes in the *Encyclopaedia of Mind*, it is fascinating to trace how Hegel attempts to reconstruct the experience of the maternal influence on the unborn by referring to his own experiences in magnetic (hypnotic) therapy.

From Hegel's point of view, the child must develop *rational habits* to escape this magic, hypnotic influence of the mother and has to become independent. From his point of view the newborn child is infected by the ideas and emotions of his/her mother when he/she comes into being.

The Female Gaze: Spiritual Motherhood vs. Bodies that Matter

As an outcome of these excavations we found that the classics of pedagogy and anthropology in the Age of Enlightenment made the earliest state of development into a fundamental task of education while at the same time leaving it to mothers, nurses and nannies as a dark continent of cultural practice. Women were chosen by nature to create the magic relation that Hegel described in his anthropology. This focus on mothers affected the collective imaginary: in the nineteenth century we can find enthusiastic references to older paintings that represented this idealised magic relation of mother and child, such as Raphael's Sistine Madonna (see Fig. 7.1).

As an example of the impact of this picture, we could read Sigmund Freud's letter to his later wife Martha, written in December 1885:

---

[2]Part of his "Encyclopaedia of the Philosophical Sciences III: The Philosophy of Mind".

Fig. 7.1 Sistine Madonna

Now I happened to know that there was also a Madonna by Raphael there and I found her
at last in an equally chapel like room and a crowd of people in silent devotion in front of
her. You are sure to know her, the Sistina. [. . .] The painting emanates a magic beauty that
is inescapable, and yet I have a serious objection to raise against the Madonna herself [. . .]
Raphael's Madonna is a girl, say 16 years old; she gazes out on the world with such a fresh
and innocent expression, half against my will she suggested to me a charming, sympathetic
nursemaid, not from the celestial world but from ours. (Freud, 1885, p. 93).

Freud again refers to this painting in his famous *Fragment of the Analysis of a Case
of Hysteria* (1905) when he describes the "magic" influence of the Madonna on his
rebellious client Dora that he noticed in her report:

She remained two hours in front of the Sistine Madonna, rapt in silent admiration. When
I asked her what pleased her so much about the picture she could find no clear answer to
make. At last she said 'The Madonna.' (Freud, 1905, p. 28).

Science historian John Forrester comments on the different perceptions related to
the gendered influence of collective imaginations in his book *The Seduction of
Psychoanalysis*: "Where Dora saw the Madonna, Freud could only see a nursemaid – that is not a mother, but a woman who takes care of a child – and was
disappointed." (Forrester, 1990, p. 50).

Philosophers of education like Johann Heinrich Pestalozzi and Friedrich Froebel also idealise the magic relation of mother and child in their ideas on pedagogy. For Pestalozzi, educational settings should be constructed like the domestic living room and left to the morals of a mother. The founder of the Kindergarten, Friedrich Froebel, equips mother and child with pedagogical tools (his "Gaben") to optimise the child's development. His concept of early childhood education and his Kindergarten movement became highly important for the women's liberation movement to professionalise the duties and responsibilities of nannies and female teachers and to legitimise women's access to higher education. Female social reformers and women's liberation activists such as Jane Addams in America or Maria Montessori in Italy developed a similar approach to motherhood", but saw a need to support it professionally.

It is an irony of history that women at the turn of the century refused to assume the task to perform an idealised motherhood for anthropological reasons. Activist Charlotte Perkins Gilman (1860–1935) states in her best-selling *Women and Economics* (1898/1994) that women of her time are not prepared, not trained, not educated to perform their reproductive and educational function properly and their task as mothers. The human mother, from her point of view, is unable to prepare the child for social life, not even being able to feed it properly because of her lack of knowledge about proper infant foods, which are produced by chemists – by men (p. 19f.). According to Gilman, women in the late nineteenth century have become "over-sexed" as a result of their economic dependency on men, or as Gilman puts it in an impressive anthropological analogy:

> In the growth of industry, commerce, science, manufacture, government, art religion, the male of our species has become human, far more than male. Strong as his passion is in him, inordinate as is his indulgence, he is a far more normal animal than the female of his species, – far less over-sexed. To him this field of special activity is but part of life, – an incident. The whole world remains besides. To her it is the world. [. . .] To make clear by an instance the difference between normal and abnormal sex-distinction, look at the relative condition of a wild cow and a "milch cow," such as we have made. The wild cow is a female. She has healthy calves, and milk enough for them; and that is all the feminity she needs. Otherwise than that she is bovine rather than feminine, she is a light, strong, swift, sinewy creature, able to run, jump and fight, if necessary. We, for economic uses, have artificially developed the cow's capacity for producing milk. She has become a walking milk-machine, bred and tended to that express end, her value measured in quarts. The secretion of milk is a maternal function, – a sex-function. The cow is over-sexed. Turn her loose in natural conditions, and if she survive the change she would revert in a very few generations to the plain cow, with her energies used in the general activities of her race and only all running to milk." (Gilman, 1898/1994, pp. 43–44)

Perkins Gilman sympathises with parts of contemporary theories of evolution. She sees the education of the young as tremendously important to human reproduction. But she argues simultaneously that motherhood is not given by nature, and that the support of motherhood faculties must be examined. To perfectly fulfil its important function for society, Gilman argues that child-rearing should become part of female (higher) education (Gilman, 1898/1994, p. 188).

The paintings of the German painter Paula Modersohn-Becker (1876–1907) also reject the ideology of "natural" motherhood. Paula Modersohn-Becker was part of the so-called "Expressionists" movement. These German artists tried to transgress the boundary between inner and outer nature with a special – and until then unknown – use of shades of colours. For them even landscapes could represent emotions. Paula Modersohn-Becker presents a "female gaze" on the construction of idealised motherhood: not transcendent and magic, but heavy, down to earth (Beuys, 2009).

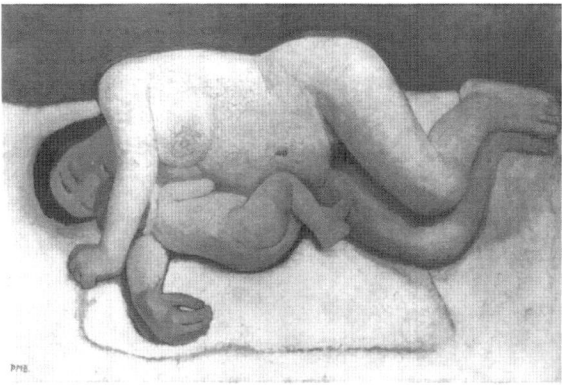

Reclining Mother and Child. Picture by Paula Modersohn-Becker, Courtesy of Kunstsammlungen Böttcherstraße, Paula Modersohn-Becker Museum, Museum im Roselius-Haus (Böttcherstraße 6–10, D-28195 Bremen)

So there was at the beginning of the twentieth century a clear demand from the "other voice", from the other half of society, to achieve knowledge for the so-called "organised motherhood"[3] and to do a better job in early childhood education. The question I would like to raise here: was it exactly this cry for "organised motherhood" from an anthropological perspective that helped to de-colonise early childhood education to the domains of medicine and psychology?

The Clinical Gaze and the Media: Ultrasound Screening as Public Viewing

After all of the speculative fantasies of the eighteenth and nineteenth centuries about mother–child relations inside and outside the maternal womb, today we have

---

[3]The contemporary American translation of the concept "geistige Mütterlichkeit" at the end of the nineteenth century was not "spiritualised" but "organised motherhood". This slight difference matched perfectly with the fact that the origin of the discourse of management and organization theory goes back to women theorists in the early twentieth century (Althans, 2007; Silverberg, 1998).

the possibility of getting a proper image of the unborn child through ultrasound screening and 3D pictures. These technologies are an outcome of clinical needs and professional practices. Ultrasounds and 3D pictures have not only produced a popular discourse in the media about pregnancy, they have had a lasting effect on the ideas about unborns in the collective imagination as well.

In the 1980s, the pictures of Swedish photographer Lennart Nilson became very popular and transformed the mental images of parents-to-be and their ideas about their unborn child. By looking at Lennart Nilson's pictures, the developmental state of parents' unborn children becomes visible, knowable, the unborn child becomes more than an idea or a bulge, it becomes "material". The warm orange and golden colours of the pictures make the unborn more alive than ever before – even though Lennart Nilson's presented objects were dead when photographed, just like the foetuses kept in test tubes in medical museums of bygone eras.

Referring to Michel Foucault, these pictures are products of the clinical gaze created by – and simultaneously creating – the discourse of medicine since the eighteenth century.

> Clinical Experience – that opening up of the concrete individual, for the first time in Western history, to the language of rationality, that major event in the relationship of man to himself and of language to things – was soon taken as a simple, unconceptualised confrontation of a gaze and a face, or a glance and a silent body; a sort of contact prior to all discourse, free of the burdens of language, by which two living individuals are "trapped" in a common, but non-reciprocal situation (Foucault, 1976, p. xvi).

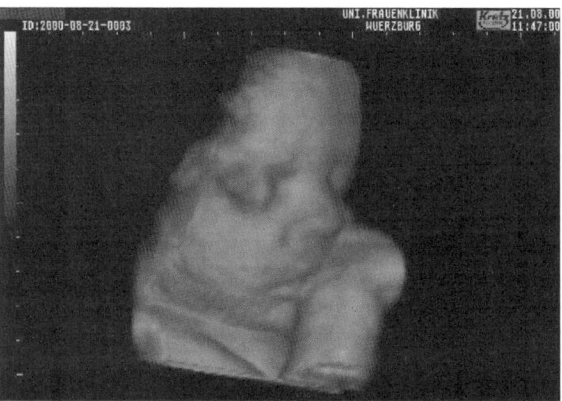

Ultrasound Picture of Unborn Child

Even if the body is not open in the context of ultrasounds and 3D pictures, the clinical gaze is able to view the condition of the unborn unhindered. It is installed as a third part in the mother–child relationship. In group discussions with families (Foltys, 2008; Foltys & Lamprecht, 2008a, b), it becomes very clear that the widespread use of ultrasound screenings during pregnancy deeply affects the relation between the unborn and his family in differing ways. In some cases, the emotional relation between mother and child becomes more stabile; fathers-to-be have expressed in interviews that they feel more involved in the pregnancy through the images of the unborn; grandparents and friends get to know the infant before he/she is born and place him in the family as an absent presence. One family created home movies with images of the unborn, presenting him/her as an acting part of the family before being born. One mother–child relation was negatively affected by the clinical gaze and its medical diagnosis when only one artery of the umbilical cord was found. The mother feared a genetic defect and proclaimed that she would watch this child and his development very carefully. As Foucault has stated, the clinical gaze has a strong impact, even if it only talks about probabilities:

> A conceptual mastery of probability in medicine implied the validation of a hospital domain which, in turn, could be recognised as a space of experience only by already probabilistic thinking. Hence the imperfect, precarious, and partial character of the calculation of certainties, and the fact that it sought for itself a confused basis that was opposed to its intrinsic technological meaning. (Foucault, 1976, p. 120)

The popular television docu-soaps and docu-dramas concerning birth (Althans, 2008; Tegethoff, 2008) show the impact of medical discourse in a double frame: we can observe families performing their family-acting by watching their new unborn member while their doctors perform their professional role and the clinical gaze. However, it is the clinical gaze that describes and defines the reality and the condition of the unborn. Hegel's "feeling souls" are separated in the clinical gaze, with the mother–womb on the table and the unborn on the ultrasound screen for all to see. Their silent dialogue is replaced by a doctoral gaze and a public viewing of very intimate details. In one episode of "Mein Baby" – broadcast on a private channel in Germany – millions of people participated in the first viewing of the penis of the unborn. The double frame of pictures of the unborn raises some questions for education theory in the twenty-first century.

Pedagogical Obligations: Reconstructing the Unborn as Other?

Is the unborn child on the screen present or absent? Is it there or not there in the outer world? From the perspective of anthropological tradition (and even for technical reasons of picture simulation practices) the child on the screen is a picture – nothing more. But pictures have as Kant states – always had "to present an object to contemplation even without its actual presence" (Kant, quoted in Wulf, 2007, p. 32). A picture creates a special presence, created by the "magical" power of images, as art philosopher Gottfried Boehm puts it:

> (This) power stems from the capacity of rendering the presence of an ephemeral and distant being to lend it such presence as to entirely take over the space of human apperception and attention. The image draws its strength from an assimilation, it creates a sameness with the represented. [...] The image and its content merge into some point where it is undistinguishable. (Boehm, 1994, p. 330).

We could answer: it doesn't matter if the unborn is there or not there in the outer world. Because we can only see the baby with the technical apparatus of the ultrasound equipment and the screen, we are faced with a problem: we cannot touch the unborn, we can only watch it. This suggests Rousseau's demand concerning education: leave the child to its actions but observe it at all times. Do the ultrasound picture and the 3D presentation help us to install the perfect setting for Rousseau's negative education?

There is a further connected question: is the image of the unborn – to speak in terms of Lacanian psychoanalysis – related to the real or to the imaginary? Maybe it is "real" – in the way French psychoanalyst Jacques Lacan defined it, as the untouchable, non-symbolic, non-imaginary centre of mental experience – because we are unable to touch it. And maybe the ultrasound and 3D artefacts help us to realise that we can always only interact in the imaginary, in the world of pictures.

The next question raised by the cultural practice of ultrasound and 3D pictures is perhaps the most important for educational reasons: is the 3D picture of an unborn an object or a subject? The "agency–patiency" concept of anthropologist Alfred Gell might help answer this question. In his art anthropology, like Bruno Latour's actor-network theoretical symmetric approach, Gell attributes agency to objects and things. He uses the example of the relationship of men and cars to explain this:

> The concept of agency I employ is relational and context-dependent, not classificatory and context-free. Thus, to revert to the 'car' example; though I would spontaneously attribute 'agency' to my car if it broke down in the middle of the night, far from home, with me in it, I do not think that my car has goals and intentions, as a vehicular agent, that are independent of the use that I and my family make of my car, with which it can co-operate or not. My car is a (potential) agent with respect to me as a 'patient', not in respect to itself, as a car. It is an agent only in so far as I am a patient, and it is a 'patient' (the counterpart of an agent) only in so far as I am an agent with respect to it. The concept of agency I employ here is exclusively relational: for any agent, there is a patient, and conversely, for any patient, there is an agent (Gell, 1998, p. 22).

If we follow Gell's advice here, the subject–object status of the unborn child depends on the context, on the use the parents-to-be make of him – sometimes the unborn will be patient, sometimes agent. It does not matter anymore. But how can education theory help to stabilise these agency–patiency processes of the mother–child relation, to keep them in a dynamic balance? Must we perhaps reconstruct the otherness of the unborn?

References

Althans, B. (2000). *Der Klatsch, die Frauen und das Sprechen bei der Arbeit*. Frankfurt; New York: Campus.

Althans, B. (2007). *Das maskierte Begehren. Frauen zwischen Sozialarbeit und Management*. Frankfurt and New York: Campus.

Althans, B. (2008). Repräsentationen von Geburt in den Medien. Zur heimlichen Alterität der Geburt in TV-Docu-soaps. In: C. Wulf (Ed.), *Geburt in Familie, Klinik und Medien: Eine qualitative Untersuchung* (pp. 207–228). Opladen: Budrich.

Beuys, B. (2009). *Paula Modersohn-Becker. Oder: Wenn die Kunst das Leben ist*. Frankfurt am Main: Insel Taschenbuch.

Boehm, G. (1994). Die Bilderfrage. In G. Boehm (Ed.), *Was ist ein Bild?* (pp. 325–343). München: Wilhelm Fink Verlag.

Bryant, W. M. (1896/1971). *Hegel's educational ideas*. Chicago: AMS Press.

de Certeau, M. (1986). *Heterologies: Discourse on the other*. Minneapolis: University of Minnesota Press.

Fluck, W. (2003). Aesthetic experience of the image. In U. Haselstein, B. Ostendorf, & P. Schneck (Eds.), *Iconographies of power. The politics and poetics of visual representation* (pp. 11–45).

Foltys, J. (2008). Geburt als körperliches und mediales Ereignis. Zur Bedeutungszuschreibung von Schwangerschaft und Geburt. In C. Wulf (Ed.), *Geburt in Familie, Klinik und Medien: Eine qualitative Untersuchung* (pp. 127–144). Opladen: Budrich. Artemis and Winkler.

Foltys, J., & Lamprecht, J. (2008a). Geburt – ein familiales Ereignis? In C. Wulf (Ed.), *Geburt in Familie, Klinik und Medien: Eine qualitative Untersuchung* (pp. 19–33). Opladen: Budrich.

Foltys, J., & Lamprecht, J. (2008b). Geburt und Familie. In C. Wulf (Ed.), *Geburt in Familie, Klinik und Medien: Eine qualitative Untersuchung* (pp. 136–148). Opladen: Budrich.

Forrester, J. (1990). *The seduction of psychoanalysis*. Cambridge, MA: Cambridge University Press.

Foucault, M. (1975). *Discipline and punish: The birth of the prison*. New York: Random House.

Foucault, M. (1976). *The birth of the clinic. An archaeology of medical perception*. London: Routledge.

Freud, S. (1885/1961). Letters to Martha Bernays, 20 December 1885. In L. E. Freud (Ed.), Letters of Sigmund Freud *1873–1939*. London: Hogarth Press.

Freud, S. (1905/2000). Fragment of the analysis of a case of hysteria. In J. Strachey (Ed.), *The standard edition of the complete psychological works of Sigmund Freud*. Part VII (pp. 7–125). New York: W.W. Norton & Company.

Gell, A. (1998). *Art and agency. An anthropological theory*. Oxford: Clarendon Press.

Gilman, C. P. (1898/1994). *Woman and economics. A study of the economic relation between woman and men*. New York: Prometheus Books.

Hegel, G. W. F. (1930). *Encyclopaedia of the philosophical science part III: The philosophy of mind*. Leipzig: Meiner.

Kant, I. (1798–1800/1986). Anthropologie in Pragmatischer Hinsicht. In W. Weischedel (Ed.), *Schriften zur Anthropologie, Geschichtsphilosophie, Politik und Pädagogik. Werkausgabe Bd. XII* . Frankfurt am Main: Suhrkamp.

Kant, I. (1869). Über Pädagogik. In G. Hartenstein (Ed.), *Sämmtliche Werke* (pp. 26–88). Leipzig: L. Voss.

Lamprecht, J. (2008). "...und jetzt hast de det größte Projekt überhaupt an ner Backe": Mutterschaftsrepräsentationen zwischen Beruf und Familie. In C. Wulf (Ed.), *Geburt in Familie, Klinik und Medien: Eine qualitative Untersuchung* (pp. 35–57). Opladen: Budrich.

Mitchell, W. J. T. (1995). *Picture theory. Essays on verbal and visual representation*. Chicago: University of Chicago Press.

Rousseau, J.-J. (1761/1988). *Julie oder die Neue Heloise – Briefe zweier Liebenden aus einer kleinen Stadt am Fuße der Alpen*. München. Artemis and Winkler.

Rousseau, J.-J., & Boyd, W. (1962). *Emile of Jean-Jacques Rousseau*. (W. Boyd Ed. & Trans.). New York: Teachers College Press.

Silverberg, H. (1998). Introduction towards a gender social science history. In H. Silverberg (Ed.), *Gender and American social science*. Princeton: Princeton University Press.

Tegethoff, D. (2008). Geburt in der Klinik. "...das hat viel mit Pädagogik zu tun...". In C. Wulf (Ed.), *Geburt in Familie, Klinik und Medien: Eine qualitative Untersuchung* (pp. 145–164). Opladen: Budrich.

Wulf, C. (2002). *Educational anthropology*. Münster and New York: Lit.

Wulf, C. (2007). Homo Pictor or the making of the human being through imagination. In S. Suzuki & C. Wulf (Eds.), *Mimesis, Poesis, and performativity in education* (pp. 25–43). Münster, New York, München, Berlin: Waxmann.

Chapter 8
A Cultural-Historical Approach to Children's Development of Multiple Cultural Identities

Mariane Hedegaard

Introduction

Cultural identity is seen as an aspect of children's psychic development that is created through their participation in everyday life in institutional practice. The primary institutions during childhood are the home, day-care and school. This conception of development of identity as multiple cultural identities is based on a theory of children's development as dependent on the conditions and demands children meet in home, day-care and school settings and how they engage in activities in the different practices in which they participate (Hedegaard, 2009). Both the general conceptions that guide daily practice and a child's concrete ways of acting in his or her historical concrete family and school create the practice traditions of which a specific child's life becomes a part. A child's development proceeds through qualitative change as a trajectory of a child's participation in new practices or contribution to change in already encountered practices. The development proceeds based on how conflicts and problems are tackled both by the child and by his or her caregivers as part of daily life activities. The interconnections between a child's engagement in social relations, appropriation of capacities, motives and self-conception are central in the child's development.

The aim of this chapter is to find a way to transcend often encountered descriptions that connect problems that children from immigrant families meet in school to children's cultural identity understood as a national or ethnic identity. Instead I want to find new ways of understanding young person's problems as connected to their participation in different institutional practice traditions both at a given period in life and through different life periods. My conception which I will argue for in the following is to see children's creation of identity as multiple cultural identities together with children's development as agents for creating activities and acquiring strategies and motives for handling demands.

M. Hedegaard (✉)
University of Copenhagen, Copenhagen, Denmark
e-mail: Mariane.Hedegaard@psy.ku.dk

M. Kontopodis et al. (eds.), *Children, Development and Education*, International Perspectives on Early Childhood Education and Development 3, DOI 10.1007/978-94-007-0243-1_8, © Springer Science+Business Media B.V. 2011

Drawing on examples from interviews with young persons of Turkish immigrant parents I will illustrate the conflicts these young persons have experienced in school as children of immigrant parents and how these conflicts have contributed to their identity of who they are today and how they see their future. The analysis will focus on what types of conflicts in the person's social situation can be seen as developmental and what types can turn into personal problems and become a hindrance – for their feeling of happiness over who they are – and for creating future plans for education and life.

Institutional Practice and Personal Development

Different phases in children's development can be related to the qualitative changes in institutional practice which take place when the child enters a new institution or an institution changes practice (Elkonin, 1999). These changes in practice provide possibilities for new activities (e.g., when a child enters kindergarten, or starts school, or enters middle school or high school). If an activity in an institutional practice like the school is to be developmental for a child, the activity has to relate to and challenge the child's capacity. A child's development is a consequence of how challenging activities proceed as part of the child's daily life activities within different institutional practices. Learning within the child's zone of proximal development (Vygotsky, 1998) contributes to the child's knowledge about the world and about himself (Berger & Luckmann, 1966). Through shared activities in social practice at home and in school, the child learns how to combine needs with cultural objects and through this process acquires collectively created *motives* (Leontiev, 1978). Activities in school and the home are not always coordinated and it can be difficult to transcend the different "worlds". For children from minority cultures the values and norms at home and at school can be so different and even in opposition or conflict, so that it is difficult for a child to participate in school activities (Phelan, Davidson, & Cao, 1991). Phelan et al. characterise family, home and peer activities as different worlds with differences in norms, values, beliefs, expectations and actions, where the boundaries are more or less difficult to transcend. To be able not only to describe but also analyse the conditions for these difficulties I will differentiate between *institutional practice* (i.e. activities connected to family and school), *value positions* (norms, beliefs, expectations) in institutions and *cultural traditions* (norms and beliefs that connects practices with imagined communities) (see Fig. 8.1).

Figure 8.1 depicts a model of the relations between different social practices within different institutions, such as the home, community clubs and school. These relations reflect different cultural traditions connected to different positions.

The first level of the model – the state – is inspired by Anderson's (1991) concept of imagined communities (see also Billig, 1998). Immigrant families living in Denmark have conceptions of themselves as coming from Turkey and feel closely connected to this society. Their concept of being Turkish is often characterised by how life was in the country when they left and not what it has become today

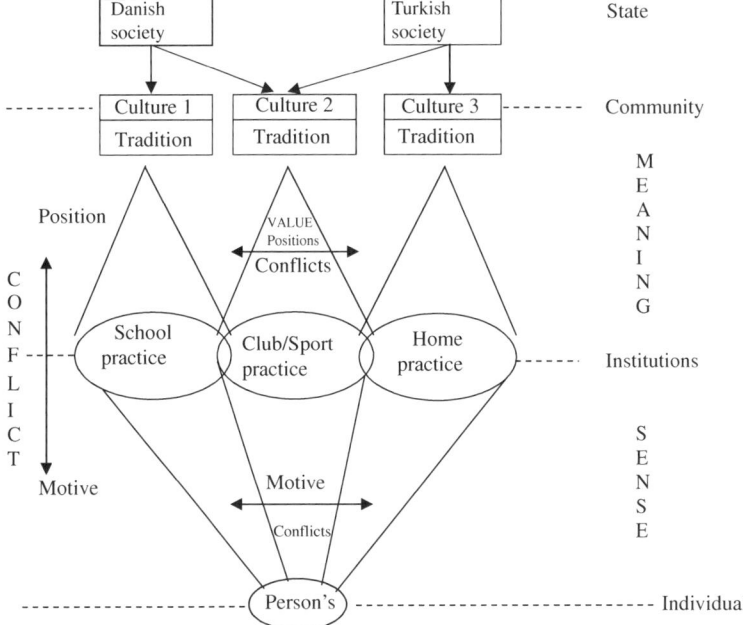

Fig. 8.1 Model of the relations between practice, positions and motives

(Hjarnø, 1988a, 1988b). At the same time they also have experiences from living in the Danish society and images of the way the Danes live. The immigrant families draw on these images and create their own cultural tradition in "immigrant communities" or "family communities" in Denmark, which create cultural value positions (Bourdieu, 1984) concerning who they are and what their traditions are and should be. They defend these positions as important for their participation in the Turkish community in Denmark. The conceptions connected to these value positions influence their actions and thereby contribute to development of practice in the different institutions – family, school, work place etc.

Introduction of a Subject Perspective as Part of a Cultural-Historical Activity Approach

One could expect that the cultural-historical activity approach of Vygotsky, Leontiev and Luria would provide some guidance to analysing culture and identity, but this has not been the case. Within the cultural-historical tradition the sense of culture is used to refer to the notion of the use of human constructs such as material and intellectual tools as components of human development (Leontiev, 1932; Luria, 1928; Vygotsky, 1929). A single research project by Luria and Vygotsky focused especially on cultural minorities (Luria, 1976). The main question was related to the influence of cultural practice on the development of thinking processes, though the empirical material also could have been used to theorise on a person's relation to the world and thereby their conception of their position in the world.

Why bother with the concept of cultural identity in relation to the cultural-historical approach?

I think that the subject's perspective as a link between the research of the formation of human consciousness, that especially was Vygotsky's project, and formulation of human activity, as Leontiev's project, need to be more explicit. A person's conception of their identity can be seen as this link that connects the description of higher psychological functions established through tool use in Vygotsky's approach (Vygotsky, 1987) with the activity as striving to fulfil collective needs in object-motivated activities (Leontiev, 1978). The concept of identity can be seen as an important concept in understanding children's development of their reflection of their activities and of their self-reflection of what person they want to be. The phenomenological tradition of Berger and Luckmann (1966) developed from Schutz (1970, 2005) can be an enrichment of the cultural-historical tradition since they are related through their basic conceptions.[1] Berger and Luckmann conceptualised how children develop both a conception of the social world and of themselves as part of the social world – a social identity. Children's conceptualisation of the social world and social identity is grounded in the same type of conceptions as Vygotsky and Leontiev's conception of how human contributes to the production, maintenance, and transmission of tools and activities in the social world.

Berger and Luckmann conceptualise the social world as a consequence of a dialectical interaction among three kinds of processes: *externalisation* – the creation of a social world in the form of institutions as products of human activity; *objectification* – one's experience of these products as "objective reality"; and *internalisation* – the process by which one learns about these institutions and how to function in them. *Social identity* is a result of an ongoing social process through which an individual internalises values and norms of the "objective world" he or she lives in. It is a "phenomenon that emerges from the dialectic between individual and society" (1966, p. 195). The internalisation process which results in the formation of social identity is the same process by which the child forms a conception of reality.

Berger and Luckmann distinguish between primary and secondary socialisation. Primary socialisation begins a process of internalisation which results in a person becoming inducted as a member of society. Significant others in the child's life (e.g., parents, siblings, extended family members) mediate the social world to the child. Secondary socialisation is the process by which already socialised individuals are inducted to the objective subworlds of his or her society (i.e. kindergarten,

---

[1]Here I will only draw on Berger and Luckmann's theoretical contribution (see Chapter 4 in Hedegaard and Fleer, 2009 for a discussion of Schutz's contribution to the cultural-historical approach).

schools, after-school clubs). The concept of secondary socialisation is important because it provides a way to get children to reflect about their immediate social world. Conflicts can arise when the values and means of action internalised from primary socialisation are not accepted by participants in another subworld that the child enters.

Berger and Luckman's conception that children encounter different cultural subworlds is especially important for cultural minority children in educational contexts. In school it is important to see that minority children live their everyday life often in relation to very different practice traditions. In this connection cultural identity and multi-cultural education can become central.

Culture Seen in Relation to a Person's Development of Identity

Berger and Luckman's conception of social identity enables a cultural-historical understanding of *personal* and *cultural identity*. In the cultural-historical tradition presented *culture is seen as traditions for practice that are recreated through a person's activities in institutional practices.* In formulating this conception I take a step further than Berger and Luckmann's conception of subworlds by introducing institutions and practices. Instead of talking about social identity I will introduce the concept of cultural identities that persons appropriate and re-create through activities in institutional practice. This fits with the cultural-historical conception that "one is not born with a personality" (Levitin, 1982; Vygotsky, 1998), it is something one creates by participating together with other persons in activities in different institutional practices. A person always has to be seen in relation to the social other persons and never in isolation. Personal identity then becomes promoted when the person starts to reflect about his or her social situations, the demands s/he meets and the competences and interest s/he has in meeting these in different practices. Personal identity also reflects a person's cultural identities as orientations towards values and norms within different practice traditions.

The term cultural identity could in itself lead to misunderstanding if it is primarily connected to the conditions set by a nation state or ethnic group. Conceptions of cultural identity as only ethnic groups or as nation state identity can lock persons both from a societal view and from their own conceptions into a special lifestyle (Hedegaard, 1999, 2005; Ogbu, 1992; Ogbu & Simons, 1998). Consequently, immigrant students can become fixed in positions created both by parents, teachers and students. Cultural identity from this viewpoint is often used as an explanatory principle connected to personal development, and can be seen as a hindrance for development of competencies in new settings (Malik, 1996).

The following interview extract from my research of immigrant children's school experiences shows how teachers change in their social relations to immigrant students leading to a change in the activities and students' self-conception. This then leads to students own creation of new practices which confirms the change in their self-conceptions leading them to maintaining fixed positions as immigrant or non-immigrant students. Thereby, they jointly accept the categorisation *foreigners*, a categorisation that the interviewed student of Turkish immigrant parents opposed and felt sad about, but at the same time started to use as a way to characterise new students and himself and thereby (perhaps nonintentionally) contributed to the change of practices.

Interviewer:	Looking back, do you remember anything that you felt sad about – if you go through all the years [you have been in school]
Mehmet:	Yes, in 4th and 5th grade when new foreigners started in our class, the teachers no longer behaved as they used to. They used to be calmer, but now if you couldn't make things out, they would get angry and say why don't you pay attention in class. One got really sad about this, when it was a teacher that one trusted.
I:	They (the teachers) started to yell at you, why do you think they did that?
M:	I don't know, perhaps because many teachers think that foreign students cannot sit quietly so the teachers get confused, that could be the reason.
I:	Did *you* also feel sad when more foreign students started in your class?
M:	Yes I did actually.
I:	Did it influence the teaching?
M:	No, not to me because in this class the Danish students outnumbered the foreign ones [in this school, several classes ended up with far more foreign than Danish students] so it went well. But during the breaks the new foreigners always went about together, and the others [the foreigners that were in the class from the beginning] were not happy about this and started to be by themselves. So then the Danes went by themselves. Normally we would meet downtown Friday after school, but this stopped completely and we stopped seeing each other.

All the different participants in a specific institution (i.e., a class in a specific school) influence the social practice that dominates the everyday activity in this institution. Children develop through participation in institutionalised forms of practice that are characterised by specialised and shared communication and activities. These practices initiate but also restrict children's activities and thereby become conditions for their development.

Cultural identity is not a factor that relates the single person directly to a specific society or ethnic group but to practice traditions connected to institutional or community practices. If researchers and educators can accept such a viewpoint, this would free many children from immigrant families from being associated directly to a special life form that is associated to a specific nation state or ethnic group. Therefore, it is important to conceptualise cultural identity as located in cultural practice that can vary between different institutions in different societies and when connected with a person then it should be understood in the sense that the person through his or her activity creates his or her own multiple and diverse cultural identities. How these multiple identities are related to a person's personal identity has to be seen in a developmental perspective.

The goal then is how to conceptualise minority children's relations to different practice traditions, and to see if the concept of cultural identities can support such an orientation in educational practice so that education can become more sensitive to children's different backgrounds and to the difference in what is important in the planning for "a good life" in the future.

This way of conceptualising personal and cultural identities does not follow completely from the research tradition as I will outline in the following. In the next section I will discuss children's development of personal identity as related to multiple cultural identities from the perspective of research traditions in anthropology and psychology. It will only be possible for me to present the main points of understanding children's development of personal identity and cultural identities. The aim with this presentation is to argue that children both deal with and become an agent in relation to demands from diverse institutional practices.

Cultural Identity – Personal Identity with Multiple Cultural Identities

Cultural identity has become a widely discussed concept within the social sciences (Friedman, 1996; Giddens, 1996; Holland & Lachicotte, 2007; Holland, Lachicotte, Skinner, & Cain, 1998; Jenkins, 2003). One likely reason is that the concept of cultural identity can be used to connect sociological and psychological approaches, and can combine aspects of a person's lived world (i.e., social, motivational, cognitive and emotional aspects of psychic life) with the content of the institutional and societal life world.

In anthropology, the ethnic identity of a person has been characterised as belonging to an ethnic group, defined through birthplace and "blood". Barth (1969) opposed this view and argued that ethnic groups can be seen as a form of social organisation. His empirical analyses of how cultural characteristics of an ethnic group change over time supports the view that ethnic identity is a creation that is conditioned by a group's change of their practice traditions and self-conception as well as the conception of other surrounding groups. The situated and context dependence of cultural identity is stressed by Hyland-Eriksen and Sørheim (1994) who follow the Barth tradition. They also point to the multiple identities that a person holds through his/her participation in the social practice within several different societal groups or institutions, such as family, school, sports club, and other specific community settings. Cultural identity is thereby created through the integration of several *sub-cultural identities,* which are created through participation in the social practice of different communities. New approaches within anthropology even enter into the psychological domain to define identity as multiple and changing with the societal context (Holland & Lachicotte, 2007; Jenkins, 2003). Holland and

Lachicotte draw on both Mead and Vygotsky's theories in their conceptualisation of a person's identities as multiple and open and not necessarily well integrated. According to Holland and Lachicotte:

> [A] Vygotskian approach values the cultural production of new cultural resources as a means, albeit a contingent one, of bringing about social and cultural change. People, banded in communities of practice, can author, intentionally or unintentionally, new selves and new cultural worlds and try to realise them (2007, p. 116).

This means that identity as a concept can transcend the idea of a homogeneous integrated identity that has been the dominating ideal in psychology (Erikson, 1950; Kroger, 2000; Marcia, 1966) by viewing people's self-conception as connected to practice.

In psychology, this ideal of a homogeneous integrated identity is present in the conceptualisation of identity as a psychological function that is unfolding in social and societal contexts following a given developmental path (e.g., Erikson, 1950). One of the questions that has been turning up in relation to Erikson's conception of identity – as self-understanding striving toward coherence formed through participating in different societal contexts, has been how the societal conditions should be conceptualised. Penuel and Wertsch look at how the sociocultural tradition from Vygotsky can contribute to Erikson's notion of identity as a sense of coherence that is mediated by cultural tools. The concept of cultural tools as a mediating concept in person's relation to the world gives, according to Penuel and Wertsch, a better understanding of identity formation in a sociocultural context. But they do not outline any ideas of how this formation takes place within different practice traditions. Penuel and Wertsch conclude their analyses with the suggestion that "identity is about realising and transforming one's purpose, using signs to accomplish meaningful action" (Penuel & Wertsch, 1995, p. 91). From a cultural-historical point of view Penuel and Wertsch still miss a central part and this is how institutional practice and person's activity relates, and how persons acquire and re-create cultural tools through participating in different institutional practices. The different practice in the specific institutions (upbringing and care at home, play and socialising in kindergarten, learning and peer activity in school) has to be taken into consideration otherwise the dynamic of a person's identity development cannot be caught.

The social interaction approach to identity formation as Craib describes it (Craib, 1998) following the Tajfel tradition (Tajfel & Turner, 1986) of identity connects identity with social roles and how persons made self-categorisations in relation to for instance nationality, ethnicity and gender. In this approach formation of social identity as a central part of a person's identity is seen as a process that develops in relation to group identification. But this approach is not satisfying as an explanation of identity formation. What again is missing is consideration for the specific practice traditions and their content that create conditions for a person's interactions. Identification, modelling and role-taking are important aspects of identity formation but without relating these processes to the practice traditions in the specific institutions where the activities take place it becomes a very abstract description. Such a description cannot count for how persons also create conditions for their own identity through their creation of and contribution to activities in the different concrete institutional practices where they live their everyday lives. The practice tradition in the specific institutions has to be taken into consideration as well as the person's concrete activities in his or her participation in specific institutional practices otherwise the dynamic of identity development as a dialectic process between institutional conditions and the person's activity cannot be caught.

Schwartz, Montgomery, and Briones (2006) present a model of how acculturation relates to cultural identity and personal identity. My aim is not to understand acculturation, cultural adaptation or integration, but to see how we in education can give children conditions for becoming agents in their own life trajectories and what possibilities differences in social practices offer children for this engagement and how concepts of cultural identities can support their active engagement in different practices. But even though the aim are different, Schwartz, Montgomery and Briones' discrimination of cultural social and personal identities can be helpful in relation to this aim. They write:

> Personal and social identity are conceptual separate, in that personal identity represents the individual's goals, values, and beliefs (which may or may not be specifically related to the ideals of a particular social or cultural group) where as social identity represents those values and beliefs that are explicitly tied to a particular in-group, as well as attitudes and behaviours toward in-group and out-group members based on these ideals. Social identity, and particular cultural identity, is likely to change as a result of acculturation as immigrant people come into contact with individuals, institutions, and customs from the new receiving society (2006, p. 10).

This is a functional description of the different aspects of identity that extend and integrate Erikson's and Taifel's traditions, but this approach does not detect how the person is an agent and creator through his or her activity in practice his or her personal as well as cultural identity.

As presented earlier personal identity is always social and part of the person's active relation to the world. Becoming cultural means that the person meets different subworlds or practices in different institutions. One of the differences between the cultural-historical approach presented here and Schwartz, Montgomery and Briones' acculturation approach is in the way culture is conceptualised. Hand describes in her comment to Schwartz, Montgomery and Briones' article that culture is seen in relation to nations and that "culture is operationalised as an entity external to the individual, that can be described, captured and quantified" (2006, p. 37). This a view of culture that I have opposed and surpassed by relating it to institutional practice, by which culture as well as persons change and develop through a person's contributions to practices.

Conflicts in a Developmental Perspective

Conflicts between different value positions connected to practice traditions in school and home can be seen as important for how children from immigrant homes develop their self-conception and personal identity. To argue for this conceptualisation I will draw on interviews conducted with young persons from Turkish immigrant homes.[2] In the interpretation of these interviews I used the three types of conflicts depicted in Fig. 8.1. Conflicts in which young persons from cultural minority families can be caught in, can be found between (1) different motives, (2) different value positions and (3) between motives and value positions (see Fig. 8.1).

For schoolchildren, the three types of conflicts are in most cases still external, connected to different practices at home and in school, but at the end of comprehensive school (in 9th and 10th grade)[3] they are gradually internalised. The last type of conflict between value positions and motives is a type of conflict that can, as I will demonstrate with Halime's case, be detrimental to development of cultural identity as multiple for a young person.

I will illustrate these three types of conflicts with extracts from the interviews with young people with Turkish immigrant parents.

Conflicts Between Different Motives

Young people born of immigrant families as well as of native-born families at one time or another come into a conflict between different motives. The young people try to solve these conflicts in different ways; some of these are not so acceptable in school context. This is also the case for several of the students interviewed (Hedegaard, 2003). Mehmet solved his conflict between opposing motives to learn English and to avoid the negative social situation of school by oscillating between running away and choosing to make an effort to learn.

Mehmet's Case

One conflict dominated Mehmet's life for several years: he wants to learn English and at the same time to be in the English class was distressing. In 5th grade he started to play truant together with some of his classmates. The reason he gave was that he did not like his English teacher. Later he got another English teacher and he stopped being truant and followed the instruction in the class. In the 10th grade Mehmet enters into a new school where both the English teacher and his relationship with his new classmates were given as reasons for renewed truancy.

---

[2] Young persons, from Turkish cultural minority families who have just finish 10 years in the Danish school have been interviewed about their experience and conceptions about school life in relation to subject matter learning, friends and teachers. Twenty young people from ten different schools in Aarhus, Denmark were interviewed. These interviews were conducted by Turkish-Danish university students. The idea was to get a diverse group of young people so that diversity in range of conceptions and problems could be outlined. All interview persons have gone through the obligatory Danish school from first grade to ninth or tenth grade, and were interviewed just after leaving public school. The interviews focus on the experiences with and conflicts between different kinds of school activities, schoolmates, teachers and parents demands (Hedegaard, 2003).

[3] In the Danish comprehensive school system 10th grade has not been obligatory before 2008, but most students have taken this grade anyhow, if they do not enter high school.

I: Why did you do this [play truant], was it because that you could not follow the
    class lessons?
Y: No! Well it happened a couple of times and then it grew into a habit. It started
    in 5th grade because of our English teacher. We did not like him, so it was
    especially in his classes.

Mehmet clearly wanted to learn English, because he said that he would have
liked to have had extra hours of English teaching in the lower grades. He also chose
English at the youth school as an after-school activity and gave English as a reason
for taking 10th grade in a new school.

I: Which subjects did you prefer in 9th grade? Did they differ from the ones you
    preferred in the lower grades?
M: Yes, they actually did because now I liked all the subjects, even English.
    Earlier I did not have such a good time with that. I learned a lot in the English
    lessons so I really liked it very much. [He got a new English teacher in 7th
    grade.]
I: Okay, so you started in 10th grade, why did you want to continue and not
    finish school after 9th grade?
M: Because then my English was not good enough and my Danish could be
    improved as well. By continuing in 10th grade, I would still have a year to
    improve my skills, so why not use it.
I: Did you make the decision together with your parents, or was it entirely your
    own decision?
M: I told them that I would like to continue, and then they asked me because they
    knew that others had finished school after 9th grade: Why don't you do the
    same? So I told them that I wanted to improve my English. And then they told
    me that they thought it would be a good idea.
I: So you continued because you wanted to improve your English?
M: Yes.

From Mehmet's description we can see that he oscillates between wanting to learn
English and leaving a situation in which he feels unsure and insulted. This conflict
is a conflict between two motives, wanting to learn English and wanting to escape
painful situations such as feeling left out or being marked as culturally different.
The conflict does not seem to be based on demands from his parents to demonstrate
their position of being Turkish and he does not describe the different events that lead
to the conflict in a way that suggests his feelings of who he is or wants to be actually
are involved. Therefore, I see this as a type of conflict that one does not need to see
as special to a child from an immigrant family, though such conflicts can often be
found in relation to that.

Challenges Between Different Value Positions

Differences between value positions are frequently encountered when a child from a
Turkish immigrant family meets the Danish school system. The cultural traditions of

home and school and their value systems are the public or shared fields of traditions that the child has to learn to handle. There can be an overlap between the practices of these two institutions. Often the overlap is small and insignificant and only takes place in the biannual contact from the Danish school system. But otherwise these two systems are rarely in contact, so that the school child has to adapt to the practice in these different institutions moving between the different worlds of home, school and peer group. The child can meet different value positions in relation to school activities in the two institutions, home and school. But if the value positions do not end up in opposite demands the challenge of the difference can contribute to the child's development as can be seen in Nilgün's case.

Nilgün's Case

I: What about camps and the like?

N: I went with the class to these things.

I: Do you think it has been important for your friendship with Danish class-mates?

N: Yes, it is as if one gets closer to them, one understands them better, it's like a door opener, when you go to these places together, that's what I think, that's what I have experienced. When we had to go to a camp they told me [the classmates]: "We thought that you were one of those girls who would not be allowed to come, because Turkish girls are not allowed to go, we're quite shocked that you're given permission. It is very nice to have you with us, you're very open and warm, some Turkish girls are so cold and don't want to talk to anybody, but you just talk and make people laugh." They also told me that I am *not* like a Turk, even if I am Turkish, so they apologised and said perhaps we've said something we shouldn't, but we don't see you as a Turk. This I have heard a 100 times.

I: What do you think, do you like it?

N: In some ways I like it, but anyhow I am a Turk, so they have to see me as a Turk, that's what I am, I cannot change it, you cannot say that you're a Dane even though you feel half Danish half Turkish.

I: Do you feel that you're Danish?

N: Yes, half of each, like when you're out of the door [of my house] you become another person; this, I believe, it has taken me a long time to understand, but I have to admit to myself that "Nilgün you can change as soon as you are out of the door, but as soon as you open the door again and go in, then you're a Turk, you're a sweet girl and do everything your mother tells you to do. But when you go out then you become another person." Anyhow, I think that everybody feels like this. It helps to know that other Turkish girls also have problems. Once I thought that I was the only one who had problems. But when I talk to other Turkish girls, from other schools as well, they actually have the same kind of problems; this is a kind of comfort.

I: So, perhaps you're dreaming of a future in Turkey?

N: No, I'm not. Only if I was forced to live there, otherwise not. I don't think
     that's where my future will be.

Nilgün demonstrated that her feeling of who "I am", is involved when she has
to orient herself in relation to the different positions of how a young girl has to
behave at home and in school. She has had trouble finding a way to live with this
difference. But at the same time the difference between value positions are also challenging and can be seen as contributing to the creation of a more complex cultural
identity.

This way of solving different value conflicts can also take place in another way
as Hayeriye's case demonstrates.

Hayeriye's Case

Hayeriye went to a Danish school since kindergarten class, but between 5th and
6th grade she was sent for 1 year to Turkey to attend a Koran school. At the time
of the interview just after finishing 9th grade in a comprehensive school she has
started at the business college. She started to wear a scarf in 5th grade imitating
her older sister, before her year of education in Turkey. She does not attend camps,
school parties, or swimming lessons. She has not been pressed by the school and she
feels that her life is in harmony with her and her parents view on these matters. She
does not feel restricted because of her religion as can be seen from the following
extract.

Playing Tennis

H: I play tennis. Many become a bit shocked that I do this, but this I do together
     with my friends. I do not care if it somehow looks awkward that a girl with
     a scarf plays tennis or badminton. I do, and I also jump around playing ball
     with my dad in the park. I can do everything that other Danish young people
     can do.

Party and Camps

H: I have never been at any camps or parties
I: Why?
H: It is because I do not fit in such places. I have my own religion and such, and
     this is where I belong. I cannot attend a party where they drink alcohol and
     just be there with a scarf and a cola. I will look quite out of place.
I: What did your classmate say to you, that you never attended?
H: But from the start I had told them that it had something to do with religion.
I: This they could accept?
H: Yes, they understood and did not ask anymore.
I: What about the camps you are supposed to participate in? Has it been so that
     you had to come with a note again and again?

H: No, because I had a head teacher, that not even asked me, because he knew everything about these matters, this was really good. He did not even ask: Are you going or not? Because he had met a lot of foreigners, so he understood us. It was the best teacher I ever have had. But every time I moved school, I had to explain how it is and things like that.

Hayeriye does not find herself in a conflict even though her parents and school have different value positions and practices. She gets support from both sides to combine practices to become Turkish and Danish in the Danish school. She does not find that she closes herself off in a Turkish cultural identity or on the other hand that she has problems in school because she chose to wear a scarf. But she does see herself as belonging to the group of foreigners in Denmark.

For both Nilgün and Hayeriye the difference between value positions is challenging and can be seen as contributing to the creation of a more complex identity. They were in different ways supported by their family, classmates and teachers to meet these challenges and to develop a cultural identity that was multiple and diverse.

Motive and Position Conflicts

The lack of contact between home and school can lead to value positions between teachers and parents that end up in conflicting demands, where the students have to administrate demands in the concrete school practice that are in conflict with their own motives.

Parents, who have not experienced the Danish school system, as well as teachers who have not experienced everyday practice in a Turkish family, will sometimes not be aware of the conflicts between opposing demands that young persons can find themselves in. Teachers and families may sometimes have problems in achieving a joint understanding based on missing communication between school and home. Immigrant parents, whose language and value system is not connected to the Danish society, may have difficulties in expressing their motives and personal sense adequately. Therefore, when conflicts arise between that which parents imagine are the activities in the school and that which their own children or the teachers communicate about the actual activities, then the imagined activities tend to be given more credence. The same may happen to teachers in case of conflicts, where their own imagined activities about immigrant home practice are trusted more than the knowledge that students give them about their home values.

This is especially the case for many girls from immigrant families in the Danish school system. A very common conflict between teachers and parents can be found when Danish school traditions have boys and girls participate together in social activities, such as camps, physical exercise and swimming lessons, while the Turkish families' positions make them forbid their girls from participating in these activities. Whatever position motivates the girl's activity she is in conflict with value positions that guide practice within school as will be illustrated with an extract from Halime's interview.

Halime's Case

When Halime came to Denmark she had attended school for 2 years in Turkey (they start at the age of five in Turkey), so when she started in the Danish school she was the same age as the Danish children in First grade, but she had to attend the "preparation class" for 1 year and then she went directly to second grade. From second to ninth grade only two foreigners attended Halime's class, so her problem was not caused by the number of foreigners in her class; on the contrary, it was caused by the fact that her teachers did not understand her problems. Halime remembers her first years in school as very good, but it changed. Halime was left out of the circles of her classmates because she was not allowed to attend camps and class events. She feels bitterness towards her parents about this and about their control of her which has to be seen in the light of the pressure put upon her by her classmates, the teachers and especially the head teacher.

H: No, so I was not given permission to go when we were to visit Prague in ninth grade and in seventh grade when we were to visit a city in Denmark, my parents didn't give me permission either.

I: What did you do when you heard that you were not allowed to go?

H: Actually I cried.

I: Did you cry in school?

H: No actually not, I told directly that I couldn't go, but that I didn't know why. I told it very coldly. They [the schoolmates] asked me why don't you ask once more. I said I didn't want to because then I would get into a fight with my father. So I had to say that I could not go on the tour, there was nothing more to say.

I: How did the teachers react?

H: They asked me if I couldn't ask again, they just wanted to have me with them on the trip. I told them I could understand that, but that I didn't want to quarrel with my father. "You have to accept that I cannot go." I told him [the head teacher].

I: Was the teacher rough, did they say that you had to go because it is part of the school?

H: Actually because I told them I didn't care, they threatened me that I could be thrown out of the school. I said that they could just do it, because I didn't care any longer. But of course they are not allowed to do this, when it is not up to me to decide if I can go, so they didn't do it.

The pressure Halime felt during her school years from teachers, her classmates and parents has made her silent which she regrets looking back. But in ninth grade she found out that perhaps her schoolmates were not as cold towards her as she had thought they were.

H: By the time we had to leave ninth grade we made a book for the class, and we had to write in the book what we thought of each other, and they wrote about me that I was very sweet. One of the girls, who wanted to be a designer, wrote that she promised me that the first dress she designed she would give to me, so that I could wear it the first time. Others wrote that I should talk more, but they all wrote nice things about me, because I was not mean, but I didn't speak that much with them.

For Halime to respect her parents value positions and at the same time to meet demands from her teachers and schoolmates that reflected her own wishes, which she could not give in to, influence not only her feeling of who she was but also her general attitude to others. She was withdrawn in relation to her schoolmates and became angry at her parents, which she expressed indirectly many times. The social conditions for participating in school practice left her with little possibility for activity and for developing her own value positions.

Conclusion

To overcome this dichotomy between concepts of identity as an internalised functional self-conception (Erikson tradition) or as an external determinant self-categorisation in relation to groups in society (Taifel tradition) and to give room for the child's own activity, the cultural-historical concept of activity and institutional practice are important. Identity can from this approach be seen as dialectic between self-understanding and understanding of the different practice traditions a person participates in. Identity has to be seen in a development perspective as taking place through a trajectory within societal institutions with multiple possibilities for activities that are created both by the institutional practice and the child.

Both the general conceptions that guide daily practice of a specific child and the child's concrete way of acting in his or her historical specific family and school creates the conditions for the child's everyday life activity and future life projects. A person's identity as multiple and cultural can be seen as anchored in the social practice of different institutions of society. The primary institutions in childhood in Western societies such as the Scandinavian countries are the home, day-care, school and after-school clubs. The children's way of living in these institutions creates their view on who they are and want to become, but their views change and become extended by appropriation of knowledge and motives. Development of multiple cultural identities can be seen from the perspective of how social relations, capacities and motives develop. This development is a function of the demands that the children meet in the institutional practices in which they participate, but it is also determined by what the child gives to this practice and how. The children not only adapt to the demands and conditions at home and school, they also contribute to them.

The conflicts that the child meets and the way s/he overcomes them are very important for his/her development. Motive conflicts will be part of all children's lives since they grow out of practice in different institutions. The conflict that children of immigrant parents meet in these cases could be characterised as specifically related to the immigration practice but there is no need to use a specific terminology of culture conflict here, the conflicts are much more about how children participate in school practice and how school practice should develop a shared practice between children coming from homes with different cultural traditions.

The position-based conflict could be identified as cultural since cultural traditions in different institutions lead to these types of conflicts. But these conflicts could also be class conflicts (Willis, 1977) or generational conflicts or subgroup conflicts (McDonald, 1999), or conflicts between religious groups. If the value positions connected to the different traditions can be separated into practice in corresponding institutions where there is no demand for overlap and if no pressure is put on the child so that traditions from one institution do not need to count in the other, as in Nilgün's and Hayeriye's case, then the child can manage to act in the different types of institutional practice. The activities in these different institutions then all contribute to the person's feeling of who they are.

The type of conflict that is detrimental to the child's development of self-worth and orientation to make use of the possibility of education in society is the one where value positions are strictly maintained by the dominant agents in the different institutions and the child's motives are not allowed to be verbalised, as in Halime's case. To give Halime the possibility to change her concept of her self and her possibilities there needs to be a loosening of the demands by the different responsible adults (i.e. that can happen if they start to communicate with each other) thereby Halime's experience of her possibilities and her self can change. Young immigrant women in these situations mostly create their own conditions by fleeing the school and becoming "silent", but they can take the initiative to change their conditions and this sometimes happens, as the news media reveals, by fleeing from the home and the parental demands, though this does not always have a happy solution.

Students are actively creating themselves as persons through participating in different practices and through this acquire different cultural identities. Identity seen from the person's perspective is continuous, but this does not mean that the person can not experience her own identity looking back at his or her development as an increase in complexity or as changed (for example, when a student gets her degree and becomes a professional). The person can also, as Nilgün describes, experience that they have to be different person's in different intuitional practices, but this does not mean that they do not see themselves as the same person, therefore I find the concept of personal identity as multiple and cultural a relevant way to conceptualise both the personal experience of a homogenous identity and the person's identity as multiple in the person's functioning in different practices.

Acknowledgments Thanks to Anne Edwards and Seth Chaiklin for discussing the paper and giving editorial comments

References

Anderson, B. (1991). *Imagined communities: Reflections on the origin and spread of nationalism* (Rev. ed.). London: Verso.

Barth, F. (1969). Introduction. In F. Barth (Ed.), *Ethnic groups and boundaries. The social organisation of culture differences* (pp. 9–38). Bergen, Norway: Bergen University Press.

Berger, P. L., & Luckmann, T. (1966). *The social construction of reality*. Garden City, NY: Doubleday.

Billig, M. (1998). *Banal nationalism*. London: Sage.

Bourdieu, P. (1984). *Distinction: A social critique of the judgement of taste* (R. Nice, Trans.). Cambridge, MA: Harvard University Press. (Original work published 1979)

Craib, I. (1998). *Experiencing identity*. London: Sage.

Elkonin, D. B. (1999). Toward the problem of stages in the mental development of children. *Journal of Russian and East European Psychology, 37*, 11–29.

Erikson, E. H. (1950). *Childhood and society*. New York: Norton.

Friedman, J. (1996). *Cultural identity and global processes*. London: Sage.

Giddens, A. (1996). *Modernitet og selvidentitet [Modernity and self-identity]*. København: Hans Reitzel.

Hand, V. (2006). Operationalizing culture and identity in ways to capture the negotiation of participation across communities. *Human Development, 49*, 336–341.

Hedegaard, M. (1999). Institutional practice, cultural positions and personal motives: Immigrant Turkish parents' conceptions about their children's school life. In: S. Chaiklin, M. Hedegaard, & J. Juul Jensen (Eds.), *Activity theory and social practice*. Aarhus: Aarhus University Press.

Hedegaard, M. (2003). *At blive frememd i Danmark. Hvordan tyrkisk-danske unge oplever deres skolegang, identitet og fremtid. (To become foreigners in Denmark. How Turkish-Danish young persons experiences their school life, identity and future)*. Aarhus: Klim

Hedegaard, M. (2005). Strategies for dealing with conflicts in value positions between home and school: Influences on ethnic minority students' development of motives and identity. *Culture and Psychology, 11*, 187–205.

Hedegaard, M. (2009). Children's development from a cultural-historical approach. *Mind Culture and Activity, 16*(1), 64–81.

Hedegaard, M., & Fleer, M. (2009). *Researching children: A cultural-historical approach*. London. Open University Press.

Hjarnø, J. (1988a). *Indvandrer fra Tyrkiet i Stockholm og København [Immigrants from Turkey in Stockholm and Copenhagen]*. Esbjerg: South Jutland University Press.

Hjarnø, J. (1988b). *Socialt arbejde blandt flygtninge og indvandrere [Social work among refugees and immigrants]*. Copenhagen: Billesø & Baltzer.

Holland, D., & Lachicotte, W., Jr., (2007). Vygotsky, Mead, and the new sociocultural studies of identity. In H. Daniels, M. Cole, & J. Wertsch (Eds.), *The Cambridge companion to Vygotsky*. Cambridge: Cambridge University Press.

Holland, D., Lachicotte, W., Jr., Skinner, D., & Cain, C. (1998). *Identity and agency in cultural worlds*. Cambridge, MA: Harvard University Press.

Hyland-Eriksen, T., & Sørheim, T. A. (1994). *Kulturforskeller i praksis [Cultural Differences in Practice]*. Oslo: Ad Notam Gyldendal.

Jenkins, R. (2003). *Social identity*. London: Routledge.

Kroger, J. (2000). *Identity development: Adolescence through adulthood*. London: Sage.

Leontiev, A. N. (1932). The development of voluntary attention in the child. *The Pedagogical Seminary and Journal of Genetic Psychology, 40*, 52–83.

Leontiev, A. N. (1978). *Activity, consciousness, and personality* (M. J. Hall, Trans.). Englewood Cliffs, NJ: Prentice-Hall. (Original work published 1975)

Levitin, K. (1982). *One is not born a personality: Profiles of Soviet education psychologists* (V. V. Davydov, Ed., Y. Filippov, Trans.). Moscow: Progress.

Luria, A. R. (1928). The problem of the cultural behaviour of the child. *The Pedagogical Seminary and Journal of Genetic Psychology, 35*, 493–507.

Luria, A. R. (1976). *Cognitive development*. Cambridge: Harvard University Press.

Malik, K. (1996). *The meaning of race: Race, history and culture in Western society*. New York: New York University Press.

Marcia, J. E. (1966). Development and validation of ego identity status. *Journal of Personality and Social Psychology, 3*, 551–558.

McDonald, K. (1999). *Struggles for subjectivity. Identity, action, and youth experience*. Cambridge: Cambridge University Press.

Ogbu, J. (1992). Cultural discontinuities and schooling. *Anthropology and Education Quarterly, 13*, 290–307.

Ogbu, J. U., & Simons, H. D. (1998). Voluntary and involuntary minorities: A cultural theory of school performance with some implication for education. *Anthropology and Education Quarterly, 29*, 155–188.

Penuel, W. R., & Wertsch, J. V. (1995). Vygotsky and identity formation: A sociocultural approach. *Educational psychologist, 30*, 83–92.

Phelan, P., Davidson, A. L., & Cao, H. T. (1991). Student's multiple worlds: Negotiating the boundaries of family, peer and school cultures. *Anthropology and Education Quarterly, 22*, 224–249.

Schutz, A. (1970). *On phenomenology and social relations.* Chicago: Chicago Press.

Schutz, A. (2005). *Hverdagslivets sociology* (Trans. from Collected works, Vol. 1, 1972). Copenhagen: Hans Reitzel.

Schwartz, S., Montgomery, M. J., & Briones, E. (2006). The role of identity in acculturation among immigrant people: theoretical propositions, empirical questions, and applied recommendations. *Human Development, 49*, 1–30.

Tajfel, H., & Turner, J. C. (1986). The social identity theory of intergroup behaviour. In S. Worchel, & W. G. Austin (Eds.), *The psychology of intergroup behaviour* (pp. 7–24). Chicago: Nelson Hall.

Vygotsky, L. S. (1929). The problem of cultural development of the child. *The Pedagogical Seminary and Journal of Genetic Psychology, 36*, 415–434.

Vygotsky, L. S. (1987). *The collected works of L.S. Vygotsky. Volume 1. Problems of general psychology.* New York: Plenum Press.

Vygotsky, L. S. (1998). *The collected works of L.S. Vygotsky. Volume 5. Child psychology.* New York: Plenum Press.

Willis, P. (1977). *Learning to labour. How working class kids get working class jobs* (pp. 11–51). Aldershot: Gower Press.

Chapter 9
Under the Sign of the Coffee Pot: Mealtime Rituals as Performative Practices

Katrin Audehm

Family Meals as Ritual Acts

Whereas journalistic essays on culture in newspapers and magazines increasingly bemoan the reduced significance of the family meal or even express concern about its total disappearance, families themselves undertake no little effort to maintain their collective mealtimes. Even though it may be becoming ever more difficult for family members to gather at the table and although having meals together may not seem very practical, eating together is one of the most important everyday rituals for families. Yet, at first glance, eating together seems to be a fully secular, continual, regular, more or less ritualized act that is part of normal, everyday life and is hardly associated with dogmatic proclamations, canonical forms, inflexible codes of behavior, or stereotypical proceedings. Moreover, typical characteristics of sacred acts, such as maintaining a reverent silence, genuflecting, expressing gratitude effusively, preaching excessively, or experiencing temporary or prolonged states of ecstasy, seem quite alien to the family meal.

But if the act of eating together becomes more than just a routinized and satiating meal for the family members, begins to have transcendental effects, and conveys values that distinguish the family as a community, then it performs the function of symbolic expression and thus the main function of rituals (Douglas, 2003, p. 39). Participating in the ritual often becomes a binding obligation with the stipulation that not every form of behavior is acceptable at the table and that certain topics of conversation remain excluded and conflicts, for the most part, repressed. In addition to its symbolic nature, then, the family meal also takes on the nature of an obligation and appeal. In this sense, then, the family meal can become indispensable, and in much the same way, the symbolic unity of the family expressed in the meal and the values conveyed by it can become sacrosanct.

K. Audehm (✉)
Free University Berlin, Berlin, Germany
e-mail: kathrin_audehm@web.de

M. Kontopodis et al. (eds.), *Children, Development and Education*, International
Perspectives on Early Childhood Education and Development 3,
DOI 10.1007/978-94-007-0243-1_9, © Springer Science+Business Media B.V. 2011

Nonetheless, the interactions at the table are not insignificantly connected to a pedagogical, generational difference, i.e., to a hierarchical difference in authority that has pedagogical effects. At the outset, the mealtime gathering involves a group of persons who embody and consummate their individual, characteristic differences, which they are not able to exclude from the ritual performance. How can the magical effect of the family mealtime ritual be explained – an effect that allows a group of diverse, individual persons to symbolically form a unit?

According to Pierre Bourdieu, speech acts and other symbolic practices such as rituals have the magical effect of invoking social actors as subjects with specific attributes, of influencing their conception of the world, and of transforming the social actors in real ways. In his studies of the linguistic field (Bourdieu, 1992), he analyzes rites of institution as symbolic borderline cases that make the source of the performative force of language most readily visible.

> One does not easily leave the spontaneously performative logic of language, which [...] helps to make (or make exist) what it says, especially through the inseparably cognitive and political constructive efficacy of classifications. (Bourdieu, 2000, p. 117)

For this performative logic is based on social magic, to which education contributes in an essential way. The following section will explain the concept of social magic and, in doing so, will focus on the interconnections between authority and education on the one hand and between language and body on the other.

On the Performative Logic of Rites of Institution

Bourdieu's studies of the linguistic field demonstrate that rites of institution are symbolic borderline cases which allow the source of language's power to become discernible. In this context, his concept of performative *logic* also provides for a critical distance to Jacques Derrida's view of the philosophy of language. Bourdieu is not concerned with a performative potential of language in and of itself, based on the gulf between signs and logical differences, with such gulfs constantly being displaced in language usage through decontextualization and supplementation, which then produce new meanings (Derrida, 1976). With Derrida, one could speak of a certain performative leeway for speech (and, above all, for writing) which guarantees that meanings are not fixed. In contrast, Bourdieu is interested in those mechanisms which provide language with symbolic power, a power that can extend to symbolic brute force and can establish symbolic differences, at the same time making meaning fixed and generally accepted.[1] As with Victor Turner's work from a perspective of Cultural Anthropology, the focus is on a process that links bodily action with social experience in rituals, resulting in symbolic statements and adapting or recalling social dramas (Turner, 1982, pp. 78–81, 116). But in contrast to Turner, Bourdieu subjects the symbolic practices, in particular the public acts of institution, to a

---

[1]On the distinction between the content and the function of the concept "difference" in Derrida and in Bourdieu, cf. Audehm and Velten (2007, pp. 17–24).

rigorous critique of power relations. For a study concerned with family mealtime rituals, Boudieu's remarks on the interconnection between authority and education are especially interesting, as this interconnection supports the assertion that the performative effect of symbolic actions is based on *social* magic – even though the family mealtime ritual is not a public act of institution.

On the one hand, Bourdieu speaks of rites of institution in terms of concrete ritual acts which immediately effect a transformation of status, such as the appointment to a new office, conferring knighthood, crowning ceremonies, or examinations. Yet, in contrast to the views expressed by Arnold van Gennep and Victor Turner, Bourdieu does not consider such rituals as rites of passage. Instead, he attributes to them the more fundamental function of instituting legitimate symbolic differences. Instituting such legitimate differences is based upon imposing boundaries and assigning an identity.

Rituals separate those who undergo such rites from those who, exactly because of the existence of such rites, are excluded from undergoing them. The separation comes about as an arbitrary imposition of boundaries that establishes fundamental divisions within a hitherto undifferentiated social order. One consequence, for example, could be that what might be called the "most effeminate" man is then separated from the "most masculine" woman. Such arbitrary boundaries appear to be natural and legitimate, for as symbolic practices rituals are traditional and widely acknowledged acts. "The separation accomplished in the ritual (which itself effects a separation) exercises an effect of consecration" (Bourdieu, 1992, pp. 118–119). The legitimate effect of such consecrations of differences is all the more certain the greater the impression is that the arbitrary boundaries are based on objective facts. In addition, instituting symbolic differences is based on assignments of identity to the person consecrated which inform that person of how he or she is expected to behave in accordance with the person's new status. Assigning an identity as a social definition becomes a veritable instance of social attribution that is imposed on the consecrated person in front of everyone.

The differences thus instituted and consecrated must be stabilized so that the temptation to transgress, to cross over the imposed boundaries, can be resisted. For this reason, the legacy of the symbolic rites of institution is entrusted to the body. The act of institution becomes the work of incorporation, which ensures that the boundaries and social definitions imposed are given a durable disposition, that in the form of a habitus they become second nature. Bourdieu refers to this inculcation and incorporation as education, as it is not simply left to chance. In addition to their practical knowledge of the norms governing appropriate conduct, the social actors also form habitual dispositions towards recognizing authority.

In order to speak with a certain authority, both what is said and the speakers themselves must have certain credentials and be respectable. Thus, what is required is a way of speaking in legitimate forms to a legitimate audience. These signs of participation in an institution or in the symbolic capital of a social group guarantee the legitimacy of the speakers. But this must also be recognized by the participants in their willingness to carry out the ritual. Recognition of authority, in turn, is a prerequisite for the efficacy of rituals. "What one might call the *liturgical* conditions, namely, the set of prescriptions which govern the *form* of the public manifestation of authority, like ceremonial etiquette, the code of gestures and officially prescribed rites, are clearly only an *element*, albeit the most visible one, in a system of conditions of which the most important and indispensable are those which produce the disposition towards recognition in the sense of misrecognition and belief, that is, the delegation of authority which confers its authority on authorized discourse" (Bourdieu, 1992, p. 113). Things have now come full circle. The performative logic of instituting legitimate differences is based on *social* magic, on the delegation of authority to speakers and their recognition through the social actors: "One only preaches to the converted" (Bourdieu, 1992, p. 126).

If the performative logic of rites of institution actually works in the way Bourdieu describes, then the actors have subjected themselves to symbolic power. Their collective belief allows them to become subjects with specific positions and specific attributes. They act in accordance with the principle: "Become what you are" (Bourdieu, 1992, p. 122). Instituting symbolic differences works as a type of social magic because it can take the dispositions of habitus as its starting point and can set all wheels in motion that promote the recognition of authority without having to repeat the work of incorporation.

From a perspective critical of ideology, social magic is "the key to explaining the transformation of social power into the concealed power of symbols" (Herkommer, 2004, p. 32). An educational perspective is primarily concerned with the question of how symbolic power becomes effective and thus focuses on the tedious and extensive work of incorporation. If the succession of various levels of acts of institution is understood as a sequence of actions, then rituals would have a magical effect because the actual work of incorporation takes place either before or after the immediate performance of the ritual. This would mean that education does not take place, or not primarily, in rituals. This could be the case, but neglects the fact that rituals are symbolic practices in the form of bodily performances. It is not only the great public spectacles that work with and on the bodies of social actors.

In his discussion of acts of institution, Bourdieu makes a generalization based on an analysis of the function of academic examinations for admission to elite educational institutions in France. With this analysis, he does refer to initiation rites, but, for the most part, the aspect of bodily force is neglected. Only in his *Pascalian Meditations* does Bourdieu, while referring to bodily pain undergone in initiation rites, explicitly agree with Foucault's account of pressures of standardization which emanate from the institutions of a disciplinary power (especially in rituals of examination) and focus on inculcation and incorporation (Bourdieu, 2000, p. 141; Foucault, 1991, pp. 238 ff.) The bodies of social actors are exposed to the mute force of social relations, the standardizing pressure of rules, or direct disciplinary interventions not only in rituals – whether these be violent tattooing practices or mutilations to be found in initiation rites, or endless training units for correcting movement patterns and game sequences, or harmless admonitions to sit up straight or not laugh so loudly at the dinner table. Yet, this is only one side of the matter. For these bodies are not only living torsos subject to precise and even violent attacks to ensure that social boundaries and symbolic differences are made durable. These are also bodies with habitus; that is to say that the social actors have a body capable of achieving insight.

> This is precisely the function of the notion of habitus, which restores to the agent a generating, unifying, constructing, classifying power, while recalling that this capacity to construct social reality, itself socially constructed, is not that of a transcendental subject but of a socialized body, investing in its practice socially constructed organizing principles that are acquired in the course of a situated and dated social experience. (Bourdieu, 2000, pp. 136–137)

Can habitual dispositions simply generate a doxic relation to one's own social world?

Bourdieu's concept of social magic has often been criticized as being so restricted that the social agents have apparently lost any subjective power to engage in a course of action. It is not only due to Bourdieu's rigorous diction that such an impression can be gained. The performative logic involved in acts of instituting symbolic differences works because it is based upon the habitual disposition of recognizing authority. In the course of the work of incorporation or education, this disposition becomes part of a habitus which in this context appears simply to be coherent and fully adapted to social conditions. But one can also refer to Bourdieu's concept itself in stating that the unadjusted and crisis-stricken nature of the habitus is actually the normal state of affairs: "The adjustment, in advance, of habitus to the objective conditions is a *particular case* ..." (Bourdieu, 2000, p. 159). Bourdieu also maintains that "habitus is not necessarily adapted to its situation or necessarily coherent" (Bourdieu, 2000, p. 160). Thus, the practical sense of the social agents need not be at the mercy of some social magic.

In his remarks on social magic, Bourdieu does, indeed, mention pedagogical action within families as an example. Yet, in his empirical research, the family itself is not a distinct issue. Hence, a question does arise as to how his general, that is, theoretically abstract and historically unspecific, characterization of education as a prerequisite of social magic, which alone can make symbolic force effective, can be related to an analysis of pedagogical forms of interaction in family mealtime rituals.

A Pedagogical Ethnography of Family Mealtime Ritual

The concept of social magic offers many and diverse opportunities to engage in related empirical research on and in families. For example, in criticism of ideology, one might inquire into where the myth of the family has gained its ability to provide orientation – even up to the present and in contradiction to real-life experience.[2] Furthermore, with recourse to the concept of habitus, the actual biographical

---

[2]The modern family is still a powerful symbol as a social institution that provides action with orientation and serves as a standard for judging the ideas and actions of social agents (cf. e.g. Haug, 2003; Hettlage, 1998, pp. 48ff.).

significance of family rituals can be examined (Friebertshäuser, 2004). Yet, for family rituals to actually be biographically significant or to effect social magic, they must have educational effects. Nonetheless, pedagogical forms of interaction or the functions of family rituals have heretofore been largely neglected in empirical analyses.

The original simple question underlying the empirical inquiry into family mealtime rituals here concerned what exactly transpires at the dinner table. This open-ended form of inquiry helps to question one's own background knowledge and expresses an inquisitive attitude that needs to be constantly applied when collecting and analyzing the data, especially since family meals are a familiar practice in one's own culture. Only gradually did the concept of social magic become the fundamental theoretical point of reference for this study, as it provided for a well-defined description of the object under study and for an in-depth analysis. At the same time, from an early inquiry into the practices of seven families, a decision to focus on mealtime rituals in three urban, middle-class, German families eventually materialized.

At the time when the research was conducted (1999–2004), the families lived in the same borough of a large city. The parents all belonged to the same generation, were around 40 years old at the beginning of the study, and, in the broadest sense, were engaged in socially or pedagogically oriented professions. In two of the families, the parents were married. In the Zobel family, the father earned the larger portion of the family income, while in the Hauser family both parents did comparable work and contributed almost equally to the family income. They also shared equal responsibilities for housework and the children's upbringing. The Zobel family consisted of the parents, their daughter Carolin, who was nine at the beginning of the study, and the 12-year-old twins Anna and Björn. The Hausers had a 5-year-old son, Erik, and a 13-year-old daughter, Friederike. The Maier family consisted of a divorced, working mother as the single parent and her 13-year-old daughter Dorothea. The main differences between the families, then, had to do with custody arrangements or family types and with the number of siblings. When the research began, at least one child from each family was attending the same elementary school, where a type of reformed pedagogy was practiced and which provided the initial contacts to the families. The families were somewhat acquainted with each other, but there was only sporadic contact and no close relationship, even though Anna Zobel and Dorothea Maier were friends.

The main methods of collecting data involved (at least five) recordings of conversations, which were done by the families themselves, and (also five) instances of participant observation in the role of complete observer.[3] These methods were complemented by group discussions and guided interviews, informal conversations,

---

[3] At this point, I would like to thank my colleague Jörg Zirfas, who undertook the fieldwork with me. To engage in fieldwork as a team whose members differed in terms of academic position, age, sex, personal family experience, and perceptions proved to be a beneficial precondition for the ethnographic analysis. The correspondingly distinct forms of contact to the families and varying ways of realizing and comprehending the mealtime rituals facilitated evaluative self-observation.

and somewhat limited participation in family celebrations such as confirmation or Christmas Eve – all of which helped to provide background information. Interactions at the dinner table were initially analyzed in accordance with the documentary method and empirically encoded (Audehm, 2007, pp. 71 ff.). Increasingly, the data were interpreted in terms of the theoretical approach and consolidated. This led to a "thick description" (Geertz, 1975) of family-specific, ritual styles of upbringing and, then, to an empirical comparison of such styles, which, in turn, facilitated a generalization of the invariant social characteristics and pedagogical functions of the mealtime rituals examined. The following remarks will explicate how the categorization of the object under study and the methodological procedures involved were oriented to Bourdieu's concept of social magic.

For ritual theory, an essential issue with respect to collective family meals is how familial unity might symbolically be produced, or, which values are conveyed in the mealtime ritual so that the family can be represented as a community. In this context, families are special social groups that can, indeed, distinguish themselves from both other families and other social factions through their rituals by creating family-specific experiences. Yet, the persons involved cannot exclude the structural differences characterizing themselves from their ritual actions. Because of such differences – social background, gender, or legally codified guardianship or custody rights – dividing lines between family members are conceivable which can become particularly significant for the performative effects of mealtime rituals. To ensure the success of the pedagogical measures intended, assignments of identity are practically unavoidable, even though these present a certain risk to the symbolic performance of the family as a community. Potential conflicts can easily arise, for example, when someone is blamed for something or obliged to carry out particular tasks. In this sense, then, the symbolic content of mealtime rituals can be reconstructed along the various dividing lines and allocations of identity among the family members. Moreover, the concept of social magic brings to mind the fact that structural differences are not simply part of the social context of the family, but also shape the familial experience created with the mealtime ritual and are instituted with the consummation of the ritual interactions. Here, the act of institution refers less to some sort of initial enactment than to a (legitimate) sort of "staging", yet just as much to intentional actions as to unintentional practices, through which theses differences are embodied, performed, represented, completed, used, confirmed, or evaded – in short, processed. Which differences characterize family mealtime rituals; how are they articulated in carrying out ritual interaction, i.e., linked to one another, represented, and brought up to date?

Although Bourdieu does not explicate the family model at the basis of his remarks, it seems that his starting point is one of fixed and unchangeable structures of authority in traditional, patriarchal, nuclear families. But Bourdieu follows a train of thought stemming from Max Weber, for whom authority is not something possessed by a competent agent as a personality trait. On the contrary, authority is conferred on someone and requires that others acknowledge it, based on belief; on a constant, everyday, inner inclination; or on extraordinary devotion (Weber, 1995, pp. 260, 315). For this reason, both the public acts of institution that are subjected to a rigorous critique of the power relations involved and the mealtime rituals within the private familial sphere can be understood as spheres of action for authority, in which the actors are competing for recognition. Then the question arises as to how the symbolic constitution of the family as a community at the dinner table relates to the acknowledgement of authority.

In Bourdieu's remarks, education seems above all to be a lengthy and, often enough, arduous task of inculcation and incorporation. In contrast to socialization, education refers to direct and intentional attempts to exert influence on the behavior of individuals which are repetitive and, in the long run, have effects on the formation of habitual dispositions. If such attempts involve appropriate pedagogical skills, the immediate effects on individuals' behavior can be planned and guided. Still, the formation of habitual dispositions exceeds the scope of singular pedagogical measures. Moreover, habitual dispositions can also contribute to resistance to pedagogical practices, especially if the severity of disciplinary interventions violates customary behavior or familiar norms, or if assertions of authority are not appropriate to such norms and thus allow power relations to become visible or otherwise perceptible. According to Bourdieu, the symbolic violence of rituals establishes communities through separation, institutes differences and educates subjects, restricts individual autonomy, and broadens no one's horizon. In terms of theoretical reflections on power, education through rituals according to Bourdieu seems to be exclusively a form of disciplining. In this sense, pedagogical authority on the one hand, is conceivable as the power of disposal in constructing pedagogical scenarios at the dinner table which provide a framework and direction for the pedagogical forms of interaction in mealtime rituals. On the other hand, the individual, concrete actions at the dinner table elude the power of disposal and individual persons' control over them. Furthermore, the forms of interaction can, in turn, have an effect on the acknowledgement of pedagogical authority within the context of the ritual, thus subjecting those with the power of constructing the scenarios themselves to the rules of the ritual.

Taking social magic as our starting point, then, we can summarize the subject of our research with the following question: How are symbolic practice, pedagogical interactions, and the authoritative structure of ritual performance interrelated at the dinner table? Since the symbolic content is just as slightly dependent on the use of language as are the social properties and pedagogical functions of mealtime rituals, ethnographic research on such rituals requires in addition to the analysis of mealtime conversations[4] the observation of non-verbal interaction and of the staged arrangement. What is to be empirically reconstructed is the interrelationship between language-based and bodily interactions, between practices involving objectified props and artifacts of ritual performance and materiality, between sensuality and the symbolic traces of the ritual scenario, an interrelationship that is constituted through mealtime ritual acts.

---

[4]Cf. a study in conversational analysis (not from a perspective of ritual theory) by Angela Keppler (1995).

Playful Asceticism Under the Sign of the Coffee Pot

This section will attempt to provide insights into the mealtime rituals of the Zobel family. The description is focused on those practices that are particularly relevant for the interconnection between authority and education and in which the ethnographic implementation of the concept of social magic is most clearly demonstrated.

When the research began, the Zobel family consisted of 9-year-old Carolin, the 12-year-old twins Anna and Björn, and the mother and father, both of whom were about 40 years of age. Every morning, this family has breakfast together in the small kitchen of their spacious apartment. Their breakfast lasts about 45 min. So the family occupies quite a bit of time, if only little space, with their shared breakfast.

At first glance, the establishment of a community at the breakfast table here seems to aim at promoting mutual conversation. Family members eat remarkably little and, as it were, only incidentally; yet, they speak a great deal, and there is nothing incidental about the way they talk. In a five-person household, it is by no means remarkable that conversation flows with virtually no breaks. Still, the logical sequencing of the focus on topics, the patient inquiries, and the composed concentration (even when conflicts arise) are impressive. The father speaks the least, not because he would have nothing to say, but because he needs to say only very little. He can rely on a condensed symbol of the pedagogical, generational difference and on a magical signifier of his authority – on the coffee pot.

Setting the table is something that the father considers his duty, but he allows the mother to help. He is solely responsible for making coffee, which is then exclusively for the parents to drink. This is the only rule that the father explicitly imposes in response to his son's occasional questions on the matter. The coffee pot and the breadbasket are the only eating utensils that have a specific place on the table. The coffee pot itself is always in the center. Even if the mother, using a table mat, has already assigned the pot its usual place, the father is the one who actually places the coffee pot on the table, and in doing so he always moves the mat, albeit perhaps only a few millimeters. The milk that the children drink and that is frequently refilled in their cups is placed on the kitchen counter opposite. The child sitting at the narrow end of the table often has to get up several times to refill the milk.

During the entire meal, the father is the focus of a number of small expressions of affection until the end of the mealtime ritual is signaled by his reading the newspaper. For this, he enlarges his own personal space by slightly pushing his chair back, leaning far back, pushing his coffee cup forwards, and, both before and after he picks up the paper, silently concentrating on enjoying his coffee in a very relaxed manner for a few moments. At these moments, no one asks him any questions, though he would otherwise occasionally intervene in a calm and humorous way, especially if the somewhat stricter mother seemed to be restricting the children's actions too much.

Taking care of contacts between the family and the outside world is another one of the father's responsibilities. Hence, he pours the observers coffee, after having decided that – since, at any rate, they do not wish to eat anything – they must at least have some coffee. From the second observation on, two coffee cups are on the kitchen counter near the door, prepared according to the preferences named by the observers. At the beginning of the individual observation sessions, the father nods toward the observers with a smile and briefly explains whose coffee is where. In this way, the symbolic trail left by the coffee is followed, showing coffee to be a stimulating drink to be consumed moderately that helps to sustain those who (need to) work, whether within or outside of the house. Enjoying coffee then begins to signify a conscious way of dealing with oneself and a competent way of stimulating one's own energies. Thus, the status of coffee as an adults' drink is reinforced by the presence of the observers.

A closer look reveals that the sequencing and meaning of the ritual are strongly determined by physical interactions. The mealtime ritual always begins with a physical game: a reversed form of musical chairs. The table is set for five persons, but only four chairs are immediately available. The seating plan involves two fixed places at which the parents always take a seat first, once they have told the children that the table is set. Only rarely are the children directly requested or even summoned to appear at the breakfast table. The first two children to appear have to squeeze past their parents. One of them – usually Carolin – even has to crawl under the table to get to her seat. The final one to appear – usually Björn – has to fetch a chair from the living room opposite. Here, too, bodily contact is not at all repelled, but, rather, sought after and practically required by the ritual scene, almost inevitable. Fetching the fifth chair completes the ritual circle and signals the beginning of the ritual. Hence, for this reversed game of musical chairs, the child that enjoys the greatest freedom in terms of appearing at the breakfast table has the greatest responsibility for beginning the communal ritual.[5] The confinement of the small kitchen space is transformed into physical proximity through which family members assure one another of belonging together and of their mutual affection. This corresponds to the father's conscious ritual intention, as he had decided that on weekdays the family should have breakfast together in the kitchen, and not at the more spacious dining table in the living room reserved for Sundays, an alternative which would not have required much more effort.

At the breakfast table, 9-year-old Carolin enjoys liberties similar to those of her father; she often lets her gaze wander at a distance and is allowed to hum or make faces. By contrast, the twins are most strongly exposed to the maternal attempts at education. The mother primarily intervenes with the aim of training a correct and appropriate way of speaking. Moreover, the parents are concerned with their children's self-education, i.e., with promoting normative competence leading to increased self-determination, even outside of familial situations. The Zobel family's education at the breakfast table aims at the children engaging in the disciplinary

---

[5] In musical chairs, there is also a chair missing, but during the game the number of chairs is further reduced. Whoever does not manage to sit on an empty seat early enough when the circling of the chairs comes to a halt, must drop out of the game. In the Zobel family, whoever arrives latest, can complement the number of chairs.

practice of behavior corresponding to the norms of the world of schooling as a pre-requisite of individual autonomy. In this way, education is staged as an achievement insured by success at school and within the bounds of individual responsibility.

The twins enjoy outdoing each other in guessing games. They frequently laugh and occasionally boast in an exaggerated way about small-scale achievements at school. During negotiations initiated and framed as a quiz game by their mother on some slight transgression committed by their father, they play the roles of the defense attorney and of a judge trying to reach a settlement. With his questions and comments, Björn, in particular, occasionally attempts to test the bounds of rules on watching television. The mother responds with brief, rational explanations; the father teases his son with ironic replies and comments. There are no debates on existing rules governing everyday behavior at the breakfast table. In stark contrast to the promotion of discipline in linguistic forms is the license accorded to the intensive physical play that takes place, for the most part, under the table. Unlike their parents, the children are conspicuously casual about how they sit at the table. Sideways on their chairs, they often let their legs dangle or touch each other or their father with their feet. Physical contact under the table hardly ever stops, while movements above the table are more effectively related to passing the food, for which explicit requests are usually unnecessary. But the mother does demand a "please" and a "thank you" if these phrases are not used while passing food around. Physical contact above the table is more reserved – but without any accompanying admonitions. Thus, education at the breakfast table is achieved in terms of a playful asceticism, i.e., as a disciplined, collective, self-directed exercise oscillating between strictness and play.

The parents have the power of disposal with regard to the ritual scene and the power to define rules of behavior, while checking conformity to such rules is primarily the mother's responsibility. Her visible authority is subject to correction by the father and to control by the 12-year-old twins. The children can also reject the maternal use of authority if it contradicts or endangers the basic principle of familial community: "one for all, and all for one." At the breakfast table, the parental hierarchy is asymmetrically distributed between mother and father. The father appears as the guarantor of the family community and has greater authority than the mother. Paternal authority is legitimized by the mother's actions and thus rendered relatively invisible, whereas maternal authority, with its visibility, must legitimize itself and is dependent on immediate, explicit acknowledgement.

Pedagogical Practice and the Performative Logic of the Mealtime Ritual

The mealtime rituals examined here convey diffuse values such as proximity and intimacy, affection and a sense of belonging, which are oriented towards a general type of experience. Moreover, the mealtime rituals involve virtually no ceremonial forms.[6] The other families involved in the research also create a separate sphere of social space for themselves at the dinner table, where they consolidate their collective bond and represent themselves as a unit. In the process, neither the boundaries of this symbolic unity nor the boundaries of the ritual behavior are put to question. With these mealtime rituals, the families do not create a fetish, but nonetheless the ritual does gain a power of its own to which all of the family members (more or less willingly) submit, though not all in the same way or to the same extent.

The mealtime ritual presents the family as a unity with differences, for both familial solidarity, on the one hand, and an asymmetrical and hierarchical structure of authority on the other are maintained. The parents have the rules of the ritual performance at their disposal, and the imposition of boundaries and the assignment of identity in the context of the ritual acts are primarily oriented to the pedagogical, generational difference.

In the Zobel family's secure ritual, generational difference is represented by a magical signifier that at the same time consecrates the father as the highest representative of the family. Whereas here a magical signifier realizes in no insignificant way the performative effect of the mealtime ritual, in the other families the pedagogical skills and the force that are necessary to establish the mealtime ritual or to assign new duties are much more visible. For the Zobel family, the father, who is consecrated in his authority, rarely needs to intervene pedagogically. Hence, his behavior at the breakfast table corresponds almost exactly to behavior typical of him in other situations. In contrast, the mother is less strict and displays much more of her sense of humor outside the context of the ritual performance. The parents do, then, determine the rules of the mealtime rituals, but are themselves subjected to the necessity of orienting their own actions to these rules. Again, this also demonstrates that the behavior of those partners who are on the subordinate level in the asymmetrical order of parental authority is more directly determined and oriented by the rules of the symbolic practice than that of the highest representatives of the familial community.

In addition to the generational difference, gender difference and social class also influence the ritual interactions. These other determinants remain in the background of the performance of generational difference, or, rather, they are dependent on it. Gender difference has a weaker effect on the dividing lines between members of the family during the mealtime ritual. The children mimetically appropriate behavior patterns typical of their parents separately, depending on their sex (cf. Chapter 1 and Chapter 6, this book). In this way, then, gender difference is not so much symbolically represented at the breakfast table; instead, it is embodied in the behavior displayed. The pedagogical action of the parents in the Zobel family reproduces a gender-specific separation typical in Germany between, on the one hand, housework and responsibility for upbringing and, on the other, gainful employment.

---

[6]Assumptions that diffuse values automatically leading to weaker (less ceremonial) or primitive (less ethically founded) magical actions are, nevertheless, dated errors common to some views in ritual theory and religious studies, errors that Mary Douglas, with her examples from practices of the pygmies, attempted to disprove when her study was first published in 1970 (Douglas, 2003, pp. 14–16).

Nevertheless, there is no assignment of identity at the breakfast table according to gender. In this sense, then, the mealtime rituals promote the processing of gender difference and can account for shifts, even though they do not disrupt its social magic.

In the mealtime rituals examined here, it is conspicuous that the sphere of work of the highest representatives remains almost completely excluded from conversation at the table. Whereas the mealtime rituals thus stage a partial separation between the spheres of work and family, no such separation is enacted between the spheres of school and family. The parents' pedagogical action is oriented to producing behavior that complies with the norms dominant at school. In the Zobel family, this manifests itself in the variant of discipline-guided upbringing at the dinner table. The family's membership in a particular social stratum is inculcated and incorporated here. Linguistic competence is valued highly; thus, a competence is favored that is related to the hierarchically organized forms of knowledge at school.[7]

The parents' attempts to exercise control over their children's behavior at school – whether expressed in the form of direct questions, well-informed advice, or general offers of help – can establish dividing lines between the siblings. Although the children try to present themselves to their parents as competent students, whenever they sense that their parents are exploiting the competition between the children to legitimize actions which do not correspond to the rules of the mealtime rituals or do not represent the values of the community adequately, the children support one another to evade parental control or to reject inappropriate use of authority. Pedagogical authority is attained by those who with their behavior succeed in appropriately representing the diffuse family values and in adhering to the basic principles of the ritual performance.

In the mealtime rituals examined here, parental authority proves to be predominantly traditional authority that is familiar and self-evident, but also a form of rational authority, which is preferably legitimized by recourse to personal figures of argumentation. The parents remain dependent on their children's recognition of their authority. In the process, the children themselves sometimes succeed in becoming representatives of the familial community. In this way, at the dinner table they also learn to make claims to authority, to see through legitimizing strategies, and to develop criteria for reliable behavior. Moreover, the mealtime rituals produce a normative interconnection between individual autonomy and collective obligation which does, indeed, limit the self-directedness of the members of the family with respect to the ritual representation of the familial community, but which, as a social experience, is also transferable to other spheres of practice. Hence, one of the most important everyday family rituals can contribute to an individual's potential to criticize authorities outside of the family.[8] In this sense, then, education at the dinner table adheres to the performative logic of: "Become what you are – outside of the

---

[7]The mealtime rituals in the other families studied demonstrate certain peculiarities (especially the mealtime ritual in the Maier family). Nonetheless, with regard to the staging of social differences, for the most part the various families are comparable (Audehm, 2007, pp. 205ff.).

[8]On the significance of mealtime rituals for forming individual autonomy as an ability to criticize authorities outside of the family, cf. Audehm (2004, pp. 224ff.).

family, too" and includes a competent and critical way of dealing with authority! From this perspective, the mealtime ritual appears as a place for negotiating pedagogical authority – within the limits of what has already been habitualized and secured with respect to its social magic by the performative effect of the mealtime rituals.

(Translation: Thomas La Presti)

References

Audehm, K. (2004). Konfirmation. Familienfest zwischen Glauben, Wissen und Können. In C. Wulf (Ed.), *Bildung im Ritual. Schule, Familie, Jugend, Medien* (pp. 211–240). Wiesbaden: VS Verlag für Sozialwissenschaften.

Audehm, K. (2007). *Erziehung bei Tisch. Zur sozialen Magie eines Familienrituals.* Bielefeld: transcript.

Audehm, K., & Velten, H.-R. (2007). Einleitung. In K. Audehm & H.-R., Velten (Eds.), *Transgression – Hybridisierung – Differenzierung. Zur Performativtät von Grenzen in Sprache, Kultur und Gesellschaft* (pp. 9–40). Freiburg, Berlin and Wien: Rombach.

Bourdieu, P. (1992). *Language and symbolic power.* (J.B. Thompson, Ed., G. Raymond and M. Adamson, Trans.). Cambridge and Malden, MA: Polity Press.

Bourdieu, P. (2000). *Pascalian Meditations.* (R. Nice, Trans.). Stanford: Stanford University Press.

Derrida, J. (1976). Signatur. Ereignis, Kontext. In J. Derrida (Ed.), *Randgänge der Philosophie* (pp. 124–155). Frankfurt am Main, Berlin and Wien.

Douglas, M. (2003). *Natural symbols: Explorations in cosmology.* London and New York: Routledge.

Foucault, M. (1991). *Überwachen und Strafen. Die Geburt des Gefängnisses.* Frankfurt am Main: Suhrkamp.

Friebertshäuser, B. (2004). Ritualforschung in der Erziehungswissenschaft. Konzeptionelle und forschungsstrategische Überlegungen. In C. Wulf & J. Zirfas (Eds) *Innovation und Ritual. Jugend, Geschlecht und Schule.* Wiesbaden: Zeitschrift für Erziehungswissenschaft, 2, 29–45.

Geertz, C. (1975). *The interpretation of cultures: Selected essays.* London: Hutchinson.

Haug, F. (2003). Ein Tag in meinem Leben in zwanzig Jahren. Lebensentwürfe von Jugendlichen. In F. Haug & W. Haug (Ed.), *Familie im Neoliberalismus.* Das Argument, 4, 44, 500–522.

Herkommer, S. (2004). *Metamorphosen der Ideologie. Zur Analyse des Neoliberalismus durch Pierre Bourdieu und aus marxistischer Perspektive.* Hamburg: VSA.

Hettlage, R. (1998). *Familienreport: Eine Lebensform im Umbruch.* München: Beck.

Keppler, A. (1995). *Tischgespräche. Über Formen kommunikativer Vergemeinschaftung am Beispiel der Konversation in Familien.* Frankfurt am Main: Suhrkamp.

Turner, V. (1982). *From ritual to theatre: The human seriousness of play.* New York: PAJ.

Weber, M. (1995). *Schriften zur Soziologie* (Ed. by v. M. Sukale). Stuttgart: Reclam.

Chapter 10
School Curriculum as Developmental Resource: Gender and Knowledge

Gabrielle Ivinson

Introduction

This chapter can be located in the growing literature on relational approaches to human development (cf. Kontopodis & Niewöhner, 2011). It argues that school curricula provide cultural resources that act as staging posts for children and young people *en route* to adulthood. Traditionally, scholarship has focused on the role of assessment in terms of tests and examinations as an inevitable measure that young people use to reflect on their progress. They use examination results to judge, "Am I more or less clever, able or talented than my peers?" We have taken a different slant by suggesting that the subject content of, for example, Science and Art, provide symbolic resources for constructing social identities as a "good enough" boy or girl (Ivinson & Murphy, 2007). Accordingly, we bring together historical legacies of knowledge that can be viewed as cultural streams and developmental concerns to suggest how the elements of the school curriculum provide material with which young people anchor themselves, maintain social identities and undertake the process of growing up as well as learning. These two processes, development and learning, are distinct yet intricately linked.

Cultural Historical Aspect of Curriculum

Each subject of the curriculum can be viewed as a cultural stream with a particular historical lineage that intertwines with historical legacies of gender. How legitimate practices are recognised by teachers is intermeshed with the *ideal* learner who historically has been recognised as the legitimate inheritor of the subject. Each element of the curriculum, such as physics, biology, art, drama, music and technology can be viewed as cultural streams in which *who* had access to the subject at *what*

G. Ivinson (✉)
Cardiff School of Social Sciences, Wales, UK
e-mail: ivinsong@Cardiff.ac.uk

M. Kontopodis et al. (eds.), *Children, Development and Education*, International
Perspectives on Early Childhood Education and Development 3,
DOI 10.1007/978-94-007-0243-1_10, © Springer Science+Business Media B.V. 2011

time is still reflected, even if only in a pale form, in the pedagogic subjectivities enacted in subject-specific classrooms today. Carol Patemen (1988) reminds us that the school reflects the social order which traditionally provided upper- and middle-class boys with routes to the public domain via male fraternity. For example, the scientific method became aligned with a particular kind of bourgeois masculinity (Harding, 1998; Walkerdine, 1988, 1989). In the nineteenth century bourgeois femininity was aligned with music and modern languages, the accomplishments required of the wives of gentlemen (Delamont, 1978; Purvis, 1991). In the UK, Design and Technology (D&T), which is a relatively modern school subject, has absorbed traditional crafts such as woodwork and metal work which act as staging posts *en route* to non-middle-class masculinity. Working-class girls generally had little or no education until the end of the nineteenth century. Their main function was to nurture and care for others within the private domain. D&T also absorbed needlework and domestic science, the subjects that previously acted as staging posts *en route* to working-class femininity. For example, our empirical studies suggested that working-class boys were given marginal social identities in science, as were girls (Ivinson & Murphy, 2007). Traditionally, girls who entered the public domain via professional jobs were in danger of being viewed as less than feminine (Delamont, 1978), a fear that has been demonstrated to continue to exert its influence in contemporary classrooms creating conflicts for "high-achieving" girls (Walkerdine, 1989).

Intersections between gender and knowledge involve a double antinomy. Alice Jardine (1985) suggested that femininity eventually came to represent "the not-male", "the other", "nature" and "maternal", which de Beauvoir (1972) termed "the second sex". While masculinity and femininity are continuously reconstructed and redefined in asymmetric relation to each other, so science is re-constructed in relation to other elements of the curriculum that are not science (Bernstein, 1971, 2000). High-status subjects protect themselves from being diluted by contaminating influences such as the "wrong type" of student and the "wrong type" of subject content including moral and spiritual issues. In this respect, science maintains strong boundaries (Bernstein, 1971, 2000) insulated from other subjects of the curriculum and from common sense knowledge(s) of everyday life (Lave, 1988; Walkerdine, 1988). High-status scientific knowledge remains decontextualised, abstract and objective, reflecting a historical legacy associated with pure and elite masculinity. The blurring of these boundaries, for example, when girls exert autonomy in science laboratories can be experienced by teachers as a threat to the social fabric buttressed, as it still is, by heterosexual, oppositional subjectivities (cf. Ivinson and Murphy, 2007, p. 96). Cultural myths of knowledge and gender remain strong and continue to be recreated in everyday classroom practices by teachers and at times by young people. The historical legacies attached to curricular elements are recognisable in the material culture of subject-specific classrooms through artefacts, equipment, furniture, spaces and time intervals. Kress, Jewitt, Ogborn, and Tsatsarelius (2001) have described classrooms as multi-modal contexts that include a range of linguistic and non-linguistic signifiers.

Classroom as Social Semiotic Space

Objects such as Bunsen burners, lathes, sawing machines or romance novels anchor subject cultures in the here and now of everyday classroom life. In order to capture the cultural-historical layering of significance imminent in matter, we can turn to recent work that depicts classrooms as semiotics fields (Bernstein, 2000; Gee, 2003, 2005; Ivinson & Duveen, 2005; Kress et al., 2001; Walkerdine, 1988). Classrooms are multi-modal and multiply layered semiotic fields in which the density of visual, oral, material, pictorial and discursive signifiers varies from one subject to another (cf. Kress et al., 2001, pp. 40–41). We shall show later that when an object such as "an information sheet" in Drama was repeatedly referred to in a girls' class yet when in the equivalent lesson boys were told to ignore the text and use their own imagination instead, then boys and girls were presented with differently textured multimodalities. The material culture of the classroom as well as pictorial clues, carried by artefacts, furniture, texts and equipment act as scaffolding (Wood, Bruner, & Ross, 1976) for students' entry into specialist subject discourse and practices. The use of visual diagrams and concrete artefacts can help to produce shared intersubjectivity between teachers and students. Kontopodis (2007) has demonstrated how visual graphs can provide mediational means to allow students to reflect back on their academic past, orient themselves in the present and project themselves forward. They act as shared resources that can ground and make concrete conversations between students and mentors in ways that otherwise can remain fuzzy and therefore devoid of meaning. Valuing school knowledge requires a student to be able to imagine a future trajectory that is in some way connected to that form of knowledge and for that identity to be valued by groups outside as well as inside school. Young people experience tensions due to the gendered identities carried by various curricular subjects and their own developing gender identities (Ivinson and Murphy, 2007; Walkerdine, 1989).

Valsiner has drawn attention to the dynamic aspect of semiotics as hybrid assemblages that come into view though activity. The use and creation of hybrid assemblages refers to young people's active engagement with the semiotic resources available to them and reflects the processes of mimesis referred to in the introduction (Chapter 1) as well as in Chapter 6. As written in the introduction:

> An important idea implied by cultural-historical research and reflected in concepts such as "mimesis" (Gebauer & Wulf, 1995), "appropriation" (Stetsenko & Arievitch, 2010), "zone of proximal development" (Chaiklin, 2003; Newman & Holzman, 1993), and "motive" (Hedegaard, 2001; Leont'ev, 1978), is *active subjectivity*, which means that children and young people as well as teachers "act according to their own intentions and motivations, actively participating in defining how signs and tools are used (Stetsenko, 2005)" (Chapter 1, this book).

Teachers and young people can realign symbolic elements to form new hybrid assemblages and create new meanings. The gender field is a good example of a ubiquitous, extended and highly available network of messages carried through lay or common sense. Many objects such as machines come already laden with gender values (Haraway, 1991). Through their classroom practice and discourse teachers can highlight or down-play the gendered affordances of artefacts such as sanding machines or Bunsen burners which come already marked as masculine. In doing so teachers can help to draw the past into the present or can override gendered cultural legacies.

Methodology

The study took place in Monks School which had introduced single-sex teaching in the lower schools, years 7–9 (students aged 11–14 years) that provided unusual conditions for exploring the interaction between gender and the construction of subject knowledge. Initial non-participant observations and informal discussions with teachers alerted us to a number of issues. Teachers were concerned that when they presented activities to boys, in comparison to girls' classes, and vice versa, the activities changed and they could not work out why. As researchers, our early observations suggested that the construction of knowledge in boys' and girls' classes was being influenced by gendered connotations attached to some activities, objects and discourses. The organisational structure of the school allowed us to investigate this in a systematic way. We designed an in-depth and highly focused study to investigate how gender was evoked and played out in classroom settings as students undertook activities across three consecutive lessons in English, Design and technology, science and drama classes. A full description of the study can be found in Ivinson and Murphy (2007).

This chapter focuses on drama lessons. The same teacher, Mrs Diamond, was observed teaching the same series of lessons to a boys' and separately a girls' year 8 class in Monks School. We employed non-participant classroom observation and used field notes to record: classroom layout; seating arrangements; movements around the classroom; peer group interaction; material culture, patterns of interaction and samples of classroom discourse. The second lesson in the series of three was video recorded and a sample of students was radiomiked to capture their discourse as they undertook the task (not reported here). Teachers were interviewed after the series of lessons about the aims of the lesson, their expectation of students and their reflections on how well lessons had gone.

We used an iterative research approach that enabled us to describe the way teachers' instructional discourse and practice provided semiotic messages for students. Our study demonstrated that across all four classrooms in Monks School teachers used instructional discourse to mark objects and practices differently in boys' and girls' classes (Ivinson & Murphy, 2007, pp. 94–97). For example, the way a teacher gave instructions about risky materials such as Bunsen burners, lighters and matches provided different messages. Girls were told more often and with more emphasis than boys not to burn themselves, to walk around the room carefully and not to touch anything that might be hot. We used classroom observations of teachers' classroom practices as the stand point from which to observe boys' and girls' practices. After the lessons we conducted individual interviews with a range of students using video footage of the lesson as stimulus prompts. Questions asked students what the teacher expected them to learn, to describe what they had done in lessons and to identify which students had done well and why.

Analysis involved working between our literature on the histories of school subjects, field notes and video footage of teachers' and students' classroom practices as well as individual interview data. We moved between planes (Rogoff, 1995, 2003) using at different points, cultural-historical planes of analysis and individual planes of analysis to demonstrate how teachers reinforced or interrupted historical legacies of curricular subjects through local classroom practice.

Subjectivities and Drama: The Historical and the Local

As a school subject drama has its origins in the experimental schools of the 1920s and the progressive pedagogies of the 1960s although it did not become a widely established school subject in the UK until the 1980s. Debates about school drama revolve around two diametrically opposed definitions of the subject; theatre studies and self-expression. The first approach focuses on technical elements such as lighting, stage-craft and theatre studies. The second emphasises role-play, improvisation, self-expression and knowledge of human relationships extending girls legitimate participation in comparison to boys. Positioned as a peripheral subject, its place in the curriculum is vulnerable and to secure it more firmly drama teachers often opt to cover aspects of the curriculum such as moral education that other subject teachers do not wish to teach. Mrs Diamond, the Head of Drama in Monks School, adopted the approach to drama that privileges self-expression and chose to use drama as a vehicle for moral development. We observed a series of lessons devoted to the topic of school truancy. Mrs Diamond wanted students to reflect about why individuals absent themselves from school and to recognise that it is a bad thing to do. She did not want to dictate this moral position, instead she told us that students' concerns, understandings and values would emerge within role-play. When asked what she valued as a good lesson Mrs Diamond spoke about drama as a community built around each person's active contribution:

> I, ...to have some sort of structure to the discussion which isn't just my question, their answer, but they're listening and they're adding their own viewpoint, their own knowledge to something so that it's growing, the discussion actually grows and is interactive. (Mrs Diamond, Head of Drama, Monk School)

Mrs Diamond introduced each class to a fictional character, Harry Roberts, first through a text, which was a diary of a typical day in the life of a school truant, next using a technique called "hot seating" in which a student played the character of Harry while others took it in turn to question him about why he truanted. In both the boys' and later the girls' class, students started off by sitting in a wide horse-shoe shape with their shoes off. The informal seating arrangements and the lack of shoes had come to signal a particular kind of practical work relating to Drama. As she started the lesson, Mrs Diamond used body postures and gestures such as sweeping the air with her arms to signal the creation of an imaginary place, which also placed a boundary between the fictional world that was being conjured into existence and ordinary classroom life. She anchored the fictional scenario by varying the tone and pitch of her voice, by her posture, facial expression and head movements as well as her instructional talk. Together these elements created a hybrid semiotic assemblage which framed and helped open an imaginary space. Students by this stage in their schooling recognised the assemblage and accepted the invitation to enter the imaginary space. However, there were subtle differences in the way she created the assemblage in the boys' and girls' classes.

Mrs Diamond started by asking the boys twice to think back to the previous lesson. She first said, "everyone is thinking about what their group" followed by a period of silence and then again by saying, "what *your* point of view was about Harry as you saw it. Remember some of the things that *you* said about Harry". In this way she made the boys bring to mind their views about Harry and so validated boys' person ideas. In the equivalent instruction in the girls' class she asked the girls to remember the roles they played in the previous lesson, as follows:

> Okay now, this is the next bit, I want you to think of the character you played last week. Which role did you play and in that role. . . . .So what did your character want to ask Harry? Okay I want you to think back to all that information on the sheet (Mrs Diamond, Head of Drama, Monk School)

She asked the girls to "remember some of the things you said about Harry" including information that had been supplied on a sheet. In the boys' class she placed more emphasis on their personal point of view rather than the information sheet. When she asked the girls to volunteer to play Harry she said:

> Now this is the next bit. I would like someone who can remember some of the details of Harry's life to offer themselves to the next piece of drama.

In comparison she invited the boys to put themselves forward, by saying:

> If you think you could put Harry's point of view across would you like to put your hand up?

In providing two distinct criteria for volunteering to play Harry she intimated that the boys' ability to put Harry's perspective across was valuable while in contrast the girls' ability to remember details from the sheet was valued. Although there were subtle differences in her instructional discourse between the boys' and girls' class, our observations detected a recurring pattern in her practice which amounted to clear differences in the balance she expected between facts and imagination. She encouraged boys to recall their personal views, while the girls were encouraged to recall the facts. By changing the emphasis between remembering facts and using imagination she introduced the activity to girls and boys in different ways.

Anchoring an Imaginative Scenario Through Shared Symbolic Resources

After the first activity students were told to work in groups of about six to create a role-play depicting scenes from "A Day in the Life of Harry Roberts". Groups had a short period of time, approximately 10 minutes, to assign each other roles and plan the scenes to perform to the rest of the class. As with all stories, each group had to find a beginning, middle and end-point. The beginning and the end of the drama had been circumscribed though the teacher's instructions. Mrs Diamond had said that the aim of the drama was either to show what Harry really felt about school or it had to finish with a scenario in which he was confronted with a plan to get him back to school and his reaction to it. The challenge was to construct scenes that would reveal his "feelings" about school and achieve a satisfactory end-point. Many students described the end-point as "the message", which constituted the "moral of the story". The actions in the middle had to prefigure and lead up to the end-point. Planning required groups to achieve a high level of intersubjective meaning in order to construct the imaginative scenarios together. We consider the socio-cultural resources boys and girls accessed to accomplish this, by focussing on, finding a role, the use of visual artefacts and agreeing an "end-point".

Finding a Role

In order for the players in the drama to achieve synchronicity in interaction they needed to know who they were and who they were talking to. Groups started by assigning each other roles such as Harry, the teacher, his mum and his friend. Some of these roles opened up access to well defined and therefore recognisable scripts (Gagnon & Simon, 1973; Plummer, 1995) such as "the authoritarian teacher", "the caring mother" or "the naughty boy". Recognition is like finding the tip of a symbolic iceberg that opens up paths of association that can be brought to the role-play. Once they had identified a recognisable cultural script a range of resources such as typical phrases, gestures and motives became available for acting out the role. Students described how they had used ideas from newspapers and from knowing specific people in their role-play. Gagnon and Simon (1973) point to three levels of scripting, cultural scenarios, interpersonal interactions and interpsychic (fantasies, plans and remembrances). Alec welded together a hybrid assemblage from the cultural scenario "the naughty boy", personal "fantasy" and his knowledge of kids who worked in Forestown market to produce Harry as a "cocky" kid with a loud voice.

Some students did not manage to find well-defined scripts. Emma played "the head of year" and she talked about the problems she had in finding things to say. When boys described problems with finding a role they put it down to not having enough time to prepare, or they blamed a peer for missing a cue. Finding a role was particularly troublesome for Lynne, and we report from her interview in depth later in the paper because it demonstrates the reflective work that girls spoke about which boys did not speak about.

The Use of Visual Artefacts

Objects, accents and roles became available as shared resources for groups and anchored imaginative scenarios in concrete ways. Don described how his group used one boy's blazer as a prop.

> Don We said like for the blanket we use a blazer and everyone just said that and we all
> thought that was a good idea. Then other people just said their ideas and we see if it's good
> ideas between the group. Then if it was, we said yes.

Another example was provided by Alec.

> Alec The way we put some accents on and where we put all the chairs and tables into like a
> stall and we were talking quite well.

Objects such as blazers and chairs were appropriated and semiotically marked
by the group with a new meaning that the group could collectively share. Boys, yet
not girls, also spoke about techniques such as "speaking loudly", "coming in on
cue" and using props. Funny voices, cultural scripts and the use of objects allowed
boys to create a high level of intersubjective meaning. The imaginative scenario
became anchored in concrete and symbolic ways. The girls did not achieve such
high levels of intersubjective meanings as the boys because roles, scripts and the
messages became matters of debate and personal reflection. The biggest obstacle
for the girls was to find an agreed end-point.

Agreeing an End-Point

The teacher had presented Harry as a naughty boy because he truanted from school.
The boys accepted this at face value and constructed a drama to show Harry being
naughty as Paul explained, "She wanted us to find out that it is better to go to school
than not go to school". Sam said that the teacher wanted, "For us to understand we
should go to school and that all boys that skip school in the end they will get in
trouble. Like bunking or losing their job". Boys understood the activity as the need
to translate a *given* message into action.

Girls on the other hand did not take the message as given. Indeed for them drama
was about trying to work out why Harry did not attend school. They debated and dis-
agreed about what Harry's motives might have been for truanting. When we asked
girls what the teacher wanted them to learn in drama, they repeatedly talked about
the need to accept that there are many different viewpoints.

Emma	That people can not want to go to school for many different reasons like bullying, or they just don't want to go to school, nothing interests them so they may want a change of school or they're just not happy and might need to be taught at home.
Researcher	And what's your view about learning that kind of thing in school?
Emma	I think it's quite important to do,
Researcher	Why?
Emma	How different, why different people don't want to go to school or if they do want to go to school and why … if not why not?

The disagreement in the girls' group about Harry's motive for not attending
school did not get resolved. By failing to agree upon the motive, the end-point
of the drama did not become a shared and fixed meaning. Girls spoke about the
need to compromise in group work and many talked about the personal cost of this.

They spoke at length about the problems of presenting ideas to the group that were overlooked, which did not get fully explored and which in the end were lost.

> Emma We worked quite well, but when we were discussing it, some people wanted their ideas in it and some people didn't like those ideas so we had to compromise a lot.

In effect "compromise" became the main work that the girls undertook. This was because within drama, girls understood the task as the need to work out hidden motives behind actions such as truanting. None of the boys spoke about compromise although we observed them having to compromise in their group work. Boys recognised the role-play activity as a need to get the message across rather than debating what the message was.

An Individual Plane of Analysis: Lynne's Account

Even though Mrs Diamond introduced the drama activities to boys and girls in different ways, the ways specific individuals recognised the hybrid assemblages of the drama setting varied greatly. This section focuses primarily on Lynne who played Harry's class teacher. In the boys' class, Dave reflected on the role of class teacher by saying:

> It was fairly easy because you know roughly how to act like them because they teach you everyday. (Dave: Boys year 8 Drama class)

Lynne started off by saying that she thought she had played the role of the teacher quite well. During her interview Lynne started reflecting on her role by talking about her personal experience of school that day. She said she had had quite a bad day and felt very "tetchy". In trying to work out how to play the teacher she considered being strict. Being strict is part of the available cultural script of the "authoritarian teacher".

> I think it was quite difficult because when you're not a teacher, it can be quite like, you're trying to sort of think now what (they are like) but they're probably not really like what you see them as. So you're trying to figure it out, how to sort it out. And I'm trying to sort of think, well because I've had a bad day, I think right I'm going to be quite hard but I'm going to be quite soft as well and just think right well, teachers can't punish them for everything they do, so () one small thing. Okay, you've had a warning sort of thing and next time you will be in trouble. You can't really act a teacher unless you *are* a teacher. I think because I mean people will say oh this is what it's like to be a teacher when they're not a teacher and the teacher will say it's nothing like that. It can be enjoyable, but it can also be awful. (Lynne, year 8 girls' Drama lesson, Monks School)

Her account revealed the tension between the cultural script of the "authoritarian teacher" and her concerns with authenticity. She reflected on what a "real" teacher might say about their job, "The teacher will say it's nothing like that. It can be enjoyable, but it can also be awful". She seemed to be concerned that her own "tetchy" mood might have influenced her to play the teacher as strict. Her reflexive awareness of her mood and her inability to accept the cultural script of the "authoritarian teacher" meant that it was not as easy for her to get into role and stay within it, unlike

Dave who did not reflect on his role-playing in this way. Instead she described the way she worried about who she was and at times this meant that she did not know what to say and at others she felt she was being "too bossy". Later in the interview she talked at length of her self-consciousness as a performer.

> Well I find if I do anything in front of a lot of people, especially if I'm on my own I get very nervous and a bit sort of all up tight but that scene, we hadn't even planned that. . . .and when I get nervous I often stutter with my words and I can't say them but I thought it wasn't bad I mean () oh just sit down for goodness sake. If I get nervous I just sort of think right look I've got to just do this, I don't really have a choice, just don't think you're just singing or whatever on your own. Nobody's listening and just get on with it. . . .But I often waffle. So it kind of when it goes on I sort of like waffle, repeating myself, I suppose I always do that, it's just the way I am. (Lynne, year 8 girls' Drama lesson, Monks School)

She depicts a struggle with herself to stay calm and "get on with it". In this extract she is clearly aware of the class as the others who may or may not judge her performance harshly. Her fantasy is that she will humiliate herself in front of her peers. Throughout her account her reflections became more complex involving an increasing number of "others". Her reflection involved: herself in role as the teacher; herself in relation to "real" teachers; herself reflecting other girls in her group acting; herself on the need to compromise; herself reflecting on her own actions as she acted; herself in front of the class acting; herself as a member of the class. We recognised her struggle to work out "who am I". She also reflected on what the teacher was looking for, which she said was to work out what is "really wrong with Harry".

Yet along with other girls we interviewed, she spoke about the need, "not to let the teacher down". Girls and not boys were taking responsibility for making sure the lesson went well by imagining what it was like to be the teacher. Girls' over-identification with teachers has been noted by other researchers (Walkerdine, 1989). Girls' excessive reflexive work, we have argued, prevented girls from partaking in the more playful aspects of drama and kept them bound to "real" life concerns and thoughts about others rather than being able to build and fully enter into fantasy worlds in the ways that the boys could.

Discussion

It could be argued that the type of drama that privileges self-expression is a cultural stream that is more in line with femininity than masculinity. According to Mrs Diamond, the aim of the drama was to make students reflect on Harry's motive for truanting and by doing so to reflect on their own behaviour. The accumulated messages in the boys' and girls' classes presented the activity in two different ways, even though Mrs Diamond reported to us that she was teaching the same lesson to both classes. In the girls' class, she insisted that they work out what Harry's "real" problem or motive for truanting was, and to act this out through scenarios. It was particularly noticeable that the girls in general worked hard at this aspect of the drama while the boys ignored it.

Mrs Diamond allowed the boys more autonomy, privileged their ideas above her lesson aims and made sure that there was time to allow each of the boys' groups to fully enact their role-play before the end of the lesson. In the girls' class, Mrs Diamond initiated a discussion after the third group had performed about why they had changed Harry to Harriett, and the bell went before two groups had performed. In interviews girls suggested that the name change was trivial from their perspective. In interview we asked Mrs Diamond why she had made sure all the boys' groups performed yet not all girls' groups.

> Umm it would be different for different lessons I think, I think it's a kind of *gut reaction* on my part to see what's the main aim here you know. I think that's, I think the boys' group there was quite umm I don't know that was *quite a pressing need for them,* it was a need for them to feel that it *was fair*, that everybody had you know had their opportunity. Whereas, I mean this is my perception, it could be wrong who knows, but *the girls had brought up issues* that you know, that were ones that were perhaps a bit I don't know, a bit too (??) but they'd expressed them in a *verbal way* so I suppose I went with that. (Mrs Diamond, emphasis added)

She described the "gut feeling" that performing was important to boys and was an issue of fairness. Mrs Diamond's seemingly intuitive decision to make sure all the boys performed yet prioritised discussion over performance in the girls' class can be viewed as a spontaneous act which nevertheless aligned with a deep cultural legacy of valuing boys' performances, and places in the public domain, more highly than girls' (cf. Pateman, 1988). In practice her *gut feeling* can be said to have worked below the level of conscious awareness.

Girls achieved fewer intersubjective markers which made it difficult for their role-play to take off into a shared imaginary realm. Instead they remained focussed on "real" problems in "real" social contexts. Because the fantasy aspects of the role-play were not well anchored through shared cultural resources the girls remained caught between two worlds: reality and fantasy. This was in line with our observations throughout the wider study that in school girls have less fun, mess about less and therefore experience flights of fancy less than boys and when they try to teachers censor them far more than boys. Girls got to exercise their imagination, autonomy and playfulness far less than boys (Ivinson & Murphy, 2007).

By colluding with the boys in not insisting that they think about what was "really" wrong with Harry the teacher allowed the boys to by-pass the need to take responsibility and to care. She tolerated and even sanctioned the negation of the feminine cultural elements of the activity. This allowed the boys to create a fantasy scenario in which the archetypal "naughty boy" was played out according to dominant and easily available scripts. Through the use of these shared symbolic resources the boys' fantasy took flight, as it were, leaving the "real" world of motives, responsibility and caring behind.

Curriculum as Symbolic Material

A relational approach to development and indeed to learning recognises that in order to achieve a sense of forward movement young people draw on the culturally available resources to map and represent change (Rogoff, 2003). In this paper we have shown how Drama was enacted in classrooms as a series of material-discursive practices (Barad, 2003, p. 18 cited in Kontopodis, 2007, p. 3). This has been operationalised as complex, multi-modal semiotic message systems that go beyond discourse to take account of the material, pictorial, iconic (Kress et al., 2001) and enacted messages such as gesture (Duncan, Cassell, & Levy, 2007). Cultural legacies are drawn into the present through a range of signifiers that align in movement for individuals as hybrid assemblages. Much of the emergence of gender in classroom practice happens beyond or below the level of discourse. Objects of the material culture of the classroom, along with patterns of practice and discourse combine to form hybrid semiotic assemblages that come into view in activity (Valsiner, 2006).

The young people's improvisation, such as Alex's performance of Harry Roberts, the school truant, created new meanings within assemblages, drawing on his experience of a real-life market, from highly available cultural scripts such as "the naughty boy" and material available in the drama studio such as chairs to signal the school bus. However, Alex's improvisation did not necessarily break with the past. Indeed, his hybrid assemblage reproduced, yet in a new form, a hegemonic social representation of masculinity (Connell, 1987). We saw how through improvisation and autonomy, indeed by ignoring the teachers' intentions to address the moral issue surrounding truancy, the boys were creative, had fun yet gained no new insights into the moral issue of truanting. Yet, Alex went away from the lesson with a strong sense of forward movement provided by a sense of being "good at drama". He told us that the other boys kept talking about his role-play days after the lesson. In terms of masculinity he was more than a "good enough" boy and he went away with a sense of satisfaction and pride. This was in one sense a developmental move forward, yet it was not a move forward in academic learning.

Lynne understood drama as a subject in which students were expected to learn about people and life including the psychology of emotions and behaviour. Her experience of drama aligned with wider cultural legacies about the caring and containing role of women in society. The effort of compromise was considerable. Lynne spoke about: having to put ideas forward even if they were rejected by the group; having to compromise her views to accommodate others "without going off in a strop"; disorganisation and having to deal with people dominating in the group. She spoke more than once in the interview about having no choice, having to get on with it and having to overcome her nervousness in relation to performing. She said, "I don't really have a choice". Lynne associated the performance with a need to take into account Mrs Diamond's position. She said, "You have to think of the teacher". She spoke of realising a performance as a kind of moral duty. She rationalised her fear of performing publicly by telling herself that she was not on her own: "just don't think you're just singing or whatever on your own".

Her account portrayed the messiness of producing a performance and the disorganisation of the group that was linked to the problem of finding a clear message. In the broader study we found that because girls worried more than boys about the psychological authenticity of the motive, the end-point of the role-play was less easy to imagine and the girls failed to create a consensus about what Harry's "real" problem was. In contrast the boys assumed that the end-point of the role-play was to persuade Harry to stop truanting and none of the boys' groups we observed spent any time discussing what Harry's "real motive" for truanting might have been. In the boys' groups the end-point of the role-play was the undisputed "fact" that had been given in Mrs Diamond's instruction. Accordingly the imaginary scenario was more strongly anchored than in the girls' group and this left the boys free to concentrate on props, timing and funny voices. Lynne did not feel that she had produced a good performance. Instead she identified with the teacher's predicament by trying to achieve a performance even although she would expose herself as unprepared, not good and even scared.

Lynne was left in a quagmire of ambiguity and some distress. Yet, according to Mrs Diamond's lesson aim she had grappled with many moral dilemmas. The problem for us as observers was that these were neither recognised nor legitimated by the teacher. Indeed they remain hidden, part of the long tradition of young women's heritage in education, struck in compromising roles. She was perhaps overly engaged with "real" social problems with less down time for play than the boys and received no recognition for these efforts. While the multimodality of subject classrooms provides symbolic resources that are used by students to show creativity, nemesis and improvisation, we cannot lose sight of power dynamics. Cultural pasts carried by different forms of knowledge that make up elements of the curriculum do not come to us as neutral resources but as value-laden. Deeply entrenched gender values still colour pedagogic subjectivities given and enacted in classrooms today. The task of teaching as Mariane Hedegaard and Seth Chaiklin (2007) have reminded us, requires a double move; first to engage the imagination and then to provide intellectual challenge, in which boys as well as girls, are confronted with difficult moral as well as technical and scientific problems.

References

Bernstein, B. (1971) *Class, codes and control. Volume 1: Theoretical studies towards a sociology of language*. London: Routledge.

Bernstein, B. (2000) *Pedagogy, symbolic control and identity: Theory, research, critique* (rev. ed.). London: Rowen and Littlefield.

Chaiklin, S. (2003). The zone of proximal development in Vytgotsky's analysis of learning and instruction. In A. Kozulin, B. Gindis, V. Ageyey, & S. Miller (Eds.), *Vygotsky's educational theory in cultural context* (pp. 39–64). Cambridge: Cambridge University Press.

Connell, R. (1987). *Gender and power: Society, the person and sexual politics*. Cambridge: Polity Press.

de Beauvoir, S. (1972). *The second sex*. Harmonsworth: Penguin.

Delamont, S. (1978). The contradiction in ladies' education. In S. Delamont & L. Duffin (Eds.), *Nineteenth-century woman*. London: Croom Helm.

Duncan, S. D., Cassell, J., & Levy, E. T. (Eds.). (2007). *Gesture and the dynamic dimension of language*. Amsterdam and Philadelphia: John Benjamins Publishing Company.

Gagnon, J. H., & Simon, W. (1973). *Sexual conduct: The social source of human sexuality*. Chicago: Aldine.

Gebauer, G., & Wulf, C. (1995). *Mimesis: Culture, art, society*. Berkeley: University of California Press.

Gee, P. J. (2003) *What video games have to tell us about learning and language.* Basingstoke: Palgrave Macmillan.

Gee, P. J. (2005) Semiotic social spaces and affinity spaces: From the age of mythology to today's schools. In D. Barton & K. Tusting (Eds.), *Beyond communities of practice: Language, power and social context.* Cambridge: Cambridge University Press.

Haraway, D. (1991). *Simians, Cyborgs, and women: The reinvention of nature.* New York: Routledge.

Harding, J. (1998). *Sex acts: Practices in femininity and masculinity.* London: Sage

Hedegaard, M. (2001). *Learning in classrooms: A cultural-historical approach.* Aarhus: Aarhus University Press.

Hedegaard, M., & Chaiklin, S. (2007). *Radical-local teaching and learning: A cultural-historical approach.* Aarhus: Aarhus University Press.

Ivinson, G., & Duveen, G. (2005). Classroom structuration and the development of representations of the curriculum. *British Journal of Sociology of Education, 26*(5), 627–642.

Ivinson, G, & Murphy, P. (2007). *Rethinking single-sex settings: Gender, subject knowledge and learning.* Buckingham: McGrawHill, Open University Press.

Jardine, A. (1985). *Gynesis: Configurations of woman and modernity.* Ithaca, NY: Cornell University Press.

Kontopodis, M. (2007). Human development as semiotic-material ordering: Sketching a relational developmental psychology? *Critical Social Studies, 9*(1), 5–20.

Kontopodis, M., & Niewöhner, J. (Eds.). (2011). Das Selbst als Netzwerk: Zum Einsatz von Körpern und Dingen im Alltag. Bielefeld: transcript.

Kress, G., Jewitt, C., Ogborn, J., & Tsatsarelius, C. (2001). *Multimodal teaching and learning: The rhetorics of the science classroom.* London and New York: Continuum.

Lave, J. (1988). *Cognition in practice.* Cambridge: Cambridge University Press.

Leont'ev, A. (1978). *Activity, consciousness, and personality.* Englewood Cliffs, NJ: Prentice and Hall.

Newman, F., & Holzman, L. (1993). *Lev Vygotsky: Revolutionary scientist.* London: Routledge.

Pateman, C. (1988). *The sexual contract.* Cambridge: Polity Press.

Plummer, K. (1995). *Telling sexual stories: Power and change and social worlds.* London: Routledge.

Purvis, J. (1991). *A history of women's education in England.* Milton Keynes: Open University Press.

Rogoff, B. (1995). Observing sociocultural activity on three planes: Participatory appropriation, guided participation, and apprenticeship. In J. V. Wertsch, P. Del Rio, & A. Alvarez, (Eds.), *Sociocultural studies of mind.* Cambridge: Cambridge University Press.

Rogoff, B. (2003). *The cultural nature of human development,* Oxford: Oxford University Press.

Stetsenko, A. (2005). Activity as object-related: Resolving the dichotomy of individual and collective planes of activity. *Mind, Culture and Activity, 12*(1), 70–88.

Stetsenko, A., & Arievitch, I. (2010). Cultural-historical activity theory: Foundational world-view and major principles. In J. Martin & S. Kirschner (Eds.), *Sociocultural Perspectives in Psychology* (pp. 231–253). New York, NY: Columbia University Press.

Valsiner, J. (2006, June, 12). *The overwhelming world: Functions of pleromatization in creating diversity in cultural and natural constructions.* Paper given at the International Summer School of Semiotic and Structural Studies, Imatra.

Walkerdine, V. (1988). *The mastery of reason.* London and New York: Routledge.

Walkerdine, V. (1989). *Counting girls out.* London: Virago.

Chapter 11
Configuration of Ontologies: An Inquiry into Learning Designs

Estrid Sørensen

A few years ago, I took part in an EU project aimed at converting the US American *5th Dimension* learning environment into European contexts[1]. 5th Dimension was developed in the 1980s in Southern California by Activity Theorists Michael Cole and Peg Griffin (1984). Since then, the computer-intensive after-school programme has been taken up by researchers and schools in various states in the USA as well as in countries abroad. Apart from computers and computer games, 5th Dimension involves a number of artefacts designed to mediate children's activity in the programme. These artefacts are the focus of this chapter.

One of the central principles of 5th Dimension is its emphasis on local adaptation. At the turn of the century, a number of scholars from Spain, Sweden and Denmark came together to set up 5th Dimension programmes in our countries. We had the task of adapting the programme to the particular conditions of our local schools and cultures. One of the several 5th Dimension sites realised as part of the EU-funded project was *Femtedit*.

Femtedit modified and integrated the variety of artefacts applied in the 5th Dimension concept into a digital environment. The core technology of Femtedit was an Internet-based 3D virtual environment where 4th grade children from Denmark and Sweden met to build up the virtual world also named Femtedit. More than moving from analogue to digital technology, the move to Femtedit was a move from Activity Theory to Actor-Network Theory (ANT). As such Femtedit was about the *configuration* of the child, while 5th Dimensions aims to *scaffold* the child. This chapter is about this difference. It is about the practical question of how different learning designs configure the ontology of the child differently, and it is about the theoretical question of what an artefact is, and in what ways we may think of artefacts as contributing to the constitution of the child, and other ontologies. As such, it is a discussion of Activity Theory and ANT. It is not symmetrical, since the

E. Sørensen (✉)
Ruhr-Universtiät Bochum, Bochum, Germany
e-mail: estrid.sorensen@rub.de

[1] The project was titled "5th Dimension: Local Learning in a Global World", and it was funded by the EU 5th Frame Programme

M. Kontopodis et al. (eds.), *Children, Development and Education*, International Perspectives on Early Childhood Education and Development 3, DOI 10.1007/978-94-007-0243-1_11, © Springer Science+Business Media B.V. 2011

vocabulary applied in the analysis is that of ANT, and indeed, the aim is to suggest a widening of the concept of the artefact in Activity Theory.

The chapter starts with an introduction to 5th Dimension, followed by a presentation of the ANT-inspired analytical frame which is then applied in the analysis of the artefacts of 5th Dimension. Subsequently, I turn to Femtedit and explain our reasons for discontinuing the 5th Dimension design and for developing Femtedit. Finally, Femtedit is presented and compared to 5th Dimension. I conclude the chapter by discussing the Activity Theory conception of artefact.

5th Dimension

The 5th Dimension concept and the first 5th Dimension after-school activities were established in 1986 in San Diego, USA, by Michael Cole, professor in cultural psychology at the University of California. 5th Dimension was a computer-mediated programme combining education and play for school children, as well as constituting an object of study for both university researchers and undergraduate students. In Star and Griesemer's (1989) terms, 5th Dimension can be characterised as a boundary object serving the agendas of several different groups. Computer games had a central role in 5th Dimension, and for children the playing of these games was accompanied by the interaction with undergraduate students who took part in the activity as well as with researchers. Moreover, a number of artefacts were scaffolding (Rogoff & Wertsch, 1984) the activity, establishing Zones of Proximal Development (Vygotsky, 1978) for the children.

Now, 20 years later, 5th Dimension is a thoroughly developed and well-described concept and design of computer-mediated after-school activity. It has been an extremely fertile ground for both discussing and developing design. While most design studies of Computer-Supported Collaborative Learning (CSCL) are inspired by Activity Theory, 5th Dimension was developed as an Activity Theory learning design even before CSCL was founded. Contrary to CSCL-scholars who tend to discuss a variety of different designs, scholars involved with 5th Dimension have spent two decades deepening the discussions and explorations of a relatively uniform design[2] (Ito, 1997; Kaptelinin & Cole, 2002; Nocon, 2005; Nocon, Nielsson, & Cole, 2004). Academic literature on 5th Dimension focuses, among other things, on sustainability, collaboration, local adaptation, learning and guidance. However, even though 5th Dimension is an artefact-rich environment, the artefacts involved in 5th Dimension are only rarely the focus of academic scrutiny. This paper remedies this. It shows how decisive the artefacts are for the practices unfolded in 5th Dimension, and it argues for a more thorough integration of artefacts in the understanding of practice.

---

[2]There are indeed variations in the ways in which the 5th Dimension design has been shaped through the years and across geographical places, not the least due to the 5th Dimension principle that each "site" must adapt to local settings while implementing general principles of the 5th Dimension design. In spite of the local differences, a continuity of the 5th dimension design is evident.

Method

The description of 5th Dimension below takes a design perspective. Activity Theory emphasises that children must be studied in their natural environment, contrary to mainstream psychology's extended use of laboratory experiments (Cole, 1996). It is important to highlight this "natural" method providing an alternative to the majority of studies on child development that tend to neglect that thinking, learning and motivation are embedded in children's practices. However, the focus on children's situated practices tend to overlook that also phenomena absent from those practices take part in constituting such practices.

Designers – as well as researchers discussing design, as we did in the EU project group – necessarily operate on the basis of an idea of how the environment is in which the design is to be inserted as well as an imaginary of its user. Moreover, this imaginary needs to depict a *generalised* image of this environment and its users. A representation of the multiple ways in which a design can possibly be applied is not a practical resource for designing a learning environment. This does not mean that an incorrect representation of user environments is applied in the designing process, but rather that representations work as a resource for designing rather than being correspondences of user environments (Suchman, 2007). Such representations are not only at work in design practices. When users are confronted with a design for the first time they apply a representation of a generalised way in which the design is to be used as a resource for doing so (Akrich, 1992). A representation does not prescribe the way in which he or she will relate to the design. It works as a resource, allowing a particular situated version of the design-in-use to be enacted in the interplay with users and their environment.

My analysis takes a design perspective by investigating the ways in which the user – artefact relationship is represented in the design rather than by looking at the design-in-use. Different representations can be generated in different practices, and the representations I create below gain their particular characteristics by emerging from an analytical practice that takes the whole design into account, which will rarely be the case in design and use practices. It is, however, not unlikely that design and use practices may generate similar or partly corresponding representations. The validity of the analysis must be evaluated in terms of its ability to relate to particular design and use practices as a resource for reflection on and intervention in design configurations.

With inspiration from Actor-Network Theory (Latour, 2005; Pickering, 1995), I describe the representation of the user – artefact relationship of 5th Dimension by analysing the *distribution of agency* between artefacts and humans inscribed in the design. The distribution of agency is given through the way artefacts are interrelated, through the *configuration* of artefacts. The material-semiotic (Law, 2009) notion of *configuration* leads us to focus not on the individual artefacts, but on the way in which artefacts relate to each other and the pattern they form when coming together (Sørensen, 2007). Concerning the root of the term "configuration", Haraway (1997) notes:

The "figure" is the French term for the face, a meaning kept in English in the notion of the
lineaments of a story. To figure means to count or calculate and also to be in a story, to have
a role… (Haraway, 1997, p.11)

Applying the notion of "figure" we are directed towards thinking about not what
the 5th Dimension artefacts mean to human beings, but what role they play in
relation with (con) the other artefacts; thus the notion of *con*figuration.

Most of the artefacts I describe below are part of several existing and working 5th Dimensions. Artefacts that are more rarely used are omitted from the
description. Each 5th Dimension site is different, and even when they use the
same artefacts, these show variations from site to site. For instance, "the maze"
is differently designed in different 5th Dimensions. In one it is formed as a papier
mâché mountain; in another it consists of a poster on the wall, a third has created
a wooden maze, and in another it is made of cardboard (Cole, 1996). Some 5th
Dimensions do not apply mazes. Similarly, many of the other artefacts, roles and
rules described below are present, in one form or the other, in some, but not all 5th
Dimensions. When no other source is mentioned, the description below draws on
the 5th Dimension Clearinghouse website, which has unfortunately been disconin-
ued, but that involved descriptions of various different 5th Dimension sites. This is
also the source of the figures that are reproduced in this chapter with permission
from Willian Blanton.

The Artefacts of 5th Dimension

This section is divided into three subsections that each describe a number of classic
5th Dimension artefacts and the configurations they form together.

Maze, Task Cards and Consequence Card

Each child attending 5th Dimension has a little figurine that he or she can place in
any of the four entrance rooms of a big wooden *maze*. The figurine indicates the
child's position in the maze. Two large posters hang on the wall of 5th Dimension.
One of them is a map of the maze. It shows the rooms and doors of the maze, and in
each room are written a few names of computer games, edutainment programmes
and board games. Figure 11.1 shows that if a child for example places her figurine
in the lower right room, she can choose to play either *Jenny's Journey* or *Word
Munchers*, or try the *Learn about Counting* edutainment programme. If she chooses
Jenny's Journey, she picks the game from a shelf and runs it on a computer. She
will also go to the box of *task cards* to find the card that is associated with *Jenny's
Journey*.

Figure 11.2 shows a task card. Each game or programme to which the maze leads
has an associated task card divided into *beginner*, *good* and *expert* levels. The child
may choose to play *Jenny's Journey* at the level she likes. First, she must read the
story that introduces the task card and the computer game. If she chooses beginners

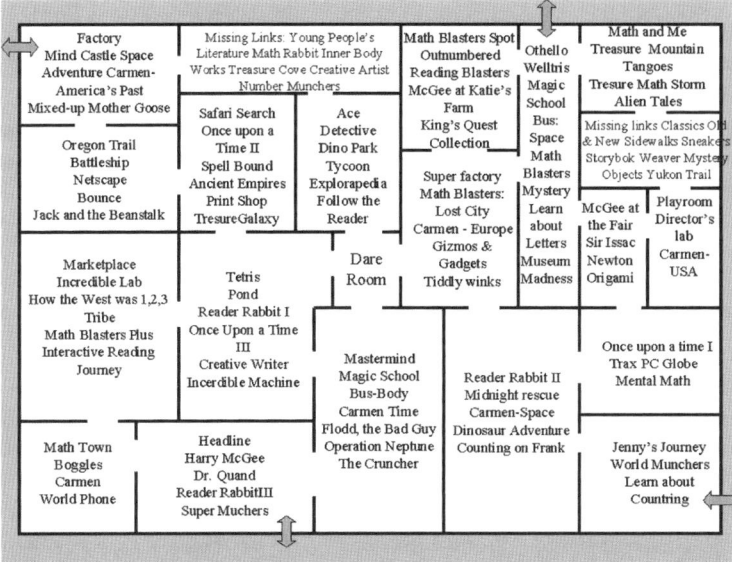

Fig. 11.1 Map of maze with names of conventional and computer games and edutainment programs. The four double arrows indicate the entrances and exits of the maze

level, she must accomplish the tasks on the task card described under this level in addition to playing the game. In the case of Jenny's Journey, this involves (a) reading the General Information, (b) looking up certain words, (c) thinking about the directions of a map and drawing a diagram, (d) naming two streets, (e) writing out a set of directions, and (f) playing certain parts of the game. The "good" and "expert" levels involve other tasks. Notice that one of the tasks under "good" asks the child to write to the *Wizard* (see below) about how she feels about running into certain problems. Task card tasks may also involve such assignments as making a video or doing artwork about the strategies used and knowledge gained while playing the game or while accomplishing the tasks on the task card. The child is not allowed to move on to other activities in 5th Dimension before completing the tasks on the task card.

After playing the game and completing the tasks of the task card, the child must look at the second poster on the wall, which like the first poster maps the maze. This poster is called the *consequence card*. The consequence card shown in Fig. 11.3 reveals that the lower right room, in which we imagined entering a figurine, has the number 6. According to the consequence map, accomplishing Jenny's Journey on beginner's level allows her to proceed to room 8. Going back to the map of the maze in Fig. 11.1, we can see that room 8 allows the participant to choose between playing *Reader Rabbit II*, *Midnight Rescue*, *Carmen-Space*, *Dinosaur Adventure* and *Counting on Frank*. If she had accomplished the game on the good level, she could have proceeded to room 8 or 16, and accomplishments on expert level would add the options of going to rooms 17 and 7.

Jenny's Journey

There are many things a person has to remember to do in a day. Sometimes there are so many we have to make a list to remind us where we have to be. It is your duty to try and complete a list of things to do AND complete them in an organized way so as not to backtrack. Backtracking will lose time, points, and YOU MAY NOT finish all the errands you have been asked to complete. Good luck and make sure you understand your directions!

> •• *RUNS ON AN APPLE II+, IIe, or IIGS.* ••
> •• *YOU WILL NEED TO GET AUNT JENNY'S MAP!* ••

BEGINNER:
Welcome to a day of shopping adventures with your Aunt Jenny...and of course some trips by yourself. Read <u>Selection #5: General Information</u> before you begin your first journey! Notice any keywords like:
　　　　detour
　　　road work
　　　dead end
　　　　map
　　random hazards
　　intersection
What do these words mean? If you don't know, look them up!!!!

Think of how North, South, East, and West are arranged on a map or compass and draw a diagram to help keep you oriented.

Prepare to go on a Short Errand with Aunt Jenny. Use the map of Lake City, your compass diagram, and a toy to follow your path!
　　　　•••
Name two streets you crossed while on your journey. Go on a second short journey (#2) with Aunt Jenny.

Write out a set of directions so Aunt Jenny can get from your house to your school!

GOOD:
You are ready for a Journey Across Town (#3)! Be sure to use the map of Aunt Jenny's neighbourhood.
　　　　•••
Did you get through the journey without running out of gas? How much gas did you have when you finished your Short Errand?
　　　　•••
Put an X on any intersection on the map and explain what an intersection is.

With a pencil, get your map of Lake City. Begin at the airport: mark an Z and head NORTH one block; then EAST three blocks. Where do you end up?

When you have completed your journey, write to the Wizard about your journey. Sometimes the Wizard messes up your plans by causing detours. Tell the Wizard how you feel about running into these problems.

EXPERT:
Take a Journey Across Town (#3)!
　　　　•••
By now you love driving and are ready to go on a "Shopping Trip" (#4) by yourself!!!!!
　　　　•••
Take a good look at the map of Aunt Jenny's neighbourhood. How much gas did you have at the end of your Shopping Trip?

Now, take a look at the map of the North County and Solana Beach.

If Carlsbad is in grid 13, what grid number should the Boy's & Girl's Club be in? Put an X where the Boys and Girls Club is located.

What grid number do you live in?

Place an X where you live.

Congratulations on you excellent driving and navigating skills!

Fig. 11.2 Task card for Jenny's journey (reproduced by author from 5th Dimension Clearinghouse Original)

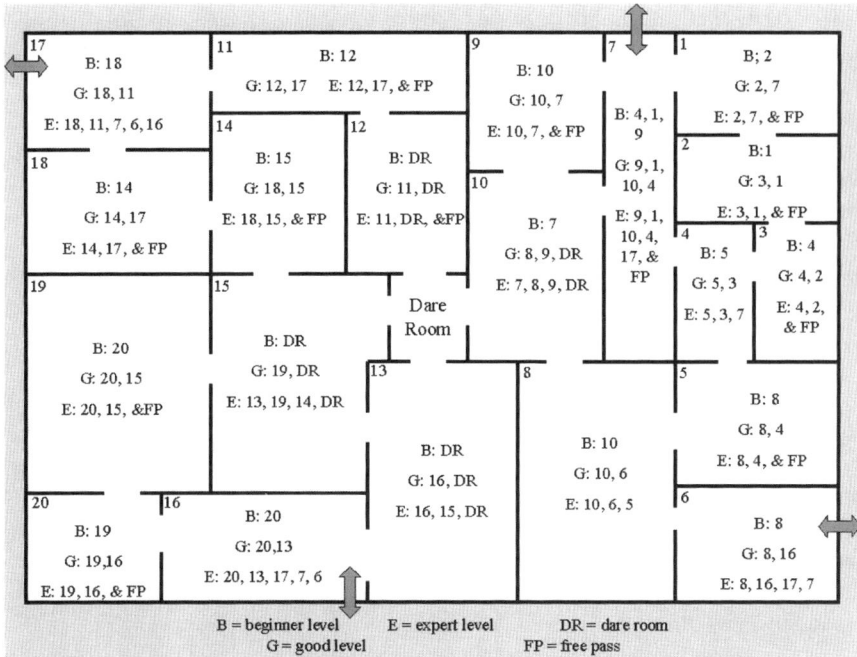

Fig. 11.3 The consequence card shows which room a child has to move to after finishing a game on either beginners (B), good (G) or expert (E) level

Ideally the child considers the consequence card before entering a room and before choosing the level. This allows her or him to outline a goal-directed path through the maze and through his desired activities (Cole, 1996). To keep track of which games the child has played on which levels, a *task card log* is filled out. Each child has his or her personal task card log that allows knowledge about the position and travel of the child to be preserved. When a minimum of 20 games has been completed, of which ten must be on expert level, the child becomes a *Young Wizard's Assistant* (Cole, 1996, p. 292).

The Maze Configuration

Latour offers the notion of *delegation* to draw attention to the work passed on from one person or thing to another (Latour, 1987, Jim Johnson (a.k.a. Bruno Latour), 1995). In this case, we can use the term to describe how the work of determining and remembering the child's position in the maze is delegated to the figurine. The figurine is in charge of that. The delegation of remembering the position of the child to the figurine has the advantage that neither the child, the researcher, the site-worker, a memo nor anyone or anything else has to remember the current activities of the child. Instead they can invest their efforts in other things.

However, the delegation of work is not without consequences. In Latour's vocabulary, the human or nonhuman to whom or which a work is delegated is a *spokesperson* who speaks on behalf of the person or thing it represents. The figurine does not speak much, but with its material presence it indicates the position of the child. Latour emphasises that any spokesperson will always express the message of the human or nonhuman he represents in its own way. When delegated to a spokesperson, the message undergoes *translation* (Law, 1994; Brown & Capdevilla, 1999; Callon, 1986). By its visual presence the figurine draws attention to the child's position in a different way than the child's memory would have, had it been in charge of remembering his or her position. The latter would be tacit and invisible until the child spoke it out. Translated through the figurine, knowledge of the position of the child is made public.

The figurine inhabits the maze. But note this: without the maze and the map of the maze the figurine cannot disclose anything about the position of the child. The maze and the map of the maze together sort the computer games. They separate the games into 20 rooms, whereby the possibility – indeed the necessity – of engaging in a journey is created for the child. However, the children cannot move freely through the maze, going to the room they fancy, picking the computer game they want. The consequence card sets up boundaries between the rooms, blocking passages between some rooms and opening passages between others. In other words, the consequence card lays out routes that specify the distances that must be travelled to come from one room to another. These distances are defined by the task cards in terms of the effort it takes to move from one position to another. More than that, the configuration of the figurine, maze, map, consequence card and task card discriminate between travellers. The consequence card divides the children into beginners, good and experts, letting only those that have accomplished certain tasks through particular passages.

Together the figurine, maze, map of the maze, consequence card, task card and task card log in their specific combination and distribution of roles of locating the position of the child, defining distances between games, laying out routes, setting up obstacles and discriminating between travellers constitute what I call the *Maze Configuration*. In this configuration the artefacts and children are bound together not simply in an inert structure, but in a dynamic interaction of distances, routes, obstacles, levels and travellers. Each artefact plays a role that contributes to the integrity of the maze configuration. Each artefact is defined and bound by the others, and when they all stay in place and fulfil their roles, the maze configuration is sustained.

Much agency is delegated to the artefacts to create distances, routes, passages, obstacles, levels, travellers and knowledge about the artefacts. In order to take part in the Maze Configuration, a child must solve tasks, identify himself as *beginner*, *good* or *expert*, he must want to play a certain game, plan how to get there and overcome the obstacles this travel implies. He can try to cheat and bypass some of the obstacles, but the figurine and the card task log will blow the whistle on this irregularity. Accordingly, the agency of the child is deeply formed through the artefacts.

The Young Wizard's Assistant

Young Wizard's Assistant, YWA Law and the List of Things

Young Wizard's Assistant is a title that children earn after having accomplished the requirements described above. The title is irreversible, and a Young Wizard's Assistant cannot lose or be freed from his title. Young Wizard's Assistants are within the jurisdiction of the *YWA Law*. The YWA Law defines the criteria for becoming a Young Wizard's Assistant. According to this law, the Young Wizard's Assistants may get special assignments from the Wizard, but when this is not the case, he or she has to follow the *List of Things*. The YWA Law furthermore defines "how to start your day" with instructions about checking if there is mail with assignments from the Wizard. The YWA Law also instructs the Young Wizard's Assistant to keep his or her records. Finally, the YWA Law defines the state of "probation", which the Young Wizard's Assistants may enter if they have not carried out their duties. During probation the assignments given are according to the YWA Law "not very much fun". The *List of Things* (Fig. 11.4) is a catalogue of Young Wizard's Assistant tasks, which mainly consist of assisting and helping other children of 5th Dimension.

The Young Wizard's Assistant Configuration

Fewer artefacts are involved in making up what I term the Young Wizard's Assistant Configuration compared to the Maze Configuration. The short description of the

List of Things

Your List of Things is a list of the activities you can do as a Young Wizard's Assistant. Use this list when you do not have an assignment from the Wizard to work on and you have finished answering all your personal mail and general Fifth Dimension mail for Young Wizard's Assistants.

Helping other Kids

1. Be good enough to help with 20 games in the Fifth Dimension. The 20 games should be 20 current games (replace any that are no longer in the Fifth Dimension); be good or expert on all of them!! If there is a game in the Fifth Dimension that you do not know well, learn it!!

2. Help out other kids with a task in the Fifth Dimension. Give hints and enjoy playing with a child or an adult newcomer. When you help other kids, write to the Wizard and me how it went!

3. Help kids in far away Fifth Dimensions. Look for letters (or ask a Chief Wizard's Assistant) from kids at other Fifth Dimension who need help with a game. Write to them and send them some hints and advice for their games or activities.

Fifth Dimension Writing and Publications

4. Write something for a Fifth Dimension publication. This is only available certain days—you will be noticed!

5. Write a story and send it to kids in other Fifth Dimension. Or write only part of a story and ask another child far away to continue it. Your story can be about Me, the Wizard, about something that happened in your Fifth Dimension or about any other topic.

Becoming More Expert with Computers

6. Learn how to use telecommunication to log into Dibishell from the Macintosh and from the IBM compatible computers.

7. Help create or improve a task in the Fifth Dimension. Make a new or better activity or task card that can be used in a Fifth Dimension. Try some new software to do this.

Representing Your Fifth Dimension

8. Read general mail regularly and see if kids at other Fifth Dimensions are doing some activity that you can join!! Write to them, and tell them that you are a Young Wizard's Assistant and you would like to participate and help them with their activity.

9. Propose an activity that other YWAs and kids at other sites can work on. Write to the Wizard about your proposal and get some help from ME! I, the Wizard, will spread the word!!

Fig. 11.4 List of things for the Young Wizard's Assistants to do (reproduced by author from 5th Dimension Clearinghouse Original)

elements of the Young Wizard's Assistant Configuration is eloquent in itself when investigating the distribution of agency. It indicates the much weaker role of the artefacts in this configuration, which leaves a greater space for agency distributed to the children compared to the Maze Configuration. The List of Things assigns the Young Wizard's Assistant to learn about new games and technologies, to help other children, to write about 5th Dimension, to write to the Wizard, to help in developing 5th Dimension, and to communicate with children in other 5th Dimensions.

Compared to the tightly interwoven artefacts of the Maze Configuration, the interrelations of the artefacts in the Young Wizard's Assistant Configuration take the form of a pool of resources that are not mutually interdependent and that can be applied in a variety of flexible ways. Even when one or more of the artefacts are not activated and some activities are not performed, this does not necessarily have any consequences for other artefacts or activities or for the Young Wizard's Assistant Configuration as a whole.

While the Young Wizard's Assistant title and the List of Things are stable and immutable, the Young Wizard's Assistant Configuration does not define a rigid way of dealing with these. The child is given the agency to fulfil the Young Wizard's Assistant title as he pleases, and to follow the List of Things as he wants. Thereby, the Young Wizard's Assistant Configuration constitutes a much clearer boundary between the child as an agent and the artefact as a resource than the Maze Configuration in which children and artefacts are interwoven, interdependent and intra-acting (Barad, 2007) in every step of the configuration. In the Young Wizard's Assistant Configuration, the artefacts are passive resources to be used by the active children.

The Configuration of Configurations

Wizard and Constitution

The *Wizard* is one of the most important features of 5th Dimension. It is a mythical figure, a "patron". In many 5th Dimensions, the gender of this figure is not clear[3]. Cole writes that disputes about the Wizard's personality are never settled, and they allow recurring discussions about gender, power and responsibility (Cole, 1996, p. 293). The Wizard is described as the creator and maintainer of 5th Dimension, it is the author of the 5th Dimension *Constitution*, and it is the provider of the board games and computer games. The children will never meet the Wizard face-to-face but only through representations, traces etc. As described above, children are asked to write to the Wizard about their activities. Depending on the technologies used in the 5th Dimension correspondence with the Wizard occurs via letters or email.

---

[3]The ambiguity of the Wizard's gender identity is intentional (Cole, 1996). The roles performed by the Wizard in most 5th Dimensions correspond, however, quite unambiguously to a Western male gender stereotype.

The Wizard is defined as a helper, prankster, mediator, and wise person. Its function is to stimulate, amuse, oversee, coordinate, encourage, praise, and bemuse 5th Dimension participants as well as to command specific activities, mediate in conflicts and maintain order in the 5th Dimension setting. The latter could for instance happen by putting Young Wizard's Assistants on probation. Children write to the Wizard to tell how they have accomplished their tasks and what they have learnt. The Wizard writes back and encourages children to go on, asks new questions about the game, suggests different ways of playing, or introduces new concepts and possibilities.

There are various other reasons for writing to the Wizard. If disputes about activities or among the participants in 5th Dimension arise, children write to the Wizard to ask for advice. They may ask the Wizard to make a decision in order to resolve the dispute. Also, if a child is sad he may write to the Wizard to unburden his heart. In some 5th Dimension sites the Wizard is a forgetful character who often neglects his responsibilities, with the result that things go wrong. For instance, the Wizard is to blame when technologies do not work and systems break down. All 5th Dimensions experience children asking questions about the existence and identity of the Wizard, but beside stories about his roles, functions and history, adults refuse to inform children about the practical materiality that constitutes the Wizard. In front of the children, adults collude with them in the pretence of the Wizard's existence in order to co-construct a playful world. Behind the backs of the children, the adults in 5th Dimension manage the Wizard's correspondence: they read the children's letters and e-mails to the Wizard and answer back. They lay out traces of the Wizard and tell the story of his or her existence, constitution and power over 5th Dimension[4].

The 5th Dimension Constitution defines the Wizard as the creator, ruler and protector of 5th Dimension. It sets the basic norms for 5th Dimension in terms of rights and rules. Members of 5th Dimensions are to be shown respect, to be cared for, and to be helped. Furthermore, they also have the right of proposing new rights. The rules maintain that everyone has to help others, share, collaborate and keep record of his or her own activities.

The 5th Dimension Configuration

What I call *the 5th Dimension Configuration* is made up of a constellation of the Wizard, the Constitution, the Maze Configuration and the Young Wizard's Assistant Configuration. The Constitution defines 5th Dimension as a region in which the rules of the Wizard and the Constitution apply, and from which children can be excluded if they do not obey these rules. Drawn together by the Constitution that applies to both of them, the Maze Configuration and the Young Wizard's Assistant

---

[4]The ethical concerns involved in concealing from the children that the adults read their confidential letters to the Wizard, and that adults secretly act through the Wizard, are rarely discussed in 5th Dimension.

Configuration each forms a subregion within the region of the 5th Dimension Configuration. Within each subregion, distinct rules, dynamics and distributions of agency exist. Between the subregions children can move linearly and irreversibly from the Maze Configuration to the Young Wizard's Assistant Configuration.

The Constitution defines the Wizard as the ruler of 5th Dimension. But it is more than that. It sets tasks, monitors, comments and sanctions practices, and it helps when things go wrong. In political terms, the Wizard holds the legislative, the judicial and the executive power as well as providing the welfare services of 5th Dimension. Possessing this variety of powers and services, the Wizard serves to integrate the three configurations into a robust structure. The 5th Dimension configuration takes a form similar to that of the Maze Configuration. It is constituted through a number of tightly knit elements: The Wizard, the Constitution, the Maze Configuration and the Young Wizard's Assistant Configuration. The relations between these elements are well defined, each element plays a specific role, and together they keep each other in place: the Maze Configuration keeps the children active in the maze and the Constitution linearly unites the Maze Configuration with the Young Wizard's Assistant Configuration, just as it also appoints the Wizard as the ruler of 5th Dimension, who guards boundaries and keeps order inside 5th Dimension.

In addition to this, the Wizard does the repair work in cases of mistakes and breakdowns, he helps when problems occur and comforts unhappy children. The Wizard's ability to move between different roles functions to configure 5th Dimension into a self-healing organism. On the one hand, the 5th Dimension Configuration keeps the artefacts and configurations together and thereby provides 5th Dimension with a strong skeleton. On the other, the Wizard's flexible repair work ensures that the skeleton is brought "back to normal" whenever social or technical irregularities in the configuration occur. This way, the configuration of 5th Dimension provides it with a strong skeleton and the flexible repair work secures the stability of the programme.

5th Dimension and the Age of Uncertainty

It was the combination of an analysis of the 5th Dimension artefacts similar to the one presented above, together with a particular understanding of contemporary societies, that gave rise to our transformation of the 5th Dimension design into the Femtedit design. The specific characteristic of contemporary society was inspired mainly by the sociologist of childhood Nick Lee (2001), who examines how childhood has changed through the past century. He notes that in Fordism adults were the representatives of the existing order while children had not yet been shaped according to that order. Referring to Harvey, Lee notes that "Fordism, with its stability, reliability and product standardisation, was not just a business strategy; it was a 'total way of life'" (Lee, 2001, p. 11) in which order was a central aspiration for human activity. Fitting the Fordist way of life, Parsons and Piaget "wove children into a universal human drama of struggle for order" (p. 43). Psychology, medicine, social science and politics were founded on the idea of one single order guided by norms and by re-integrating what was seen as deviant behaviour. Adulthood represented the *end*, stability, the norm that children could – and should – reach through development and education. In Lee's terms, adults were *beings* while children were *becomings*.

Today, however, adulthood can no longer be understood as the state of stable completion and self-possession on which being-hood once rested. Deleuze (1995) describes contemporary subjects as engaged in life-long processes of learning and continuous flexibility, in an endless process of becoming. Society and norms are seen as being in continuous change, and thus there is no clear guideline of what to aim for, or of where to direct development as well as learning. In what Lee calls the *age of uncertainty* adults and children share the fate of being beings as well as becomings. Note, however, the difference between Fordist becomings and the becomings of the age of uncertainty: While the former were *becomings-towards-an-end*, contemporary becomings are *becomings-without-an-end*. This is not only a question of temporality. We find different norms spatially distributed, in different cultures and subcultures. Breaks on norms are no longer unequivocally treated as deviant (compared to a norm's end), but can be seen as expression of a different culture in a landscape of multiple norms.

Lee's categorisation of our age rests on a thorough analysis of contemporary and past societies in which a complex web of factors are at play. In this chapter I shall not discuss these further, but focus on the overall picture of the contemporary way of life as characterised by a plurality of norms and a continuous becoming-without-an-end. This is in contrast to the integrated Fordist society, whose characteristics include the aspiration for a singular norm and the treatment of not normal behaviour as deviance (see also Beck, 1992; Giddens, 1991).

In light of these considerations, becoming-towards-an-end is implied in the 5th Dimension's Maze Configuration. As long as the child stays within the Maze Configuration, he or she is intimately entangled with the artefacts, without a strong agency of his or her own. Such agency can, however, be achieved when granted the Young Wizard's Assistant title. The move from the Maze Configuration to the Young Wizard's Assistant Configuration is analogous to developing from child-becoming to adult-being in the Fordist way of life. Both establish a normal and an irreversible path from the former to the latter. This path moves from less agency to more agency, from developing to developed, from becoming to being. Indeed, the Young Wizard's Assistant is granted rights and has responsibilities similar to a citizen of a nation state, compared to the child in the Maze Configuration who acts within protected space of actions and consequences.

The Young Wizard's Assistant is entangled with the Constitution, the List of Things and the YWA Law. These artefacts are indeed stable. They keep each other and the Young Wizard's Assistant in place. The Young Wizard's Assistant can contribute to creating new activities, but only as long as they would leave the Constitution, the List of Things and the YWA Law untouched. The Young Wizard's Assistant's activities strictly have to be enacted within the boundaries of 5th Dimension. Ito (1997) describes how a boy in one 5th Dimension struggled hard to achieve the Young Wizard's Assistant title in order to be able to play the computer game *SimCity2000* without interruption. However, the director of 5th

Dimension repeatedly interrupted his playing, reminding him that he had to help the others learn, and not simply play himself. The stability of the 5th Dimension Configuration is at risk of being undermined by the unbound agency of the Young Wizard's Assistant if this is not bound by the 5th Dimension rules. The being of the Young Wizard's Assistant is accordingly a being within a closed frame.

Apart from this temporal becoming-towards-an-end 5th Dimension establishes an integrated stability that entails mechanisms to bring the system back into place, to the given norm, whenever irregularities appear. Variation and diversity is indeed possible and even highly wanted in 5th Dimension (Cole, 1996), but only to a certain degree. There is a clear point at which variation and diversity stop being this and turn into being irregularities. This point is when the system is at risk of losing the integration between its various parts. At that point irregularities must be conquered in order to re-establish the system. Also at this point the 5th Dimension Configuration has similarities with Fordism. It establishes a single norm and employs mechanisms to re-integrate what or whoever is not adhering to the norm.

It was on the basis of a similar analysis that my research team concluded that 5th Dimension's stable and singular configuration would not correspond well to the age of uncertainty. In order to design a learning material that would be adequate for—and co-constitute—the child as a *becoming-without-an-end*, we would have to modify the configuration of the 5th Dimension artefacts to constitute a becoming, transforming and multiple way of life. In the following I present Femtedit as such a design, developed with the 5th Dimension artefacts as its point of departure.

Femtedit: Becoming-Without-an-End

Contrary to the detailed analysis of the distribution of agency in the 5th Dimension design, the discussion of Femtedit will focus only on those aspects of design which could be transformed from the stable and singular configuration of 5th Dimension into a configuration of becoming-without-an-end.

The project ran for seven weeks, and was initiated by telling the 9 to 10-year-old children a frame story, which in a condensed version goes like this:

> On the Internet is a virtual world called *Femtedit*. Its citizens are the *Femteditians*. They come into being as a result of programme errors on the server hosting their virtual world. When they arrive in Femtedit they are curious, but empty. Soon they start building a home and surfing the Internet. From their homes they make links to web pages they have visited. This fills them up. As an effect of building their homes and linking to web pages, they build up their identities. A Femteditian's identity corresponds to the complete content of the web pages they have linked to.

> Everything was fine in Femtedit until the day a virus attacked the server. Slowly but unmistakably, the buildings in Femtedit disappeared and with them the links. The Femteditians' identities were deleted. Eventually the virus was eliminated, but Femtedit had almost vanished, and the Femteditians had become empty like zombies. They could not move, they could not act, they could not save their world. Just in time, however, the youngest of the Femteditians, *Jaga*, managed to write to the researchers asking for help to save Femtedit by building up new homes and making hyperlinks from their homes. The latter would reanimate the Femteditians, slowly making them able to go on living in their treasured world. The researchers realised this task was larger than they could manage. They gathered a Danish

and a Swedish fourth-grade class, explained the situation and entrusted the children with the rescue operation.

The children were each provided with a little virtual figurine (an avatar) with which they could enter the virtual world Femtedit via a school computer and start building up the virtual world. They could build buildings and landscapes and to these they could add a variety of surfaces, images and sounds, as well as link to Internet web sites. The children were divided into ten groups, each responsible for reanimating one Femteditian and rebuilding its home. Each group consisted of children from both countries. Situated several hundred kilometres apart they could communicate with their Scandinavian colleagues in the virtual world through avatar gestures, through chat and digital telegrams. The Femteditians had just enough energy to provide each group with a short blog message of feedback every week concerning the children's buildings and links.

The *frame story* was Femtedit's version of 5th Dimension's Constitution. Like the Constitution, the frame story was related to all participants who were thus united through this relation. Different to what I described concerning the Constitution, however, the frame story did not serve to keep elements together. Contrary to an integrating function, the frame story was a point of departure of the activity from which the development of the world and the activity could set off. As such the frame story only had an initial function and could later be abandoned. It defined an origin for a journey – a becoming – not a territory for beings.

The integrating function of the 5th Dimension maze and task cards was redesigned in Femtedit into a *guideline* for the researchers and teachers. The guideline constituted a sequential plan for how the feedback from Femteditians to the children should unfold: at the second session, feedback should regard the choices of individual links for the Femteditians, after that the relations between links were questioned and finally the interrelations between one Femteditian's links and those of other Femteditians were inquired after. This sequence of feedback was Femtedit's version of the task cards. Like the task cards in 5th Dimension which functioned to make children reflect and further develop their thoughts about the games they played, Femteditians made the Femtedit children reflect on their work through their *feedback*. Contrary to 5th Dimension where children acted in interrelation with task cards and a maze that were set and settled prior to the children's engagement with these artefacts, the Femteditians' feedback and the guideline involved in organising this feedback were recurrently reviewed and therefore always only temporary.

As was the case in 5th Dimension, the researchers wrote field notes in Femtedit after each session. But contrary to 5th Dimension, in which students wrote field notes mainly for their own study purposes, the field notes in Femtedit were resources for further development of the programme. In Femtedit the researchers uploaded their field notes to a closed discussion *forum* on the Internet. We read each other's field notes and on the basis of these data we discussed what had happened during the previous session and what the relevant next feedback from the Femteditians would be. In the same way as the adults in 5th Dimension wrote the Wizard's answers to the children, the researchers and teachers in Femtedit also wrote the feedback from the Femteditians to the children.

We need to consider Femtedit's version of task cards further in order to understand how these together with the guideline contributed to shaping becomings-without-an-end contrary to the more mechanical function of the task cards. Because the children were collectively building up the Femtedit world, this world changed as the project progressed. The changing landscape and identity of Femtedit and the Femteditians were the basis for the researchers' and teachers' field notes and for their feedback to the children. This condition of continuous change implied that the researchers could not rigidly follow the given guideline when giving feedback. Not only was it impossible to introduce the steps at the same pace for all groups due to their different work rhythms, furthermore some steps made less sense for some groups and new steps had to be introduced. Contrary to the configuration of maze and task cards, which was stable and a priori settled, the configuration of guideline, researchers, forum and feedback was indeed a continuous becoming.

There is more to say about Femtedit's version of the task cards. The configuration of guideline, researchers, forum and feedback was related to a particular organisation of the children. They were divided into groups whose members worked at different times and across national boundaries. Such an organisation in which participants cannot experience the practices of the others requires of its participants that they articulate their distributed individual activities (Schmidt & Bannon, 1992; Star & Strauss, 1999). In 5th Dimension, reflection was cultivated through the task cards, while in Femtedit communication was promoted through the *blog* that was used for feedback and communication between group members. Whereas the task cards were individual and were to be answered by each game player of 5th Dimension, the blog was a means of communication that allowed the children to discuss how to continue the activities. Through the children's discussions, new ideas and plans would develop and thereby contribute to the ongoing development of the activity, whereas the task cards mainly worked to keep individual children active within the Maze Configuration while at the same time learning and developing towards the completion of the 5th Dimension curriculum.

It is difficult to find one element in Femtedit that corresponds to the Wizard. Being virtual, and to some extent mystical creatures, the *Femteditians* did display some of the Wizard's characteristics. While the latter, however, was the sovereign of 5th Dimension, the Femteditians were not much more than participants, who uttered their wishes, needs and gratitude, but who did not hold any power to sanction good or bad behaviour[5]. The Femteditians could to some extent be seen as holding judicial power, but they lacked the legislative and executive power wielded by the Wizard. Without this integration of powers, Femtedit lacked an arrangement that could keep the activities within a certain frame. It also lacked a rescuer that could secure the stability of the world or activity.

The virtual environment could endlessly be changed in interaction with the children, and endless communication could take place within the virtual world to which

---

[5]Like the adults in the 5th Dimension behind the back of the children acted as the wizard through letters and emails, it was the researchers in Femtedit that - behind their back - wrote to the children in the name of the Femteditians.

there was thus only becoming, only transformation, no end-point. Compared to 5th Dimension, Femtedit lacked a mechanism to re-integrate irregularities. However, from the point of view of Femtedit, re-integration was a less important mechanism and what in 5th Dimension counted as irregularities were in Femtedit resources for the ongoing change of the Femtedit configuration (see Sørensen, 2009). With its lack of integration mechanisms Femtedit did indeed come to display the characteristics of the way of life of the age of uncertainty.

Conclusion

Arranging a comparison between two technologies – highlighting differences, scaling down similarities – as I have done in this paper generates an expectation of concluding that one or the other is better. I shall not conclude in this way. One of this chapter's lines of argument explains why my research group chose to change the 5th Dimension design into Femtedit. We changed the design because we thought the 5th Dimension design was inadequate for the age of uncertainty. Whether the way of life of the age of uncertainty is worth pursuing has, however, not been decided upon.

Instead of pointing to a better design, I would like to draw a practical and theoretical conclusion of this chapter's analyses. I have treated children and materials as co-constituted by and through the configuration of heterogeneous elements. I have analysed how different configurations of artefacts in 5th Dimension and in Femtedit gave rise to different distributions of agency between materials and child. When the agency of the material changed, so did the agency of the child.

The notion of configuration, and thus of co-constitution of humans and artefacts, is foreign to Activity Theory. Cole (1996) describes three modes of interacting with artefacts that he observed in 5th Dimension: "orientational", in which the child treats the artefact as a thing in itself; "instrumental", in which the thing is incorporated as a mediator for the child's goal-directed action and finally "reflective", in which mindfulness is involved in working with the artefact. This tricotomy corresponds to Wartofsky's (1979) division of artefacts into three categories. According to this, primary artefacts are tools directly used in human activities. Secondary artefacts are representations of objects and of modes of operation and action involving such objects, applied in activities concerning preservation and transmission of acquired skills, modes of action or practices of production. Tertiary artefacts are imaginative, abstract representations involved in play or artistic activity whose original representational role (as secondary artefacts) has been bracketed. The three different types of artefacts share the characteristic with Cole's account of modes of interacting with artefacts, in that they are productive and perceptual resources for and mediators of human activity.

Wartofsky's account of artefacts corresponds to the Activity Theory definition of the relationship between subjects, artefacts and objects. Famously, Engeström (1990) illustrated Leontiev theory of activity through a triangle of subject, object and tool that symbolises how artefacts mediate the subject to act towards the object. Activity is defined as the trinity of subject, object and artefact, which may lead to an understanding of these three entities as playing equal roles in configuring the activity. This is, however, not the case, since the subject is granted the role of an agent, while the artefact is a mediator, and the object the goal.

Locating a priori agency in the child and defining artefacts as scaffoldings, Activity Theory predetermines what kind of configuration the interplay of design and practice can possibly have. It will always be a configuration of humans using, making or manipulating artefacts. According to Activity Theory, artefacts are indeed mediating these human activities, but this does not change the fact that the human in Activity Theory analyses will never escape the role of the agent, while artefacts are granted a passive role. Applying the notion of configuration, however, my analysis has allowed us to see that there are variations in the ways in which agency is distributed. As discussed, Activity Theory understands the maze as scaffolding the child, yet it is, however, no less active than the child in the Young Wizard's Assistant arrangement. No space is left for an empirical investigation of how materials and children may mutually be formed, as I have shown was the case with the child in the two configurations gaining very different agencies. Accordingly, the option that multiple ontologies of children as well as of artefacts might emerge is not given in Activity Theory.

This is not only a theoretical question. It is indeed a practical question. An Activity Theory approach asks which technology best scaffolds a child's development, and thus it defines the ontology to be developed prior to answering the question. Consequently, it is only those artefacts that in interrelation with the child give rise to the expected ontology that can possibly be concerned. I suggest the notion of configuration in the study of children because it allows us to investigate how agency is distributed differently by and through different practical sociomaterial arrangements, whereas I with Activity Theory have to stick to one type of configuration, with one set of ontologies given by the theory. But what if application of other artefacts would lead to other ontologies? And what if their combination would contribute to forming what a child could possibly be? I have argued that this is the case, and with this approach we gain the opportunity to ask how different ontologies could emerge, what they would look like, and whether they correspond to a way of life we like. We might be surprised and learn about new ways of life that could be inspiring, that could be good. I therefore close this chapter by asking my fellow Activity Theory researchers: are you in for a surprise?

References

Akrich, M. (1992). The de-scription of technical objects. In W. Bijker & J. Law (Eds.), *Shaping technology/building society: Studies in sociotechnical change* (pp. 205–224). Cambridge: MIT Press.

Barad, K. (2007). *Meeting the Universe Halfway: Quantum Physics and the Entanglement of Matter and Meaning*. Durham, NC: Duke University Press.

Beck, U. (1992). *Risk society: Towards a new modernity*. London: Sage Publications.

Brown, S. D., & Capdevilla, R. (1999). Perpetuum mobile: Substance, force and the sociology of translation. In J. Law & J. Hassard (Eds.), *Actor network theory and after* (pp. 26–50). Oxford: Blackwell Publishers.

Callon, M. (1986). Some elements of a sociology of translation: Domestication of the scallops and the fishermen at St. Brieuc Bay. In J. Law (Ed.), *Power, action and belief* (pp. 196–233). London: Routledge and Keagan Paul.

Cole, M. (1996). *Cultural psychology: A once and future discipline*. Cambridge, MA: Belknap Press.

Deleuze, G. (1995). *Negotiations*. New York: Columbia University Press.

Engeström, Y. (1990). *Learning, working and imagining*. Helsinki: Orienta-Konsultit Oy.

Giddens, A. (1991). *The consequences of modernity*. San Francisco: Stanford University Press.

Griffin, P., & Cole, M. (1984). Current activity for the future: The Zoped. In B. Rogoff & J. V. Wertsch (Eds.), *Children's learning in the 'zone of proximal development'* (pp. 45–64). San Francisco: Jossey-Bass Inc. Publishers.

Haraway, D. J. (1997). *Modest_Witness@Second_Millennium.Femaleman©_Meets_OncoMouse^{TM}: Feminism and technoscience*. New York: Routledge.

Ito, M. (1997). *Kids and simulation games: Subject formation through human-machine interaction*. Presented at annual meeting of the society for the social studies of science.

Johnson, J. (a.k.a. B. Latour) (1995). Mixing humans and nonhumans together: The sociology of a door-closer. In S. L. Star (Ed.), *Ecologies of knowledge: Work and politics in science and technology* (pp. 257–277). Albany: State University of New York Press.

Kaptelinin, V., & Cole, M. (2002). Individual and collective activities in educational computer game playing. In T. Koschmann, R. Hall, & N. Miyake (Eds.). *CSCL 2, carrying forward the conversation* (pp. 303–316). Mahwah, NJ: Lawrence Erlbaum Associates.

Latour, B. (1987). *Science in action*. Cambridge, MA: Harvard University Press.

Latour, B. (2005). *Reassembling the social: An introduction to actor-network-theory*. Oxford: Oxford University Press.

Law, J. (1994). *Organizing modernity*. Oxford: Blackwell Publishers.

Law, J. (2009). Actor network theory and material semiotics. In B. S. Turner (Ed.), *The new Blackwell companion to social theory*. Oxford: Wiley-Blackwell.

Lee, N. (2001). *Childhood and society: Growing up in an age of uncertainty*. Buckingham: Open University Press.

Nocon, H. (2005). The role of network in the school of tomorrow. In M. Nilsson & H. Nocon (Eds.), *School of tomorrow: Teaching and technology in local and global communities*. New York: Peter Lang.

Nocon, H., Nielsson, M., & Cole, M. (2004). Spiders, firesouls, and little fingers: Necessary magic in university – community collaboration. *Anthropology & Education Quarterly, 35*(3), 368–385.

Pickering, A. (1995). *The Mangle of Practice: Time, Agency and Science*. Chicago: University Press.

Rogoff, B., & Wertsch, J. (Eds.). (1984). *Children's learning in the 'zone of proximal development'*. San Francisco: Jossey-Bass Inc. Publishers.

Schmidt, K., & Bannon, L. (1992). Taking CSCW seriously: Supporting articulation work. *Computer Supported Cooperative Work: The Journal of Collaborative Computing, 1*(1), 7–40.

Sørensen, E. (2007). STS goes to school: Spatial imaginaries of technology, knowledge and presence. *Outlines – Critical Social Studies, 1*, 15–27.

Sørensen, E. (2009). *The materiality of learning: Technology and knowledge in educational practice*. New York: Cambridge University Press.

Star, S. L., & Griesemer, J. R. (1989). Institutional ecology, 'translations' and boundary objects: Amateurs and professionals in Berkeley's Museum of Vertebrate Zoology 1907–39. *Social Studies of Science, 19*(3), 387–420.

Star, S. L., & Strauss, A. (1999). Layers of silence, arenas of voice: The ecology of visible and invisible work. *Computer Supported Cooperative Work: The Journal of Collaborative Computing, 8*, 9–30.

Suchman, L. (2007). *Machine reconfiguration*. Cambridge, MA: Cambridge University Press.

Vygotsky, L. S. (1978). *Mind in society: The development of higher psychological processes*. Cambridge, MA: Harvard University Press.

Wartofsky, M. (1979). *Models: Representation and scientific understanding*. Dordrecht: Reidel.

Chapter 12
Enacting Human Developments: From Representation to Virtuality

Michalis Kontopodis

Time, Development and Re-presentation

On considering the wide range of developmental psychological and educational research (see e.g. recent issues of *Child Development*), it can be inferred that the performative turn in the social sciences (Butler, 1997; Conquergood, 2002; Wulf, Göhlich, & Zirfas, 2001, cf. also Kontopodis, Wulf, & Fichtner, Chapter 1, this book) has had little effect on developmental psychology and educational science. What the performative turn strongly criticized is the deep-rootedness in modernity of the epistemology of *representation*. Building upon the epistemological grounds of objectivism, modern science (including pedagogy or educational science and developmental psychology) has until now tried to *represent* reality and to explain the world as a *meaningful whole*. According to historical anthropological approaches, standing behind this idea of a universal order is a dominant instance of God (Nietzsche, 1882/1974) or of the white male European adult (Foucault, 1971/1972; Wulf, 2004). As Hess argues, "modernist sciences tended to share a few general patterns: they developed theories that conceptualized their objects in terms of closed system dynamics, often with equilibrium principles. . . ." This "modernist style in science was consistent with the modernist culture of the surrounding societies" (Hess, 1997, pp. 131–132). The other way round, science played an important role in stabilizing and organizational principles of modernity (Law, 1994).

The concept central to the representation of the world as a meaningful order has been that of *linear* or *irreversible time*. According to Hess, while Newtonian physics was "in a sense timeless and reversible" (Hess, 1997, pp. 130–131), in the nineteenth century the concept of irreversible time entered physics through thermodynamics. In this way, in the scientific discourse, time became perceived as irreversible and

M. Kontopodis (✉)
Humboldt University Berlin, Berlin, Germany
e-mail: michaliskonto@googlemail.com

M. Kontopodis et al. (eds.), *Children, Development and Education*, International Perspectives on Early Childhood Education and Development 3, DOI 10.1007/978-94-007-0243-1_12, © Springer Science+Business Media B.V. 2011

symbolically depicted as an arrow.[1] This concept has spread to a number of disciplines which conceptualized the world in evolutionary terms (biology, geology, anthropology, sociology, political economy, etc.). Piaget introduced the concept of irreversible time in psychology which in this way became "Developmental."[2] As Perret-Clermont and Lambolez write:

> [Piaget...] instituted the so-called 'genetic' approach. Inspired by biology, he transposed to psychology the time inherited from natural sciences, reinterpreted the concept of evolution, and imported the concepts of assimilation, accommodation, and equilibration, investing them with an explanatory function (Perret-Clermont & Lambolez, 2005, p. 3)

On the basis of the principles of assimilation, accommodation, and equilibration, the concept of development in mainstream psychology implies a linear time that moves toward a given end in which the minimum of possible activity is achieved, as depicted in Fig. 12.1.

As a result, the child's actions and experiences, seen from a developmental-psychological point of view, form a continuum, a meaningful entity. This developmental continuum should lead to a rational universal individual – the conception of man that modern pedagogy is grounded on (Wulf, 2002). In terms of Vygotsky:

> Piaget represents the child's mental development as a process in which *the characteristics of the child's thought gradually die out.* For Piaget, the child's mental development consists of the gradual replacement of the unique qualities and characteristics of the child's thought by the more powerful thought of the adult. The beginning of the child's mental development is represented in terms of the solipsism of the infant. To the extent that the child adapts to adult thought, this infantile solipsism gives way to the egocentric thought of the child [...] With age, the characteristics of the child's thought begin to disappear. They are replaced in one domain after another and ultimately disappear entirely. [...] [D]evelopment is portrayed as a process through which one form of thought is gradually and continuously being forced out by another. The socialization of thought is viewed as an external, mechanical process in which the characteristics of the child's thought are forced out. In this sense, development is comparable to a process in which one liquid – forced into a vessel from the outside – replaces another that had previously filled the vessel. [...] Development is reduced to the dying out of the characteristics of the child's thinking. What is new to development arises

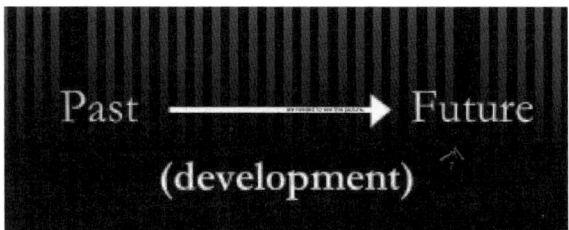

Fig. 12.1 Linear representation of time

---

[1] Prior to thermodynamics, other domains of human thought such as mythology (e.g. 'Chronos') and religion (e.g. Christianity) also envisaged time as irreversible.

[2] For the conceptualization of time as irreversible in other fields of psychology see Kontopodis, 2006; Pourkos & Kontopodis, 2005.

from without. The child's characteristics have no constructive, positive, progressive, or for-mative role in the history of his mental development. Higher forms of thought do not arise from the characteristics of the child, but simply take their place. According to Piaget, this is the sole law of the child's mental development (Vygotsky, 1934/1987, p. 175)

Vygotsky here criticizes Piaget for proposing that a child's characteristics gradu-ally die out while the potential higher forms establish themselves. Exactly the same criticism is to be found in the work of the famous science and technology scholar Latour:

[Development in Piaget] is the realization 'in time' of what was already there *in potential* (...) [it] unfolds determinations, but nothing really happens, exactly as it is possible to calculate all the positions of the pendulum from its initial position without the actual fall of the pendulum adding any new information (Latour, 2005b, p. 185)

Latour here claims that the past and the future in education and in developmental psychology are presupposed and that development is conceptualized as an arrow connecting them. In such a paradigm, it is impossible to create a situation with completely new properties – only another way of combining the already known properties is possible. Such a concept of time, as Ansell-Pearson argues, "sees in a new form or quality only a rearrangement of the old and nothing absolutely new" (Ansell-Pearson, 2002, p. 85; Stengers, 1997, p. 66).

Not only the concept of "development" but also the broader idea of continuous linear temporality and the epistemology of representation that underlie the con-cept of evolution have been much criticized by the so-called process-philosophical approaches of the late nineteenth and early twentieth centuries. Implicitly or expli-citly taking critical distance from modern natural-scientific understandings of time (such as thermodynamics and, later, relativity theory) and from continental sub-stance philosophies (for example Plato, Aristotle, St. Augustine, Descartes, or Spinoza), scholars in different contexts and disciplines tried to establish new epistemologies. They did not focus on *time per se* but on the *processes* that interlace matter and science, "matters of fact" and "matters of concern," nature and history. One could think in this respect of Whitehead's process philosophy (Whitehead, 1929/1978), Peircian semiotics (Pape, 1988; Peirce, 1958), Bergson's concept of virtuality (Bergson, 1896/1991), or Tarde's theory of invention, imitation and opposition[3] (Tarde, 1897/1999). The concept of "representation" has also been strongly criticized in the context of quantum physics by Heisenberg and Bohr (Bohr, 1928/1983; Heisenberg, 1927) and recently by the feminist scholar Barad (2007).

All of these approaches claim that realities (and linear time or development in concrete) exist neither prior to nor outside of methodologies. As Law put it, sci-ence "is performative. It helps to produce realities" (Law, 2004, p. 143). Building upon these approaches, it seems to me that the concepts of "enactment" or of "per-formativity" are central in rejecting the epistemology of representation and the concept of linear time which "unfolds out-there." The concepts of "enactment"

---

[3]For secondary literature on these approaches see: Ansell-Pearson, 2002; Koutroufinis, 2007; Latour, 2005a; Sandbothe, 1998; Stengers, 2002.

or of "performativity" embody the above-mentioned process-philosophical tradition implying that:

1. Reality is at the same time single but also multiple; everything is virtually related to everything but actually only some relations are performed[4] (cf. Deleuze, 1988; Deleuze & Guattari, 1980/1987).
2. Reality does not exist objectively "out-there" in the course of a linear temporality, but its very existence requires *action* for the reason that relations do not exist without action (cf. Latour, 1987).
3. Humans and objects, tools or materials are symmetrically involved in action (cf. Latour, 1994).
4. Different kinds of action enact or perform different relations between signs and things or doings and thus enact different realities. In this regard, what scientific action does is not to re-present reality but to create different forms of presence and absence in the sense that some relations between signs and things/doings are enacted and others are not (cf. Law, 2004).
5. Re-presentation is sometimes so well organized that we can neither perceive the "absence" nor imagine how different relations between signs and things could be enacted.

Elaborating on the concepts of "time" and "enactment," in this chapter I will search for alternatives to the modern developmental approaches in psychology and elaborate on what could be a non-modern approach (Latour, 1995). Drawing on the analysis of written documents produced in two different school contexts, I will deconstruct modern practices of "re-presentation" of development and suggest a relational understanding of development not as a phenomenon that is not "out-there" but as a process of relating signs and things or doings on different levels. Taking under consideration the recent problems and challenges of the education of ethnic and class minorities and different genders (Benites & Fichtner, 2006; Kontopodis, 2009c, cf. also Chapter 13 by Chronaki, this book; Chapter 8 by Hedegaard, this book; Chapter 10 by Ivinson, this book), the aim of my study is to provide possible answers to the political question of how time and human development can be conceptualized so that freedom, imagination and movement are reflected and generated at school.

For this I will mainly contrast the narratives of three young women with immigrant backgrounds. I will also contrast the performative effects of these narratives and how these promoted further developments or actions on school organizational level. The narratives concern their everyday experiences. The first two were written as daily reports at the School for Individual Learning-in-Practice (Germany) and the other was composed as a diary section in the context of the "Freedom Writers"

---

[4]The term 'virtuality' has been much popularized in the context of new media and computer technologies. Maintaining a critical distance from this popular understanding, I use here the concept of virtuality to refer to human development as the actualization of endless possible social relations in terms of the philosophy of Deleuze and Guatarri (1980/1987).

project at the Woodrow Wilson High School (California, US). These narratives could be seen as typical, in the sense that they were similar to many other students' narratives that I had in my research materials. But following holistic methodological principles, one could anyway argue that these materials are "parts of the whole" and reflect more general trends and phenomena I observed in the field. For this reason they may be used as exemplarily in the context of a more general analysis (cf. Vygotsky, 1927/1997).

Research Fields and Methodology

The School for Individual Learning-in-Practice (name modified) is an experimental school that combines social work, teaching in the classroom, and vocational education. I conducted ethnographic fieldwork during the school year 2004–2005 at this school and those experiences are the basis for the following analysis. As a school psychology trainee and a PhD researcher, I participated in the everyday life of this school in most cases for 5 days per week during the whole school day as well as in official and informal teachers' meetings which took place outside the school timetable for one school year. The school, based in one of Germany's biggest cities, served students who had hitherto been unsuccessful in their school career and had failed more than once to be promoted to the next grade. The school curriculum valued reflection or reflectivity in combination with a practical orientation: students were supposed to have various vocational experiences in "real-life" contexts in order to find out for themselves where their interests lay in order to make serious decisions about their future.

Soon after the beginning of the school year my research project was approved by the school director and local authorities. After this approval, the students who wanted to participate in my research signed an informed consent. All students were older than 16 years of age and according to German law no parental consent was necessary. My friendly and trusting relationship with the students allowed me access to all documents that they produced. Teachers also trusted me because I had already finished studies in psychology at MA level and had a good understanding of the practical problems of the students' and teachers' everyday lives at school. The fact that teachers soon regarded me as a colleague, in addition to my respect for laws (such as anonymizing or pseudonymizing the students' names), enabled me to access most school documents.

The students of this school usually had an immigrant background or they were German students from problematic home environments affected by alcoholism and/or unemployment. The process of student selection resulted in approximately the same number of male and female students, and a balance of students of German and foreign (mainly Turkish) ethnicity. Most families were from lower socio-economic layers as becomes clear from the school's own statistics. In most cases, the students were about 18 years old but continued to pursue a school education ending with a certificate that would normally be obtained by students who are 15 years old. Below I will concentrate only on the female students of this school, with a focus on how ethnicity, gender and social class interrelated to each other (cf. Chapter 9 by Audehm, this book; Linstead & Pullen, 2006; Walkerdine, 1988, 1990).

The second educational practice I focus on here emerged in one class of the Woodrow Wilson High School in Long Beach, California, USA, from 1994 till 1998. The main teacher involved in this practice was Erin Gruwell[5] (English language teacher). Under her guidance, students began reading and writing anonymous diaries in the classroom about their everyday lives. This practice introduced issues for classroom discussion on a number of social problems such as racial segregation, appearance and discrimination, domestic violence, misogyny, dyslexia and attention deficit disorder, homosexuality, loss of friends and family members in shootings.

The students who participated in the Woodrow Wilson High School like the students of the School for Individual Learning-in-Practice, to whom I referred above, came together in their late teens from different ethnic backgrounds and shared experiences of social exclusion, minimal economic and unappreciated cultural resources, family-related problems, and low educational levels. Many of the students of both schools had engaged in violent activities, although the students of the School for Individual Learning-in-Practice had not been confronted with the tragedies of shootings and killings faced by the students of the Woodrow Wilson High School in Long Beach. The materials that refer to the Freedom-Writers project come from the books the teacher Erin Gruwell published about this project (Gruwell, 1999, 2007a, 2007b) as well as from an a posteriori examination of a series of other sources such as webpages and reports by other people.[6]

My research materials from the School for Individual Learning-in-Practice involved 17 h of audio-recorded and later transcribed teachers' organizational meetings that took place every week, 21 audio-recorded and transcribed semi-structured, open-ended expert interviews with the students, and plenty of ethnographic research material that consisted of video-recordings of class activities and fieldnotes. The analysis of the fieldnotes, interviews, and video-recordings as well as of the circulation and use of written documents at the School for Individual Learning-in-Practice has been inspired by ethnographic and science and technology studies approaches (Emerson, Fretz, & Shaw, 2003; Jessor, Colby, & Shweder, 1996; Latour, 2005a). My methodology assimilated critical ethnography, i.e. "the reflective process of choosing between conceptual alternatives and making value-laden judgments of meaning and method to challenge research, policy and other forms of human

---

[5]Real name mentioned in her own books: Gruwell (1999, 2007a, 2007b).

[6]*The Freedom Writers'* project soon became very popular and even led to a commercial film production with Hilary Swank by Richard LaGravenese (2006). The Freedom Writers' approach, especially as it was presented in the film, has been criticized because of reproducing the romantic understanding of the teacher as a hero who should sacrifice her/his personal life to overcome broader social and educational deficits, which state institutions are responsible for (Chhuon and Carranza, 2008). The book, however, may also be perceived as a richer source of information if not analyzed from a hero-centered perspective but in combination with other sources – which I try below.

activity" p. 147 (Levinson, Foley, & Holland, 1996; Thomas, 1993; Thomas & O'Maolchata, 1989).

I also used a variety of methods to document semiotic and material agency, emphasizing the "connections between the actants" (Latour, 1987, 2005a) and the interdependencies of semiotic and material aspects of agency.[7] A particular focus of this ethnographic observation was the movement of students, teachers and school documents between different places. Another aspect on which I regularly focused was the use of technological equipment (mainly PCs but also phones, mobile phones, etc.) and the use of files. In particular settings, I also documented the use of other artifacts, for example drawings, films, drinks, clothes, etc. I also documented the circulation and use of all possible sorts of written language employed at school (e.g. learning materials, apprenticeship reports, etc.) and collected its photocopied versions. I tried to study development as material-semiotic ordering (Kontopodis, 2007b), focusing on the question of how new relations come out of old ones, and how a qualitatively different future can emerge out of the past (Bowker, 2005; Deleuze, 1994; Deleuze & Guattari, 1980/1987; Stengers, 2002).

In the following section, I will employ parts of these research materials as examples for the purposes of the present argumentation. I do not want, however, to compare the different educational practices in the context of which these narratives emerged. I believe that both have been developed in unique ways in particular local contexts so that it would be impossible to compare them on the ground of common principles, values, and methodologies. Very different people with different motives (cf. Chapter 7 by Hedegaard, this book) were involved in each educational practice, making it impossible to "copy" either the one or the other practice and transmit it to the other context. I will try, however, to refer to the practice followed at the Woodrow Wilson High School in order to reflect upon the fabrication of development at the School for Individual-Learning-in-Practice from a "meta-perspective" (Fichtner, 1996, 2007).

Representing Everyday Life and Development at the School for Individual Learning-in-Practice

The female student I will refer to below is Samira (pseudonym), a young working-class woman of Turkish ethnicity and German nationality. She had not had a successful school career, and this was the reason she was a student of the School for Individual Learning-in-Practice. In comparison, however, to the other students of the School for Individual Learning-in-Practice, her school performance at this school had been high for the past year. She was rarely absent and overall "self-responsible" in the way teachers expected a student to be. Like many other female students of the School for Individual Learning-in-Practice, Samira was doing an

---

[7] One can notice here a series of similarities to the school ethnography of Sørensen (Chapter 11, in this book), see also Sørensen, 2009.

internship at a hairdressers. During her time at school, in the context of the German language class she was expected to write daily or weekly reports for her supervising teacher on her activities carried out at the internship. The purpose of this activity was at the same time practicing in writing in German as well as reflecting about one's internship and professional orientation. For example, she wrote on the 18th of February, 2005:

> On the third day I actually did nothing special. As always, I was there at 9.45. I immediately folded the towels, then I [...] The first customer came at ten o'clock – he had a dog with him which barked and got on our nerves the whole time. In the meantime I took off the curlers (off the doll head), which I'd put on yesterday: it looked really good. In short, I was proud of myself, the curls looked really great and well done, right to the roots. Mike (pseudonym) said so too! [...] With the haircut it didn't work so well, but fortunately a customer came, and Anna (pseudonym) was doing the same for her. I observed attentively from the beginning till the end. And on Wednesday I am going to try this again [translation by author from German].

Samira documents here, in writing, the tasks in which she was engaged as well as their evaluation by the adults working at a hairdressers, the location of her Learning-in-Practice project. It is the third day of Samira's internship; the narration starts at 9:45 a.m., then moves to 10:00 a.m., etc. A continuous temporal past space is enacted here by means of mediation. Throughout the report, everyday life events are *objectified* into sentences written in (German) past tense and put in a sequence to produce continuity. A connection to future events is also made: "And on Wednesday, I am going to try this again."

What is disclosed here is that Samira (re-)views what happens "out-there" from "in-here" in the context of a concrete situation. She is sitting at her desk in the classroom (in-here) and under the guidelines of the supervising teacher *translates* a multiplicity of events that have taken place during her internship (out-there) into a meaningful whole which is temporally ordered. The relation between the "in-here" and the "out-there" is mediated and materialized by the report. Information is not just transported but is condensed, generalized, individualized, and modified so as to be used in further settings for different purposes (Law, 1997; Serres, 1980/1982). An important element of this translation is the fact that action is individualized and the writing subject is put at the center of the narration. Another important element of the translation is the enacted temporal order that makes what has happened during Samira's internship meaningful to her and to the teacher who is going to read her report.

The enacted temporal order not only considers the past, it also considers the future. The events and ongoing actions that have taken place during Samira's internship are meaningful in regard to a future state which should be achieved, the state of being rational (Wulf, 2002), of being adult (Holzkamp, 1993), of being a job-seeker (Rose, 1999). Such a report is supposed to support the student's own self-reflection about her past as well as support her in developing an orientation for the future. This is clearly revealed in further research materials about Samira as well as in another report, apologetic in tone, which recounts the failure of another student in her vocational education at a hairdressers. This report, entitled "My Last Day at the

Hairdresser Salon…," was written by Huriet (pseudonym), another female student of Turkish ethnicity:

> I decided not to continue my internship at the hairdresser's #name#. There were very many reasons why I wanted to change my internship: e.g. because it is located too far away – I wanted a site of internship that is close to where I live. (Another reason was that) it was not for me, the hairdressers simply was not my world. I had the impression that I was like a cleaner. They gave me only cleaning tasks […]. I am now completing my internship in the cafeteria and it is a lot of fun. I hope that I can also orient myself for my future [translation by author from German].

Huriet here narrates an unsuccessful internship at a hairdressers that she broke off. Given the fact that the internship at a hairdressers has been unsuccessful, the student informs the supervising teacher about the present situation in a second internship and expresses her concern about her future professional orientation. The student uses informal language ("was not my world," "a lot of fun") and tries to apologize to the teacher to whom the report is directed. Reading the report, we cannot know what (has) happened exactly, but only what the student is writing to the teacher. What is hereby forgotten is the richness and probably the ambiguity of the student's ongoing and dispersed experience (Stephenson & Papadopoulos, 2006), which many times – as manifested in my field notes – was related to exclusion, lack of respect, and other negative experiences often complained about by marginalized young subjectivities (cf. Hansen & Jarvis, 2000).

The report answers implicit questions such as: "where do events and actions lead to?", "is the internship successfully leading to what is predefined as a successful end?" The state of being a worker is here the implied successful future that is at stake and to which the different events, experiences, and actions should lead. The reports presented above go together with a series of other mediating tools such as files, cards and registers of absences, CVs, and certificates. The enacted temporal order is not only narrative and semiotic but also *material*; it is *materialized* in the written report which is saved in the student's personal file so as to be circulated in various settings and taken into consideration in future activities such as counseling and evaluation (Kontopodis, 2007a; cf. also Middleton & Brown, 2005).

Samira and Huriet were expected by their families to marry and become housewives, possibly maintaining a low-paid part-time job. Teachers, however, motivated them to accomplish a professional training as a hairdresser in order to later be able to work and become financially independent. They were in a way "captured" in this "either–or" discourse but were not able to reflect about its conditions of possibility in a radical-critical way (Fairclough, 1992). To concentrate on the case of Samira – she should have made a decision between two choices, either being a housewife or a hairdresser – but nothing beyond this. As she explained to me during an interview:

I: And how do you experience success or why is success important to you?
S: I just don't want my life to become boring.
I: Mm

S: Well, I don't know, what am I supposed to say, erm (2 seconds pause) I just don't want to sit at home and become a housewife, like other Turks, I also want to have a career – a successful professional life, and although hairdresser is not always such a successful occupation, but, if one really manages it then one can become a really good hairdresser, and receive awards or the title of "master," I don't know.

One could say that the subjectivity of a Turkish woman is performed here. Samina saw her emancipation in her professional career as a hairdresser, but was also not very convinced whether this choice would be the best. However, she did not have any other choice. If all would go well, on finishing the school, she, as all other students of this school, would have a certificate of the lowest level of non-specialized education and be 18 years old. This "either housewife or hairdresser" dilemma belonged to a dominant discourse which excluded other possibilities – for example those of political activism and radical societal change and transformation. The only history enacted in the narratives presented above and in most of the narratives produced and circulated at the School for Individual Learning-in-Practice is that of success or failure of concrete individuals. There is no space for the enactment of collective memories of exclusion, gender-based discrimination, or racial segregation. In the Introduction I mentioned that different kinds of action (in this case: different narrations and forms in which they are materialized) would enact or perform different relations between signs and things or doings, i.e. different histories, memories, imaginations and realities (Kontopodis & Matera, 2010b). Seen from this point of view one could claim that in the cases of Samira and Huriet different narrations (and forms of materialization) would have enacted different pasts as well as different futures.

Referring to the context or the situatedness of these narratives one should say here that about 15 years ago, the teachers of what later became the School for Individual Learning-in-Practice were politically active in promoting a new learning method and school model for all the students of Germany. Their political-educational project would have created possibilities inside and outside the school environment for individual learning with an everyday life orientation. The School for Individual Learning-in-Practice in Germany was initially conceived by engaged teachers as a political-educational reform project, but after long bureaucratic processes was turned into a school for excluded students. The teachers were confronted with huge bureaucracy and law-related limitations and in the end a school was established that fulfilled the wishes of the municipal educational administration – which was very different from what was initially imagined. This has also been the fate of numerous other progressive or radical local educational initiatives in Germany. This situation manifests the reluctance of political and educational authorities to allow new learning methods and educational models to be developed and reflects also a broader educational and social crisis in Germany (Nolan, 2001) and the entire developed world, a crisis which is manifested by increased failure rates, low social mobility, the failed integration of generations of migrant populations and, last but not least, by school shootings (Pourkos, 2006).

How can different pasts and futures and different developments be enacted? To examine different developmental orderings and possibilities I will consider in the following the case of another young woman who was expected by her family to become a housewife and by the teachers to enter the job market – however in a very different context, that of the Freedom Writers' project in California, which enacted radical visions of future societal change and transformation.

"Growing up Chicana"

Students in both projects presented here engaged in describing their everyday life in writing – in both cases during the English or German language lesson. However, significant differences can be observed. An extract from one of the Freedom Writers' diaries is presented below:

> Growing up, I always assumed I would either drop out of school or get pregnant. So when Ms. G. started talking about college, it was like a foreign language to me. Didn't she realize that girls like me don't go to college? Except for Ms. G., I don't know a single female who's graduated from high school, let alone gone to college [...]. I always thought that the only people who went to college were rich white people [...]. After all, I live in the ghetto and my skin is brown. But Ms. G. kept drilling into my head that it didn't matter where I came from or the color of my skin. She even gave me a book called *Growing up Chicano* (Lopez, 1995) about people who look like me, but made it out of the ghetto. In class today she made us do a speech about our future goals. I guess some of her madness was rubbing off on me because I found myself thinking about becoming a teacher. I began to think that I could teach young girls like me that they too could 'be somebody' [...] (Gruwell, 1999, pp. 202–204)

An anonymous female "Freedom Writer" of Chicano background wrote the extract presented here. According to her self-biographical account, she had been expected to either drop out of school or get pregnant because of her ethnicity (cf. Garcia-Reid, 2007). However, instead of accepting this "future" as self-evident, she views from a meta-perspective how this "future" is fabricated. As in most diary extracts created at the Woodrow Wilson High School, and in contrast to the daily reports written by the students at the School for Individual Learning-in-Practice, the anonymous writer does not try to produce an "objective" account about what has happened somewhere "out-there." The reflection here is about how the "out-there" (in this case: ghetto) relates to the "in-here" (high school, where she is writing the diary) and how this relation is mediated by what people say about living in the ghetto and skin color.

What is going on here, is not reporting or reflecting on the school performance as in the narratives of Samira and Huriet, but reflecting about the conditions of discourse production and self-reflection itself. The reflection is about the ghetto in relation to its outside and also about the anonymous Freedom Writer's development not as something happening "out-there" or "in-here" but as the process of relating the "out-there" and "in-here" thus changing both the "out-there" and the "in-here" and their relation. It is thus possible to view reality from the standpoint of the new

(Fichtner, 2005, 2007) and to imagine very different futures that would not only concern the student's individual development but broader social transformations. In contrast to the usual limited expectations of students of Chicano ethnicity, the anonymous "Freedom Writer" writes that she will follow higher education and "help build the human nation":

> For the first time, I realized that what people say about living in the ghetto and having brown skin doesn't have to apply to me. So when I got home, I wrote this poem: *'They Say, I Say: They say I am brown/I say I am proud/They say I only know how to cook/I say I know how to write a book/So don't judge me by the way I look/They say I am brown/I say I am proud/They say I'm not the future of this nation/I say/Stop giving me discrimination/Instead/I'm gonna use my education/to help build the human nation'*. I can't wait to read it to the class tomorrow (Gruwell, 1999, pp. 202–204 – continued from previous extract)

Latour suggests that if "the sorts of connections, short-circuits, translations, associations and mediations that we encounter daily" (Latour, 2005b, p. 181) are revealed, then difference is possible: potentiality turns into virtuality. This has been the case for the anonymous "Freedom Writer" presented above and for the other "Freedom Writers."

The question poses itself here, what was the context of this narrative production? The Freedom Writer's project[8] emerged in a situation of institutional deficits and educational as well as broader social problems in Long Beach, California (cf. Houck, Cohn, & Cohn, 2004), which had been expressed in an outbreak of interracial gang warfare. The development of this project as a whole as well as of the relations between the students and the teachers was unpredictable, as well as *dramatic* in the sense of Vygotsky (1925/1971, 1929/2005, 1934/1999 see also: Chapter 1, this book).

A few months into the school year, one of Erin Gruwell's students passed a note depicting an African-American classmate with extremely large lips. The teacher Gruwell got hold of the paper and became infuriated, telling her students the thick-lipped cartoon was like the propaganda the Nazis used during the Holocaust. A student then asked her, "What's the Holocaust?" In that instant, a radically innovative educational practice began which is very difficult to adequately present in a few lines. As Gruwell recalls, "I immediately decided to throw out my meticulously planned lessons and make tolerance the core of my curriculum" (Gruwell, 1999, p. 3).

Gruwell took the students to see *Schindler's List*, an American film drama from 1993 directed by Steven Spielberg (1993) and based on the historical novel *Schindler's Ark* by Thomas Keneally (1982). The film is about Oskar Schindler, a German businessman who saved the lives of more than a thousand Polish Jewish refugees during the Holocaust by employing them in his factories. Gruwell also

---

[8]The name *Freedom Writers* is a metaphor, connecting the students participating in this project in the Woodrow Wilson High School to the *Freedom Riders* of the 1960s who fought against segregation during the Civil Rights Movement also in California.

invited elderly survivors of the Holocaust as guest speakers to her class. She then had the students read books written by and about other young people in times of war, such as Anna Frank's *The Diary of a Young Girl* (Frank, 1995[1947], cf. Lee, 2006), Zlata Filipovic's *A Child's Life in Sarajevo* (Filipović, 1994), and Elie Wiesel's *Night* (Wiesel, 2006(1960)). Like Anne Frank, Zlata, when she was only 11 years old spent her days cooped up in a room (of an apartment), often never seeing day-light and lived through constant bombings – not to mention severe food and water shortages. "My students saw that these other kids, living in real wars, had picked up pens, chronicled their pain, and made their story immortal," Gruwell comments (Anonymous, 2002, online).

Later on, at her initiative, students began to write diaries about their everyday lives, following the examples of these other young people. Of particular importance for the Freedom Writer's diaries, as in the one presented above, was that the diary was anonymous and was not addressed toward a teacher who embodied institutional control but toward potential readers (the other students and the teacher) who might have shared similar experiences or faced similar problems. A box at the back of the classroom where students could anonymously place their diaries was a very impor-tant material-semiotic ordering that added a new element to the history of diaries as mediating tools (Roth, 2007; Vygotsky, 1924/1993).[9] It supported students not only in expressing themselves, but also in moving beyond their identities and under-standing how their everyday experiences were similar to students from different racial groups or from different social strata. Individuals or groups of youths were not conceived only in terms of their ethnic identity, but also in terms of shared experiences of social exclusion, economic and family-related problems, ages and low-educational levels.

Writing an anonymous diary was a kind of emancipatory memory work that regarded individual experience(s) from a collective perspective (Haug, 1987, 1992; Stephenson & Papadopoulos, 2006). Students here were not seen from the point of view of their past leading linearly to the future, but the opposite: they perceived themselves from a future point of view as *witnesses* of the racial war around them as well as of a series of other forms of repression. One could say here that witnessing took place from an imagined or virtual future point of view (Kontopodis, 2009a). Doing this, they did not reflect about their performance or their individual develop-ment and professional orientation in the closed way the students of the School for Individual Learning-in-Practice did, but they were given open space to reflect about their relations to the other students and, broadly speaking, about the history of these relations. Holocaust and the resistance to it were enacted anew as seen in relation to

---

[9]Diaries were written anonymously and, although the writers remained anonymous, the teacher collected them out of the black box and students took turns reading aloud each other's entries as well as editing them. "I constantly used their stories to teach [English]," teacher Gruwell says. "We read aloud, edited aloud. I could take something from a journal and compare it to a story by T.C. Boyle or Amy Tan or Gary Soto. We could look at the work side-by-side, juxtaposing themes or comparing literary techniques. It's an authentic way to teach" (Anonymous, 2002, online).

those concrete students' presents and futures. Individual history and future development on the one hand and societal history and future societal development merged
into each other and led to radically new realities. The relation between one's past
and one's future and development in general was radically redefined: not as individual development but as the social development of new relations between different
subjectivities (Daniels, 2001; Lave & Wenger, 1991).

Students realized that these latter shared social experiences were what make them
vulnerable more than any particular ethnic identity. It was thus revealed that a series
of everyday problems were not private, but public and related to citizenship. A series
of associated activities of the Freedom Writers, such as circulating and reading
books (e.g. *Growing up Chicana*), watching films, or looking at pieces of art were
further practices that supported this kind of social reflectivity (cf. van Oers, 2007).
Diaries, books, and works of art *mediated* the communication between various subjects who were confronted with similar problems and enabled thus an enactment of
reality not in developmental terms, i.e. in terms of *potentiality* (development towards
a given end) but in terms of *virtuality* (Bergson, 1896/1991; Deleuze & Guattari,
1980/1987) – "virtual" in the sense that the written narration mediated the presence
of non-present subjectivities, creating multiple temporalities and relations between
places "in-here" and "out-there."

Following Bergson, from the viewpoint of theory there is no difference between
the potential and the real. Something is *already given* as "potential" and simply
has existence or reality added to it when it is "realized." Conversely, the virtual
is real but not actual (Bergson, 1896/1991). In actualizing itself, it does not proceed by limitation or exclusion but rather must *create* its own lines of actualization
in positive acts that require such "a process of invention" (Ansell-Pearson, 2002,
p. 72) that it diverges or differentiates itself from itself.

Although it is not easy to analyze this philosophical idea in a few lines, in my
view, a student's development is virtual if it is radically redefined: not as individual
development but as development of qualitatively new socio-material relations, i.e.
as development towards the coming community (Agamben, 1993). Etymologically,
virtual (Virtue, virtuous) means full of virtue, i.e. the capacity to act: "By the virtual
we understand the set of powers to act (being, loving, transforming, creating) that
reside in the multitude" (Hardt & Negri, 2000, p. 357). The fact that in 1998, the
Freedom Writers received the Spirit of Anne Frank Award for their commitment
to combating discrimination, racism, and bias-related violence, as well as the fact
that many of the "Freedom Writers" have graduated with college degrees, some
have earned master's degrees or Ph.D.s and continue to contribute to the day-to-day
running of the Freedom Writers' Foundation, a non-profit organization which offers
teacher-training workshops and scholarships, could be seen as an example of how
"virtual" social relations may look.

Following Stephenson & Papadopoulos, we could define what happened in the
Freedom Writer's project as "Outside Politics": "Outside politics is contingent,
unpredictable, and unintentional." It refers to work "with unrealized trajectories,
possibilities which do not yet exist (not even in the symbolic, nor the imagination), potentials which may never manifest [themselves]" and suggest that such a

work requires an "expanded, slowed-down present [which] fuels new relations with other actants and new forms of action..." and not a clear "vision of an alternate future" (Stephenson & Papadopoulos, 2006, p. 205). Development conceptualized in these terms can vary endlessly: "The connections developed between people can fundamentally alter those involved, without necessarily making each 'more like' the other" (Stephenson & Papadopoulos, 2006, p. 107). In this sense, it is possible that development be "un-limited" and institutional memory and biography be fused with imagination (Kontopodis & Matera, 2010a).

Outlook: From Potentiality to Virtuality

According to modern ontologies and temporal orderings, time and human development are objective phenomena "out-there." In this context, development is represented, assessed, spoken about, etc. The argumentation presented above elaborates on the concept of "mediation" and challenges the idea of representation of time and development as such. The analysis claims that time and development are *enacted relations*. Such an approach renders the role of mediating tools visible, showing how mediating *creates* times and realities – instead of just representing them.

In his detailed study of the work of Vygotsky Papadopoulos concentrates on the notion of "mediation" (Papadopoulos, 1999) and regards the work of Vygotsky as "antimodern." He focuses on the relations of the notions of subjectivity, mediation, context, and performativity[10] in Vygotsky's work, and examines their strong political implications. Advancing Vygotsky's understanding by referring to the cases of the students of the School for Individual Learning-in-Practice in Germany, Samira and Huriet, and to the case of the anonymous "Freedom Writer" of the Woodrow Wilson High School in Long Beach, California presented above, we could claim that reports, diaries, as well as photos, teachers' memos and other tools, to which I could not refer here, mediate "development," applying a particular material-semiotic temporal order upon action. They filter what is transmitted from "out-there" to "in-here" and vice-versa, thereby generating institutional remembering and forgetting (Middleton & Edwards, 1990). Development is thus a material-semiotic ordering taking place in school and in other educational institutions. Material-semiotic orderings that enable freedom and imagination are those which do not regard development as something happening out-there, but as a mediated relation between the "in-here" and the "out-there" enabling unthinkable socio-material futures to be imagined and achieved.

The written narratives presented above *mediate* the relation between the past, the present, and the future as well as the relation between an "in-here" and an "out-there" (Law, 2004; Middleton & Brown, 2005). Different mediating tools would

---

[10]I use this term to summarize in one word an aspect of Vygotsky's approach Papadopoulos refers to periphrastically, for details s. Papadopoulos (1999, p. 322).

Fig. 12.2 Time as seen from a relational point of view

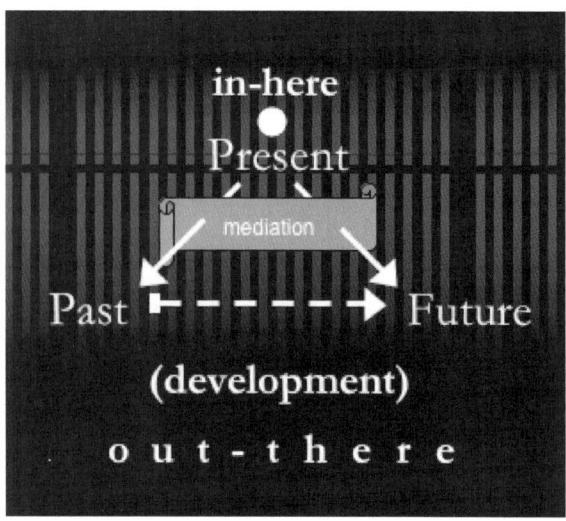

have promoted different temporal and spatial orderings, different organizations of subjectivity and different developments. What is concealed in the above-mentioned examples is that Samira and Huriet are somewhere "in-here," for example in the classroom, and regard what is happening "out-there" at the places of their vocational training witnessing an either "successful" or "unsuccessful" future. Notes and memos, reports and other material-semiotic tools such as CVs, students' files, questionnaires, etc. (Kontopodis, 2007b, 2009b) *mediate* the relation between the in-here and the out-there as depicted in Fig. 12.2.

Moving a step futher, I would like to argue that reports, memos, and other material-semiotic tools – "maps" or "images" according to Deleuze and Guattari – belong to time and do not represent time. In his critique of the modern notion of representation in *Cinema 1 and 2*, Deleuze introduces a new concept of time: that of time-image (Deleuze, 1986, 1987). The hyphen in the compound word "time-image" designates that image belongs to time and does not just represent time (Kozin, 2009). Following Deleuze (1986, 1987) and Deleuze and Guattari (1980/1987), one could argue that a written narration, a picture, a diagram etc. – in their terms a "map" – is not a *representation* of reality. *Mediating* does not just *represent* something already existing but *creates* new realities – virtual ones. However, usually this kind of mediation remains invisible, so that the past appears to lead linearly and automatically into the future. Multiple pasts and futures, i.e. "virtual realities," are thus excluded. What happens as a result is, according to Latour, a "fabrication" of time (Latour, 2005b). It is exactly this mediation that becomes visible in the case of the Freedom Writer discussed above.

Even if the above-presented material is very brief and has only an exemplary function, one could however argue that in the context of the modern educational organization, teachers and students but also educational science and developmental psychology usually try to explain what adolescence, youth, and development are. Mediating tools such as the narratives presented above are of particular importance because they enable concrete enactments of pasts and futures while rendering other enactments impossible. Usually mediating tools used in school settings (i.e. discourse, school files, students' reports, teachers' memos, etc.) fabricate linear time and development towards a final pre-defined state. This concept of development of *potentialities* (and not of *virtualities*) dominates developmental psychology, educational science, and modern education and is grounded on the epistemology of representation as well as on the model of irreversible time, which stems from thermodynamics and evolutionary theory. The Freedom Writers' project can be seen as a small example of an exception to this rule and the same can be said for some other projects such as the practice research presented by Chronaki, Chapter 13, this book or for educational projects that emerge in the context of broader socio-political movements (Kontopodis, 2009c, 2010).

Even non-mainstream alternatives such as the anthropology of childhood or cultural psychology, which otherwise differ greatly from mainstream approaches, often claim to *represent* youngsters, adolescences and/or developments. Scientists, teachers and students usually ignore or conceal the mediations required for this and believe that what they represent as development of a particular student "in-here" is identical with what happens "out-there." In this way, development is objectified and "either–or" dilemmas such as that of Samira analyzed above are constructed. In the context of reflection tasks, consultation, and evaluation practices, students and teachers accept the semiotic linear temporal order as the only possibility – which in turn shapes their further motives, decisions, and actions. In such a paradigm, it is thus impossible to create a situation with completely new properties and development unfolds towards the known and not towards the unknown. The open question poses itself thus: how is it possible to undo or remake this "fabrication of time" thus enabling multiple virtual developments and better educational opportunities for current peripheral subjectivities (Latour, 2005b)?

Acknowledgments I would like to express my graditude to the students and teachers of the "School for Individual Learning-in-Practice" (name modified) for their support, cooperation and trust during the field research, to which this article refers. I am also very thankful to B. Althans, B. Fichtner, M. Hildebrand-Nilshon, M. Pourkos, D. Papadopoulos, E. Sørensen, A. Stetsenko, and C. Wulf for their support and inspiration in writing this article.

References

Agamben, G. (1993). *The coming community*. Minneapolis: University of Minnesota Press.
Anonymous. (2002). Keepin' it real. *Northwest Education Magazine, 8*(2), Accessed August 14, 2009, http://www.nwrel.org/nwedu/08-02/real.asp
Ansell-Pearson, K. (2002). *Philosophy and the adventure of the virtual: Bergson and the time of life*. London: Routledge.
Barad, K. (2007). *Meeting the universe halfway: Quantum physics and the entanglement of matter and meaning*. Durham: Duke University Press.
Benites, M., & Fichtner, B. (Eds.). (2006). *Vom Umgang mit Differenz: Globalisierung und Regionalisierung im interkulturellen Diskurs*. Oberhausen: Athena.

Bergson, H. (1896/1991). *Matter and memory* (N. M. Paul & W. S. Palmer, Trans.). New York: Zone.

Bohr, N. (1928/1983). The Quantum postulate and the recent development of atomic theory. In J. A. Wheeler & W. H. Zurek (Eds.), *Quantum theory and measurement* (pp. 87–136). Princeton, NJ: Princeton University Press.

Bowker, G. (2005). *Memory practices in the sciences*. Cambridge, MA: MIT Press.

Butler, J. (1997). *Excitable speech: A politics of the performative*. London and New York: Routledge.

Chhuon, V., & Carranza, F. (2008). Book review: Conchas, G. Q. (2006). *The color of success: Race and high-achieving urban youth*. New York: Teachers College Press. Publication. Retrieved August 15, 2008, http://uex.sagepub.com/cgi/rapidpdf/0042085907311018v1.pdf

Conquergood, D. (2002). Performance studies: Interventions and radical research. *The Drama Review, 46*(2), 145–156.

Daniels, H. (2001). *Vygotsky and pedagogy*. London and New York: Routledge Falmer.

Deleuze, G. (1986). *Cinema I: The time-movement* (H. Tomlinson & B. Habberjam, Trans.). London: Continuum.

Deleuze, G. (1987). *Cinema II: The time-image* (H. Tomlinson & B. Habberjam, Trans.). London: Continuum.

Deleuze, G. (1988). *Bergsonism*. New York: Zone Books.

Deleuze, G. (1994). *Difference and repetition* (P. Patton, Trans.). London: Athlone.

Deleuze, G., & Guattari, F. (1980/1987). *A thousand plateaus: Capitalism and schizophrenia* (B. Massumi, Trans.). Minneapolis: University of Minnesota Press.

Emerson, R. M., Fretz, R. I., & Shaw, L. L. (2003). *Writing ethnographic fieldnotes*. Chicago: University of Chicago Press.

Fairclough, N. (1992). *Discourse and social change*. Cambridge and Cambridge, MA: Polity Press.

Fichtner, B. (1996). Ein Dialog zwischen Vygotsky und Bateson oder: Interdisziplinarität als Methodologie. In J. Lompscher (Ed.), *Entwicklung und Lernen aus kulturhistorischer Sicht: Was sagt uns Wygotski heute* (pp. 195–206). Marburg: BdWi-Verlag.

Fichtner, B. (2005). Reflective learning: Problems and questions concerning a current contextualization of the Vygotskian approach. In M. Hoffmann, J. Lenhard, & F. Seeger (Eds.), *Activity and sign: Grounding mathematics education* (pp. 179–190). New York: Springer.

Fichtner, B. (2007). Wirklichkeit vom „Standpunkt des Neuen" sehen – das Beispiel Albert Einstein. In M. Benites & B. Fichtner (Eds.), *Vom Umgang mit Differenz. Globalisierung und Regionalisierung im interkulturellen Diskurs* (pp. 145–158). Oberhausen: Athena.

Filipović, Z., & Pribichevich-Zorić, C. (1994). Zlata's diary: a child's life in Sarajevo. London: Penguin Books.

Foucault, M. (1971/1972). *The archaeology of knowledge and the discourse on language* (M. Sheridan-Smith, Trans.). New York: Harper and Colophon.

Frank, A. (1995 [1947]). The Diary of Anne Frank (Original Title: Het Achterhuis: Dagboekbrieven van 12 Juni 1942 – 1 Augustus 1944/ The Annex: diary notes from 12 June 1942 – 1 August 1944). (S. Massotty, Trans.; O. H. Frank & M. Pressler, Editing.) New York: Doubleday.

Garcia-Reid, P. (2007). Examining social capital as a mechanism for improving school engagement among low income Hispanic girls. *Youth & Society, 39*(2), 164–181.

Gruwell, E. (1999). *The freedom writers diary: How a teacher and 150 teens used writing to change themselves and the world around them*. New York: Broadway Books.

Gruwell, E. (2007a). *Teach with your heart: Lessons I learned from the freedom writers*. New York: Broadway Books.

Gruwell, E. (2007b). *The freedom writers diary: Teacher's guide*. New York: Broadway Books.

Hansen, D. M., & Jarvis, P. A. (2000). Adolescent employment and psychosocial outcomes – A comparison of two employment contexts. *Youth & Society, 31*(4), 417–436.

Hardt, M., & Negri, A. (2000). *Empire*. Cambridge, MA: Harvard University Press.

Haug, F. (1987). *Female sexualization: A collective work of memory*. London: Verso.

Haug, F. (1992). *Beyond female masochism: Memory-work and politics*. London; New York: Verso.

Heisenberg, W. (1927). Über den anschaulichen Inhalt der quantentheoretischen Kinematik und Mechanik. *Zeitschrift für Physik, 43*, 172–198.

Hess, D. J. (1997). *Science studies: An advanced introduction*. New York: New York University Press.

Holzkamp, K. (1993). *Lernen: Subjektwissenschaftliche Grundlegung*. Frankfurt am Main: Campus.

Houck, J. W., Cohn, C. K., & Cohn, A. C. (2004). *Partnering to lead educational renewal: High-quality teachers, high-quality schools*. Long Beach, CA: Teachers College Press.

Jessor, R., Colby, A., & Shweder, R. (Eds.). (1996). *Ethnography and human development: Context and meaning in social inquiry*. Chicago, London: University of Chicago Press.

Keneally, T. (1982). *Schindler's Ark*. New York: Simon & Schuster.

Kontopodis, M. (2006). Theoretical approaches to the study of time: Time as a socio-historical and cultural phenomenon and its implications. In M. Pourkos (Ed.), *Socio-historical and cultural approaches in psychology and education* (pp. 227–251). Athens: Atrapos (In Greek).

Kontopodis, M. (2007a). Fabrication of times and micro-formation of discourse at a secondary school. *Forum: Qualitative Social Research (Online Journal), 8, 1, URL (consulted June, 2008):* http://www.qualitative-research.net/fqs-texte/1-07/07-1-11-e.htm

Kontopodis, M. (2007b). Human development as semiotic-material ordering: Sketching a relational developmental psychology? *Critical Social Studies, 9*(1), 5–20.

Kontopodis, M. (2009a). Editorial: Time. Matter. Multiplicity. *Memory Studies, 2*(1), 5–10.

Kontopodis, M. (2009b). Documents' memories: Enacting pasts and futures at the school for individual learning-in-practice. *Memory Studies, 3*(2), 11–26.

Kontopodis, M. (Ed.). (2009c). *Children, culture and emerging educational challenges: A dialogue with Latin America*. Berlin: Lehmanns Media.

Kontopodis, M. (2010). *Contradictions, emerging dynamics, and open questions of the landless worker's movement in Espirito Santo, Brazil 2010: A multimedia anthropological scape*. Online Publication. Retrieved May 10, 2010, http://landlessmov2010.wordpress.com/ (Accessed May 18, 2010)

Kontopodis, M., & Matera, V. (2010a). Doing memory, doing identity: Politics of the everyday in contemporary global communities (introduction to special issue). *Outlines: Critical Practice Studies, 3*, Accessed August 14, 2010, published online: http://ojs.statsbiblioteket.dk/index.php/outlines/index

Kontopodis, M., & Matera, V. (Eds.). (2010b). *Doing memory, doing identity: Politics of the everyday in contemporary global communities. Outlines: Critical Practice Studies, 3*(special issue), Accessed 14 August 2010, published online: http://ojs.statsbiblioteket.dk/index.php/outlines/index

Koutroufinis, S. (Ed.). (2007). *Prozesse des Lebendigen: Zur Aktualität der Naturphilosophie A. N. Whiteheads*. Freiburg and München: Karl Alber.

Kozin, A. (2009). The appearing memory: Gilles Deleuze and Andrey Tarkovsky on 'Crystal-image'. *Memory Studies, 3*(1): 103–117.

LaGravenese, R. (Writer) & DeVito, D (Producer) (2006). Freedom writers. Washington, DC: Paramount Pictures.

Latour, B. (1987). *Science in action: How to follow scientists and engineers through society*. Cambridge, MA: Harvard University Press.

Latour, B. (1994). Les objets ont-ils une histoire? Rencontre de Pasteur et de Whitehead dans un bain d' acide lactique. In I. Stengers (Ed.), *L'effet whitehead* (pp. 197–217). Paris: Vrin.

Latour, B. (1995). *Wir Sind Nie Modern Gewesen: Versuch Einer Symmetrischen Anthropologie*. Berlin: Akademie.

Latour, B. (2005a). *Reassembling the social: An introduction to actor-network-theory*. Oxford and New York: Oxford University Press.

Latour, B. (2005b). Trains of thought: The fifth dimension of time and its fabrication. In A. N. Perret-Clermont (Ed.), *Thinking time: A multidisciplinary perspective on time* (pp. 173–187). Göttingen: Hogrefe & Huber.

Lave, J., & Wenger, E. (1991). *Situated learning: Legitimate peripheral participation*. Cambridge and New York: Cambridge University Press.

Law, J. (1994). *Organizing modernity*. Oxford, UK and Cambridge, MA: Blackwell.

Law, J. (1997). *Traduction/Trahison: Notes on ANT*. Lancaster: Department of Sociology, Lancaster University.

Law, J. (2004). *After method: Mess in social science research*. London: Routledge.

Lee, C. A. (2006). *Anne Frank and children of the Holocaust*. New York: VIKING and Penguin Group.

Levinson, B., Foley, D., & Holland, D. (Eds.). (1996). *The cultural production of the educated person: Critical ethnographies of schooling and local practice*. New York: SUNY Press.

Linstead, S., & Pullen, A. (2006). Gender as multiplicity: Desire, displacement, difference and dispersion. *Human Relations, 59*(9), 1287–1310.

Lopez, T. A. (Ed.). (1995). Growing Up Chicana/-o. New York: Harper Paperbacks.

Middleton, D., & Brown, S. (2005). *The social psychology of experience: Studies in remembering and forgetting*. London and Thousand Oaks, CA: Sage.

Middleton, D., & Edwards, D. (Eds.). (1990). *Collective remembering*. London, Newbury Park and New Delhi: Sage.

Nietzsche, F. W. (1882/1974). *The gay science: With a prelude in rhymes and an appendix of songs* (W. Kaufmann, Trans.). Vancouver: Vintage Books.

Nolan, M. K. (2001). 'Opposition Machen Wir!' – Youth and the contestation of civic and political legitimacy in Germany. *Childhood-a Global Journal of Child Research, 8*(2), 293–312.

Papadopoulos, D. (1999). *Lew S. Wygotski: Werk und Wirkung*. Frankfurt am Main: Campus.

Pape, H. (Ed.). (1988). *Ch. Peirce: Naturordnung und Zeichenprozess: Schriften über Semiotik und Naturphilosophie*. Aachen: Alano Rader.

Peirce, C. (1958). *Values in a universe of chance: Selected writings of Charles S. Peirce*. Garden City and New York: Doubleday.

Perret-Clermont, A. N., & Lambolez, S. (2005). Time, mind and otherness. In A. N. Perret-Clermont (Ed.), *Thinking time: A multidisciplinary perspective on time* (pp. 1–14). Göttingen: Hogrefe & Huber.

Pourkos, M. (2006). The role of socio-historical-cultural context in the interpretation and understanding of the columbine tragedy: Towards an eco-bodily-experiential approach. In M. Pourkos (Ed.), *Socio-historical and cultural approaches in psychology and education* (pp. 573–596). Athens: Atrapos.

Pourkos, M., & Kontopodis, M. (2005). How 16-year-old students experience time at school. *Psychology (The Journal of the Hellenic Psychological Society), 12*(2), 249–275.

Rose, N. (1999). *Powers of freedom: Reframing political thought*. Cambridge: Cambridge University Press.

Roth, W.-M. (2007). On mediation: Toward a cultural-historical understanding. *Theory & Psychology, 17*(5), 655–680

Sandbothe, M. (1998). *Die Verzeitlichung der Zeit: Grundtendenzen der modernen Zeitdebatte in Philosophie und Wissenschaft*. Darmstadt: Wissenschaftliche Buchgesellschaft.

Serres, M. (1980/1982). *The parasite*. Baltimore and Maryland: Johns Hopkins University Press.

Sørensen, E. (2009). *The materiality of learning: Technology and knowledge in educational practice*. New York: Cambridge University Press.

Spielberg, S. (Writer) & Spielberg, S., Molen, G. R., Kennedy, K., & Lusti, B. (Producers) (1993). Schindler's List. USA: Universal Pictures.

Stengers, I. (1997). *Au nom de la flèche du temps: Le défi de Prigogine*. Paris: La Découverte.

Stengers, I. (2002). *Penser avec Whitehead: une libre et sauvage création de concepts*. Paris: Seuil.

Stephenson, N., & Papadopoulos, D. (2006). *Analysing everyday experience: Social research and political change*. London: Palgrave Macmillan.

Tarde, G. d. (1897/1999). *L'opposition universelle essai d'une théorie des contraires*. Le Plessis-Robinson: Institut Synth. pour le Progres de la Connaissance.

Thomas, J. (1993). *Doing critical ethnography*. Newbury Park, CA: Sage.

Thomas, J., & O'Maolchata, A. (1989). Reassessing the critical metaphor: An optimist revisionist view. *Justice Quarterly, 6*, 143–172.

van Oers, B. (2007). Helping young children to become literate: The relevance of narrative competence for developmental education. *European Early Childhood Education Research Journal, 15*(2), 299–312.

Vygotsky, L. S. (1924/1993). The fundamentals of defectology. In R. Rieber (Ed.), *The collected works of Vygotsky* (Vol. 2). New York and London: Plenum.

Vygotsky, L. S. (1925/1971). *The psychology of art*. Cambridge, MA: MIT Press.

Vygotsky, L. S. (1927/1997). The historical meaning of the crisis in psychology: A methodological investigation (R. van de Veer, Trans.). In R. Rieber (Ed.), *The collected works of Vygotsky* (Vol. 3, pp. 91–107). London and New York: Plenum.

Vygotsky, L. S. (1929/2005). Concrete human psychology: An unpublished manuscript. Publication. Retrieved May 25, 2009, from The Laboratory of Comparative Human Cognition: http://lchc.ucsd.edu/MCA/Paper/Vygotsky1986b.pdf (Accessed May 18, 2010)

Vygotsky, L. S. (1934/1987). Thinking and speech (N. Minick, Trans.). In R. Rieber (Ed.), *The collected works of Vygotsky, Vol. 1 problems of general psychology* (pp. 39–288). New York and London: Plenum.

Vygotsky, L. S. (1934/1999). The teaching about emotions: Historical-psychological studies (S. Sochinenij, Trans.). In R. Rieber & M. J. Hall (Eds.), *The collected works* (Vol. 6, pp. 69–235). New York and London: Plenum.

Walkerdine, V. (1988). *The mastery of reason: Cognitive development and the production of rationality*. London: Routledge.

Walkerdine, V. (1990). *Schoolgirl fictions*. London and New York: Verso.

Wiesel, E. (2006 (1960)). Night *(Original Title: Un di Velt Hot Geshvign)* (M. Wiesel, Trans.). New York: Bantam Dell.

Whitehead, A. N. (1929/1978). *Process and reality: An essay in cosmology*. New York: Free Press.

Wulf, C. (2002). *Educational anthropology*. Münster and New York: Lit.

Wulf, C. (2004). *Anthropologie: Geschichte, Kultur, Philosophie*. Hamburg: Rowohlt.

Wulf, C., Göhlich, M., & Zirfas, J. (Eds.). (2001). *Grundlagen des Performativen: eine Einführung in die Zusammenhänge von Sprache, Macht und Handeln*. Weinheim: Juventa.

Chapter 13
"Troubling" Essentialist Identities: Performative Mathematics and the Politics of Possibility

Anna Chronaki

Identity-Work, Performativity and School Mathematics

During the last few years I have been engaged in ethnographic research concerning mathematics learning within the complexities of multicultural classrooms. I have become particularly interested in Tsiggano[1] children and their communities as they still seem to experience extreme marginalization from what is taken to mean mainstream state benefits such as the "right" of education. It is striking how the vast majority of studies in the area adopt a "gypsiologist" perspective (see Dafermos, 2006; Okely, 1997) and how current "innovative" curricula policies emphasize enculturation by means of regulating and disciplining Gypsy-Tsiggano bodies and minds according to what is taken as "normal" development within a "modern" society.

In a number of studies, I have concentrated on analyzing critical episodes concerning Tsiggano children's participation in formal school mathematical practices. These episodes were realized as part of organizing specific "teaching experiments" undertaken in the context of ethnographic research – aiming to tackle issues of

---

A. Chronaki (✉)
University of Thessaly, Volos, Greece
e-mail: chronaki@uth.gc

[1]Tsigganoi (τσιγγάνοι) is the name most commonly used in Greece and in continental Europe (e.g. Cigány in Hungary, Cigano in Portuguese, or Zingari in Italian) for Romani people, also known as Roma, Gypsies or Travelers (see Wikipedia; http://en.wikipedia.org/wiki/Names_of_the_Romani_people). Today the term Romani or Roma is formally used in most organizations including the United Nations and the Council of Europe. For this paper, the term Tsiggano is mostly used, interchangeably with Gypsy and Roma, in order to reflect how people in the community still refer to themselves. However, the term Gypsy (Γύφτος) – although avoided as it has a derogatory sense in Greek) – has not disappeared and the emerging term Roma is used hesitantly due to its emphasis on creating a common identity amongst diverse communities in Europe. A related term is Chicano or Xicano. It is used in American-English language and context, and although it seems related, it refers to American-born people of Mexican decent and is associated with the striving of the Chicano movement in the late 1960s for social, economic and political equality (see Armando Navarro, 1974).

M. Kontopodis et al. (eds.), *Children, Development and Education*, International   207
Perspectives on Early Childhood Education and Development 3,
DOI 10.1007/978-94-007-0243-1_13, © Springer Science+Business Media B.V. 2011

knowledge development as related to human development and identity. The notions of "learning identities" (Chronaki, 2003, 2005) and of "hybrid identities" (Chronaki, 2008a) were discussed as ways to capture the ontological character of learning mathematics. It was an attempt to emphasize, on the one hand, how deeply endorsed narratives about identity relate to participation in school mathematical activities, and on the other hand, how "self" and "other" positions embodied in those formal learning practices are polyphonic and potentially dialogical. This endeavor grew along with the premise that mathematical knowledge can no longer be seen as an objective entity "out there," primary to, and independent of human discursive and material practices. Moreover, one cannot continue seeing mathematics merely as a universal tool for solving problems that apply to "real life." Instead, its socio-historical character in the making of significant contributions towards conceiving and organizing modernity needs to be appreciated as culturally and politically situated (Law, 2004; Mimica, 1988; Restivo, 1991; Walkerdine, 1988).

The present chapter brings together earlier work (e.g. Chronaki, 2003, 2005, 2008a)[2] and re-reads interpretations by considering performativity theory (Butler, 1990, 1993, 1997). In the first research project, Maria and Giannoula, two girls at the ages of seven and nine, are engaged in a "teaching experiment" introducing formal arithmetic problem-solving based on everyday selling–buying examples with money-use. The ethnographic study lasted approximately 2 months, and combined observations and interviews both at home and school settings The teaching experiment was implemented as part of small group interactions amongst the two girls and Sofia – the adult educator – in their homes as this is where the girls felt most comfortable. It has been noted that part of the process of participating in school arithmetic practice involves constructing a certain "learning identity" that reflects the "norms" of mathematical culture. This encompasses the learning of rituals including ways of using (and valuing the use of) old and new arithmetic tools (i.e. finger-use, lines, counting, strategies for arithmetic operations with two and three digits etc.). The second research project discusses an ethnographic teaching experiment (called Mathematics in Tsiggano words) where Panagiotis, an 11-year-old Tsiggano boy, in a series of three lessons, is invited to become the teacher of the class and to teach mathematics in the Romani language – his mother tongue. Whilst the teaching experiment lasted for three teaching slots of approximately 40 minutes each, the overall ethnographic study took place over about 2 months in a primary school located in an urban Greek city. The two experiments utilize language and selling–buying problems as "funds of knowledge" aiming to create a space for dialogicality amongst Tsiggani and non-Tsiggani students, as well as, amongst informal and formal mathematical knowledge.

The ethnographic teaching experiment methodology espoused in those studies was close to the perspective of cultural-historical psychology (see Hedegaard &

---

[2]For more details concerning the methodology in each one of the teaching experiments one needs to refer to Chronaki (2004) for the cases of Maria, Giannoula and Sofia, and to Chronaki (2008) for the case of Panagiotis.

Chaiklin, 2005) where subjects and artifacts interact in purposefully organized zones of proximal development and, thus, trajectories of development can be not only narrated, but also acted upon. Here, I will argue that teaching experiments can also be seen as "performative acts" where humans-with-mathematics co-create potentialities for both identity-work and knowledge development. Because of a simultaneous presence of active interventionist and ethnographic approaches to knowing, a teaching experiment methodology comes close to what Diawara (1996) calls "performance ethnography." In this regard, the performative approach contributes deliberatively towards creating a "dialectics" in which people through communicative action, create and re-create themselves within the spheres of dominant and marginalized cultural discursive experiences.

Judith Butler (1988), in her early philosophical essay, discusses phenomenological, anthropological and theatrical evidence and argues that performative acts (based on the notion of "acts" as espoused by Edmund Husserl, Maurice Merleau-Ponty or George Herbert Mead and "speech acts" as maintained by John Searle) consist of verbal and gestural semiotic systems through which social agents constitute social reality. Recent developments of the "performative turn" emphasize a shift from representational epistemology – the urge to *represent* reality, to explain the world as a *meaningful* whole and to capture development *as a continuous linear temporali*ty (see Chapter 12 by Kontopodis, this book). Butler (1988), discussing gender identity, argues that "*an identity tenuously* [is] *constituted in time – an identity* [is] *instituted through a stylized repetition of acts*" (p. 519). One could extend her views from gender, to Tsiggano identity, and to learning mathematics identity as something one *does* through repetitive "acts" and not as something one inherits from birth. In this sense, one might assume that Tsiggano learning identity in the mathematics classroom could move from the dominant stereotyping of Tsiggano as "weak" and "unmotivated" learners towards more fluid, hybrid and thus open subject positionings to include alternative possibilities mediated by alternative acts and actions.

Performativity refers to an embodied culturally scripted character of identity where its main focus is to expose hegemonic conceptions of identity as fictions generated by power through repeated reproductions of norms. Currently, social theorists talk about "performative acts" as multiple genres of evolving bodily actions and discursive enactments that have both the potential of being imitative and disruptive to hegemonic discourses (Butler, 1997; Chronaki, 2008b; Haraway, 1997; Law, 2004; see Chapter 12 by Kontopodis, this book). In this sense, the teaching experiments discussed here can be captured as performative for they resemble the "norm" of school mathematics (e.g. teaching arithmetic problem solving) and at the same time, they seek to create a "utopian" space that troubles this very "normality" (e.g. resisting disciplining with "normal" mathematical culture, introducing a utopia such as teaching mathematics in the Romany language). The way performances are enacted describe performative behavior as a related whole amongst appearances and facts, surfaces and depths, illusions and substances, appearances and actualities. Schechner (1985) explains further that performances as fluid ongoing events "*mark and bend identities, remake time and adorn and reshape the body, tell stories and allow people to play with behavior that is restored, or 'twice-behaved'"* (p. 361). Performances, thus, can be seen as cultural practices that repeat and reaffirm, but also resist, transgress, and *"re-inscribe or passionately re-invent"* (Diamond, 1996, p. 2) repressive understandings that circulate in daily life (cited in Denzin, 2003, p. 10). As Butler (1988) explains;

> [i]f the ground of gender identity is the stylized repetition of acts through time, and not a seemingly seamless identity, then the possibilities of gender transformation are to be found in the arbitrary relation between such acts, in the possibility of a different sort of repeating, in the breaking or subversive repetition of that style (p. 520)

The motive in this text has been to imagine what might be the "possibility of a different sort of repeating" school mathematics. And specifically, what might be the potential of moving beyond an essentialist view of identity that serves to construct, on the one hand, Tsiggano children as incompetent in doing school mathematics, and on the other hand, mathematics as a static body of objective knowledge. Performative theory, as outlined above, permits us to imagine identity-change as a potential possibility affecting both human and knowledge, or subject and object transformation and development. Not only human subjects but also material objects are performative as they are active participants and have the potential to move, shift and change life trajectories. As Law explains science is performative as it helps to produce realities (Law, 2004, p. 143). In this sense, mathematics is performative and along with Tsiggano children becomes a participant in a complex assemblage. It enacts simultaneously the reproduction and disruption of norms, and performs a stage that "troubles" in Judith Butler's words hegemonic discourses about who is able, and who is not, to do well in school mathematics. As such, the present chapter aims to discuss a politics of possibility. In other words: Can we create, by means of a "teaching experiment," a stage that "breaks," in Judith Butler's words, essentialist images about who is able to do school mathematics? Can we "trouble" hegemonic discourses concerning who sets priorities and principles?

In the following, two teaching experiments will be discussed as two cases of performing school mathematics; *first* the performing of school arithmetic based on selling–buying word problems by Maria, Giannoula, and Sofia, and *second* the performative act of teaching arithmetic in the Romani language by Panagiotis. Subsequently, the effects of these teaching experiments as cultural resources for troubling essentialist identities and providing an alternative politics of possibility are discussed.

Performing School Mathematics: The Case of Maria, Giannoula, and Sofia

"Identity," and in particular identity-work, can be recognized as multi-voiced in nature and as a coproduction amongst "self" and "other" narratives. As Pereen (2007) says: "Identities oscillate between exterior and interior, as the self takes on the determinations offered up by others and fashions them into provisional self-narratives" (p. 17). She cites Hitchcock (1992) who argues that dialogicality

> ...suggests a potential for intersubjectivity in which the 'I' becomes 'I' not by canceling or relegating its Other. Instead, it continually redefines itself and others in a dissonance that has its material expression in the *struggle over signs* (my emphasis, cited by Peeren, 2007, p. 17).

The "struggle over signs" becomes also evident in school mathematics practices and in particular when participants learn to utilize formal mathematical tools. It was argued in Chronaki (2003, 2005), that Maria and Giannoula, the two Tsiggano girls, as they try, in the realm of a teaching experiment implemented by Sofia, to appropriate "new" tools (e.g. the algorithm for adding or multiplying three digit numbers) they imitate what the adult offers. The process of appropriating "new" tools was emotionally invested since the girls are invited to consider identity-change. The analysis indicates that they are invited not only to use "new" tools but also to learn "new" behavioral habits. In a sense, Sofia, the educator, urges the girls to adopt a specific "learning identity" in order to become acculturated to the rituals and lifeways of school mathematics. For this, she guides them closely by judging, correcting, and assessing their behavior throughout and by framing the proper use of bodily gestures and semiotic codes to support Maria and Giannoula in making a move from "spontaneous" to "scientific" or from "informal" to "formal" mathematics. Some indicative episodes can be seen in Table 13.1, where Sofia stresses the importance of checking answers for validity, of counting as a disciplined and systematic way of working, of replacing body-based counting (e.g. fingers, objects) with mental arithmetic, and of avoiding distractions such as eating whilst studying.

Table 13.1 Performing school arithmetic (adapted from table 2 in Chronaki 2005 p. 68)

Utterances	Translation	Interpretation
Σοφία: Λοιπόν. Για λίγο ξαναμέτρα απ' την αρχή!	Sofia: Okay. Well. Count again from the beginning!	Sofia wants to stress the importance of providing valid answers. One needs to count again and again in order to double check the truth of our answer.
Γιαννούλα: Δεν τα έκανα καλά;	Giannoula: Didn't I do it well?	
Σοφία: Όχι! Ξαναμέτρα τα! Να είσαι σίγουρη θέλω!	Sofia: No. Count again! I want you to be sure!	
Σοφία: Να μετράς! Έτσι να σκέφτεσαι!	Sofia: You must count! You must think this way!	Sofia encourages a disciplined, careful and systematic way of working.
Σοφία: Όχι με τα χέρια – κάντο με το μυαλό τώρα...	Sofia: Not using your hands. You must use your brain now...	Sofia discourages the use of fingers in counting and, instead, promotes the use of mental arithmetic.
Σοφία: Συγκεντρώσου τώρα. Θα φάμε αργότερα.	Sofia: Concentrate now. We will eat later.	Sofia stresses the importance of concentrating on work Eating should not distract the activity.

The "stylized repetition of acts" – in Butler's words – as they become constituted over time, stresses a process of re-affirming certain rituals in the mathematics
classroom but also of re-shaping body and mind and transforming learning identities. This allows us to conceive Maria, Giannoula, and Sofia as performing school
mathematics.

Diamond (1996) describes performances as cultural practices that reaffirm, resist,
transgress, *"re-inscribe or passionately reinvent"* repressive understandings that
circulate in daily life (cited in Denzin, 2003, p. 10). In a similar vein, Maria
and Giannoula re-affirm and resist the enculturation to school mathematics, as
performed by Sofia. At times, the two girls experience performing mathematics as an emphasis to identity change or a colonialization of their body and
mind (see Bauchspies, 2005). According to Schechner (1985) performances mark
identities as they remake time, reshape bodies, and retell stories. On the basis
of the above, we can argue that the "struggle over signs" runs deeper and can
be identified also in ways of telling stories about "self" and "other" as they
become part of public narratives. Two vignettes, based on interviews with a Greek
teacher and a Greek-Tsiggano parent, also discussed in Chronaki (2008a), were
revealing:

> Gypsies laugh at the idea of school... They participate as they like... They place no hope
> in education ....They regard education as a lost game. A game they do not even try to play.
> This can be an unbearable feeling of failure, not for them, but for us who try to quell them
> (Vignette A: A Greek teacher, April 2005)
>
> They want us to sit still in the classroom...They want us to speak little, but how little is
> little?...We try to be like them... But we are still not good enough. They call us names. They
> ask us to produce paper, too. We don't know how to do it. But we're good at selling things
> on the street. We cheat them there. (Vignette B: A Tsiggano Greek parent, April 2005)

At a first level reading, the two vignettes represent dominant discourses in
terms of "who are the Tsiggano students" and how they relate to schooling.
Despite diversities within the Gypsy-Tsiggano community itself, when compared to
Gypsies-Tsigganos, people tend to identify differences in terms of everyday habits,
values, and desires. As the above vignettes denote they discern segments marking
the broader discourse of "gypsiologists" as described by Okely (1983, 1997) and
recently by Dafermos (2006) on the basis of orientalism (Said, 1978). Through the
perspective of "gypsiologists," Tsiggano people are constructed as "insufficient" in
their attempts to participate in varied practices of the hegemonic culture such as
schooling (see also Said, 1978 on "orientalism" and Young, 2001 for a critique).
This is the genre of a monologic discourse and tends not only to exoticize but
mainly to naturalize how Tsiggano people live and experience everyday lives. The
discourse of a fixed Tsiggano identity reflects an essentialist perspective, where all
social dynamics (such as class, gender, and race) operate simultaneously towards
producing its coherence and unification. However, Hall & du Gay (1996) argue that
identity is not simply a personal quality but needs to be considered as relational
to interactions with others where the focus moves towards the processes by which
identity becomes re-constructed. Identity has been reformulated into

…a lived category that harbors a crucial political dimension without thereby ignoring the way identities – even oppositional ones – often manifest themselves as constitutive enforcements of sameness that exclude both internal and external difference. In arguing for a 'conjectural understanding' of identities capable of taking into account the shifting political relations and specific historical and material circumstances that contextualize all identity constructions, post colonial theory creates a new perspective of identity that acknowledges the way 'identity can be a basis for connection as well as disconnection (Clifford, 2000, p. 106).

A further reading of the evolving utterances amongst Maria and Giannoula and their educator, as they were trying to solve mathematical tasks permits a conceptualization of "learning identity" as a fluid, non-static and hybrid category in a continuous moving amongst "self" and "other" positions. These positions were repetitively rehearsed by the humans-with-material unit reproducing (but also breaking) performativities. More specifically, the girls were, at times, meticulously engaged in imitating the performance of certain behaviors with mathematical objects and rituals (e.g. making sense of words, using tools, symbolizing, checking, verifying, organizing, being silent and listening to the adult, talking in certain ways, working out the arithmetic in a disciplined way). And, at other times, they resisted by either being silent, ignorant, or diverting the focus from the mathematical task. These processes spanning long periods of time and mediated by the educator, involved identity-work for the girls as learners, since they have to accommodate a second "voice" – that of formal arithmetic discourse – in tandem with appropriating "new" tools and positions.

The stress over developing a certain fixed "learning identity" in the mathematical practice is comprised of two interconnected aspects. On the one hand, the girls had to be convinced that formal arithmetic tools (and their material signs) are valuable and useful for certain activities. On the other hand, but interwoven with the first, they have to abandon their own "home" tools for doing mathematics considering them as second rate and derivative. This was a stressful and often painful situation that would lead either to silence or resistance. The demand for immediate replacement with "new" tools results in feelings of incompetence and insecurity. It was noted that a significant aspect that sustains participants in this complex and at times painful process is a deep motivation for getting to know the "other." Overall, one can say that what Tsiggano children experience with the school arithmetic practice is not familiar territory. It can be realized as a hybrid space that creates "virtual" realities. Kontopodis (Chapter 12, this book) based on Deleuze and Latour explains how multiple pasts and futures inhabit reality almost invisibly. On the basis of the case of Tsiggano students I will argue that this invisible reality creates uncertainty and that the potential for gaining entry to school arithmetic practice depends also on the degree that they become aware of imagining alternative realities. A possible passage to development is "fabrication of time" as coined by Latour (2005) where potential past and future is re-narrated and where reality takes the form of virtuality.

Performing a certain "identity" is interwoven with their potential for learning. An image of oneself and in particular of how one *is* or *could be* or even *can imagine being* positioned within a practice has the potential for shaping learning trajectories and directs attempts along certain paths of inquiry and action. Identity and learning feed each other. Learning shapes identity itself since it can assist realizing, imagining and performing alternative positions. Is it then reasonable to assume that, since Tsiggano people are often judged on the basis of narrow and negative identities, their potential for shaping a learning trajectory in school mathematics is rather weak? Taking into account that the dominant images of the "mathematically able" or talented (see Damarin, 2000) are far apart from mainstream Tsiggano learning identities, it becomes easy to appreciate the gap amongst the two and provide an affirmative answer.

But, a different possibility is being painted by Peeren (2007) along with Bakhtin who assists her to argue that the correspondence of subjectivity to a durable, complete, continuous and immobile identity-as-unity is an absolute impossibility. She cites Bakhtin's discussion of "the image of the hero" who is characterized in literary texts by a strange combination of identity and metamorphosis:

> This combination sees the hero develop in a temporal sequence that proceeds 'spasmodically' like a line with 'knots' in it, where the knots mark points of transformation. The hero does not stay the same; his subjectivity is distinguished precisely by his ability to be transformed into someone or something else and back again (p. 12).

The image of a "hero" can also apply to Maria and Giannoula, the girls mentioned above, or to Panagiotis and his classmates who we will meet in the next section, as well as to any other student who struggles to cross borders amongst varied "realities" of in/formal schooling.

A "Performative Act" as the "Right" to Mathematics: The Case of Panagiotis

In March 2004 a teaching experiment was devised under the theme "Mathematics in Tsiggano words," as part of my undergraduate teaching, and implemented at a nearby primary school with the explicit purpose to encourage Tsiggano children's active participation in school mathematics. As explained in Chronaki (2008a) the teaching experiment involved Panagiotis, an 11-year-old Tsiggano boy who was required to become the teacher of mathematics and teach both his Tsiggano and non-Tsiggano classmates arithmetic and selling–buying problem-solving by means of Romani number words. The experiment can be interpreted, in socio-cultural terms, as using the Romani language as a resource or as "funds of knowledge" (Chronaki, 2008a). In this way, Tsiggano culture is not seen as a constraint, but as enabling since children's own space of competences (e.g. numbers in Romani, selling and buying in the streets) can provide bridges to formal mathematical practices. However, at the same time, the teaching experiment becomes a stage for performing school mathematics from an alternative viewpoint – that of doing mathematics in the Romani language – and providing an alternative image for Tsiggano students – that of becoming competent participants in the mathematics class.

Panagiotis' performance as the teacher showed great responsibility. Having done the basic numerals (1, 2, 3, ..., 10), he moved on to 11, 12, 13 etc. He then stopped, and to our surprise, he asked his classmates, or rather his "pupils," to carry out smaller tasks. Knowing the names of the first numerals, he asked them to create numerals above ten such as 11, 12, 13, 14, 15, 16. . . up to 50. This was a triumph! Panagiotis, a low-level, marginalized and silent participant had now managed to handle very gentle instructional situations. It was obvious that he could perform his role as a teacher quite seriously. At the end of this teaching slot (it lasted 35 min approximately) all the children could count numbers in Romani. Panagiotis was very proud. He was so eager to explain every word and assist them all in any way he could (see Figure 13.1).

During the second teaching period the aim was indeed to practice with the number words they had just learned. One idea pursued was constructing bigger numbers. Iraklis, an Albanian boy was surprised to find how easy it was to learn numbers in Romani. He noticed a method (due to the ten-base arithmetic system) of building up any number by knowing only a few word numbers (see Nunes (1997). At the end of lessons, Panagiotis asked if we could continue. It was obvious that this experience was unique for him and it was also certain that he was happy as most of the non-Tsiggano children assured us. Having practiced number words in Romani and having learned how to build big numbers using these words the next step was to apply what they had learned in situations of selling and buying – a familiar practice especially to Tsiggano boys (as opposed to girls) due to their early involvement in family jobs. Indeed, when we introduced the idea of setting a small market place in the classroom, all Gypsy kids were able to contribute with ideas about what type of market place this should be, what products to sell (e.g. carpets, clothes, fruit, flowers etc), and how to organize it. After discussion, whereby issues such as the type and size of objects were considered bearing in mind that they needed to be easily moved in the classroom, the children decided that selling decorative objects and cosmetics (e.g. vases, little statues, perfume bottles, cards etc) was more appropriate. This was due to the fact that these objects could be easily brought to school and thus we agreed that during the next lesson, each of them should bring one such object. At this point, Panagiotis was chairing the discussion. It was quite interesting how well he tried to make sure opinions from all classmates, and currently his pupils, were heard and represented (see Figure 13.2).

By the next lesson, which took place the following week, most of the children had brought various objects from home in order to set up the "shop." Nikos, a Tsiggano boy, insisted on being the shop owner and was asked to put prices on the objects – transforming them into sellable goods. The rest of the class would assist the shop-owner and Panagiotis would carry on being the teacher. Panagiotis realized that besides the numbers, he had to teach some new phrases, such as; "I want to buy this. . ."? or "How much does it cost"? He wrote these phrases on the board for his classmates to use. This way, if anyone forgets a word, they would find it on the board. He also asked them to practice the words by re-writing them in their books. After more practice with these phrases, each child would come to the "shop." Nikos was standing at the shop performing the role of the "shop-owner." Each child

Fig. 13.1 Three different students' worksheets: learning number-words in Romani

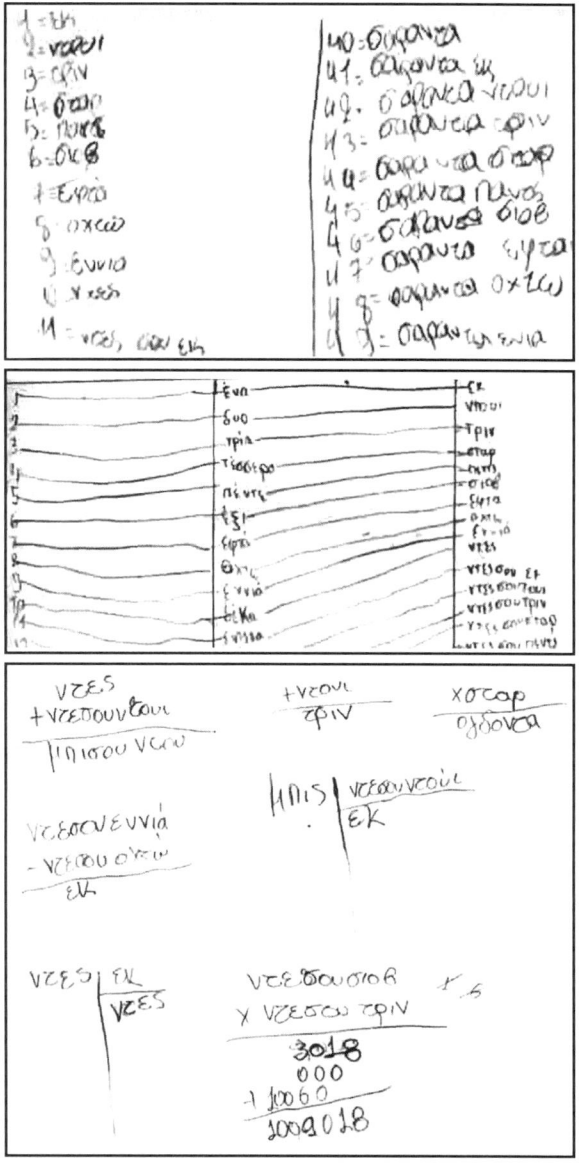

performed the role of buyer asking Nikos about the goods displayed in front of him by using the Roma phrases they just learned. All kids seemed to enjoy this dramatization process. The act of selling–buying was interpreted by some of them as learning mainly a new language. For this reason, some kids expressed an interest and found the task helpful. As one of them commented: "...it will be helpful when I go to the market." In the market, Roma people sell their goods and as a non-Tsiggano

Fig. 13.2 Panagiotis performs the teacher

child mentions this is a possibility for enhancing communication based on using some Romani phrases. We agreed that this was a good idea, and after spending some time practicing the new phrases, we moved into the role-playing of selling and buying goods using the newly learned Romani phrases and word numbers (see Figure 13.3 and Figure 13.4).

So, what might be the significance for both Tsiggano and non-Tsiggano children of being-in-the event of performing Romany mathematics words? What are

Fig. 13.3 Acting out the market: selling and buying in Romani

Fig. 13.4 Learning words useful for creating sell and buy problems (Two different worksheets)

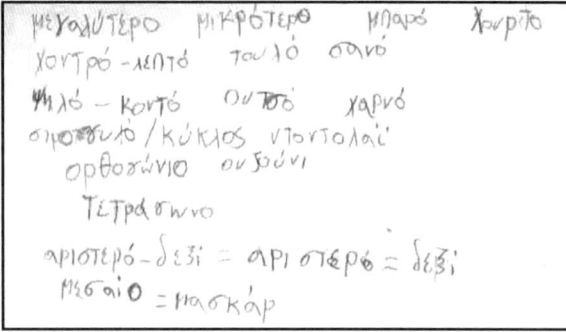

the unfolding significations for their identity work as mathematics learners? Is this "performative act" merely about teaching Romani numbers as a foreign language, or does the performing of Tsiggano-math-words opens up "alternative" ways of embracing self–other narratives and challenge the status of hegemonic discourses? Is it merely about performing street commerce or does this performative act have deeper effects for the subjects who enact the teaching and learning in Tsiggano mathematics words? As said before, a socio-cultural perspective emphasizes multilingualism and "funds of knowledge" as resources for mathematical learning development. However, I would stress here that performing mathematics in one's own mother tongue, and especially when this tongue is marginalized and excluded from state practices, has an additional potential. It can serve to a deeply political and ethical responsibility. Tsiggano children performing school mathematics in Romani at the public space of a school classroom resembles a protest by illegal immigrants who in May 2006 took to the streets in Los Angeles and started to sing the national anthem of the United States in both English and Spanish. As Butler and Spivak (2007) explain in a short book entitled "Who sings the nation-state" the event travelled widely via the web and created media debates in a context where political battles over language hegemony in a multi-lingual country such as the US are not settled. Specifically, in the state of California, debates concern whether English should be the obligatory language for all public services including all public schools. One can imagine how the act of singing the US national anthem in Spanish becomes an outrage for those who are strong advocates of "English-only" policies.

In a similar vein, when Tsiggano children perform mathematics in the Romani language, it's almost as if they are "singing" a western national anthem! On the one hand, the public use of the Romani language in a school classroom carries risk. Its use in state schools is not (officially) permitted and those who dare to break this rule could be prosecuted. On the other hand, the Romani language exists only as an oral code and as such is regarded as an inadequate mediator for formal schooling and especially for scientific learning. Thus, for Panagiotis, a Tsiggano boy, to perform the teacher and to teach the whole class how to count in Romani was certainly not only a huge, but a risky or even a precarious in Judith Butler's words, step to take. Panagiotis performs, in a series of teaching slots, the teacher who organizes a mathematics lesson based on knowledge from his own culture and language. But, he also performs authority and competence to deal with formal practices. Such a "performative act" can be conceived as utopian since Tsiggano culture and language are not utilized as a resource in state education. For some it might entail the risk of ridiculing a traumatic reality, but for others it might entail the hope of an alternative possibility (see Figure 13.5).

Butler and Spivak (2007), when discussing the street singing of illegal immigrants in the US argue, based on Hannah Arendt that singing in Spanish performs several functions including the "right to have rights" (Arendt, 1958/1988). The performative act of signing is not only about asserting the multi-lingual reality of the public sphere in the US, but it also presents a way of articulating the human subject's *right to have a voice and become visible*. A street performance, thus, is related directly to processes of reclaiming agency. Similarly, the school mathematics classroom performance of "singing" numbers functions equally as a way of reclaiming agency as mathematics learners by means of voicing their "right to mathematics."

Fig. 13.5 Classroom and students during the teaching experiment

Troubling Essentialist Identities: Discussing a Politics of Possibility

A politics of possibility is discussed by Denzin (2003) as part of "performance" ethnographic research. He cites Madison (1998) who discusses the impact of performing the story of two African American female cafeteria workers. In 1968 at the University of North Carolina they led a strike protesting for better work and pay conditions. Although their struggle as "strike leaders" was never acknowledged by the university, the performance itself

> ..allowed these women and their families to bear witness to their suppressed history. This performance did not create a revolution, but it was 'revolutionary in enlightening citizens to the possibilities that grate against injustice (Madison, 1998; p. 280).

Denzin (2003) argues that the importance of these performances is that they

> . . .interrogate and evaluate specific social, educational, economic and political processes. This form of praxis can shape a cultural politics of change. It can help to create a progressive and involved citizenship. The performance becomes the vehicle for moving persons, subjects, performers, and audience members into new, critical, political spaces (p. 19).

In the context of the "Mathematics in Tsiggano words" teaching experiment discussed here, children's experiences were sought by asking them to discuss, reflect on, and evaluate what had happened. Since, the potential of performing teaching and learning school mathematics in alternative ways indicated a potential of embracing the "other," the children's own experiences could be unlocked. When talking to non-Tsiggano children about their feelings for Tsiggano children, one realizes that aspects of the dominant discourse genre (e.g. racist feelings) are still apparent. For example, Aggeliki says:

> My parents do not suggest anything in particular but only that I have to be careful because they may rob me.

Martha:

> I haven't discussed this [with my parents] (...) but I know they do not like them. . . My mum says that if I am friends with them, I should not speak Greek (...) I will lose touch with my language.

Stella:

> They say that I have to be careful with them because they might have a disease and so I should stay away. I must stay far away because they hit.

And Tasoula:

> No, they do not like them because they do not know them. We do not meet and so they do not like them. (...) I do not like them too. They hit and they say bad words.

Parental "voices" are mediated through these kids who themselves act as cultural tools perpetuating the power of a hegemonic discourse about Roma people. Cultural hegemony has been coined by Gramsci (1971) in order to bring to the fore the ideological function of social representations, emphasizing the role of power in the cultural production of meaning. However, the very same children express a will to learn the Romani language as a means to communicate with Roma people in the market. They add: *"(...) we can now understand what is happening in the corridors, in break-time and outside school."* Both positions seem antithetical and almost in opposition to each other. At the same time, these oppositional stances entail hybridity and as such they carry potential for moving positions and thus for engaging in dialogicality. The comment made by Antonis indicates such a move:

> He [Panagiotis] liked it, because they can never use their language here. Only outside....

The normalized irony that Tsiggano kids enter school and classrooms by leaving their mother tongue outside now appears to be a paradox. Panagiotis explains:

> We can only speak our language during breaks. But even then, teachers think we shout or swear at each other. And they get angry at us. They tell us to stop speaking tsigganika at school.

This highlights the oppression Tsiggano children face when they try to communicate in school. The present teaching experiment was a rare event in children's life where their mother tongue was not forbidden but, instead, encouraged to be performed in the public sphere of a school classroom. This performance could potentially work towards creating an entry to the possibility for dialogicality. This could be materialized through making explicit aspects of heteroglossia (i.e. focusing on the presence of multiple social languages, embracing alterity, challenging the dominance of monolingualism). It comes as no surprise that kids with a non-Greek cultural background are quite content with this innovative teaching intervention. For example, Iraklis, an Albanian boy, and Vassilis, who is Bulgarian, could associate themselves with Panagiotis more than any other classmate. They both were asking if we could teach numbers in their language, too. Iraklis, for instance, mentioned that:

> (...) He [Panagioti] was much calmer... Something, like a first time. I believe he liked it. Because he will study and if he wants to be a teacher, he knows now how to start. . ..

And Vasilis said:

> He liked being a teacher... And he wanted to say many things in his tsiggano language and he liked it.

Perhaps, we could consider the cases not only of Panagiotis, but of all children, as indicative of a politics of possibility that opens up a dialogue amongst "self" and "other". More specifically, children's narratives revealed a possibility for dialogue by means of creating hybrid and multi-vocal space(s) for identity-work or intersubjectivity (Bakhtin, 1979/1986; Kamberelis, 2001) at several levels; cultural, linguistic, pedagogic, epistemological, ethical, or political. Identity-work is primarily about constructing a sense of belonging and constructing this belonging is never an individual act. Instead, it performs publicly and the classroom locality provides the foreground for setting up the scene for identity-work in a public sphere.

Concluding Remarks

Taking into account that, on the one hand, oppressive learning experiences felt by most children who belong to marginalized groups due to ethnicity, class or gender are not scarce, and that, on the other hand, an essentialist nature of formal school mathematics that tends to capture human learning development in static terms is still prevalent amongst curricula practices such as learning content and assessment procedures, the present study aimed to open up an alternative politics of possibility. Specifically, by means of discussing the effects of two ethnographic teaching experiments as performative acts, the aim was to explore the possibility of breaking dominant discursive narratives in constructing certain fixed learning identities for children in monologic mathematics classrooms (see Matusov, 2004, in preparation). Contrary to hegemonic images about either subject (Tsiggano children) or object identities (school mathematics), identities are becoming produced in a liminal space between traditional and modern practices. In this sense, not only Tsiggano learning identities but also mathematics become performative in the school mathematics classroom and this means that children-with-mathematics become active participants in a complex assemblage. As Latour (2005) has claimed objects, tools, and materials are also actors along with humans as part of scientific and everyday practices.

Although this chapter is based on earlier work (e.g. Chronaki, 2003, 2005, 2008a), here, I re-work an added notion of the ethnographic teaching experiment methodology as a location for performative mathematics. Mathematics, as all science and technology, is performative. Law (2004) reminds us that science has the potential for transforming our realities and, thus, our lives. Humans and objects, tools or materials are symmetrically involved in action (Latour, 1994). The way number, in a broad sense, has influenced the development and realization of modernity could be a manifestation of this (see Chronaki, 2010). But how does mathematics becomes performative in the lives of children such as Maria, Giannoula, and Panagiotis? What type of performativity enables them to argue that "mathematics runs in our blood"? And what performative acts constitute them as incompetent for formal school mathematics?

Greek Tsiggano or Roma culture develops at the borders amongst varied traditional and modern forms of Gypsy and Greek culture. It is in this space that "voiceless" Tsiggano children, as the subaltern in Spivak's (1988) words[3], struggle for recognition. And it is also within the same space that "hate speech" in Butler's (1997) words, as a category of illocutionary act, generate as acts of naming with

---

[3]Gramsci originally coined the term 'subaltern' in order to address the economically dispossessed. Currently, Ranajit Guha has reappropriated Gramsci's term in an effort to locate and re-establish a voice or collective locus of agency in post-colonial India. In her essay "Can the Subaltern Speak?", Spivak acknowledges the importance of understanding the 'subaltern' standpoint but also criticizes the efforts of certain subaltern studies' emphasis towards creating a 'collective voice' through Westernized mediating practices. Spivak's essay "Can the Subaltern Speak?" was originally published in Nelson and Grossberg (1988).

sinister (and violent) implications and produce institutional conditions (e.g. curricula practices) for violence and racism to function. Ethnographic observation and interviewing, as seen in the previous sections, indicates how children from both cultures perform varied stereotypes about not only Gypsy learning identities, but also Greek and other ethnic minorities' identities. Identities, as seen above, are not chosen, negotiable or shared at will and dialogism is not always achieved. It is necessary, based on the previous section and in particular for the cases of Tsiggano children mentioned, to ask how social agency relates to a repertoire of social skills and cultural resources that mediate its fabrication over time.

What makes us who we are is not a pre-existing, invariable core of identity, but a series of reiterative identity effects that allow us to act in the world. Captured through the same lenses the identity of the so-called mathematically able or the so-called Roma learner are constructed as "marked categories" and seem to represent two opposites of a pendulum. In other words, even though Tsigannos people admit favorably that "mathematics runs in our blood," the image of a mathematically able Gypsy pupil becomes almost an impossible fantasy. Butler's politics of performativity as a way to talk about politics of identity has received considerable critique (see Boucher, 2006; McNay, 1999) on the grounds that subject agency is mainly conceived as culturally and not institutionally or collectively formatted. As Boucher (2006) argues, an exclusive emphasis for

> the interpersonal and intrapsychic dynamics of identity conflict [...] evacuates the materiality of institutions and reduces the social field to the sum of dyadic interpersonal collisions (p. 113).

McNay (1999, 2000), in her attempts to understand subject production in relation to subject agency and change, explains that Judith Butler's thought, as rooted in Lacanian and Foucaultian theory, frames subjectivity mainly as "lack." She further suggests the need to deploy Butler's theory along with more sociological and philosophical accounts on identification (e.g. Pierre Bourdieu, Paul Ricouer, and Cornelius Castoriadis) that could support imagining agency, not as monadic, but as a dialectic interaction amongst subject and historical context.

Certainly, these claims need further attention. Teaching experiments as "performances" can be seen as cultural resources that have the potential to create a passage to such dialectical interactions (or performativities) where subject relate to historical texts. Clearly, performativity and performance exist in tension with one another, in a tension between doing, or performing and the done, the text produced by the performance. Whilst performance is sensuous and contingent, performativity *"becomes the everyday practice of doing what's done"* (Pollock, 1998, p. 43). This can also be observed as part of my research in the context of the ethnographic teaching experiments either as a "performative act" aiming to design for a "disruption" of hegemonic images or as "performativity" where identity-work becomes captured by what is already done in the past and what can be imagined for the future.

Performances tend to act as "troubling mirrors" for performativity and although they have the potential for disrupting hegemonic discourses, they cannot guarantee a smooth transition towards dialogicality. However, they create a location for a politics of possibility as seen in previous sections. Pollock (1998) asserts that performativity is "what happens when history/textuality sees itself in the mirror – and suddenly sees double; it is the disorienting, [the] disruptive" (p. 43). Performativity derives its power and prerogative in the breaking and making of the very textual frameworks that give it meaning in the first place (p. 44). Could we, by following the above line of thinking, argue that children's identity-work is captured along the terms of a performativity that is constantly informed by history and textuality and is *almost* beyond their agency? This *almost* can be a pivotal point when a mirror appears as Pollock says above – a mirror that enables the performative to avoid obedience to the grand discourses and become disruptive. It might be that only when a "performance" acts as a mirror for "performativity" that it entails a possibility for disrupting what is taken to be shared as *"normal" learning identities*. And, as such it can set notions of culture and identity "in motion." Performative mathematics as political acts of performances can then be seen as "troubling mirrors" that disrupt hegemonic discourses and thus can create locations for a politics of possibility.

Acknowledgments The present chapter is based on a meta-analysis of previous studies. I would like to thank all students, teachers, and student-teachers who have enabled this study in a wide variety of ways. At the same time I would like to thank three very close colleagues Manolis Dafermos, Panagiotis Kanellopoulos, and Michalis Kontopodis for their support, strength, and inspiration towards a better way of living in academia.

References

Arendt, H. (1958/1988). *The human condition*. Chicago: University of Chicago Press.

Bakhtin, M. (1979/1986). *Speech genres and other late essays*. (C. Emerson & M. Holquist, Eds., V. McGee, Trans.). Austin, TX: University of Texas Press.

Bauchspies, W. (2005). Sharing shoes and counting years: Mathematics, colonialisation and communication. In A. Chronaki & I. M. Christiansen (Eds.) *Challenging perspectives on mathematics classroom communication* (pp. 237–260). Connecticut: IAP press.

Boucher, G. (2006). The politics of performativity: A critique of Judith Butler. *Parrhesia, 1*, 112–141.

Butler, J. P. (1988). Performative acts and gender constitution: An essay in phenomenology and feminist theory. *Theatre Journal, 40*(4), 519–531.

Butler, J. P. (1990). *Gender trouble: Feminism and the subversion of identity*. New York: Routledge.

Butler, J. P. (1993). *Bodies that matter: On the discursive limits of 'sex'*. New York: Routledge.

Butler, J. P. (1997). *Excitable speech: A politics of the performative*. London and New York: Routledge.

Butler, J. P., & Spivak, G. C. (2007) *Who sings the Nation-State?: Language, politics, belonging*. Calcutta and New York: Seagull Books.

Chronaki, A. (2003). *Developing mathematical learning as mastering new tools and entering new discourses: Some thoughts on a very complex process*. Paper presented in the EARLI (European Association of Research in Learning and Instruction). August 2003, Padova, Italy.

Chronaki, A. (2005). Learning about 'learning identities' in the school arithmetic practice: The experience of two young minority Gypsy girls in the Greek context of education. *European Journal of Psychology of Education: Special Issue on "The Social Mediation of Learning in Multiethnic Classrooms"*, *20*(1), 61–74.

Chronaki, A. (2008a). An entry to dialogicality in the maths classrooms: Encouraging hybrid learning identities. In M. Cesar & K. Kumpulainen (Eds.), *Social interactions in multicultural settings* (pp. 117–145). Rotterdam: Sense Publishers.

Chronaki, A. (2008b). *Mathematics, technologies, education: The gender perspective*. Volos: University of Thessaly Press.

Chronaki, A. (2010). Revisiting mathemacy: A process-reading of critical mathematics education. In H. Alro, O. Ravn, & P. Valero (Eds.), *Critical mathematics education: Past, present and future* (pp. 31–50). Rotterdam: Sense Publishers.

Clifford, J. (2000). *Routes: Travel and translation in the late twentieth century*. Cambridge, MA: Harvard University Press.

Dafermos, M. (2006). *Marginalisation and Educational Inclusion*. Athens: Atrapos.

Damarin, S. (2000). The mathematically able as a marked category. *Gender and Education, 12*(1), 69–85.

Denzin, N. K. (2003). *Performance ethnography: Critical pedagogy and the politics of culture*. Thousand Oaks, CA: Sage Publications.

Diamond, E. (1996). Introduction. In E. Diamond (Ed.), *Performance and cultural politics*. New York: Routledge.

Diawara, M. (1996). Black studies, cultural studies: Performative acts. In J. Storey (Ed.), *What is cultural studies? A reader* (pp. 300–306). London: Arnold.

Hall, S., & du Gay, P. (Eds.). (1996). *Questions of cultural identity*. London: Sage Publications.

Haraway, D. (1997). *Modest_Witness@Second_Millennium. FemaleMan©_Meets_OncoMouse^{TM}*. New York: Routledge.

Hedegaard, M., & Chaiklin, S. (2005). *Radical-local teaching and learning: A cultural-historical approach*. Aarhus: Aarhus University Press.

Hitchcock, P. (1992). *Dialogics of the oppressed*. Minneapolis, MN: University of Minnesota Press.

Kamberelis, G. (2001). Producing heteroglossic classroom (Micro)cultures through hybrid discourse practice. *Linguistics and Education, 12*(1), 85–125.

Latour, B. (2005). *Reassembling the social: An introduction to Actor-Network-Theory*. Oxford and New York: Oxford University Press.

Law, J. (2004). *After method: Mess in social science research*. London: Routledge.

Madison, D. S. (1998). Performances, personal narratives, and the politics of possibility. In S. J. Dailey (Ed.), *The future of performance studies: Visions and revisions*. Washington, DC: National Communication Association.

Matusov, E. (2004). Bakhtin's dialogic pedagogy (Guest Editor's Introduction). *Journal of Russian and East European Psychology, 42*(6), 3–11.

Matusov, E. (2009). Pedagogical chronotopes of monologic conventional classrooms: ontology and didactics. In *Journey into Dialogic Pedagogy*. Hauppauge, NY: Nova Publishers.

McNay, L. (1999). Subject, psyche and agency: The work of Judith Butler. *Theory, Culture, Society, 16*(2): 175–193.

McNay, L. (2000). *Gender and agency: Reconfiguring the Subject in feminist and social theory*. Cambridge: Polity Press.

Mimica, J. (1988). *Intimations of infinity: The mythopoeia of the Iqwaye counting system and number*, Oxford, New York and Hamburg: Berg.

Navarro, A. (1974). The evolution of Chicano politics in Aztlan. *Chicano Journal of Social Sciences and the Arts*, 5, 72.

Nelson, C., & Grossberg, L. (Eds.). (1988). *Marxism and the Interpretation of Culture* (pp. 271–313). London: Macmillan.

Nunes, T. (1997). Systems of signs and mathematical reasoning. In T. Nunes & P. Bryant (Eds.), *Learning and teaching mathematics: An international perspective*. Oxford: Psychology Press/Taylor and Francis.

Okely, J. (1983). *Changing cultures: The traveller-gypsies*. Cambridge: Cambridge University Press.

Okely, J. (1997). Some political consequences of theories of gypsy ethnicity: The place of the intellectual. In A. James, J. Hokney, & A. Dowson (Eds.), *After writing culture: Epistemology and Praxis in contemporary anthropology*. London: Routledge.

Pereen, E. (2007). *Intersubjectivities and popular culture: Bakhtin and beyond.* Stanford. Stanford University Press.

Pollock, D. (1998). Performing writing. In P. Phelan & J. Lane (Eds.), *The ends of performance.* New York: New York University Press.

Restivo, S. (1991). Mathematics in society and history: Sociological inquiries. Dordrecht, Boston and London: Kluwer Academic Publishers.

Said, E. (1978). *Orientalism: Western conceptions of the orient.* London: Penguin Press.

Schechner, R. (1985). *Between theater and anthropology.* Philadelphia: University of Philadelphia Press.

Spivak, G. C. (1988). Can the subaltern speak? In C. Nelson & L. Grossberg (Eds.) *Marxism and the interpretation of culture* (pp. 271-313). Urbana/Chicago: University of Illinois Press

Walkerdine, V. (1988). *The mastery of reason: Cognitive Development and the production of rationality.* London: Routledge.

Young, R. J. C. (2001). *Postcolonialism: An historical introduction* (1st ed.). Oxford: Blackwell Publishing.

Chapter 14
The Role of *Practice* in Cultural-Historical Science

Seth Chaiklin

> *Es wird sich zeigen, dass es sich nicht um einen großen
> Gedankenstrich zwischen Vergangenheit und Zukunft handelt,
> sondern um die Vollziehung der Gedanken der Vergangenheit.
> Es wird sich endlich zeigen, dass die Menschheit keine neue
> Arbeit beginnt, sondern mit Bewusstsein ihre alte Arbeit
> zustande bringt.*
>
> (Marx, 1843/1975, pp. 56–7)[1]

The Main Idea in Brief

All sciences have an *object* toward which they are directed. *Cultural-historical science* is directed to the study of human practices. *Human practices* are manifest in institutionally structured traditions of action, which are organised in relation to the production of collectively needed products. Cultural-historical science is directed to investigating these institutionally structured traditions of action. This chapter elaborates some general conceptual, philosophical, and practical considerations for making these investigations more concretely.

The expression *cultural-historical science* has been adopted to reflect a generalisation of a line of thinking grounded in cultural-historical psychology, and subsequent theoretical developments inspired by this psychology. Cultural-historical science has its own conceptual foundation and justification; it does not depend

S. Chaiklin (✉)
University of Bath, Bath, UK
e-mail: s.chaiklin@bath.ac.uk

[1]It will become evident that it is not a matter of a large hyphen between past and future, but of *realising* the thoughts of the past. It will become evident finally that mankind is not beginning a *new* work, but is consciously carrying into effect its old work.

M. Kontopodis et al. (eds.), *Children, Development and Education*, International
Perspectives on Early Childhood Education and Development 3,
DOI 10.1007/978-94-007-0243-1_14, © Springer Science+Business Media B.V. 2011

directly on the history of other social sciences that have included *practice* within the scope of their object. This chapter clarifies (a) some of the research problems that have led to the formulation of this science, (b) the meanings of *object* and *practice*, (c) some of the first social scientific developments that focus on *practice*, and (d) some general principles of investigation in cultural-historical science. It concludes with some brief remarks about orienting points for further work.

The Road to Cultural-Historical Science: Practical Origins

The general notion of *practice* has been present within cultural-historical psychology from its beginning in the 1920s, because of its focus on historically developed practices – both as a necessary part of the process of forming psychological capabilities and as the source of psychological contents acquired by individuals. For example, Vygotsky and Luria, focused on the mastery of cultural forms of behaviour, with Vygotsky (e.g., 1929) drawing methodological consequences in his historical-genetic method, which focused on the genesis of psychological capabilities. Drawing on materialist ideas from Marx (cf. *The German Ideology*) about the important role of practice for the development of many psychological capabilities, and continuing Vygotsky's historical focus, Leontiev (1973/1959, 1978/1975) argued that psychological studies have to recognise that psychological processes (e.g., thinking and cognition) are inseparably bound with the processes of human life. This view was extended even further by one of Vygotsky's research collaborators, who asserted the need to study children's development in the actual processes of formation, such as in school classrooms (El'konin, 1961, p. 4). In all these instances, however, *practice* is treated as a background or precondition for understanding the development of psychological capabilities, rather than a central focus of investigation in its own right. As will be discussed later in this chapter, Vygotsky (1997b/1926) gave a brief paean to practice as being central for the development of psychology, but in general, there has not been direct attention to practice as an object of study.

My own entry into questions about practice first started with an interest to better understand what it means to understand human action in meaningful practices (e.g., Chaiklin & Lave, 1993). That interest continued as many researchers pointed at the importance of practices, and the need to understand their historical development, but often it came no further than pointing at or describing the problem (e.g., Rockwell, 1999; Scribner, 1985).

My awareness for the need to focus on *practice* as an object of study became particularly acute when I started to work with practitioners on trying to solve problems within their practice. The particular concern – which became formulated as *practice-developing research* (Chaiklin, 2006) – was how to make cooperative actions with practitioners that concurrently address an immediate practical problem, while giving a platform for "developing" a practice. In working on such problems as what it means to "develop" a practice, both theoretically and practically, and in working with practitioners to make a model of their own practice, it became more apparent that existing theoretical resources for describing practices were barely existent. The need and importance to focus more directly on practice arose against this background. The theory of activity could be one way to address these problems, but the *activity* concept, as developed by Leontiev, is used to address too many issues. It looked productive to separate a *practice* concept from an *activity* concept, which has led to the present formulation of cultural-historical science.

The Meaning of "Object"

Every science investigates a range of specific substantive phenomena, where each science is differentiated from another by an overall defining characteristic that articulates "to what" the science is directed generally. Some European traditions use a word to refer technically to this "what". For example, in the German tradition, one speaks of the *Gegenstand* of a science (e.g., Laucken, Schick, & Höge, 1996). Similarly, in Scandinavian traditions, one formulates the *genstand* (Danish) (or *gjenstand* [Norwegian]) of a science (e.g., at the University of Copenhagen, the first semester of psychology includes a course on the *genstand* of psychology).

There does not seem to be a specific English word for this purpose. Perhaps *object* is the closest translation to this idea. One of the definitional entries for *object* in the *Oxford English Dictionary* reflects this general idea of "the end to which effort is directed; the thing sought, aimed at, or striven for". But the normal connotations of *object* in English do not include the idea of *topic* or *subject matter*, and the *Dictionary* does not indicate any sense of *object* as a technical or theoretical term. For example, the definitions and examples of the noun *object* given in the *Oxford English Dictionary* do not mention the words *science*, *research*, *academic*, *knowledge*, *topic* or *subject matter*. In short, the use of the word *object* in English does not seem to call forth the intense focus on articulating the general objective toward which a science is directed.

Perhaps brief mention of this linguistic lacuna in English is sufficient for overcoming it – or at least introducing the idea of "object of a science" in a technical sense. To take some of the social scientific disciplines that originated in the nineteenth century, the object of psychology is sometimes defined as the "science of human behaviour" or the "science of the human mind and its functions"; anthropology is described broadly as the "science of humanity", or in some more specific versions, as a "science of culture and social organisation of a particular people". These crude dictionary definitions serve to illustrate the idea of *object* as outlining the general category of phenomena that a science seeks to investigate, where different sciences are directed to different overarching objects.

Specific aspects within a particular science's object may overlap with another science (e.g., some problems, such as personality, have been investigated by psychologists, sociologists and anthropologists), but, in general, different sciences are formed in relation to different objects.

Any particular science is defined by the "object" on which it is focused, even if there are fundamental differences in the theoretical assumptions used to address the object. For example, in relation to psychology as a study of human behaviour, or the mind and its functions, some researchers use a cognitive psychological approach (e.g., committed to ideas of representations, uses of representations, and near-decomposability of mental processes and structures in relation to a context in which they operate) to explain human action (e.g., Anderson, Reder, & Simon, 1997, pp. 20–21), while others use a cultural-historical theory that focuses on mastering systems of signs and actions that have developed historically. Both are pursuing (roughly) the same object (e.g., explanation of human cognition and action), and often can use the same empirical material, but interpret or explain the empirical material differently. The visible differences between theoretical perspectives arise in the forms and kinds of knowledge sought about its object, where the formulation and investigation of specific questions depend on the theoretical choices used to delimit or select phenomena (i.e., ontological assumptions), which in turn usually engender particular epistemological assumptions or requirements for investigating these phenomena.

In cultural-historical science, the object is human practices, including both their collective development and their interaction with individual development. This object is formulated with its own positive intellectual roots, drawn in part from the nineteenth century, but cutting across the categories typically found to differentiate nineteenth century social science conceptions (e.g., individual vs. societal). In other words, this science is not simply a combination of (parts of) previous social sciences or a delimitation of a special subfield within one or more of these social sciences.

Whether psychology and anthropology, as presently conceived, will continue to survive and thrive as coherent sciences is irrelevant to the question of whether cultural-historical science can be formulated and pursued. The relation of cultural-historical science to these historical categories is addressed in the concluding section.

The general idea of *object* has now been introduced, along with the idea that the object of cultural-historical science is focused centrally on human practices; the next step in introducing cultural-historical science is to elaborate the meaning of *practice*.

The Meaning of "Practice"

Given that practice is conceived as an object of research, it is necessary to define or delimit the phenomena encompassed by this term. At the same time, because practice is a research object, a comprehensive, a priori definition is not expected nor intended. The following discussion provides (a) six conditions to be considered when formulating a definition of practice, (b) some initial indications about the meaning of practice, and (c) comments on theoretical implications of this definition.

Conditions for Defining Practice as a Theoretical Term

A first condition in defining *practice* is that the word has been used in the English language for at least 600 years. A variety of connotations and traditions of use for this word have arisen over this time, both in everyday and scientific contexts.

A second condition is that scientific meanings may or may not overlap with everyday meanings (i.e., there can be differences between everyday and scientific meanings). The problem is not a choice of words; we have little choice, but to use words, possibly ones with everyday meanings. Therefore, it is important to note that everyday word such as *practice* can be used in a scientific conception without intending an everyday meaning. This condition is not restricted to the social sciences. Consider this observation from Bohr (1950):

> [P]hrases often found in the physical literature, like "disturbance of phenomena by observation" or "creation of physical attributes of objects by measurements", represent a use of words like *phenomena* and *observation* as well as *attribute* and *measurement* which is hardly compatible with common usage and practical definition and, therefore, is apt to cause confusion. (p. 53)

But as Bohr also notes:

> [O]ur task can only be to aim at communicating experiences and views to others by means of language, in which the practical use of every word stands in a complementary relation to attempts of its strict definition. (p. 54)

A third condition is that the meaning of a word, when it serves as a concept, is not delimited by the definition of the word itself. The meaning of a word referring to a scientific concept is defined in part by its relation to a system of concepts. For example, as Bohr points out with his concept of complementarity, definitions of concepts are tied to measurement procedures. The problem is to articulate the system of ideas being defined, rather than trying to find the true meaning of *practice*.

A fourth condition arises because different theoretical perspectives within scientific traditions can engender definitions or ways of using the term *practice* to refer to different relations. Multiplicity of terms and definitional problems has been an ongoing problem in psychology (e.g., J.M. Baldwin, 1910, proposed a committee for unification of terminology in psychology with the idea of making a standardised dictionary of terms; multiple different meanings for the concept of intelligence among two dozen researchers, Sternberg & Detterman, 1986).

A fifth condition is that even if a standard definition is made, the meanings of technical terms do not always remain static; they transform as the system of theoretical concepts is developed. Vygotsky (1997b/1926, p. 282), while praising the contribution of Baldwin's dictionary (from 1901 to 1906), also notes that attempts to read contemporary books (in the mid-1920s) with this dictionary is impossible, because the meanings of words have changed.

A sixth condition is the peril of working in a pluralistic theoretical environment, especially when one wants to establish a theoretical definition that runs against standard usage. This condition should be familiar to researchers in the cultural-historical tradition who must explain, for example, that the meaning of *personality* refers to motives and personal sense, not to traits (cf. Chaiklin, 2001).

Given these conditions, there is no intention to provide an ultimate or comprehensive definition of *practice* that incorporates or covers the scope of existing usage and connotation. The meaningful formulation developed here does not necessarily have to be reduced to or equated with other definitions of *practice*. Some researchers may ignore or misinterpret explications and reasons for this specific definition, or continue to presuppose that there is a true, or primal, or essential meaning for *practice* – but then they must explain why this definition should dominate or why there cannot be a multiplicity of meanings. There is no suggestion that others should stop using their definitions or meanings of practice and adopt the one presented here, but researchers who want to use a different meaning of practice must elaborate and clarify their intended meaning (as attempted here).

Practice: A Dictionary Investigation

One way to formulate a concept of practice as an object of scientific investigation is to look in a standard dictionary, such as the *Oxford English Dictionary*. The meanings presented in the dictionary are formed in an historical way, reflecting the richness and embeddedness found in the everyday meanings associated with practice. That is, examples of "everyday use" of this term from over the centuries are collected, with linguists making a reductive analysis of the main themes in how this word has been used (comparable to a social scientific researcher who makes a reductive analysis of the main themes in an interview). In this way, it is possible to become aware of the range of issues and themes commonly intended with the everyday use of the word *practice*.

There is no expectation that the dictionary has discovered or recorded the true or more primal meaning of practice. One must form the scientific object from theoretical analysis, rather than accept uncritically the everyday meanings expressed in a dictionary as an adequate theoretical account for the idea of practice. While not denying or denigrating the value of everyday language, there is no reason to be restricted by existing conventions and consciousness associated with its definitions of *practice*. The remainder of this section explicates the inadequacy of these definitions, which helps clarify what is needed in a definition of practice for cultural-historical science.

In the analysis, all definitions, of *praxis* and *practice* (as nouns) in the *Oxford English Dictionary* (and not marked as obsolete) were examined. The main ideas in these definitions are listed under the heading "Characteristic" in Table 14.1. The number of each dictionary entry is identified in the top row of Table 14.1, with the x subscript marking the *praxis* definition. The $\sqrt{}$ indicates which characteristics are given for that definition. For example, the definition for the first column ($1a_x$) is: "Action or practice; *spec.* The practice or exercise of a technical subject or art, as distinct from the theory of it; (also) accepted or habitual practice or custom".

Table 14.1 Simple analysis of definitions of *praxis* and *practice*

Characteristic	$1a_x$	$1b_x$	$1c_x$	$1d_x$	$1e_x$	1	2a	2d	3a	3b	3c	4
Action / carrying out / doing	✓	✓	✓	✓	✓	✓	✓	✓	✓	✓		✓
Distinct from theory	✓	✓		✓			✓	✓				
Voluntary		✓			✓							
Skilful					✓							
Habitual / custom	✓									✓	✓	
Technical skill / profession	✓					✓						
Systematic / procedure											✓	✓

The main elements of this entry are noted with a ✓ as seen in Table 14.1. Similar classification was made for the other definitions. Table 14.1 covers more or less all the variations that appear in these definitions.

As can be seen from Table 14.1, most of the dictionary definitions focus either on actions in general or more specifically on traditions of habitual, professional, technical, or skilful action. These actions may be conscious and wilful, but they do not need to be, especially if they are customary and habitual. This is fine, as far as it goes, but these everyday conceptualisations of the meanings of practice are focused mostly on observable aspects of practice, without giving an account or indication for why these actions exist or to what purpose they are directed. There is no account for the dynamics of actions. In other words, the dictionary does not include a theory of "practice" (as defined in the next section) as part of its definitions of *practice*. The following formulation of *practice* addresses these problems, trying to give a clear idea of the object to which cultural-historical science is directed.

Theoretical Definition of "Practice"

As just noted, one significant failure with the dictionary definitions is that they do not include any mention or indication of the object to which practice is directed (neither generally nor specifically). In the notion of practice developed here, this is an important defining characteristic.

All practices are organised around producing particular objects or products, where these objects are necessary for reproducing some conditions of life. Practices arise when, over time, these needed objects are repeatedly lacking (e.g. because they are consumed or new persons appear).

The assumption is that collectively (i.e., as a species) humans respond to these lacks by making material transformations that produce material objects or conditions that overcome the lack, thereby satisfying the need. Although a need may be satisfied in a particular instance (e.g., *your* house is built, *your* shoes are made), this general need (and associated lack) continues to appear for others, and may reappear again for you. A practice is reflected in a historically developed tradition of action that grows up around producing products that satisfy a generalised need (in relation

to reproduction for conditions of life). The term *generalised* is meant to empha-
sise that a need is found among many persons, as opposed to a single individual.
Conditions of life is meant to be understood historically, in that conditions for life
now include many objects and products that go long past pure physiological need[2].

For example, most societies use symbolic forms in their reproduction of conditions of life, where many societal practices depend on these symbolic uses.
Knowledge of these forms is a repeated lack, in that all humans are born without
this knowledge. Traditions of action (e.g. manifested as instruction in schooling
organisations) address this lack by aiming to produce an object (e.g. specific ability to work with necessary forms) that overcomes this lack, thereby satisfying a
generalised need in relation to the reproduction of life conditions.

Note that practice is conceptualised here as an ideal[3] that is manifested or
reflected in actions. The challenge of practice analysis is to formulate the ideal
embodied in a tradition of action.

A second (and related) failure in the dictionary definitions is that the general
idea of practice is not differentiated from specific forms of practice. The notion of
practice explicated here is understood as embodying three forms. The first form –
just described – is an abstract universal form. (All) practices appear as traditions of
action that aim to produce objects or products that satisfy collective or generalised
needs.

This universal characterisation of practice is not particularly useful as an object of
scientific investigation. Some might even consider it a metaphysical assumption that
can only be asserted but not substantiated. While it is possible to investigate the idea
of practice in this general form, it is often more interesting and important to study a
specific practice, in relation to particular generalised needs and products that satisfy
these needs. This second form (embodying the universal idea of practice) is a *specific practice*, where a specific practice is organised in relation to producing objects
for specific generalised needs. As a rule, specific practices become institutionalised
in specific societies.

Production of bread, providing legal advice, teaching school children are specific practices found in many parts of the world. To study a specific practice in
general is difficult, if not impossible. These specific practices must be analysed as
concrete practices in relation to local historical conditions (e.g., laws, traditions,
customs). The *concrete practice* is the third form (within a specific practice), which
is grounded in the historical characteristics of a specific practice. For example, the
need historically to preserve or rework legumes or grains so that the foodstuff is both
preserved and palatable has been solved differently according to whether one, for
example, produces tortilla in Mexico, pappadum in India, or knäckebröd in Sweden.

---

[2]Note that oxygen is not usually a need (from the point of view of practice), even if it is a need
(from a physiological point of view). In some limited cases (e.g., medical practices, welding),
where this gas is needed, then there are actions to produce it. But in these cases physiological need
is not motivating its production. At another historical time, it may be necessary to produce oxygen
as part of creating conditions for reproduction of life.

[3]Meant in a dialectical sense of the term, such as elaborated by Ilyenkov (1977).

A Few Theoretical Implications of the Conception

Although the preceding propositions for conceptualising practice are sparse, they yield many important implications and consequences. Here are a few of them.

The idea of need provides a hypothesis for the origin and essential defining features of a given practice. A need is satisfied by an object. The practice aims to produce the object. Without the need, there is no practice. The objects (or products) that satisfy needs serve to give a direction to actions, not in a deterministic way, but by providing an idea toward which actions are directed.

The relations between actions, product and generalised need are important for differentiating individual actions or collections of actions from a practice. The professional baker and the family may use some of the same physical actions in making bread, but the significance of these individual actions are understood differently because they are two different practices. Even though the physical product (the loaf of bread) is superficially the same, these are different objects, in that the baker is producing loaves for commodity exchange, which responds to different needs than the family which is producing loaves for their use-value in relation to their need for nutrition or aesthetic experiences.

The present discussion about generalised need has not considered concrete forms of need in any systematic way. Many spurious (or dubious) questions can arise once concrete examples are considered. Can "different" practices produce the same object? Must each need engender only one practice? Or can different practices satisfy the same need? With such abstract questions, one can quickly create classificatory nightmares. But it is easy to awaken from this bad dream, by recognising that the task is not to classify practices into mutually exclusive categories (unless one has some metaphysical reason, such as a divine plan). The external or surface forms of practices (i.e., relations between needs, practices, and objects) are understood as historical consequences of human efforts to respond to needs. It would be surprising not to find overlaps in the course of historical developments, in that generalised needs can arise that are not dependent on a single practice; and different practices can respond to these needs (e.g., consider the range of health professionals such as doctors, nurses, physiotherapists, nutritionists whose practices may be organised in part in relation to the same needs). This situation clarifies that the object of cultural-historical science is not to describe practices, but to conceptualise the processes of production and development of a practice, and the traditions of action to realise the product.

Summary Statement about Cultural-Historical Science

Cultural-historical science is the general science of the origins, development, and transformations of practices, both from individual and collective perspectives. It is directed at studying practice as an ideal, expressed in historically developed traditions of action organised to produce products that satisfy collective needs. The aim is to understand the structural dynamics that organise these actions (e.g., the needs and products around which a practice is organised; the traditions of action used to realise these needs; the processes by which individuals acquire the ability to work within a practice).

This summary statement of cultural-historical science can be elaborated further after considering some of the conceptual issues that have motivated the formulation of this science.

Historical Developments that Led to a Focus on Practice

Given that there has not been a systematic scientific tradition that has taken *practice* as its object, it is difficult to point to a particular historical event or publication that was the initial or key event for establishing this focus. Nonetheless within dialectically oriented intellectual traditions, with their focus on the historical formation of empirical phenomena, one finds many relevant ideas and insights that lead to or underpin a focus on practice as an object. One could, somewhat arbitrarily, choose to start with Vygotsky (e.g., "Practice pervades the deepest foundations of the scientific operation and reforms it from beginning to end." 1997b/1926, p. 305), or Marx's eighth thesis on Feuerbach (e.g., "All mysteries which lead theory to mysticism find their rational solution in human practice and in the comprehension of this practice[4]" 1988/1845, p. 122).

To give an impression of some of the details of these historical sources and inspirations, this section considers some works from Karl Marx in the period from 1843 to1845, and continues with a discussion of a section of Vygotsky's 1926 analysis of a crisis in psychology. These considerations bring forward some of the conceptual roots for cultural-historical science, and illuminate some historical origins of a scientific focus on practice. They also show that a central focus on human practices as an object in scientific investigations has been present for a long time in world history, even if this focus has not been a basis for extensive theoretical and empirical investigations.

Human Practice as a Starting Point for Philosophy

The first theme to be addressed is the choice of a starting point for analysis of issues concerned with human action and experiences. Often the origins of psychology are described as an empirical break with and from philosophy. For one of the conceptual roots of cultural-historical science, the break occurred within philosophy itself, where arguments arose for the necessity to start from and with human practices as a way to address philosophical problems.

---

[4]Alle Mysterien, welche die Theorie zum Mystizism[us] veranlassen, finden ihre rationelle Lösung in der menschlichen Praxis und in dem Begreifen dieser Praxis.

The following brief discussion highlights some of Karl Marx's considerations that direct a focus on human practices as the way to address philosophical problems. Perhaps the most important formulation of this idea is found in the *German Ideology*:

> The premises from which we begin . . . are the real individuals, their activity and the material conditions under which they live, both those which they find already existing and those produced by their activity. These premises can thus be verified in a purely empirical way. (Marx & Engels, 1988/1845, p. 42)

This statement comes immediately after Marx criticises German philosophers for not considering the relation between their philosophy and the German reality, "the relation of their criticism and their own material surroundings" (p. 41).

The important consequence or implication of Marx's intention is that philosophy must start from exploring the empirical consequences of human practices (cf., the eighth thesis cited previously). In other words, philosophy must be conducted through analysis of the empirical conditions of human life and its implications. This "obvious" step – to move philosophy from the critical reflection and assertions of philosophers to the analysis of the consequences of human practices for human life – is still not widely recognised among philosophers and social scientific researchers (for an exception, see Jensen, 1999).

Some of the considerations leading to this formulation can be seen in a letter that the young Marx wrote in September 1843 to Arnold Ruge, just prior to his move to Paris to collaborate with Ruge in the short-lived production of the *Deutsch-Französische Jahrbücher*. During this period Marx was engaged in an intensive program of reading about political economy, socialist thought, economic history, and political philosophy – which he continued in Paris (see McClellan, 2006, pp. 59–71). This letter – which was later published in the *Jahrbücher* – expresses the substantive tasks in front of them.

The letter contains many important topics and issues, which are well worth reading. For now only a few selected quotes (see Table 14.2) are discussed to bring out two important points. The first is a contrast that will appear again later in the discussion about the crisis in psychology at the beginning of the twentieth century, namely the relation between intellectual work (whether as philosophy or empirical research) and societal practices. The second (and related point) is their assertion of the limitation of rational analysis (as philosophy had been largely practiced), and the reconfigured role (or form) of philosophy, which methodologically must engage with the reality that it is studying.

These quotes exemplify this line of thinking about the role of practice in philosophy, rather than bear the entire burden of the argument. They were chosen because they are some of the earliest examples in which Marx starts to direct attention to the empirical processes of human interaction (both as a method and an object of study). While they do not formulate the idea of *practice* per se, they help to understand why attention was directed to the processes of societal life.

For easier reference, though perhaps at the expense of literary force, fragment A in Table 14.2 is separated into numbered sentences. The reading strategy is to

Table 14.2 Quotations from Karl Marx's letter to Arnold Ruge, September 1843

Fragment A

1.   Not only has a state of general anarchy set in among the reformers, but everyone *will* have to admit to himself that he has no exact idea what the future ought to be.
2.   On the other hand, it is precisely the advantage of the new trend that we do not dogmatically anticipate the world, but only want to find the new world through criticism of the old one.
3.   Hitherto philosophers have had the solution of all riddles lying in their writing-desks, and the stupid, exoteric world had only to open its mouth for the roast pigeons of absolute knowledge to fly into it.
4.   Now philosophy has become mundane, and the most striking proof of this is that philosophical consciousness itself has been drawn into the torment of the struggle, not only externally but also internally.

Fragment B

The critic can therefore start out from any form of theoretical and practical consciousness and from the forms peculiar to existing reality develop the true reality as its obligation and its final goal.

Fragment C

[O]ur motto must be: reform of consciousness not through dogmas, but by analysing the mystical consciousness that is unintelligible to itself, whether it manifests itself in a religious or a political form.

apply reflexively the principle in Fragment B to Marx's own work (i.e., seeking to elaborate ideas embedded implicitly in these formulations).

Fragment A.1 refers to a kind of crisis among persons who are proposing socialist and communist solutions (i.e., "the reformers") to societal conditions, because, as Marx asserts, there are no concrete ideas of what the future societal form should be. Previously the intent (of philosophers), in Marx's view, was to produce and impose "some ready-made system" on societal life. "The new trend", named in A.2, shifts to a process in which a "new world" is found through "criticism". In cultural-historical science, research (i.e., criticism) is directed toward developing practice (i.e., "new world") by engaging with currently existing conditions ("the old one"). A.3 continues to reproach the a priori approach of philosophers (especially those committed to Hegel's thought), while A.4 again emphasises that philosophy has become worldly, it can no longer stand outside, reflecting on societal practices, but must become part of, and act within, the phenomenon it is studying.

Fragment B again emphasises the point in A.4, that existing societal practices are the starting point, and focuses on elaborating the possibilities in these conditions. Fragment C reiterates the rejection of a priori thought (A.2), and the need to analyse existing societal practices as a way of forming consciousness, rather than proclaiming solutions to problems through "dogmas".

The collective emphasis of these fragments focuses on the need to be engaged in and with societal practices as a focus of attention, where the "goal" or the "insight" of this engagement is not the imposition of pre-formed plans, but to understand practices, or the consequences of practices (e.g., in the form of "mystical consciousness"), and through these analyses, aim to bring improvements back into practices (A.2).[5]

Marx's concern in this letter was to argue that philosophical problems cannot be solved with "ready-made" solutions. But what consequences, if any, arise for those who want to make scientific research about societal practices? One answer can be formulated in part by taking a starting point in Marx's *Theses on Feuerbach*. The main point is that some problems are not solved by "thinking" through, but by transforming material conditions that are the source of the problems. Hence the analysis of societal practices (i.e., theory) is only a moment in the process of developing practice.

By the end of 1844, Marx had produced several manuscripts about economic and philosophical issues. In the beginning of 1845, he needed to leave Paris, when he and other German expatriates were expulsed by French authorities, moving to Brussels, where he continued his intense reading and writing, formulating ideas that were to become the basis of his materialist theory of history. During this period in the spring 1845, Marx wrote down 11 theses about materialism in a notebook. The direct, pithy style in which they are written suggests they were an *aide memoire* – meant to remind the writer of the key ideas to be elaborated and argued in a final text. While many of the ideas formulated in different theses were embodied in Marx's subsequent work, their compact formulation remained for 40 years in his notebook, until 1886, when Friedrich Engels was preparing a pamphlet, *Ludwig Feuerbach and the End of German Classical Philosophy* (which was based on two articles he published in *Neue Zeit* in 1884, just after Marx's death). As Engels explains in the foreword to this pamphlet, he had decided to find and look over the unpublished manuscript of *Die deutsche Ideologie* that Marx and he had produced in 1845–1846. In doing so, he encountered Marx's notebook with these 11 theses, and decided to publish them (after making some editorial adjustments)[6].

The *Theses* are a rich set of propositions, addressing many philosophical issues about materialism, the role of religion, the nature of human beings, the role of philosophy (see Brudney, 1998, Chapter 7; Hook, 1936 for comprehensive discussions). In several places, ideas are formulated in a single sentence or phrase that can be seen retrospectively to reflect key assumptions in contemporary social scientific traditions. The present discussion does not try to address all the aspects in the *Theses*

---

[5]This perspective on studying existing practices does not reify them, because clarification can bring new understandings that were not initially imagined implicitly or explicitly, which introduces new ideals to be realised (cf. Hegel's discussion of the Absolute). For a similar reading of this letter, see Carver (1983, p. 30), which brings out the idea that Marx is focused on human practices, and development through those practices.

[6]The original theses from Marx were subsequently published in 1924. The original German version is available at: http://www.marxists.org/deutsch/archiv/marx-engels/1845/thesen/thesfeue-or.htm. An English translation is available at: http://www.marxists.org/archive/marx/works/1845/theses/index.htm.

that might be relevant for a cultural-historical science (e.g., the tenth thesis's focus on "social humanity" as a standpoint for society, the third thesis's consideration of the role of material conditions for thought, or the sixth thesis's description of persons as an "ensemble of social relations").

For now, the intention is to highlight an aspect of the theses, which Brudney (1998) has called a "simultaneity model" of interaction with the world. The main idea is that individuals (as persons, including researchers) cannot stand "outside" the world, as if it were an external object to grasp. Rather "the fundamental relation to the world is that of an agent continually changing and being changed by it, and a correct understanding *of* this fact is to be obtained in and through the process of changing the world" (p. 237). This perspective contrasts with a "feedback model" in which one acts, gets feedback, refines one's model and acts again. The critical point is that "understanding inheres in one's actions. There is no separate theoretical standpoint" (p. 237)[7]. In other words, because a researcher is already embedded in practical relations, before research starts, it is necessary to act in these relations as part of coming to understand them. This conception in the *Theses* has an important implication for cultural-historical science. The *Theses* are directed against philosophers, but the argument can be interpreted, as done here, as going beyond the simple point that one needs to have empirical material as part of understanding or interpreting the world. The issue being raised is the need to intervene in practices as part of the process of understanding them.

This idea is formed mostly compactly in Marx's eleventh thesis, "Philosophers have hitherto only interpreted the world in various ways; the point is to change it". This thesis is often quoted alone, where, out of context, it would seem to suggest that one should be working for practical transformation of societal conditions. This may also be implied in this formulation, but more important in the context of the other theses is that philosophical problems cannot be solved simply by interpretation, but by changing material conditions. Hence the importance of understanding practices and the importance of understanding changes in practices, and the limitation of a purely intellectual approach to addressing philosophical questions. From this point of view, Hegel is correct to note that philosophy, as a purely analytic activity, does end with him. Cultural-historical science can be understood as the science that seizes the implications of this analysis, focusing on practices as its object.

Vygotsky and Crisis in Psychology

Another important resource for understanding the conceptual roots of cultural-historical science is Vygotsky's (1997b/1926) text on the crisis in psychology about the object of psychology. The designation *crisis* started around the end of the 1890s,

---

[7]Brudney analyses all the theses in detail, concluding that the balance of evidence lies with the simultaneity model over the feedback model. I agree with this conclusion (even if I disagree with the overall thesis of the book in which this argument appears).

peaking in the mid-1920s, and continuing through the early 1930s. While much of the discussion was located in Germany, it was part of an ongoing international discourse that captured the attention of psychologists at the beginning of the twentieth century. This underlines the point that forming the object of a science is not a trivial matter.

Against this background, Vygotsky, the most important originator of cultural-historical psychology, wrote a book-length manuscript about this crisis. The main theme of this book was a discussion of this international crisis in the intellectual development of psychology, centred around the tension between a natural-scientific (usually behaviourist) perspective which sought law-like relations and a humanistic, subjective approach that sought to describe and understand human experience. (These tensions remain today.)

Of particular interest is Section 12 (in the subsequently published version of the manuscript), in which there is an extended discussion and argument for the importance of societal practices in relation to scientific psychology. The heart of Vygotsky's analysis is the need to put practice into the centre as the focus of psychology, with the need for a methodology that is appropriate to study human practices. In Vygotsky's analysis, these two aspects – focus on practice and an appropriate methodology – are what brings about the crisis and also provides the solution! It brings about the crisis because researchers wanted their basic research to be relevant for practice, in part as a societal legitimation of psychology as a science. Yet other investigators, outside academic psychology, were actually confronting societal practices, using psychotechnical approaches. These approaches were not particularly grounded theoretically, nor drawing on academic research, but possibly refined through decades or centuries of practical experience. The crisis arose in Vygotsky's view, because of the need for an applied or practical psychology that could meet the demands of societal practices:

> [Psychology] which attempts not so much to explain the mind but to understand and master it, gives the practical disciplines a fundamentally different place in the whole structure of the science than the former psychology did. (p. 305).

This new role for psychology creates new demands for methodology ("practice as the constructive principle of science which requires a philosophy, i.e. a methodology of science", p. 306). These methodologies, which were not generally available, are the source and the solution of the crisis in psychology. As Vygotsky notes, "Practice pervades the deepest foundations of the scientific operation and reforms it from beginning to end" (p. 305) and "reforms the whole methodology of the science" (p. 306).

One might expect – given Vygotsky's song of high praise about the importance of practice – that this concept would have a significant role in his written work. However, despite Vygotsky's dramatic and repeated assertions and challenges in Section 12 about the importance of practice as a way of conceptualising a new approach to psychology, there does not appear to be any insight or discussion about how to approach this problem, not even in other parts of the manuscript about the crisis. And discussion of this issue simply disappears from his subsequent writings.

That is, although Vygotsky's subsequent research was oriented to practical situations (e.g., concept use) and drew on the idea of practice as the main source of functional development, the idea of practice does not figure in any significant way in Vygotsky's theoretical or methodological discussions, nor does he refer to this discussion from the *Crisis* manuscript. While not excluding the possibility of finding such a discussion, its rarity suggests that the task formed by Vygotsky – of working out methodology appropriate to practice – still remains to be done.

Summary about Historical Roots

This section has shown some of the conceptual roots that motivate a general orientation to practice as an object for a science. A theme that until now has been allowed to run *sotto voce* in several of the discussions here arises from a juxtaposition of problems concerning knowledge production (an epistemological problem) with an interest to produce knowledge that is relevant to human concerns (a practical or substantive problem). The epistemological problem concerns the role of human action in producing knowledge. Lektorsky (1999) outlines this issue as a matter of *activity* (though not in the theoretical sense connected with the theory of activity, e.g. Leontiev, 1978/1975). The practical problem is focused on how research and action can be relevant to human practices.

For the most part, these roots only reflect on the importance of and need for focusing on practice. This is not the same as having concrete principles or a programme of work for how to investigate or work with such a science. The next section in this chapter assembles some general principles for working in this direction.

Some General Principles of Cultural-Historical Science

The discussion of the historical background in the previous section elucidates some of the considerations that motivate the formulation of cultural-historical science as the general science of practices. This section presents some of the general principles that characterise studies in cultural-historical science (Table 14.3).

Table 14.3 Some general principles of cultural-historical science

1. Researchers have often only looked at the consequences of practices; the point is to develop them.

2. Practices arise to produce objects that satisfy societally-meaningful needs.

3. It is necessary to start by analysing a practice as a whole.

4. A scientific task is to formulate and concretise objects on the basis of historical and empirical analysis.

5. The interactions by which objects are realised must be explicated, through a differentiation of the whole.

These principles provide one way to understand Vygotsky's suggestion that by putting practice in the centre, the entire methodology of science must be reorganised.

The first principle articulates the main aspects of the science, namely the development and transformation of practices. On the surface, this principle seems uncontroversial (in that most researchers would claim that their research, at some point, would be relevant to this interest). The controversy starts when the "at some point" must be specified. Much research on practices remains at a descriptive or analytic stage, sometimes justified with the claim that one must first understand or describe a practice, before it is possible to intervene. This strategy may be appropriate or sensible, in some cases, but when is the description adequate or sufficient? This strategy can also serve as a way to avoid both confronting what knowledge already exists in relation to a practice, considering the purpose of a practice, what is needed to realise it, and daring to enter into developing that practice. Even more critical: what if some kinds of knowledge about a phenomenon can only be discovered from confronting the problems of attempting to form the practice, rather than trying to describe what others are doing? These matters will not be solved by description. Cultural-historical science, drawing on the analysis of Marx's *Theses on Feuerbach*, is oriented to the consequences of taking the "some point" to be "now". The first principle is meant to reflect an important epistemological assumption: significant knowledge of a practice can often only be gained through an engagement in trying to develop the practice.

The second principle simply reiterates the definition of practice presented before, but it is important to formulate this idea as a principle, because of its implications and consequences for the subsequent principles.

The methodological importance of the third principle arises from the assumption that a practice must be understood, in the first instance, as a unitary phenomenon (i.e., the system of necessary relationships or interactions that define a practice). It is not productive, even if it is possible, to decompose or select out particular aspects of a practice, without considering the relations and interactions within the whole of the phenomenon, because these relationships are interconnected, and mutually influential. This perspective is reflected in Vygotsky's (1934/1987) discussion of "analysis by units" and "analysis by elements": "In contrast to the term "element", the term 'unit' designates a product of analysis that possesses all the basic characteristics of the whole. The unit is a vital and irreducible part of the whole" (p. 46). This particular quote comes from a text in which Vygotsky was analysing the relationship between thinking and speech, but the general idea is discussed elsewhere (e.g., "to proceed not from a thing and its parts, but from a process to its separate instances", Vygotsky, 1997a/1931, p. 68). In the present case, the second principle gives an important starting point for arguing that one is addressing the "whole" of a practice[8].

---

[8] A comparable discussion, described in terms of working with "the totality of the relevant elements of an object" versus a "limited fragment of that theoretical ensemble" can be found in Bourdieu and Wacquant (1992, pp. 232–233).

The fourth principle emphasises the commitment to understanding practice(s) through a grounding in historical conditions, rather than simply appealing to "common sense" as a sufficient way of identifying objects. Maybe it is practically necessary, at present, to start with common sense – it seems as though this is often what happens – but in the long run, it would be better to ground objects in historical analysis. To illustrate the problem with using common sense or everyday understandings, consider the situation where, in most countries around the world, children go many days of the year to a special place where subject-matter activities take place (i.e., reading and writing in relation to natural and human sciences). What is the practice? Is it education? Schooling? Instruction? One risks a plethora of overlapping "practices". Given the second principle, where one understands practices in relation to its object, then one needs to engage in further analysis, to identify objects, and differentiate the historical responses to those objects. See Chaiklin and Hedegaard (2009) for an analysis of education as a practice, where schooling and instruction are one particular form of practice. That analysis still does not have an adequate historical background, but its complexity should be sufficient to underline that we cannot continue to approach the question of practice as a definitional (i.e., dictionary) exercise.

The fifth principle is a continuation of the third principle. One cannot stop with identifying the necessary structural relations that embody the whole, one must continue to address analytically the principles of interaction (i.e. dynamics) among these relations in relation to producing the product of a practice. These dynamics may or may not be explicit or conscious among practitioners.

To take a simple example, if the object of cooking is the production of (tasty) food, then the dynamics may involve an interaction between the quality of raw ingredients, the availability of appropriate tools for the purpose (e.g., a convection oven), the conditions for preparation (e.g., enough room in the kitchen, how much time), and the technical skill of the cook. The critical point here is that these relations between these general concepts are always present in all cooking practices. That is, their presence does not depend on the consciousness of the practitioner. At the same time, in realising a product, the practitioner must work in relation to these conditions. To understand the dynamics, is to understand the processes by which a cook works with the material conditions to produce the object. The research problem is to better understand the principles of interaction among these relations in the production of the object.

More specific principles must necessarily be worked out in practice. This suggestion reflects an important theoretical point that principles should be formed from reflection over our actions (cf. Vygotsky's general science; Marx's letter to Ruge). In short, there are no methodological "roast pigeons" flying toward the open mouths of researchers; one must start hunting in the forest of practice.

Concluding Remarks

Practice is the object of cultural-historical science. This chapter, as a first introduction to cultural-historical science, has explicated the meaning of *practice* and *object*, and presented some general principles for addressing this object. The chapter was motivated in part because of a series of meetings and workshops (see Acknowledgments of Chapter 1) to confront questions about methodological development of the cultural-historical tradition. In the 1970s and 1980s, it was possible to define one's interests in more oppositional terms ("We will not be like 'them'!", where "them" included some combination of characteristics as "positivist", "mechanical", "ahistorical", or "asocial", "unsituated", and so forth). In the first decade of the twenty-first century, when faced with the diversity of papers and interests from persons who are oriented more or less in the same theoretical direction, more difficult challenges arise in relation to formulating the general frame of one's science.

It would be convenient if one could make a few precise statements about the right kinds of research actions to make, together with short, clear justifications for the actions (such as this chapter has attempted). This reasonable expectation to achieve clarity about assumptions and principles used to conduct scientific investigation is undercut, however, by the endless mass of intricacies that arise – ontological assumptions about the phenomena under investigation, epistemological assumptions about what kind of knowledge should be produced, specifications of the objectives and purposes of the research, clarifications in relation to existing ideas and approaches. Thus, there was no intention to provide and defend a comprehensive methodological theory, with all the philosophical foundations addressed and clarified. Indeed such a goal would not be possible. If cultural-historical science is a living science, then these issues must be developed constantly; this is one of the consequences of the transformation of methodology that moves away from the foundational goals that have characterised much of (philosophy of) science in the past. Rather than resolve the foundational issues, which is seen as validating the science; this chapter works in the spirit of Vygotsky's point that truth is in practice, so these philosophical analyses cannot be an end in themselves or a validating foundation for cultural-historical science, they can at best give some orienting points toward developing practice.

Acknowledgments   Thanks to Mariane Hedegaard and Ray McDermott, whose editorial and conceptual insights have helped in the quest to express my intentions in this chapter. Additional thanks to Stuart Gallagher, Tim Leighton, and Christine Schweighart.

References

Anderson, J. R., Reder, L. M., & Simon, H. A. (1997). Situative versus cognitive perspectives: Form versus substance [Rejoinder]. *Educational Researcher, 26*(1), 18–21.
Baldwin, J. M. (1910). Report on terminology. In E. Claparède (Ed.), *VIme congrès international de psychologie (Tenu à Genève 2 au 7 Août 1909)* (pp. 480–481). Geneva: Librairie Kündig.
Bohr, N. (1950). On the notions of causality and complementarity. *Science, 111*, 51–54.
Bourdieu, P., & Wacquant, L. J. D. (1992). *An invitation to reflexive sociology*. Cambridge: Polity Press.
Brudney, D. (1998). *Marx's attempt to leave philosophy*. Cambridge: Cambridge University Press.
Carver, T. (1983). *Marx & Engels: The intellectual relationship*. Brighton: Wheatsheaf.

Chaiklin, S. (2001). The category of 'personality' in cultural-historical psychology. In S. Chaiklin (Ed.), *The theory and practice of cultural-historical psychology* (pp. 238–259). Aarhus: Aarhus University Press.

Chaiklin, S. (2006). *Practice-developing research: Introduction to a future science.* Unpublished manuscript. Danish University of Education.

Chaiklin, S., & Hedegard, M. (2009). Radical-local teaching and learning: A cultural-historical perspective on education and children's development. In M. Fleer, M. Hedegaard, & J. Tudge (Eds.), *Childhood studies and the impact of globalization: Policies and practices at global and local levels* (World Yearbook of Education 2009) (pp. 179–198). London: Routledge.

Chaiklin, S., & Lave, J. (Eds.). (1993). *Understanding practice: Perspectives on activity and context.* Cambridge: Cambridge University Press.

Hook, S. (1936). Marx and Feuerbach. *New International, 3,* 47–57. (accessed from http://www.marxists.org/history/etol/writers/hook/1936/04/feuerbach.htm)

Ilyenkov, E. V. (1977). The concept of the ideal (R. Daglish, Trans.). In *Philosophy in the USSR: Problems of dialectical materialism* (pp. 71–99). Moscow: Progress.

Jensen, U. J. (1999). Categories in activity theory: Marx's philosophy just-in-time. In S. Chaiklin, M. Hedegaard, & U. J. Jensen (Eds.), *Activity theory and social practice* (pp. 79–99). Aarhus, Denmark: Aarhus University Press.

Laucken, U., Schick, A., & Höge, H. (1996). *Einführung in das Studium der Psychologie: Eine Orientierungshilfe für Schüler und Studenten* (7th ed.). Stuttgart: Klett-Cotta.

Lektorsky, V. (1999). Historical change of the notion of activity: Philosophical presuppositions. In S. Chaiklin, M. Hedegaard, & U. J. Jensen (Eds.), *Activity theory and social practice* (pp. 100–113). Aarhus: Aarhus University Press.

Leontiev, A. N. (1973/1959). *Problems of the development of the mind* (M. Kopylova, Trans.). Moscow: Progress.

Leontiev, A. N. (1978/1975). *Activity, consciousness, and personality* (M. J. Hall, Trans.). Englewood Cliffs, NJ: Prentice-Hall.

Marx, K. (1970/1859). *A contribution to the critique of political economy* (M. Dobb, Ed., S. W. Ryazanskaya, Trans.). New York: International Publishers.

Marx, K. (1975/1843). Karl Marx and Arnold Ruge, September 1843. *Karl Marx, Friedrich Engels Gesamtausgabe* (Bd. 12, pp. 54–57). Berlin: Akademie Verlag.

Marx, K., & Engels, F. (1988/1845–1846). *The German ideology* (C. J. Arthur, Ed., W. Lough, C. Dutt, & C. P. Magill, Trans.). New York: International.

McClellan, D. (2006). *Karl Marx: A biography* (4th ed.). Basingstoke: Palgrave Macmillan.

Rockwell, E. (1999). Recovering history in the study of schooling: From the *longue durée* to everyday co-construction. *Human Development, 42,* 113–128.

Scribner, S. (1985). Vygotsky's uses of history. In J. V. Wertsch (Ed.), *Culture, communication, and cognition: Vygotskian perspectives* (pp. 119–145). Cambridge: Cambridge University Press.

Sternberg, R. J., & Detterman, D. K. (Eds.). (1986). *What is intelligence? Contemporary viewpoints on its nature and definition.* Norwood, NJ: Ablex.

Vygotsky, L. S. (1929). II. The problem of the cultural development of the child. *The Pedagogical Seminary and Journal of Genetic Psychology, 36,* 415–434.

Vygotsky, L. S. (1987/1934). Thinking and speech (N. Minick, Trans.). In R. W. Rieber & A. S. Carton (Eds.), *The collected works of L. S. Vygotsky: Vol. 1. Problems of general psychology* (pp. 39–285). New York: Plenum.

Vygotsky, L. S. (1997a/1931). *The collected works of L. S. Vygotsky: Vol. 4. The history of the development of higher mental functions* (M. Hall, Trans., & R.W. Rieber, Ed.). New York: Plenum.

Vygotsky, L. S. (1997b/1926). The historical meaning of the crisis in psychology: A methodological investigation (R. van der Veer, Trans.). In R. W. Reiber & J. Wollock (Eds.), *The collected works of L. S. Vygotsky: Vol. 3. Problems of the theory and history of psychology* (pp. 233–343). New York: Plenum Press.

Biographical Notes

B. Althans

Birgit Althans (PhD) is a professor of social pedagogy at the University of Trier. From 2000 to 2008 she was a scientific associate at the Free University of Berlin, where she wrote her habilitation comparing the relationships between gender, social work and management in the early decades of the last century. She also worked on a project about rituals as part of the Centre of Excellence "Cultures of the Performative", and on a second project about representations of birth. Other areas of interest include cultural and gender studies, historical and pedagogical anthropology and poststructuralism in educational science. Selected publications include *Das maskierte Begehren: Frauen zwischen Sozialarbeit und Management* [The Masked Desire: Women between Social Work and Management] (2007, Campus) and *Der Klatsch, die Frauen und das Sprechen bei der Arbeit* [Gossip, Women and Talking at Work] (2000, Campus).

K. Audehm

Kathrin Audehm (PhD) studied pedagogy, philosophy and educational science in Leipzig, Berlin and Dundee. Her dissertation, *Erziehung bei Tisch. Zur sozialen Magie eines Familienrituals* [Education at the Table. On the Social Magic of Family Rituals], was published in 2007 with Transcript. She now works with the excellence research cluster "Cultures of the Performative" at the Free University in Berlin. She has published a number of articles about rituals, pedagogical ethnography and educational philosophy.

S. Chaiklin

Seth Chaiklin (PhD) is a reader at the Department of Education, University of Bath, UK. He has been trained as a psychologist and has done research on mathematical problem-solving, subject-matter learning in natural science, history and physics, as well as some work with cultural minorities and the development of societal relations. He is currently interested in theoretical conceptions for describing and analysing practice as well as in strategies for the development of professional practice. Chaiklin was the president of the International Society for Cultural and Activity Research (ISCAR) from 2002 to 2008. Selected publications include *Radical-local teaching and learning* (2005, with Mariane Hedegaard, Aarhus University Press) and *Understanding Practice: Perspectives on Activity and Context* (1993, edited with Jean Lave, Cambridge University Press).

A. Chronaki

Anna Chronaki (PhD) is an associate professor at the University of Thessaly, Department of Early Childhood Education. She graduated from the University of Patras and continued with her Masters and PhD at the University of Bath, UK. She has worked at the University of Bath, University of Aalborg and Open University in Milton Keynes. Her publications include articles in journals such as *Educational Studies of Mathematics* and the *European Journal of Educational Psychology*. She recently edited a book entitled *Challenging perspectives on mathematics classroom communication* (2005, Information Age Publication Inc.). She is currently teaching undergraduate and postgraduate level courses about mathematics education, gender and technology use as well as ethnographic approaches to researching mathematics and technology practices.

B. Fichtner

Bernd Fichtner (PhD) is professor of educational science at the University of Siegen, Germany. He is also the director of the International Education Doctorate Program and the co-founder of the International Society for Cultural Research and Activity Theory (now ISCAR). Since 1993 he has cooperated extensively with federal universities in Brazil on various research projects. Selected book publications include *Lernen und Lerntätigkeit* [Studying and the Learning Activity] (1996, Lehmanns), *Kinder und Jugendliche im Blick qualitativer Forschung: Kulturhistorische Schule, Phänomenologie und Ethnografie in Brasilien und Deutschland* [Children and Youth in qualitative research: the cultural-historical School, Phenomenology and Ethnography in Brazil and Germany] (2003, co-edited with Maria Freitas and Roberto Monteiro, ATHENA-Verlag) and *Vom Umgang mit Differenz: Globalisierung und Regionalisierung im interkulturellen Diskurs* [On Dealing with Difference: Globalization and Regionalization in Intercultural Discourse] (2006, co-edited with Maria Benites, ATHENA-Verlag).

M. Hedegaard

Mariane Hedegaard (PhD) is a professor of psychology at the University of Copenhagen. She is also the head of the research centre PPUK (Person, Practice, Development, Culture). Her research focus is on child development in a cultural-historical perspective and the formation of personality (i.e. concepts, identity and motives) through school teaching. She is also interested in the position of Middle Eastern children in Danish schools, their learning, development and conceptions about school life, as well as the teaching of social science to minority children. Recently published books include *Graffiti som Engagement* [Graffiti as Engagement] (2007), *Radical-local Teaching and Learning. A Cultural-historical Approach.* (2005, with Seth Chaiklin, Aarhus University Press), and *Elevens*

Alsidige Personlige Udvikling – et Dialogredskab [Students' General Personal Development – a Tool for Dialogue] (2007, with J. Bang and Niels Egelund, Dansk psykologisk forlag).

M. Hildebrand-Nilshon

Martin Hildebrand-Nilshon (PhD) was a professor for developmental psychology at the Free University of Berlin till 2008. His research focuses on developmental and cultural psychology, especially on the ontogenetical development of language and on prelinguistic and linguistic communication in different cultural contexts. Selected publications include *Kultur (in) der Psychologie. Über das Abenteuer des Kulturbegriffs in der psychologischen Theoriebildung.* [The Culture of Psychology. On the notion of Culture in psychological Theorizing] (2002, published with Chung-Woon Kim and Dimitris Papadopoulos, Asanger) or the article *Zum Kontext von Sprache und Kommunikation in den Arbeiten von L.S. Vygotskij und A.N. Leont'ev. Anmerkungen zur Debatte um Kontinuität oder Diskontinuität beider Positionen* [Language and Communication in the Works of Vygotskij and Leont'ev. Comments on the Debates on the (Dis)continuity of both positions] (2004, in: *Die Aktualität des Verdrängten. Studien zu Geschichte der Sprachwissenschaft*)

G. Ivinson

Gabrielle Ivinson (PhD) is a lecturer in psychology in the Cardiff University School of Social Sciences. She is a social and developmental psychologist whose main interest is in the way knowledge is socially represented and constructed, particularly focussing on gender and knowledge in education. Currently she is researching pedagogic strategies in secondary schools. This involves ethnographic work in secondary school classrooms using various observation methods and in-depth interviews with students about undertaking tasks teachers set them in lessons. She recently published the book *Rethinking Single Sex Teaching: Engendering Critical Pedagogy* (2007, with Patricia Murphy, Open University Press).

S. Klasen

Sigrid Klasen is currently a scientific associate and doctoral student at the Department of Anthropology and Education at the Free University of Berlin. She is also a teacher at a school for German as a foreign language as well as a psychologist. Her research focuses on the development of emotions, preverbal communication processes and aesthetic learning in early childhood. In her thesis, she examines practices that families use to establish a relationship to a newborn baby. She recently published the book *Mimesis in der frühen Kindheit: Mikroanalyse einer Spielsequenz zwischen Mutter und Kind.* [Mimesis in Early Childhood: the Microanalysis of an Interaction between Mother and Child, 2009].

M. Kontopodis

Michalis Kontopodis (PhD) studied Psychology in Greece, France, Poland and Germany and works as a research associate at the Institute of European Ethnology at the Humboldt University of Berlin. He is engaged in both theoretical and empirical work on anthropological and cultural-psychological approaches to human cognition and development. In 2009 he was a visiting research associate at the City University New York and at the New York University and in 2010 at the Pontificia Universidade Católica de São Paolo, Brazil. He is the Secretary of the International Society for Cultural and Activity Research (ISCAR) as well as editor of the ISCAR Newsletter and member of the editorial board of *Outlines: Critical Practice Studies.* Kontopodis has co-edited the Special Issue "Materializing Times: from Memory to Imagination" of *Memory Studies* (January 2009, Vol. 2, Number 1) as well as the Special Issue "Doing Memory, Doing Identity: Politics of the Everyday in Contemporary Global Communities" of *Outlines: Critical Practice Studies* (June, 2010). He is also the editor of the books *Das Selbst Als Netzwerk: Zum Einsatz Von Körpern Und Dingen im Alltag* (with J. Niewöhner, 2011, transcript) and *Culture and Emerging Educational Challenges: A Dialogue with Brazil* (2009, Lehmanns Media).

C. Moro

Christiane Moro (PhD) directed the educational science laboratory at Nancy 2 University in France from 2002 to 2005. Since 2005 she has been ordinary professor in developmental psychology at Lausanne University in Switzerland where she directed the Institute of Psychology over the last three years. She is the co-founder of the LARPsyDIS (LAboratoire de Recherche en Psychologie des Dynamiques Intra- et InterSubjectives) de Lausanne. Specialized in development in early infancy and preschool children, she is interested in the role of materiality as source and resource for semiotical development; her themes of research concern the status of the object and their social (canonical and symbolic) uses in development, the production of gestures in preverbal development as well as related to the development of speech and, more recently, to joint attention. Her works are based on the cultural-historical theory of L.S. Vygotsky. Selected book publications include *L'objet et la construction de son usage chez le bébé, une approche sémiotique du développement préverbal* (2005, co-écrit avec Cintia Rodríguez, Peter Lang); *Situation éducative et significations* (2004, co-edited with René Rickenmann, De Boeck); *Unité et pluralité des sciences de l'éducation. Sondages au cœur de la recherche* (2004, co-édité avec Gisela Chatelanat et Madelon Saada-Robert, Peter Lang).

F. Seeger

Falk Seeger (PhD) studied psychology and sociology at the University of Münster. He has been a senior lecturer in psychology and mathematics education at the Institute of Mathematics Education at the University of Bielefeld, Germany, since 1980. His current research focuses on external representations, semiotics and cultural-historical psychology. He recently edited a book with L. Radord and G. Schubring: *Semiotics in Mathematics Education* (2008, Sense). Other publications include: *The Culture of the Mathematics Classroom* (1998, edited with J. Voigt and U. Waschescio, Cambridge University Press) and *Activity and Sign: Grounding Mathematics Education* (2005, M. Hoffmann and J. Lenhard, Springer).

E. Sørensen

Estrid Sørensen (PhD) holds a junior professorship of cultural psychology in the Mercator Researchgroup "Spaces of Anthropological Knowledge: Production and Transfer". In her current research she investigates how knowledge about the harm of violent computer games to children are produced and circulate among different fields of society: science, media regulation, game industry and children's media practices. She holds a PhD from the University of Copenhagen where she was also a research leader of the EU-funded project "5D: Local Learning Communities in a Global World". She is affiliated with the Department of European Ethnology in Berlin, and she has held various other research and teaching positions at universities in Germany and Denmark. Her publications include the book *The Materiality of Learning: Technology, Knowledge and Presence in Educational Practice* (2009, Cambridge University Press) and numerous articles in such journals as *Comparative Sociology, Forum Qualitative Social Research,* or *Outlines – Critical Social Studies.*

Stetsenko, Anna

Anna Stetsenko (PhD) is a professor in developmental psychology at The Graduate Centre City University New York. Her research is concerned with the development of cultural-historical Activity Theory (with roots in the works of Vygotsky, Leont'ev and Luria) through combining knowledge of its diverse international contexts and interpretations. She focuses on learning and development, development of mind and language, the self, gender, epistemology and history of psychology, attempting to re-conceptualize these topics from the standpoint of Activity Theory. Selected book publications include: *The Birth of Consciousness: Early Stages in the Development of Systems and Meanings* (2005, CheRo Press) and *Vygotsky's Psychology: Voices from the Past and Present* (2002, edited with Dorothy Robbins).

Ch. Wulf

Christoph Wulf (PhD) is a professor of anthropology and philosophy of education and co-founder of the Interdisciplinary Centre for Historical Anthropology at the Free University of Berlin. He is a member of the "InterArts" Research Training Group, the "Cultures of Performance" Collaborative Research Centre (SFB) and the "Languages of Emotion" Centre of Excellence at that same university. He is the founder and vice-chairman of the Society for Historical Anthropology. He is a founding member of the Commission on Educational Anthropology of the German Society for Educational Science, vice-president of the UNESCO commission in Germany, a member of the Conseil scientifique of the Institut National de Recherche Pédagogique (Paris/Lyon) and a member of the International Research Centre for Cultural Sciences (Vienna). Dr. Wulf's areas of research include historical and educational anthropology, mimesis, aesthetics, intercultural education, performativity and ritual research, and research on emotions. He edits the *Zeitschrift für Erziehungswissenschaft* [Journal for Educational Science] and *Paragrana. Internationale Zeitschrift für Historische Anthropologie* [Paragrana. International Journal for Historical Anthropology], as well as the series "Historische Anthropologie", "European Studies in Education", and "Pädagogische Anthropologie". He has enjoyed guest professorships in the USA, the Netherlands, the UK, Sweden, Italy, Austria, France and Japan. He is especially well known for his comprehensive works *Mimesis: Culture, Art, Society* (1995, with Gunter Gebauer, University of California Press) and *Anthropology of Education* (2002, Münster/New York), but is also the author/editor of numerous other books such as *Tanz als Anthropologie* [Dance as Anthropology] (2007, co-edited with Gabriele Brandtstetter, Fink); *Pädagogik des Performativen* [Pedagogics of the Performative] (2007, co-edited with Jörg Zirfas, Beltz); *Pädagogische Theorien des Lernens* [Pedagogical Theories of Learning] (2007, co-edited with Michael Göhlich and Jörg Zirfas, Beltz), *Dynamics and Performativity of Imagination: The Image between the Visible and the Invisible* (2009, co-edited with B. Hüppauf, Routledge) etc.

Name Index

Subject Index

Printed by Printforce, the Netherlands